REENGINEERING IN ACTION

REENGINEERING IN ACTION

The Quest for World-Class Excellence

Editor

Chan Meng Khoong

National Computer Board, Singapore

ICP

Imperial College Press

Published in India by

Cambridge University Press India Pvt. Ltd.
under the imprint of Foundation Books
Cambridge House
4381/4 Ansari Road
Daryaganj,
New Delhi - 110 002

This reprint edition 2010

ISBN- 13: 978-81-7596-787-8

This edition of *Chan Meng Khoong / Reengineering in Action,* is published by arrangement with World Scientific Publishing Co. Pte. Ltd.

Published by Manas Saikia for Cambridge University Press India Pvt. Ltd.
and printed in India at Mehta Offset Pvt. Ltd. A-16 Naraina , New Delhi -28

Preface

Business process reengineering was first popularized as an organizational change paradigm in 1990. While many ingredients of the paradigm were already well developed in business schools in the '80s, a timely dose of information technology and industrial engineering at the turn of the decade gave reengineering the fresh new holism that was soon to captivate corporate leaders the world over. The popularity of reengineering has spread globally like wildfire ever since.

Despite the numerous debates by scholars and managers regarding the effectiveness of reengineering, there is little dispute that reengineering is probably the closest among management paradigms to a panacea that corporations can depend on to eradicate their ills. Reengineering has also graduated from its early role in the era of downsizing and other corporate disasters. The mission of reengineering today is to help corporations in their quest for world-class excellence. The aim of this book is to provide concrete pointers for the road ahead in this quest.

This book is an international showcase of reengineering in action, with a collective wisdom spanning five continents. It contains a collection of 25 writings from reengineers reporting from the battlefield of corporate transformation. These writings are organized into five sections, namely Introduction, Concepts & Tools, Public Sector Experience, Private Sector Experience, and Future Prospects. The writings are rich in vivid descriptions of real-world experience. The collection of methods, tools, principles, and case studies in the public and private sectors, are weaved into a synergistic fieldbook tailored to meet the needs of reengineers today and tomorrow.

The target readership for this book includes chief executive officers, chief operations officers, chief information officers, information systems managers, human resource managers, management consultants, industrial engineers, and educators in management and information systems. The book aims to help corporate decision makers take stock of where reengineering has been, as well as to prepare for future applications of the paradigm.

Part I provides an introductory, contemporary perspective of reengineering that is critical for appreciating the rest of the book. I lay the foundation for understanding reengineering as a process of organizational transformation to attain world-class excellence. Eleven key principles for achieving high-impact reengineering are presented.

Part II provides a spectrum of state-of-the-art concepts, techniques and tools that span reengineering practice. Wolfgang Deiters *et al* propose a classification and modeling approach for semi-structured processes, and discuss IT support for their enactment. Hélène Bestougeff and Amel Bouaissi present a generic software tool for modeling processes that supports multiple perspectives. Jurgen Vanhoenacker *et al* propose an integrated framework for codifying organizational process knowledge. Leslie Johnson and Maria Stergiou show how the concepts of evolutionary delivery and evolutionary development help to link reengineering with systems engineering. Shigeki Umeda and Albert Jones adopt a supply chain management perspective for reengineering, and propose methodologies for analysis and simulation. Freimut Bodendorf *et al* develop a framework for process design using reusable building blocks. Pedro Ramos and José Fiadeiro show how formal logic can be used to validate process designs against organizational rules. Jaakko Virkkunen and Kari Kuutti provide a critical assessment of the pitfalls in defining the unit of analysis, and discuss concepts to overcome these pitfalls. Kaiyin Huang examines the influences of electronic commerce on organizational transformation, and proposes methods for identifying the pivots for transformation. Luigi Benedicenti *et al* propose a new methodology for object-oriented process modeling and activity-based costing.

Part III is devoted to successful reengineering applications in the public sector. I share some experience in Singapore, where a very high success rate has been achieved in reengineering projects. Daryll Prescott describes US DoD experience in reengineering records management. William Underwood *et al* draw insights from the same DoD experience to develop extensions to IDEF methodology. Pin-Yu Chu and Chun-Hung Yang discuss the use of data envelopment analysis for civil service efficiency evaluation, a technique that can be added to the reengineering toolkit. Veronika Thurner relates lessons learnt on the softer aspects of reengineering from studying a public sector firm. Tien Hua Yim-Teo presents rigorous findings from a wide-ranging public sector survey on success factors for change.

Part IV is focused on reengineering applications in the private sector. Roger Sor and Dieter Fink examine the impacts of IT and process interdependencies in four contrasting corporations. Matt Barney *et al* present the experience of Lucent Technologies in reengineering the HR systems and procedures supporting a chip factory. Lauri Forsman relates the experience of Nokia Telecommunications in reengineering end user support processes. M. P. Jaiswal examines the roles of IT, TQM, and business vision in the reengineering of two large agribusiness enterprises. Monika Calitz and Andrékwen Calitz review the use of sophisticated software tools in the reengineering of a textile manufacturer. Chester Warzynski describes case studies of reengineering in higher education establishments.

Part V examines the continued relevance and prospects for reengineering practice in the next millennium. Ted Lewis discusses five critical success factors for achieving excellence in the 21st century organization. In the final chapter of this book, I paint visions of the look and feel of organizations and the nature of reengineering practice in the 21st century and beyond.

The process of developing this book proved to be a fascinating project in itself. Starting from the initial inkling of the concept for this book some 18 months ago, a community of potential contributors was gradually cultivated, and gathered opportunistically to meet at a symposium last July. Following the symposium, the resolve to publish this book gained a quantum leap, and a process of global coordination ensued to piece together the contributions into a single volume while negotiations with the publisher were in progress. Remarkably, close to one hundred percent of the development process was carried out electronically, using the Internet.

I would like to thank the 43 contributing authors for their commitment to the success of this book, without which this book would not have seen the light of day. Many thanks also to David Sharp and his team at Imperial College Press for the highly professional work in the publication process. This book is a milestone in the reengineering literature, an achievement to remember for all of us involved.

Finally, I would like to dedicate this book to my wife, Serene, for all the wonderful love and inspiration that she has given me throughout this challenging journey.

C. M. Khoong
May 1, 1998

Contents

PART I

INTRODUCTION

Chapter 1

Reengineering for World-Class Excellence

CHAN MENG KHOONG

Centre for Strategic Process Innovation, National Computer Board,
71 Science Park Drive, Singapore 118253, Republic of Singapore
E-mail: chanmeng@ncb.gov.sg

A large part of reengineering practice has focused on fixing organizational problems, and much scholarly debate has centered around the relevance and strengths of the paradigm for serving such purposes. However, the true value of reengineering lies in organizational transformation, which will be missed by practitioners who use reengineering only to address mundane factors of operational process efficiency. The contemporary role of reengineering is to reinvent organizations in order to attain world-class excellence. Eleven key principles for high-impact reengineering, drawn from many years of hands-on experience, are outlined in this chapter: reengineering while being successful; reengineering without risks; reengineering for strategy; reengineering as a synergy of the best methods; envisioning; process thinking; systems thinking; creative rethinking; change management; preparation; and reengineering for the future.

1. Introduction

Business process reengineering has been defined as 'the fundamental rethinking and radical redesign of business processes to bring about dramatic improvements in performance.' The term reengineering was first coined in 1990 to describe the ultimate panacea for many of management's problems. Hammer's article in the *Harvard Business Review* and Davenport's article in the *Sloan Management Review* are now recognized as classics that brought the paradigm to the attention of organizations worldwide.

Over the years, the practice of reengineering has remarkably survived the onslaught of skeptics and counter-paradigm proponents to become the management paradigm of the decade. No other management paradigm has attained the same expanse of reach across cultures, across professional disciplines, and across rungs of management in such a short period of time and with so much excitement generated over it.

If the reengineering paradigm has been infamous in any way, it was the perception that reengineering is used primarily to fix broken organizations. This is perhaps a result of the paradigm's coincidental coexistence with the early '90s era of downsizing and other corporate disasters. The reengineering paradigm has since graduated from this stigma — there is much more for organizations to gain from reengineering today. The mission of reengineering today is to help organizations in their quest for world-class excellence.

Organizations today, be they in the private or public sectors, are captivated by the notion of world-class excellence. Being world-class means being second to none. Achieving world-class excellence is an intricate challenge. How do we measure or benchmark performance? How do we get from where we are today to being world-class? And, after getting there, how do we sustain world-class excellence? Reengineering can help answer these questions. This paper surfaces several facets of reengineering that will illustrate, and hopefully convince, how reengineering can be the paradigm of choice.

2. Successful Organizations Need Reengineering

Cases of organizations which were previously prosperous but have now fallen into hard times abound. These lessons suggest throwing away the adage — *'if it ain't broke don't fix it'* — for the new principle which says *'fix it while it's still okay.'* Reengineering for world-class excellence embodies the spirit of the new principle. The same methods and tools of reengineering continue to apply, but serve the new objectives of helping successful organizations take a further quantum leap to unprecedented levels of excellence.

Of course, it is not trivial for the new principle to sink in, at least in the case of private sector organizations. Organizations constrained by urgencies of the bottom line are inclined to minimize their exposure to initiatives of substantial cost and risk if they believe that they are in the pink of health. However, in the public sector, where bottom line pressures do not exist and it is often possible for the organization to stand on the edge of disaster for extended periods, the perspectives on reengineering are rapidly changing. Forward-looking government officials now realize that reengineering for world-class excellence may be the only strategy at their disposal to rescue their organizations from the doldrums.

3. Reengineering Need Not Be Risky

Some anecdotal evidence in the early to mid '90s indicated that reengineering projects have a high risk of failure. Failure rates of 70% have been quoted widely, and perhaps irresponsibly, as such reports have significantly tainted the reputation of the paradigm. More recent surveys suggest the exact opposite — that the success rate of reengineering projects is closer to 70%. This appears to be the case even in Europe, where complex labor laws and industry-government relationships have made the continent an unlikely hotbed of reengineering practice in the past. Over in Singapore, where the public sector has embraced reengineering openly, the success rate is practically 100%.

It is therefore conceivable that the known failures in reengineering are a result of faulty use of the paradigm, rather than a limitation of the paradigm *per se*. To exploit the paradigm fully, one must invest time and effort to understand its workings. The following sections serve to help improve this understanding. Organizations must also understand the downside of *not* implementing reengineering, rather than be discouraged by the hypothetical downsides of reengineering.

4. Reengineering for Strategy

A common misconception about reengineering is that it is intended only for improving the cost-effectiveness of operational processes, through examination of time, cost, and quality factors, while strategic business planning is an entirely separate exercise that takes care of market positioning and other long-term organizational priorities. This misconception is unfortunate, as the disconnect between reengineering and strategic planning would yield similar disconnects between operations and strategy, barriers between management and employees, and poor linkages among the many interdependent indicators of corporate performance.

The essence of business strategy is differentiation. Differentiation does not lie in the organization's knowledge of markets, customers, or competitors, as such information depends on external, uncontrollable factors. Furthermore, such information is accessible to many other organizations as well. The key to differentiation — the organization's core competence — lies in its processes and the (human and systems) capabilities used to operate those processes. Reengineering is therefore the strategic tool — crafting the world-class processes and capabilities that form the organization's *secret weapons*. Without having these secret weapons to be deployed, market positioning would be a blind process.

5. A Potent Mix of Old Wines in a Sexy New Bottle

Certainly, reengineering cannot be a totally new management paradigm. Similar concepts were proposed in the '80s. The spectrum of methods and tools employed in reengineering are essentially 'old wines.' What is really new about reengineering is the holistic application of these old wines all at once — thus the potent mix. One cannot appreciate the wonderful flavor of this potent mix if the constituent wines are drunk separately. The rest of it is packaging — thus the sexy new bottle.

In simple terms, other management paradigms that attack a few hard or soft organizational issues in isolation tend to offer lower impact than reengineering. By addressing all facets of an organization holistically, the many dependencies across organizational functions can be taken into account, and uncertainty in knowledge of future external scenarios minimized. One may then ask: this being the case, does reengineering cause chaos? Chaos can certainly set in if change implementation is not properly managed. Someone has likened reengineering to 'changing the engines of a flying airplane' — technically feasible (if the airplane has more than one engine), but extremely challenging.

Sometimes, reengineering is pitched competitively against other paradigms, e.g. reengineering versus total quality management. If we subscribe to the potent mix concept, then such competition should be a non-issue, as reengineering is all of the other management paradigms plus more — more in the sense of drinking the potent mix all at once.

6. Reengineering Requires Envisioning

A reengineering initiative without a business vision goes nowhere. The formulation of a vision statement for the new organization is a critical first step in reengineering. An organization's vision statement is an expression of its strategic intent — the desired future state of affairs. This desire is ideally expressed in terms of the level of excellence to be attained, and the time frame for attaining that level. The reengineering exercise will develop strategies to bring the organization from the current state to that defined by the vision.

The vision statement should provide concrete, measurable performance targets. The targets should be ambitious — something that is beyond the realm of what is possible today. The vision should also be inspirational and easy to communicate, and should ignite the imagination of people to picture how differently the organization will operate in the future.

The vision may be expressed along customer segment, product/ service type, or activity type dimensions. It is good to frame the vision around the core competence of the organization, as this ensures that the organization will focus the energies of limited resources on doing what it can do best.

Vision statements are commonly confused with mission statements. An organization's mission statement is an expression of its core purpose — its reasons for existence, its charter, and its social responsibilities. The mission statement should have a sense of permanence, like a reflection of the 'eternal soul' of the organization. It is within the boundaries of the organization's mission that the vision and strategies would operate.

As a consequence of the mission-vision confusion, it is common to find mission statements containing both elements of core purpose as well as vision or strategies. Ideally, if the mission statement is to incorporate an expression of a desired future state, that state should be such that reaching for it is an endless journey — a level of excellence so high that no time frame would suffice.

7. Reengineering Requires Process Thinking

A process is a set of activities that, taken together, produce a deliverable of value to a customer. This simple definition has four important keywords: *activities*, *deliverable*, *value*, and *customer*. A concept that lacks any of these four components cannot be considered as a process, and can at most be a slice of a process.

The customer is at both the start and end points of the process. At the start point, the customer triggers the process with the request for some deliverable. At the end point, the customer receives the deliverable, out of which some form of value is derived. Everything in between the start and end points are the activities that are needed to generate the deliverable of the required value. Very often, this suite of activities can span across functional as well as organizational boundaries. End-to-end process visibility and ownership is a central tenet of reengineering.

Sometimes the term *procedure* is used interchangeably with *process*. But in business parlance, a procedure is quite different from a process. A procedure is a set of rules that define the right and wrong ways to perform activities. Procedures are normally well documented, but processes are rarely documented. Procedure flow is prescriptive (i.e. 'thou shall not') and vertical, while process flow is descriptive (i.e. 'how to') and horizontal.

Procedures applied on activities of a process are not value adding, but tend to impose checks and controls to ensure consistency and quality in those activities. Procedures, if not aptly applied, tend to affect the efficiency and effectiveness of processes. If the process is a water pipe, then procedures are valves along the pipe.

Also note that, once a process design is cast in concrete as *the* standard way to deliver the results to the customer, the process design becomes equivalent to a procedure if it is to be religiously followed. Therefore, one must to careful not to place processes under ISO 9000 certification until they have been optimally designed. The question remains, though, that processes need to be designed to support future changes, if future reengineering cycles are to be avoided.

The apparent emphasis on processes in the reengineering paradigm gives the impression that application is limited to routine, operational, and microscopic business activities. It is appropriate to view reengineering analysis as being anchored on core business processes, but the influence of the analysis can encompass all facets of the organization, including strategy, partnerships, and even core values. Said another way, reengineering can be applied to all levels and perspectives of an organization's business. The impact of reengineering is strategic, giving the organization a new positioning that should remain relevant for many years to come.

8. Reengineering Requires Systems Thinking

A system is a set of interconnected elements, such that the set exhibits properties as a single whole. The important thing to remember in this definition is that a system is more than the sum of its parts — dividing an elephant into two does not yield two elephants. Every organization is a system, and often a complex one. Events in an organization are a result of patterns of behavior, and these patterns are a result of some underlying systemic structure. The underlying structure may not be readily visible or attributable to any subset of the organization, and yet surrounds everyone in the organization. The complaint that '*no one is to blame but the system as a whole*' is a familiar one.

Systems thinking, therefore, is a process of discovering and developing the underlying structure that generates patterns of behavior in an organization. Many of the problems faced by management or workers are really symptoms of deeper problems. With systems thinking, we can navigate the sea of causes and effects that span across space and time. In the process analysis phase of reengineering, systems thinking is needed to uncover the root problems to be addressed. In the process redesign phase, systems thinking is again needed to examine the implications of organizational change, before, during, and after implementation.

The systems thinking field has been around somewhat longer than reengineering, and can be traced back to the work of Forrester in the '60s. Until the '80s, the field has been applied mainly to policy simulation and analysis, and was more commonly known as system dynamics. In the '90s, in parallel to the emergence of the reengineering paradigm, systems thinking has been rediscovered as a strategic tool for leadership, and is seen as synonymous with the concept of learning organizations. Systems thinking, leadership, and learning are all critical success factors for reengineering.

9. Reengineering Requires Creative Rethinking

Reengineering requires us to fundamentally rethink the need to do things, and about the way things are done. Rethinking requires not only an open mindset, but also plenty of creativity in order that radical, out-of-the-box ideas can be generated constructively. The field of creative thinking has a traditional presence in education and more recently in the professional development of executives. Reengineers need to be equipped with creative thinking skills — which is easier said than done, given that most executives are just too busy with the day-to-day chores and responsibilities to have any time for thinking.

How do we apply creativity in reengineering? In the real world, we solve ill-defined problems in continuously dynamic environments. Solutions are often useless by the time problems are completely specified. Even as we bring a wealth of information into the reengineering process, uncertainties in business boundaries and the future environment will remain. The creative reengineer finds ways to harness these uncertainties, rather than be constrained by them. We live in a world of conflicting objectives and constraints, and creative are those who can walk the tightrope of contradictions toward constructive progress.

Although reengineering has a lot to do with problem-solving, the creativity needed in problem understanding may be more critical than that required for generating solutions. The ability to transform problems, to look at problems from different angles and to select the best angle to attack the problem, is a very advanced level of creative thinking. Once the problem 'handle' is grasped, matching a solution to the problem requires much less creative thinking. A valuable spin-off from creative problem understanding in reengineering would be the evolution of a set of reusable reengineering strategies that can be applied across diverse business domains. In a sense, we need a systematic way to learn from reengineering experience.

10. Reengineering Requires Change Management

The stage in which the reengineering project crosses over from planning into implementation is a critical one. At this time, external consultants leave the scene, and members of the reengineering project tend to refocus their energies back on their day-to-day duties. At this crossover point, the reengineering blueprint must stipulate very clearly the implementation deliverables, milestones, deadlines, persons responsible for the deliverables, and internal and external dependencies. Without identifying and agreeing on these basic conditions, the blueprint may not be implementable.

Of course, the blueprint is but a theoretical concept until implementation of change has taken place. While development of the blueprint is achieved within months, full implementation of the blueprint may take years. It is not possible to transform an organization overnight. Physical changes, such as restructuring, job re-packaging, or refurbishment of the workplace are easy and low in risk. Less straightforward are the implementation of new IT systems and training of staff for the new systems and processes. Such implementation is costly and takes substantial calendar time.

The toughest challenge, though, is in changing the mindsets of people to operate in the new organization. In the change process, the attitude of people will evolve from uninformed optimism to informed pessimism to challenge and ambivalence and finally (if we manage to get that far) hope and acceptance. Management needs to continuously motivate and guide the staff to help them through the period of change. In times of chaos and uncertainty, the best people may leave the organization, such that the benefits of reengineering are cancelled out in the end. Change management requires aggressive follow-through by senior managers and executives, and cannot be outsourced. Otherwise reengineering implementation can lose momentum rapidly, or the implemented changes may be cosmetic and wear off easily.

11. Reengineering Requires Preparation

Before an organization embarks on reengineering, there is a host of preparatory activities to undertake. First of all, management needs to be clear about the need for reengineering. The need may be raised by anyone in the organization, but developing a common goal for reengineering and communicating the goal takes time. Getting the buy-in of all stakeholders and staff in the reengineering project takes time. Putting up a good case for reengineering requires substantive background study to be done on both the external and internal environments. Equipping management and staff with the prerequisite skills and perspectives also takes time. Finally, the organization must be prepared for the costs of implementing change, which are normally very high. It would be shameful to see a reengineering initiative terminated suddenly just because of budget limitations.

The topmost challenge in preparing for reengineering is in psychological preparation. Change works against the comfort zone that human beings by their nature enjoy. Much effort is needed to psych employees for the breadth and depth of changes that may soon sweep across the organization. It is natural for people to resist change if they believe that their own sense of security, esteem, or achievement will be affected by the reengineering exercise. Management must accept that resistance to change is inevitable in reengineering, and find ways to manage the resistance over an extended period of time.

12. Reengineering for the Future

Some critics claim that reengineering can only be used to fix today's business problems, but not to prepare the organization for the future. Certainly, if reengineering is undertaken as a project with explicit start and end dates, the extent to which the project can help the organization prepare for the future depends on the information that is brought into the reengineering process during the project duration. There is always the possibility of a 'horizon effect' that may not be anticipated, unless the organization is locked into a journey of perpetual reengineering.

Several complementary strategies need to be applied in order to reengineer for the future. Firstly, during the reengineering planning phase, the organization must be resourceful in formulating projections of the future scenarios within which it may have to operate. Secondly, during the reengineering implementation phase and the post-reengineering continuum, the organization must have in place robust mechanisms to adapt itself constantly to the changing demands of its stakeholders. Last but not least, the organization must view reengineering as a prospective, rather than retrospective, exercise. It is useful to learn about the past in order to prepare for the future. However, to take the leap into the future, the organization must also be able to *forget* and *unlearn* the past.

13. Conclusion

The points raised in this chapter highlight the fact that reengineering is a complex process in itself. Nevertheless, when viewed positively, reengineering can be a powerful approach to achieving world-class excellence. With a good vision, appropriate thinking methods and tools, adequate preparation and follow-through, and, most importantly, the best people involved in the team, the reengineering journey can be a thoroughly rewarding experience.

References

1. S. Aggarwal, Re-engineering: a breakthrough or little new, *International Journal of Technology Management* **13**(3), (1997) 326–344.
2. B. Caldwell, Missteps, miscues, *Information Week*, June 20, 1994, 50–60.
3. J. C. Collins and J. I. Porras, Building your company's vision, *Harvard Business Review*, September–October 1996, 65–77.
4. T. H. Davenport and J. E. Short, The new industrial engineering: information technology and business process redesign, *Sloan Management Review* **31**(4), (1990) 11–27.
5. J. W. Forrester, *Industrial Dynamics* (MIT Press, Cambridge, MA, 1961).
6. R. Gibson (ed.), *Rethinking the Future* (Nicholas Brealey Publishing, London, 1997).
7. M. Hammer, Reengineering work: don't automate, obliterate, *Harvard Business Review*, July–August 1990, 104–112.
8. C. M. Khoong, A framework for executing reengineering step zero, *International Journal of Business Performance Management*, Vol. 1, 1998, to appear.
9. J. Peppard, Broadening visions of business process re-engineering, *Omega* **24**(3), (1996) 255–270.
10. M. E. Porter, What is strategy?, *Harvard Business Review*, November–December 1996, 61–78.
11. C. K. Prahalad and G. Hamel, The core competence of the corporation, *Harvard Business Review*, May–June 1990, 79–91.
12. P. Senge, The leader's new work: building learning organizations, *Sloan Management Review* **32**, Fall 1990, 7–23.

PART II

CONCEPTS & TOOLS

Chapter 2

Applying Workflow Management Technology to Semi-Structured Business Processes*

WOLFGANG DEITERS
Fraunhofer-Institut für Software- und Systemtechnik,
Joseph-von-Fraunhofer-Str. 20
D-44227 Dortmund, Germany
E-mail: deiters@do.isst.fhg.de

THORSTEN LÖFFELER
Fraunhofer-Institut für Software- und Systemtechnik,
Joseph-von-Fraunhofer-Str. 20
D-44227 Dortmund, Germany
E-mail: loeffel@do.isst.fhg.de

RÜDIGER STRIEMER
Fraunhofer-Institut für Software- und Systemtechnik,
Joseph-von-Fraunhofer-Str. 20
D-44227 Dortmund, Germany
E-mail: striemer@do.isst.fhg.de

*This work was partially funded by the German Federal Ministry for Education, Science, Technology and Research BMBF within the cooperative project MOVE.

The workflow management technology is one enabling technology for achieving IT-support for business process oriented information systems. However, currently available workflow systems focus on solutions for well-structured business processes, the execution of which are known a priori, *i.e. before enacting the processes. One main disadvantage of such systems is their deficiency in coping with some real-life situations which demand for a flexible process support. Today's systems usually strictly distinguish so called build time components (for process definition) and run time components (for process enaction). In order to deal with the aspect flexibility of business processes, it is important to overcome this phased model of process management. In this chapter, so-called semi-structured business processes are introduced. Furthermore a classification scheme is introduced for identifying different kinds of semi-structured process models. For some of the classes of semi-structured business processes, examples for a suitable IT support are given.*

1. Introduction

The workflow technology is an enabling technology for achieving business process oriented IT systems. Workflow management systems support the enaction of business processes on the basis of an explicit process description called the workflow model. This workflow model is enacted (usually interpreted) by a dedicated component of a workflow system called the workflow engine,[1] thus driving the business process ahead. The workflow engine stores all information in a workflow database. By that is becomes possible to record the process history (for example, for quality assurance reasons), to identify the current process step (for example, in order to answer requests like 'how long will the process still be running?'), and so on.

However, most of the systems that are available today on the market offer system support for handling business processes the structure

[1]An architecture for workflow management system is given by the workflow management coalition [1].

of which are strongly defined, i.e. process steps and schedule, people that are involved, and the information base needed, are known. The systems mostly distinguish between a build time phase when the processes are being described and defined in a workflow model and a run time phase when the modeled processes are being enacted. In practice, however, during enaction, unplannable situations often arise, either in exceptional cases or when a certain situation occurs for the first time. That means it is quite often necessary to overcome the strict separation between build time and run time phases. Sometimes information about how to proceed in the process only becomes known during the process, i.e. at run time. So, a technology that would allow to interwave build time and run time phases would contribute much to a more flexible management of processes, allowing the process to be partially defined before start of the enaction, and the models to be completed when knowledge about how to perform the processes becomes available. This late modeling, however, is only one concept for achieving flexibility in process management. Other concepts can be thought of and are needed in specific situations. That means a whole set of different concepts is needed in order to obtain an approach to achieve flexible process management. Within this chapter such concepts and solutions for supporting flexibility are discussed.

Achieving flexible support for business processes is one major topic in workflow managememt research. The work presented here is related to a project funded by the German Ministry of Education, Science, Research and Technology. This project, called MOVE (Improvement of business processes with flexible workflow management systems), is a cooperative project with several research institutes and more than eight industrial companies. It consists of two threads — a research thread and an application thread. In the application thread workflow management is introduced and — among others — problem situations in the business processes supported by the current state workflow management systems are observed. Based on the experiences made in the application thread, new concepts toward a flexible handling of business processes and toward a continuous improvement process for the customers´ business processes and the supporting IT systems are being determined in the research thread. By that it is intended in the project to expand the scope of available technology to the more comprehensive idea of flexible organizations supported by a flexible, process-centered technology.

The argument of this chapter is structured as follows: In Sec. 2 the conceptual framework for distinguishing and managing business processes is given. In Sec. 2.1 a classification scheme for business processes is defined first. This classification scheme is given based on a terminology that distinguishes different kinds of business processes. Following that, the way how to identify to which class of the scheme a given process has to be associated with is discussed in Sec. 2.3. After that, IT support for the different process classes is sketched in Sec. 3, before a case study shows an application of the methodology (Sec. 4). Finally, Sec. 5 concludes and gives an outlook on further work to be done in the scope of the subject of this chapter.

2. Classifying and Identifying Business Processes

2.1. *A classification scheme for business processes*

To enable the modeling, analysis and enaction of business processes, the structuredness of these processes must first be examined. Structuredness can be classified according to the presence of certain process characteristics. The process characteristics we use — information base, cooperating partners, solution path — were identified in an empirical study [2].

By 'solution path' we mean all tasks which have to be carried out in the course of a process and their sequence. The 'cooperating partners' are all those involved in a process, cooperating in any way whatsoever. 'Information base' refers to all documents, data, knowledge, etc. available to or required in the process.

By taking these three characteristics and differentiating further according to whether they are *a priori* plannable or unplannable (i.e. at build time of the model), eight process classes are created. We visualised these process characteristics using a system of coordinates on three axes (Fig. 1).

Process classes for which the information base, the solution path and the cooperating partners are all plannable are called structured processes (# 0 in Fig. 1). Processes for which all three characteristics are unplannable are referred to as unstructured (# 7 in Fig. 1). These two classes are not dealt with in the following, because the scope of this chapter is the examination of semi-structured processes. We therefore restrict ourselves to the remaining six classes of the classification scheme:

Processes belonging to class 1 have in common, that a specific solution path is given and that it is known, what kind of information the process performers should use, while it is unknown which

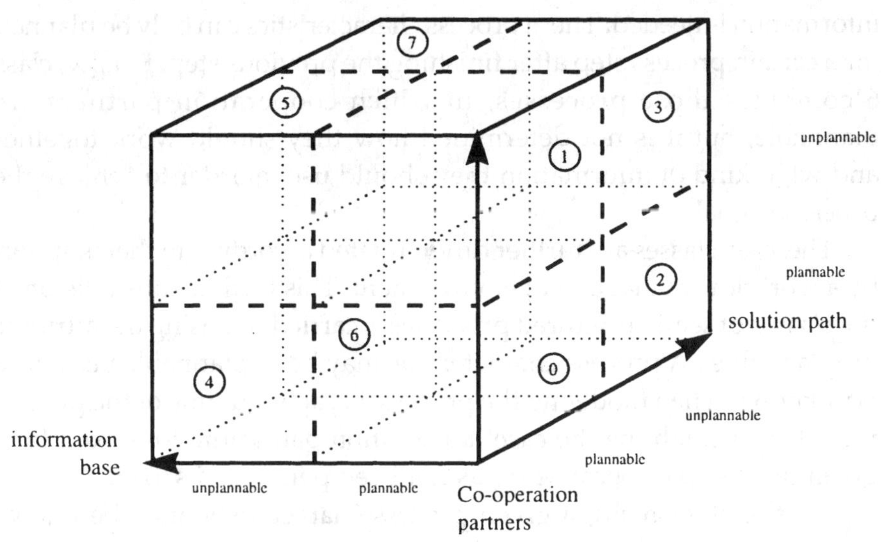

Figure 1 A process classification scheme

persons or roles should perform the process. Situations like these can arise, for example, when a person once defined drops out due to illness. For the processes in class 2, cooperating partners and information base is plannable, but the way how to deal with a certain problem is not defined. The degree of freedom for the process performers is consciously kept large. For the processes of class 3 only the information base is planned. The solution path is, like in class 2, not determined and it is also unknown who will perform the process.

Situations in which certain information objects cannot be planned are addressed in class 4. In such processes it is determined which cooperating partners work together and how they should act. What kind of information they should use is not planned. The solution path is the only known process characteristic for the processes in class 5. A classical process of this class is to plan the introduction of an information system for an enterprise. The steps to introduce the system are well known but it may not be determined, for example, whether there are external consultants necessary or which kind of information is needed. These process characteristics can only be planned for a certain process step after finishing the previous step. Finally, class 6 combines those processes, in which cooperation partners are plannable, but it is not determined how they should work together and what kind of information they should use in order to achieve the processes goal.

These six classes are further differentiated according to their support by a workflow management environment. This further sub-division of the classes of semi-structured processes is carried out using the attribute 'unplannable.' A process characteristic may be unplannable because it is unknown when modeling the process, i.e. at build time of the process model. This might be the case if a solution path cannot be fixed for a given process part because it has not been performed so far.

On the other hand, a given process characteristic may be known when modeling the process, but it can change during the process. We then call the process characteristic unplannable, too. For example,

Class	Sub-class	Plannable characteristics	Unplannable characteristics
1	a	solution path plannable information base plannable	cooperating partners change
	b	solution path plannable information base plannable	cooperating partners unknown
2	a	cooperating partners plannable information base plannable	solution path changes
	b	cooperating partners plannable information base plannable	solution path unknown
3	a	information base plannable	cooperating partners change solution path changes
	b	information base plannable	cooperating partners unknown solution path changes
	c	information base plannable	cooperating partners change solution path unknown
	d	information base plannable	cooperating partners unknown solution path unknown
4	a	solution path plannable cooperating partners plannable	information base changes
	b	solution path plannable cooperating partners plannable	information base unknown
5	a	solution path plannable	information base changes cooperating partners change
	b	solution path plannable	information base changes cooperating partners unknown
	c	solution path plannable	Information base unknown cooperating partners change
	d	solution path plannable	information base unknown cooperating partners unknown
6	a	cooperating partners plannable	information base changes solution path changes
	b	cooperating partners plannable	information base changes solution path unknown
	c	cooperating partners plannable	information base unknown solution path changes
	d	cooperating partners plannable	information base unknown solution path unknown

Figure 2 Subclasses of semi-structured business processes

although the basic set of potential cooperating partners within a process may be known, the person available to actually execute the process at a given time may change from case to case.

By distinguishing whether the different process characteristics are plannable or not, the six classes are subdivided into 18 subclasses: two subclasses for each of the classes with only one unplannable characteristic, and four subclasses each for classes with two unplannable characteristics (Fig. 2). In Sec. 3, for each subclass one possible solution for realizing the problem depicted by the subclass in a workflow management system is shown.

2.2. *Identification of semi-structured business processes by means of process descriptions*

So far we discussed that it is one important issue to appropriately distinguish structured from semi-structured processes and (for semi-structured processes) to assign them to the respective class in the classification scheme when building process models.

Thus it is necessary to provide means to a process modeler in order to enable him to associate processes with classes of the scheme defined above. This association has to take place when building the process models. Building process models means describing them using a given process modeling language. For the classification of a process it becomes necessary to relate the different characteristics of the classification scheme to the entity types of a given process modeling language. Entity types of a process modeling language are defined in a metamodel for this language. In order to cover as many process modeling languages as possible the Workflow Management Coalition's metamodel [3] is used in the following (Fig. 3).

The process characteristics we use for distinguishing semi-structured business processes are related to the metamodel of the Workflow Management Coalition as follows:

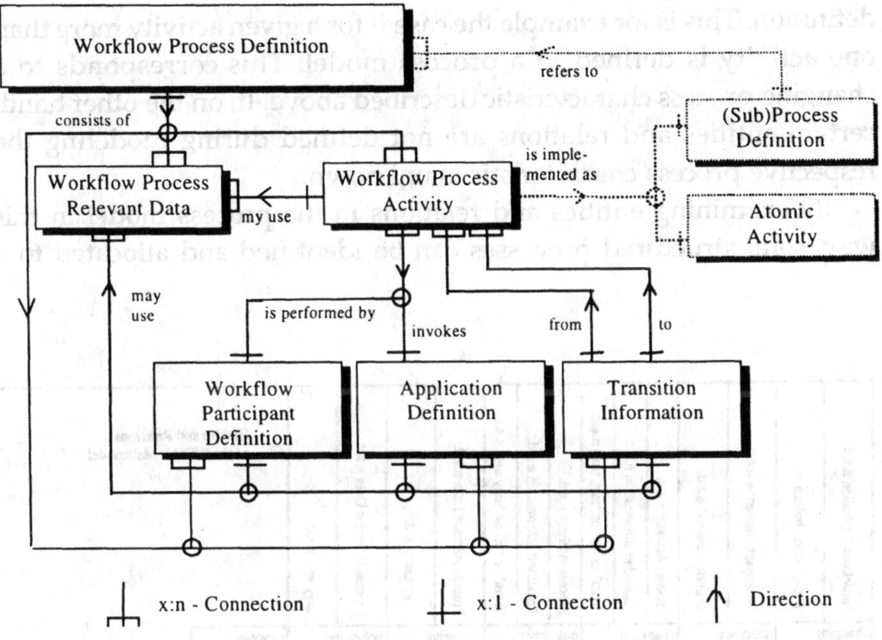

Figure 3 The WFMC-Metamodel of business process models

- The process characteristic 'cooperating partners' is represented in the metamodel by the entity 'participant definition' and the relations defined for this entity.
- The information base corresponds to the entity 'process related data' and its relation to other entities.
- The process characteristic 'solution path' is represented in the metamodel by the entities 'process activity' (and therefore by the entities '(sub)process definition' and 'simple activity') and 'transition information' and their relations. Depending on the granularity of the process description, the process characteristic 'solution path' may also have to include the entity 'application definition'.

During process modeling, situations arise in which it is *a priori* impossible to give certain entities an unambiguous or adequate definition. This is for example the case if for a given activity more than one activity is defined in a process model. This corresponds to a changing process characteristic described above. If, on the other hand, certain entities and relations are not defined during modeling the respective process characteristic is unknown.

By examining entities and relations in the process model in this way, semi-structured processes can be identified and allocated to a

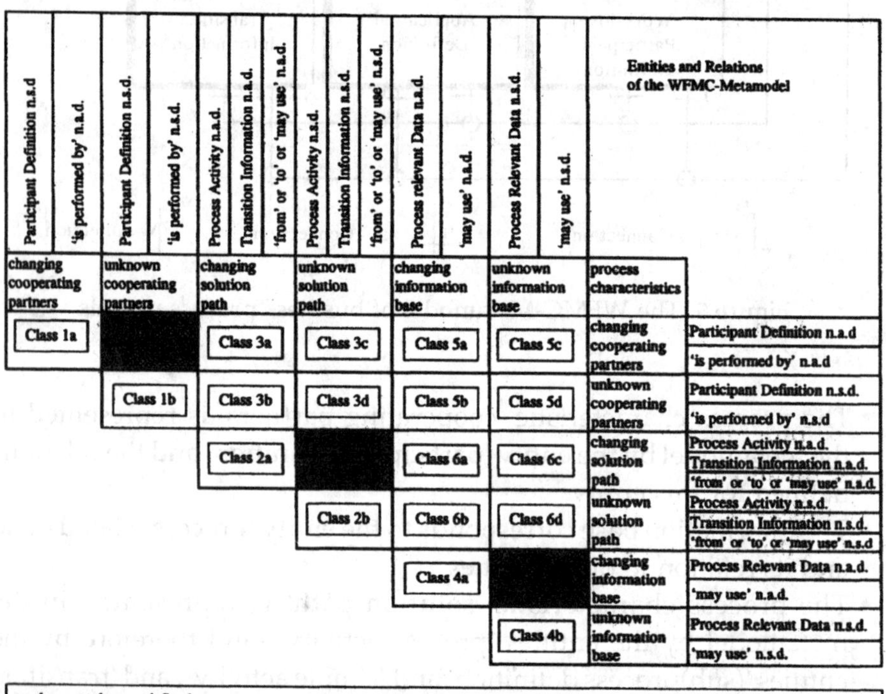

Figure 4 Reference table for the identification of semi-structured business processes

class of semi-structured processes (Fig. 4). Identification and classification will be clarified further with the use of examples.

2.3. *Examples for semi-structured business processes*

- **Example 1**: A project report has to be written by an independent, self-organizing team. It is not fixed which information, documents, etc. serve as a basis for the project report.
  In this example only the participant definition is known and defined adequately. The process activity must be implemented as a subprocess definition, but it cannot be defined, because the process activities performed by the self-organizing team are *a priori* not determined. The process relevant data cannot be fixed too, because the information, documents, etc., which serve as a basis for the report are not known. For these reasons, this business process is a semi-structured process of the class 6d.
- **Example 2**: Within the business process of dealing with applications, a specialist requests another specialist. The requests occur in irregular and unspecifiable intervals.
  In this case it is not known under which circumstances what information is required. The process relevant data can be defined, but the relation 'may use' cannot be defined adequately. This business process is a semi-structured process of the class 4a.
- **Example 3**: An employee with a particular qualification for dealing with a certain process gets ill. The process has to be taken over by other employees. Each of the process activities are performed by another employee in dependency on their qualification, work load, etc.
  Here the participant information and the relation 'is performed by' cannot be defined unambiguously, because e.g. the work load cannot be specified *a priori*. So this business process is a semi-structured process of the class 1a.

3. IT Support For Semi-Structured Business Processes Within Workflow Management Systems

3.1. Overview: IT support for certain process classes

Unlike classification, IT support for semi-structured processes must be considered in a tool-specific manner. The solution frameworks for the various classes are described using the CORMAN business process management environment [4–6], developed at the Fraunhofer Institute for Software Engineering and Systems Engineering. The system supports the modeling, analysis and enacting of business process models described in the process modeling language FUNSOFT [5–7] based on high-level petri-nets.

First, various solution frameworks are described for the classes with only one semi-structured characteristic, as the solutions for the classes with more than one such characteristic result from corresponding combinations. In the following only a brief outline of the solution frameworks is given here. A detailed explanation of this solution framework goes beyond the scope of this chapter.

- **1a Processes with changing cooperating partners:** In this case, different persons must be able to select the tasks to be performed at enaction time. Functions to manage task delegation and personnel replacement must also be provided. To realize this functions the basic concept of workflow transaction provided by FUNSOFT is needed [8].
- **1b Processes with unknown cooperating partners:** At enaction time, it must still be possible to involve new persons who were not involved in the process up to this point.
- **2a Processes with changing solution path at model build time:** In processes of this type, it is necessary to offer the choice between alternative process parts to those persons who are involved in the process.
- **2b Processes with unknown solution path:** The solution path is to be identified during enaction time, i.e. at that point in time when the

process part is to be performed. Modeling and enactment are therefore intertwined. We call the model definition that takes place during enaction late modeling. This class is described in Sec. 3.2.

- **4a Processes with changing information base:** Information which is only used occasionally during the enaction of a process must be available on demand. This means that the information is not automatically available at enaction time, but that it is made available only when it is required.
- **4b Processes with unknown information base:** At enaction time, the necessary information must be searchable with tool support so that it can then be further processed in the workflow environment. For the investigation of these information it is possible to provide functions known from help desk systems [1] within the workflow environment.

3.2. *Example: late modeling*

In this section we describe the realization of a specific class of semi-structured processes, namely processes with unknown solution paths. In these cases, it is not possible at build time, to fully specify the workflow activities of a partial process and their chronological order. This may be the case because the process has not been performed so far or the process modeler wants to retain a large degree of freedom for the people performing the process. For this kind of semi-structured processes, we propose the modeling of the solution path at run time, called 'late modeling.'

Late modeling is the possibility of defining, changing and removing workflow activities of a partial process while the enaction of the main process still runs. In order to provide this possibility, the process parts, that may be modified, have to be marked. Special events signaling the need of process modification have to be created. After all, the persons who are permitted to define changes of the partial process have to be identified. In case one of the modification triggering events occur during the enaction of the process, the marked activities are disabled for the current process enaction instance, while the enaction of the main process is still running. The disabled activitites may now be changed by the defined persons. A set of rules guarantees that the process model cannot get to an inconsistent state and the interface to the main process may not be modified.

The modification of process parts usually affects a number of people performing following activities within the process model. In order to model a process alternative, which satisfies the needs and requirements of all these people, a negotiation mechanism is needed [8]. After the modification is done, the modified process part is set back to the enaction of the main process.

4. Case Study

Within the MOVE project, we are currently developing a workflow application for the Contract Management business process of DHL Worldwide Express GmbH in Germany. The business process starts with a request from the salesperson for special rates to be offered to a customer. It is mandatory that special rates are agreed by the pricing committee afterwards. If the special rates are approved, the contract will be prepared for signature — both of the customer and DHL. Details of the signed contract such as special rates have to be entered into different systems.

When modeling the business process, we recognized that there are two semi-structured parts within the process. Both parts occur during the approval of the special rates:

- To decide whether the special rates can be approved, the margin has to be calculated. Depending on the calculated margins, different people have to approve the special rates. Who this may be depends on the margin. Therefore it cannot be predicted in advance who is entiled to approve the special rates. It can only be determined when the margin is known.

Because of this, we identifed that this subprocess is a semi-structured one belonging to class 3c in our classification scheme: processes with an unknown solution path and changing cooperating partners.

- If the special rates are refused, the salesperson has the oportunity to file an objection against the refusal by triggering a subprocess 'escalation.' The aim of the escalation is to approve a refused request for special rates although it has been refused before. The escalation subprocess is similar to the approval subprocess. The difference between these subprocesses is that there are no rules according to which calculated margins must be approved by given persons. Because of the similarity of both subprocesses, the escalation also belongs to class 3c of the classification scheme: semi-structured processes with an unknown solution path and changing cooperating partners.

Besides the challenge of mapping semi-structured processes onto a workflow model and enacting such processes, there is another organizational issue that we had to keep in mind when designing the workflow application: the persons who are entitled for the approval are only involved in the whole process when a certain margin requests their involvement or when an escalation occurs. These activities have only to be performed a few times per month. Therefore it is questionable whether to provide a workflow client to these persons or to let them use their normal communication mediums to inform them about new activities that they have to perform.

For these reasons, we decided to enact the subprocesses approval and escalation using the intranet technique. That means, the subprocesses are performed outside the control of the workflow management system. When the subprocesses terminate, the results are returned to the workflow management system.

The following technology is planned for realization: The persons that are entitled for the approval are informed about new activities by an e-mail, that is automatically generated by the workflow application. The e-mail contains a hypertext link to a HTML-page in the intranet.

This page is also automatically generated providing all necessary information for performing the approval or the escalation. On the other hand, it supports the decision whether to approve or to refuse the special rates. The decision is returned to the workflow application by using a CGI-Script. After that, the decision can be evaluated by the workflow management system. Further work is done under the control of the workflow management system.

The advantages of this solution are the following:

- The persons that are entitled for the approval do not have to learn to use new tools for their work. They only use their mail tool and their internet browser.
- Special workflow management system, offering the functionality to handle such semi-structured processes, are not needed for this process.
- Because standard internet technologies are used, this solution can be realized in an inexpensive way.
- The procedures and scripts that were developed for enacting the semi-structured processes can be reused for archiving the requests for special rates.

The disadvantage of this option is, that the exact status of the subprocesses is not available (e.g. for customer information) as it is handled outside the control of the workflow management system. It is only possible to give a statement that the subprocess 'approval' or 'escalation' is performed.

5. Further Work

In this chapter we propose an approach for the classification, identification and IT support of semi-structured business processes. The IT support for processes of this kind is defined and realized in existing workflow management systems like the process management environment CORMAN in a stepwise manner. A second generation of workflow management systems may provide a larger scale of built-in flexibility than currently available systems do. Besides developing solutions as extensions of existing systems, it is therefore important to define flexibility requirements for this second generation workflow tools, derived from our experiences described in this paper. Flexible workflow management systems are one goal of the project MOVE (Improvement of business processes with flexible workflow management systems), which is a cooperative project with several research institutes and enterprises, funded by the German Ministry of Education, Science, Research and Technology. In this project we currently expand the scope of this work from semi-structured business processes to the more comprehensive idea of flexible organizations supported by a flexible, process-centered technology.

References

1. M. Kriegsmann and R. Barletta, Building a case-based help desk application, *IEEE Expert*, December 1993, 18–24.
2. A. Picot and R. Reichwald, *Bürokommunikation. Leitsätze fuer Anwender* (in German) (Hallbergmoos, 1987).
3. P. Lawrence (ed.), *Workflow Handbook 1997* (John Wiley & Sons Ltd, Chichester, 1997).
4. R. Adomeit, W. Deiters, M. Gera, B. Holtkamp, R. Jägers, H. Weber and N. Weißenberg, Kernel/2r — A reference model conformat factory support environment, in H. Weber (ed.), *The Software Factory Challenge*. (IOS Press, Ohmsha, 1997) pp. 93–205.
5. W. Deiters and V. Gruhn, Process management in practice — applying the FUNSOFT net approach to large-scale processes, *Automated Software Engineering* **5**(1), January 1998.
6. V. Gruhn, validation and verification of software process models, Ph.D. thesis, University of Dortmund, 1991.
7. W. Deiters, A view based approach to software process management, Ph.D. thesis, Technical University of Berlin, 1993.
8. W. Deiters, V. Gruhn and H. Weber, Software process evolution in

MELMAC, in D. Cooke (ed.), *The Impact of CASE on the Software Development Life Cycle* (Singapore, 1994).

9. T. Herrmann, Workflow management systems: ensuring organizational flexibility by possibilities of adaption and negotiation, in *Proceedings of COOCS ´95* (Milpitas, California, USA, ACM SIGOIS , 1995) pp. 83–94.
10. W. Deiters, Transactions in the FUNSOFT net approach for process management, in F. Leymann, H. Schenk and G. Vossen, *Transactional Workflows* (Dagstuhl-Seminar-Report, 1996).

Chapter 3

The RARE System: A Multiview to Model and Reengineer the Business Process

HÉLÈNE BESTOUGEFF and AMEL BOUAISSI
Marne La Vallee University — 5 Bd Descartes,
Champs-sur Marne 77454 Marne-La-Vallee Cedex 2- France
E-mail:bestoug@ladl.jussieu.fr

Business process reengineering is becoming a widespread practice, but there is not yet a general approach which can be used in all environments. The central problem is related to differences in process definition and available tools to support the process redesign. This chapter presents a task/communication model based on task workflows and communication loops. By separating the analysis of the process into two views and using the object-agent paradigm, alternative reengineering solutions to achieve business objectives and task assignment can be tested dynamically. A prototype system called RARE (Role, Activity, Resource, Event) is described. First, a basic set of relevant modeling primitives is clearly defined, then to each concept, generic objects or agents are associated in order to have a uniform logical description of the whole system. Finally, a simple example of BPR using RARE is given.

1. Introduction

Today a company must be competitive with respect to such factors as cost/productivity, quality/service, speed/flexibility. To meet these objectives, organizations have often evolved in response to their business environment without real analysis, leading to a patchwork approach. In fact, organizations should rethink their business processes in order to adapt them to changes in customers' and suppliers' needs, as well as to technological innovation. This state of affairs has led to innovative management proposals for the next millennium.

Business Process Reengineering is a recently emerged management concept introduced by Hammer and Champy [1], who claimed drastic performance improvements if organizations were ready to comply with their approach. Although many debatable issues have been raised concerning the relevance of such an approach and many failures have been reported, the development of applications with associated models and tools has flourished in the past few years [2].

In a recent book, Hammer and Stanton [3] discuss what they consider to be the ten top mistakes that lead to failure. In our view, two of them are of particular interest :

- Ignoring the concerns of employees.
- Failure to adequately prototype and test before implementation.

It is clear that employees often view BPR as a source of insecurity and therefore, in any reengineering project, there is a strong need to manage the individual, social and organizational issues. In short, it seems important to analyze processes as a set of behaviors required to support successful business relationships, and to develop modeling and simulation tools which can be used for rapid prototyping and validation before actual implementation.

Our general framework is based on a model where on the one hand, the actor dependency makes the relationship between actors explicit in terms of their dependence on other actors to achieve their goals, and on the other hand, the task structure emphasizes the constraints between actors and activities.

Hence, business process can be represented and simulated along two views: the 'What' view and the 'How' view. The first one translates a business problem into business objectives carried out by actors through conversations and commitments. The latter describes business objectives in terms of work procedures.

To implement this approach, we have defined a three-level model:

- The **concept level** where basic primitives and their relationship are defined.
- The **logical level** which corresponds to the design step in terms of an object-agent architecture.
- The **implementation level** characterized by a user-friendly interface.

2. Task/Communication Perspective of a Process

A large spectrum from process improvement to radical redesign can be considered for business process reengineering. In the first case, an understanding of the existing process is essential, while the latter approach is based on a new strategic vision of the business, and analysis of past structures may not be necessary.

However, to conduct any reengineering, methodologies and/or modeling of business process are necessary.

Traditional modeling techniques concentrate on the modeling of activities and flows. This leads to an 'assembly line' model. However, in analyzing the causes of inefficiency, it is common to note that the main problem is not the tasks themselves but the communication between people in charge of those tasks. Hence, in process modeling it is important to consider the actors as entities who can make decisions and deal with multiple tasks.

Processes have been described in the literature along different perspectives: functional, informational, organizational and behavioral.

The first perspective is related to the classical task decomposition with respect to resource availability and management. Resource's description (material and informational) and their relationship constitute the main part of the informational perspective. The organizational perspective models the communication and cooperation between actors (or roles) of an organization. Finally, the behavioral perspective represents the dynamic aspect of the process [4].

In order to model a business process, the following questions must be answered:

- Who is involved in the process?
- Which tasks are part of the process?
- Who is responsible for which task?
- Which events trigger which tasks?

In our framework, we define a process as a structured flow of *conversations* and *associated tasks*. We call this two views approach the *task/communication perspective*. The idea of conversation flows in business modeling was initiated by F. Flores and T. Winograd [5]. Since then, several researchers have used and extended the basic ideas [6]. A conversation is a process step describing communication and commitments between two roles. The possible types of conversations used in our model are detailed in Sec. 3. A task represents a coherent structured set of uninterrupted activities under the responsibility, at a given moment, of a role.

In order to achieve a relevant redesign and enable process innovation, several steps are required [7]:

1. to identify existing processes,
2. to evaluate current problems,
3. to define and optimize new processes.

The analysis starts by delimiting the scope of each process and then the design of a new business process must include the following aspects :

- Business goals and objectives.
- Organization of people to support the process.
- Interactions between the environment and the process.
- Information created and stored.
- Performance measurement involving measuring improvements as a basis for further advance.

In general, what is available, as a start for redesign, is some sort of work procedure description, which can be translated into a task view. In our framework, in order to reengineer a process, one may build the conversation model associated with the tasks. Dysfunction in communications can help to point out bad human organization leading to poor results in task's performance. A new organization is then designed depending on people's ability and inherent constraints, and consequently tasks can be restructured or modified (Fig. 1).

Another approach for redesign could be to ignore the past task's structure and work directly toward a new organization, at the conversation and task levels simultaneously. The resulting model at the task level can afterwards be compared with the initial task's structure for assessment or adjustment (Fig. 2).

Both approaches must be seen as iterative procedures and not as a one-shot application. In Sec. 4, we give a small example to illustrate the different required steps for the first approach.

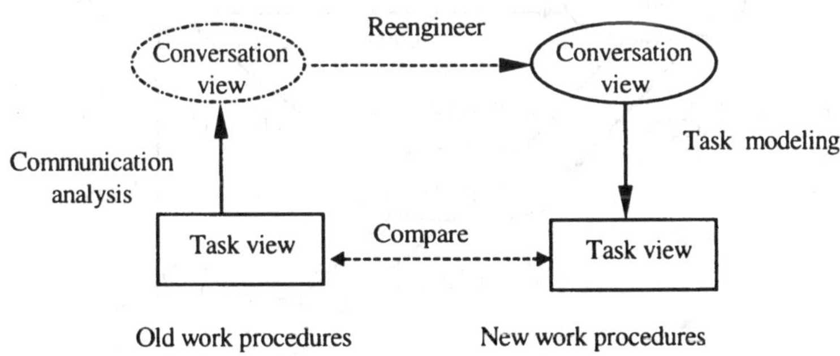

Figure 1

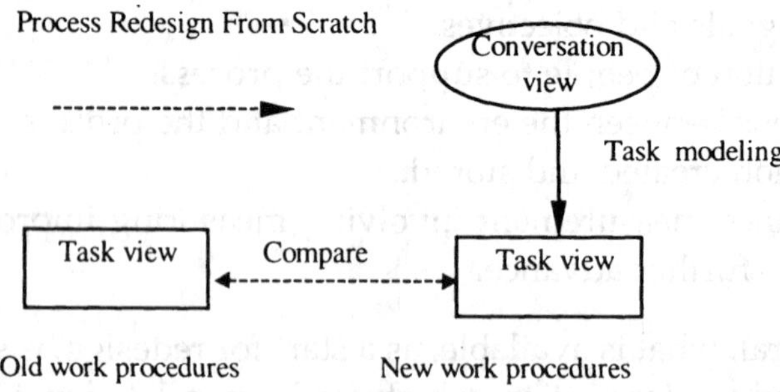

Figure 2

3. The RARE System

3.1. *General framework*

In order to describe conversations and tasks, we have precisely defined four primitives: **role, activity, resource, event**. To choose these primitives, we have tried to take into account the different concepts presented in the literature [8] and seen how they can be integrated into a simple coherent set.

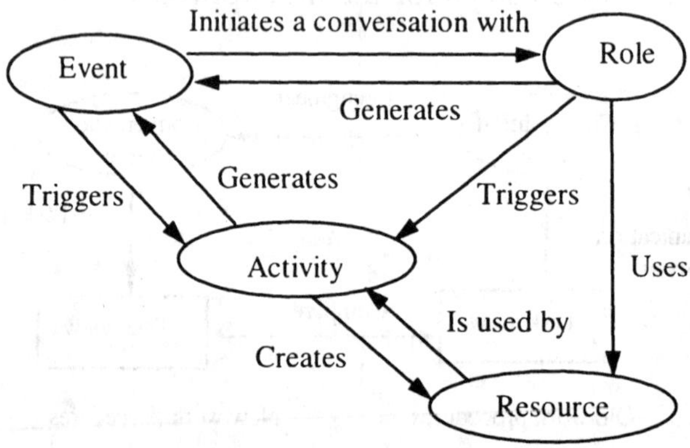

Figure 3 Relationship between RARE primitives

- A **role** is a set of objectives, obligations and responsibilities associated with an actor at a given moment. Roles are related to other roles through conversations.
- An **activity** is a transformation which, when given some input resources delivers output resources after a given time, subject to some business rules. Simple activities can be combined in a complex one, which is described only through global input/output resources and a combined business rule.
- A **resource** is a material or informational entity. Two main types of resources can be defined: dynamic and static. A dynamic resource corresponds to a flow between activities. A static resource is given *a priori* and can be sharable, consumable, or fixed.
- An **event** corresponds to a change of state in the organization. A state being a recognizable or definable condition of the organization.

3.2. *Concept level*

The concept level models conversation and task. A conversation is a *sequence of phases* (ordered set of phases) involving *two roles* named 'speaker' and 'hearer.' A conversation has one main objective attached to it. This objective is satisfied if a completed conversation occurs between the speaker and the hearer. If needed, each phase can be decompozed into sub-phases.

Another way to define conversations is to introduce the different *states* of a conversation. A phase is then defined by two states: beginning of a phase, completion of a phase (and, if needed, a given duration). For instance, the most popular diagram is the 'Customer and Supplier — Conversation for Action' [6] which has in its simple form four phases to which can be associated four states.

- Phase 1: opening of the conversation by a request or an offer.
- Phase 2: commitment or negotiation.
- Phase 3: performance associated with the request or the offer.
- Phase 4: assessment and acceptance.

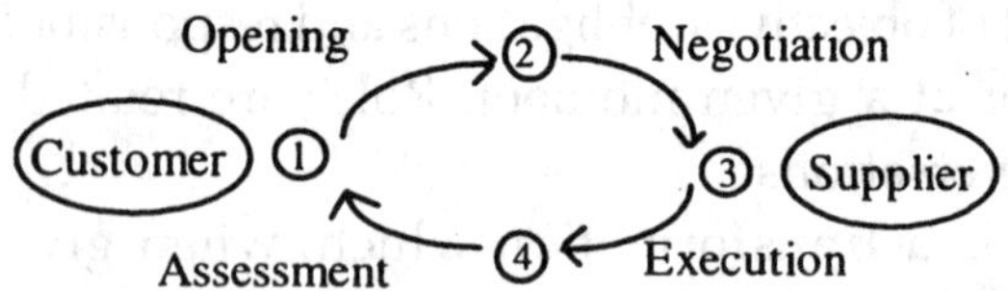

Figure 4 Conversation for action

The label attached to each phase denotes intentional performatives as introduced by Austin and Searle in the speech act theory [9]. The fact that the conversation concludes in state 1 is considered, here, as a 'satisfactory conversation.' Generally, one or more states in the state diagram can be defined as 'final' or satisfactory.

Although the expected conversation has a given number of phases, say four, when analyzing a particular application some phases may be absent. This can be interpreted as a dysfunction or a local fact. For instance, when the assessment phase is missing, it means that from the 'customer' viewpoint the result is not satisfactory, even though the required task has been performed (the non-satisfactory situation may be due to delays or quality problems).

In Fig. 5, the negotiation phase is missing: in this process, orders have to be executed as soon as uttered, the agreement is implicit and no negotiation can take place.

Normally, a conversation develops *forward* by going from one phase to the next one. Besides the possibility to divide a phase into subphases, (where the conversation can halt), one can define a 'way-back' by starting anew from a given phase, and canceling some already acquired results. For instance, from state 4, we can define a way-back step asking for a new performance phase (dotted line in Fig. 6).

The notion of phase is more natural to the user than state diagrams. However, at the formal level, conversations are particular finite state automaton with some constraints due to the nature of phases and way-back transitions. Each state of the automata describes in detail the transactions between the two roles. In particular, it is indicated whether

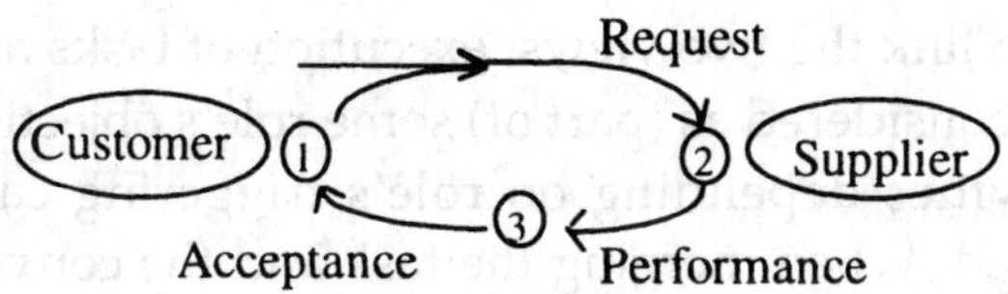

Figure 5

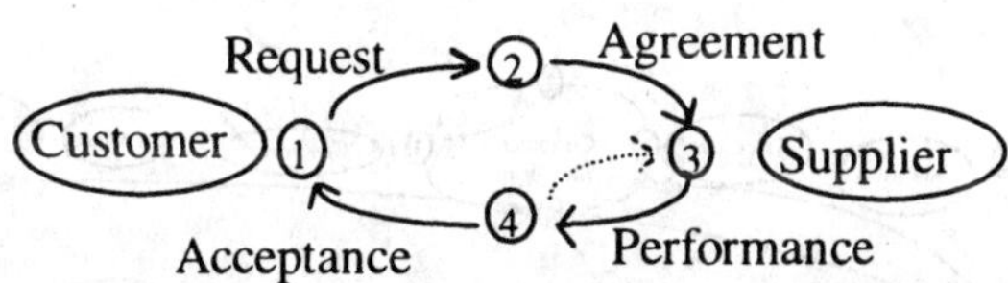

Figure 6

at this stage another conversation can be started (by whom and with whom), whether some task can be triggered and by whom, duration or admissible delays for a phase, etc.

The graphical representation used in the RARE system enables, by clicking on roles, phases or states to list the associated information which will be detailed at the logical level. The conditions on transitions between phases' states are used for the simulation, and may interrupt the conversation's flow if they are not satisfied.

Tasks are described as a serial or parallel combination of activities. An activity is described by its name and its informational structure: input/output resources, triggering events, triggering role, generated events and a business rule. This rule gives the needed calculations for performance evaluation.

The flow of resources between activities is not explicitly described, but results from the triggering conditions associated with the activities. Although on the diagrams, arrows are shown between activities, they only represent *possible or desired flows* and may be different during simulation. When a task is triggered, the result of a task is always some resource (material or informational).

In order to link the two views, execution of tasks are triggered by roles and are considered as (part of) some role's objective. Constraints between activities depending on role's triggering can therefore be explicitly stated. When merging the task and the conversation views, we have a concept level diagram. An example which will be commented upon in the next section, is given in Fig. 7.

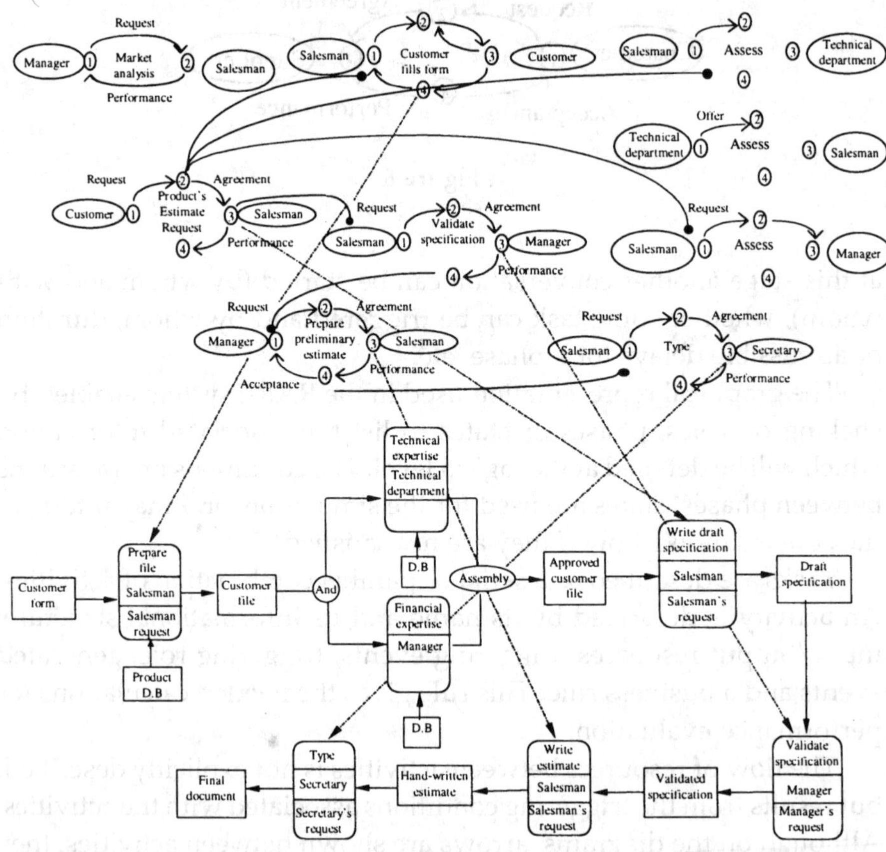

Figure 7

3.3. *Logical level: objects and agents*

The previous level is only an overall vision of a process. In order to evaluate, simulate and reorganize we need more information which is given by the logical level. This level, however, should be free from implementation details.

Two paradigms for design are much in use now: object model and agent model. While methodologies to design objects are already available, agents are still in the development stage [10]. We have chosen to use both paradigms: agents for roles and objects for the other primitives [11]. On the other hand, shifting totally to a multi-agent architecture, as advocated by some approaches [12], leads to more complex and less readable models of activities and resources.

In fact, agents can be seen as a specialization of objects [13].

- An object is an entity that comprises a set of *attributes* and a set of *operations*.
- An autonomous agent is an object together with an associated set of *goals* and an associated set of *motivations*.

Communication between objects or agents is performed by message passing, but the meaning of individual messages is interpreted in a different way. In particular, motivations for agents can be defined as filters on agent's messages [14].

We have seen that to each role is attached a set of objectives, and that roles engage in conversations with other roles. In a given simulation, a role must then satisfy a local objective it agreed upon. To do so, the role must choose an optimal plan, which is described by conversations with other roles and/or execution of tasks. However, a plan is conditional over possible reactions of other roles and may be updated afterwards. Hence, using objects and agents is fruitful because reorganization can then be clearly and explicitly studied from two perspectives. For a given business objective, several actors can potentially satisfy the request and a task is not attached to an actor: the

Taylor's principle does not apply any more. A task represents one of the many steps of some actor's plan. Therefore, when looking for some work reorganization (satisfying local and global constraints) one can choose and distribute in an optimal manner business objectives and tasks [15].

3.3.1. Dynamic

A static model can give some information about the organization of a process. It is a snapshot. A process is dynamic in nature. Simulation is useful to determine measurements of quality and business performance [16]. It can show, under alternative scenarios deadlocks, useless tasks or activities, redundant conversations, bad conversations structures, etc.

The reengineering can be simulated and evaluated before a real implementation is undertaken. Moreover, some improvements, based on structural properties of the concept and logical levels can be automatically suggested: remove cycles, remove unused nodes, create teams working on common tasks or activities, etc.

The dynamic of the model is driven by events and events can be described in an homogeneous manner at the task and conversation level. External events are listed in an agenda and have predictable occurrence time; they generally initiate conversations. At the conversation level, events can be generated by a conversation and can trigger a task, i.e. the head activity of a task. Each activity is activated either by an explicit, or an implicit event (completion of some previous activities in a chain, for instance).

3.4. Implementation

Two different modes of specification are present in RARE, the graphical mode and the dialogue mode. In the graphical mode, the user draws the diagrams by choosing from different graphical object types corresponding to the different concepts defined above.

In the dialogue mode, all inputs are given by dialogue boxes (instantiation of the logical level). This way, we have an incremental construction of the entire model.

The agent-object architecture of the RARE system makes it easily extensible. Moreover, by selecting which object to show and which ones to hide, the system supports a *selective visualization* of the different aspects of a process.

4. Reengineering Using RARE

The RARE system can be used for diagnosis and redesign. The concept and logical level diagrams are a support for communication and discussion between the different people involved in the BPR process.

To explain how to use the RARE system for reengineering, we shall discuss a simple example adapted from a real case analyzed in Ref. 17.

4.1. *Analysis of the AS-IS situation*

The firm under consideration manufactures products with specific features given by the different customers. One simplified business process is the description of the working out of an estimate. First, the customer defines his needs with a salesman, then detailed analysis normally involves the technical department and the manager for feasibility assessment. If there is an approval, it is then worthwhile for the salesman to write a draft for the specification and validate it with the manager. Finally, the salesman writes out an estimate, and a secretary must type it.

Although the work procedure seems simple at the task level (Fig. 7), the customers are not satisfied.

To build a task/communication model of what really happens, information has been collected through interviews with the staff of the enterprise in order to :

- Identify the conversations and associated roles.
- Describe the goals of conversations.

The first problem arises when we want to connect the conversations and the tasks. Although some tasks are supposed to take place in the work procedure, they are not really performed (the assessment tasks). Another problem is found when some given task is claimed to be performed by two different persons. Usually it is not executed at all!

The resulting model shows how people working in this firm see their communication activities.

Considering the diagram, several remarks can be made :

- Many conversations are not completed (assess, validate specification, type estimate).
- Some conversations are not coherent, two different roles take care of the same objective (technical assessment).
- The market analysis is not connected to the rest of the process.
- These problems can arise from different causes.

First, there is clearly a lack of understanding of what a commitment means in a conversation. Incomplete conversations give rise to delay and complaints. There is somewhere an implicit way the actions described are completed, but it is not clearly stated.

Incoherence comes from conflicts between people's responsibilities: who is in charge of what?

Disconnected conversations shows a lack of communication or concern between people supposed to work together on the same process, or a misunderstanding of the process.

4.2. *Suggestions for reengineering*

The previous remarks can be used to improve the process (close the conversation and eliminate incoherent conversations). It is only when the diagram is coherent and complete that a simulation can take place. To really reengineer the process a more drastic approach must be taken. There are no universal rules to succeed. The BPR team must explore alternatives by discussing with the involved staff. The previous analysis and diagram can help in answering the following questions:

- Are there useless conversations?
- Can some conversations be replaced by access to common information facilities or adequate tools?
- What are the different skills of actors involved in the process?
- Can some tasks be performed by different people depending on variable dynamic constraints?

This last point leads to dynamic reorganization, where the multi-agent architecture of the system is very important in order to simulate different organizations where actors can exhibit different abilities in the course of a process.

In our example, several remarks were made after the preliminary analysis. Due to delays and unclear respective responsibilities of the actors involved, the assessment procedures were often bypassed. The manager considered that the validation was not always necessary, although the salesman felt more secure to have it. But due to delays no one was really satisfied. The secretary was generally overloaded with work and could not type the estimate on time. Finally, the market analysis should be connected to another process.

What can be proposed is to reorganize the process into two procedures, whether the customer's request is a simple case or a more complex one. Figure 8 gives the new diagram for the simple process, where the salesman should take the responsibility of presenting an estimate without the manager's approval, but with a real technical

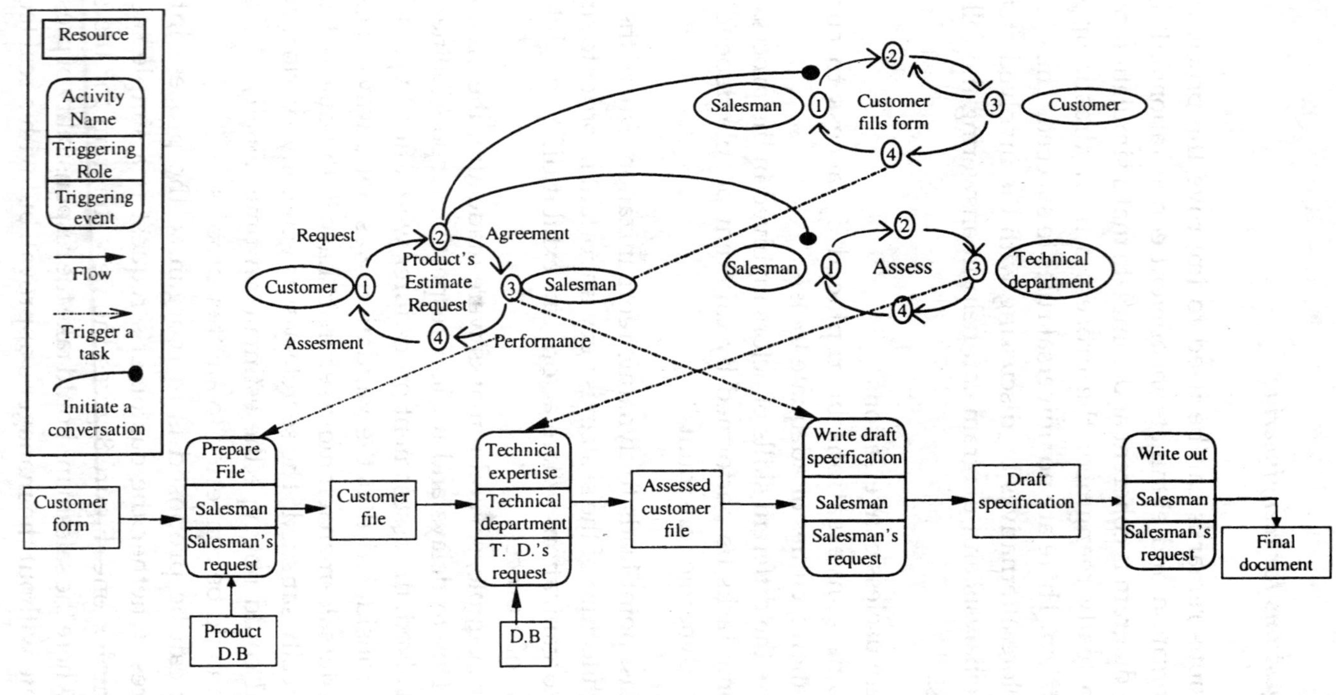

Resource
Activity Name
Triggering Role
Triggering event
Flow
Trigger a task
Initiate a conversation
Salesman
Customer fills form
Customer
Request
Customer
Product's Estimate Request
Agreement
Salesman
Assesment
Performance
Salesman
Assess
Technical department
Customer form
Prepare File
Salesman
Salesman's request
Product D.B
Customer file
Technical expertise
Technical department
T. D.'s request
D.B
Assessed customer file
Write draft specification
Salesman
Salesman's request
Draft specification
Write out
Salesman
Salesman's request
Final document

Figure 8

assessment, and type himself the document. Another diagram will give the description for the complex cases.

5. Conclusion

Enterprises have to adapt to the new market needs. Modeling and simulation tools can help to capture dysfunction and test new organizational structures. We have presented the RARE system as an original approach to the problem of business modeling and simulation. The two-views description has the capability to model the communication and the task organization of an enterprise. By separating the two views, alternative solutions to business objectives and task assignment can be analyzed and tested by simulation using the coordination actions of the intelligent agent architecture.

References

1. M. Hammer and J. Champy, *Reengineering the Corporation. A Manifesto for Business Revolution* (Nicholas Brealey, London, 1993).
2. K. Spurr, P. Laysell, L. Jennison and N. Richards (eds.), *Software Assistance for Business Reengineering* (John Wiley & Sons, 1993).
3. M. Hammer and S. A. Stanton, *The Reengineering Revolution* (Harper Collins, New York, 1995).
4. B. Curtis, M. I. Kellner and J. Over, Process modeling, *Communications of the ACM* **9** (1992) 75–90.
5. R. Medina-Mora, T. Winograd, R. Flores and F. Flores, The action workflow approach to workflow management technology, *Proceedings of CSCW* (1992) 281–288.
6. T. Schal, Workflow management systems for process organizations, *Lecture Notes in Computer Science 1096* (Springer, 1996).
7. T. H. Davenport, *Process Innovation* (Harvard Business School Press, Boston, MA, 1993).
8. Workflow management coalition, *Terminology and Glossary* (1996).

9. R. Searle, *Expression and Meaning. Studies in the Theory of Speech Acts* (Cambridge University Press, 1979).
10. H. Bestougeff, Intelligent agents: a new step towards data and knowledge organization, in *Modeling Complex Data for Creating Information* (Springer, 1996) pp. 9–14.
11. H. Bestougeff and A. Bouaissi, A multi-agent architecture to model and simulate a business network of recurrent conversations and associated tasks, *Proceedings of EMCSR '98* (Vienna, 1998).
12. T. J. Norman, N. R. Jennings, P. Faratin and E. H. Mamdani, Designing and implementing a multi-agent architecture for business process management, *ECAI'96 Workshop, LNAI 1193* (Springer, 1997) pp. 261–275.
13. M. Luck and M. d'Inverno, A formal framework for agency and autonomy, *Proceedings of the First International Conference on Multi-Agent Systems* (1995) 254–268.
14. M. Barbuceanu and M. S. Fox, Integrating communicative action, conversations and decision theory to coordinate agents, *Proceedings Autonomous Agents* (ACM Press, 1997) pp. 49–58.
15. H. Bestougeff and M. Rudnianski, Games of deterrence and satisficing models applied to business process modeling, *AAAI Spring Symposium* (AAA I Press 1998) 8–14.
16. K. Tumay, Business process simulation, *Proceedings of the 1995 Winter Simulation Conference*, pp. 55–60.
17. S. V. Bronfman, Réseaux de communication dans les organisations: une méthode d'analyse fondée sur l'approche langage/action, doctoral thesis, Université de Paris I (1996).

Chapter 4

Integrated Business Process Management: 'How It All Fits Together'

JURGEN VANHOENACKER
Pricewaterhouse Coopers Management Consultants,
16, Rue Eugène Ruppert, L-1014 Luxembourg, Luxembourg
E-mail: jurgen.vanhoenacker@lu.pwcglobal.com

ANTONY BRYANT
Leeds Metropolitan University,
The Grange, LS6 3QS Leeds, United Kingdom
E-mail: a.bryant@lmu.ac.uk

GUIDO DEDENE
University of Leuven (K.U. Leuven),
Leuven Institute for Research on Information Systems (LIRIS),
Naamsestraat 69, B-3000 Leuven, Belgium
E-mail: guido.dedene@econ.kuleuven.ac.be

Much of the current debate around BPR centers on its claims for successful implementation, and its distinctive novelty. In this chapter we seek to move the debate forward by observing that the methodological basis for BPR lacks transparency and, very often, fundamental justification. Most methodological support advanced in the literature is taken too often for granted, and needs to be specified far more exactly and appropriately. As a consequence, many business process professionals can no longer appreciate how the endless list of modeling techniques, the variety of decision making guidelines and the numerous staffing prescriptions 'fit together' into a comprehensive whole to facilitate their decision making. Not surprisingly, many fail to mobilize, exploit and capitalize on the organizational knowledge base, which is needed for inducing business process change. In this chapter, we will explain some of these methodological shortcomings, and offer the SPARTA framework for developing a far more inclusive, integrative and adaptive approach to the field of I-BPM — Integrated Business Process Management. Illustrations from an I-BPM effort in the Financial Services Industry will accompany our understandings.

1. Towards a Broader Discussion on the Business Process Phenomenon

Despite a decade of experience with the business process phenomenon, certain fundamental problems still beset its successful application and cause concern to practitioners. Considering the enormous financial and intellectual investments made in the 'business process issue', it is no surprise that the prime conceptual quest for BPR advocates — and critics — has been focused around this aspect. The result is an ever-growing bibliography of research findings from authors, each with their own list of pitfalls, success factors and avoidance strategies for successfully implementing redesigns [1–6]. Amongst many others can be cited the difficulties in ensuring top management commitment or the technical problems involved in developing a responsive workflow management system.

Although we understand the importance of this stream of research, we are convinced that there is another critical aspect that has been largely ignored in the business process debate so far. Our reasoning is based on the belief that most implementation problems are the result of a defective decision making process, prior to any consideration of implementation issues. As such, the point of departure for our research was an inquiry into the adequacy of current methodological support for BPR decision making, and whether this provides sufficient capabilities for the business process professional. If such support is inadequate or inappropriate, it will be a critical weakness in any BPR application. We have the impression that the effectiveness of a vast number of 'classical' BPR methodologies has mostly been taken for granted. Moreover, the overwhelming existence of sophisticated methodological support for BPR lacks transparency. Many business process practitioners face a 'methodology overload' and fail to appreciate when, why and how, one or another business process technique should, or can be used in their efforts.

Overall, we feel that current characterizations of the business process phenomenon and its methodologies are too narrow in focus. They reflect a highly normative, mechanical perspective on business reality whereby IT has been elevated to the role of primary, or even sole change vector. The current rhetoric largely assumes that business processes can be pulled apart and redesigned like Lego [7]; an influence partly inherited from Software Engineering approaches [8–12]. Despite caveats to the contrary in the early writings of BPR advocates, that warned against 'throwing computers at problems,' classical BPR can still be found deficient in its own terms. Furthermore, there is the paradox that many guiding concepts of the business process movement retain large 'Taylorist' influences, and many enthusiastic 'reengineering czars' mistakenly assume that business processes have been engineered in the first place. All this leads to a contradiction between the practice and recent research [11, 13–16]. Attending to the neglected aspects of BPR should resolve some of these contradictions, and may redeem BPR for a wider group of practitioners. In short, there is a need to broaden both the context and concept of BPR and to reconsider some of the basic principles underlying the business process phenomenon.

In the first place, we wish to introduce the notion of Integrated Business Process Management (I-BPM) as an amalgam of general managerial action concerned with business processes. As such, we deliberately take a non-partisan stand. We want to avoid the seemingly endless discussion on the exact differences between BPR, TQM, etc.; which has been raging — in a largely futile manner — for many years. Rather, depending on the specifics of each situation, I-BPM can appear under different forms and labels. At times, this might consist of a radical reengineering in the strict sense of the concept, a trimming or reorientation of processes, an implementation of a total quality management system or even a combination of the above concepts.[1] The bottom-line is that, in each of these cases, the central theme is effectively managing and changing business processes — whether or not they are thought to need 'reengineering.'

2. Getting Back To Basics: The Methodology Triangle

Simply stated, managing business processes involves questioning the validity of existing working practices (cf. the 'AS-IS' picture) and justifying potential changes (cf. the 'TO-BE' picture). Various methodologies and tools can be used to support the above decision making process. Consequently, it might be that one way to improve our ability to manage business processes would be to improve the guiding methodological vehicles underlying these tools and methods.

We consider a methodology to be a prescriptive device that guides our actions and decisions. As such, a methodology could be a generic and highly formal concept such as the 'SHAPE/Integrated Process Engineering methodology' of Coopers & Lybrand, or an informal and largely tacit mental model used by a single organization. Regardless of the exact form in which a methodology appears in reality, three

[1]For instance, our experience reports on reengineering efforts preceding the implementation of ISO 9001-compliant quality systems.

fundamental building blocks should be explicitly integrated. We refer to this as *the Methodology Triangle*:

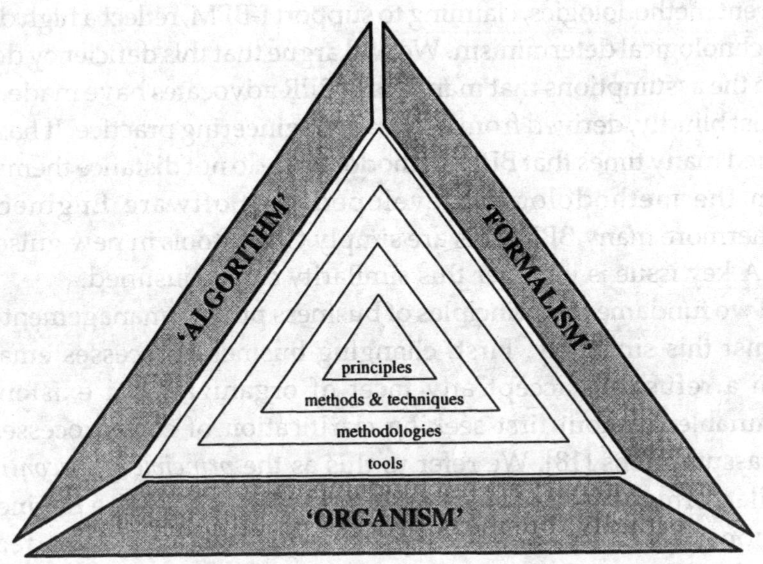

Figure 1 The 'Methodology Triangle'

A first, and most straightforward component of any methodology is what we call the 'Formalism.' This refers to the means of representation and communication (e.g. process flowcharts). Secondly, the 'Algorithm' component deals with the decision making as a whole, thereby indicating the different phases, activities and steps in the process (e.g. simulating a redesign). Finally, the 'Organism' component refers to the different roles, actors and skills required during the decision making processes (e.g. a process champion). In short, we consider any piece of methodological support as something more than a collection of sophisticated modeling and diagram techniques. However, the most difficult part is to see how all these elements, stemming from different disciplines, 'fit together' into a comprehensive whole.

3. Organizing for I-BPM Methodologies: The SPARTA Framework

Current methodologies, claiming to support I-BPM, reflect a high degree of technological determinism. We will argue that this deficiency derives from the assumptions that many early BPR advocates have made, often almost blindly, derived from Software Engineering practice. It has been argued many times that BPR methodologies do not distance themselves from the methodologies developed for Software Engineering; furthermore many BPR tools are simply CASE-tools in new guises [13, 17]. A key issue is whether this similarity can be justified.

Two fundamental principles of business process management work against this similarity. First, changing business processes emanates from a refusal to accept any facet of organizational existence as immutable, without first seeking clarification of core processes and key assumptions [18]. We refer to this as the *principle of discontinuity*. Similar forms of inquiry are not fundamental for Software Engineering practice. Secondly, business process practitioners face decision situations that are highly unstructured. The problem has to be fitted into a 'frame' before any solution can be developed. We refer to this as the *principle of dynamic complexity* [19]. This is distinct from the principle of *detail* complexity in Software Engineering, where the practice is quite correctly focused on the technicalities of the potential solutions. As such, whereas I-BPM addresses elements of discontinuity and dynamic complexity, embedded in business processes; conventional Software Engineering methodologies focus on issues of stability (cf. the need for a stable data-model) and detail complexity (cf. the stepwise refinement principle), excluding other aspects. Simply stated, an I-BPM methodology should be thought of more as an organizational double-loop learning device for acquiring the crucial understanding of 'why?' a business process exists in the first place rather than a tool for solely describing the details of 'how?' a business process operates in itself. At the very least, any SE methodologies need some fundamental reorientation if they are to be applied to I-BPM contexts.

Moreover, our understanding of the Methodology Triangle suggests the need to validate and integrate knowledge from different disciplines into comprehensive methodological support. Therefore, developing effective BPR methodologies should be founded on an interdisciplinary basis, and cannot simply re-use SE approaches. Proponents claim that Systems Theory offers a viable foundation for integrating elements of various disciplines [20–22]. We approach Systems Theory as a language that can be used to describe all sorts of phenomena in terms of a set of interrelated components that, together, form a comprehensive whole and manifest an emergent property. Consequently to describe a phenomenon such as I-BPM as a 'system' means that a model, stated in systems terms, needs to be created. We have developed such a model that contains six fundamental functional components that provide the bases for any form of methodological support for I-BPM [23, 24]:

I-BPM as a System of Systems	**'ORGANISM'**	**'ALGORITHM'**	**'FORMALISM'**	
Feedback System	*Reporter*	*Observation*	*Flow-Activity-Flow (FAF) Construct*	'SOLICITOR'
Abstraction System	*Sensemaker*	*Introspection*	*Intention-State (IS) Construct*	'PROCESSOR'
Openness System	*Diplomat*	*Diversion*	*Intention-State-Intention (ISI) Construct*	'ACCEPTOR'
Questioning System	*Troubleshooter*	*Discursion*	*Positive State-Intention- State (+SIS) Construct*	'RESISTOR'
Leverage Identification. System	*Animator*	*Deracination*	*Negative State-Intention-State (-SIS) Construct*	'TRAFFICATOR'
Servomechanistic System	*Negotiator*	*Conversion*	*Inverted Activity Intention-Activity (AIA^{-1}) construct*	'ASSESSOR'
	Organizational System	**Decision Making System**	**Modelling System**	

We have coined the acronym 'SPARTA' for this framework:

1. **S**olicitor: a methodology should enhance the 'soliciting' of information with respect to the underlying business process problem situation and the business process environment.
2. **P**rocessor: a methodology should enable the 'processing' of information in terms of the dynamics of business processes instead of the infinite details.
3. **A**cceptor: a methodology should encourage and 'accept' different interpretations of the same problem situation instead of expressing an early judgement.
4. **R**esistor: a methodology should 'resist' taking for granted the seemingly familiar and the obvious elements that underlie business processes.
5. **T**rafficator: a methodology should point out directions ('a trafficator') and leverages for changing the underlying problem situation.
6. **A**ssessor: a methodology should provide a mechanism for 'assessing' the nature of a proposed redesign and the resulting changes once achieved.

4. Going a Step Further: Developing a Meta-model for Sparta

So far, the above presentation of SPARTA only provides an outline against which we can locate our understanding of I-BPM. In order to provide the framework with the prescriptive power needed for methodology development, we should formalize each cell into a common language. In other words, a *meta-model* should be developed that formalizes the content of each cell and enables integration with the other cells. A similar meta-model in its turn could furthermore be used as a conceptual data-schema for I-BPM tool builders to organize their repositories. Recently, a renewed interest has emerged concerning the outlook and way of organizing a BPM-tool repository. Whereas the early BPR tools were somewhat revamped versions of popular CASE-tools, increasingly they are being positioned within the realm of corporate knowledge systems, Group Decision Support System (GDSS) or organizational learning systems.

Considering the above, each SPARTA dimension of Formalism, Algorithm and Organism can be treated as the object of a meta-modeling exercise. For each dimension, we will inquire into the nature of the constituent components, how to represent them as meta-concepts, how they are linked and how they can become a comprehensive whole, manifesting an emergent property. Below, we provide a brief overview of this exercise in meta-modeling.[2] Since a detailed account of the meta-modeling strategy lies beyond the scope of this paper, we will focus on the interpretation of some meta-model concepts, in particular the ones concerning the underlying systems concept of components, interrelations and emergent properties.

5. The SPARTA Formalism Meta-Concepts

The SPARTA Formalism addresses the required set of presentation and communication vehicles in I BPM settings. In practice, practitioners use a variety of modeling techniques. Whereas some stick to plain textual descriptions (i.e. a special type of model), others resort to highly sophisticated diagramming techniques. In many cases, these modeling techniques often serve as nothing more than a descriptive role to document decisions once they have been made. They do not offer much support for understanding the rationale — the 'why' — underlying the business process itself. The SPARTA Formalism attempts to counterbalance this phenomenon.

---

[2]We have adopted the M.E.R.O.DE. methodology to structure our meta-modeling effort [25, 26].

A basic component of our Formalism is what we call a *'business process dimension.'* This represents different ways to look at business processes, whereby each dimension addresses a specific type of information to be captured within a (model) representation. As such, we can address a business process in a number of ways; the logical sequence of its activities, the information structures they act upon, the people who execute the business process activities, and so on. Considering the cognitive and information processing limitations of humans, modeling theory has argued that one should beware of combining multiple process dimensions into one single model representation [27, 28]. It is neither possible nor desirable to gather all the views in one and the same model. Therefore, each representation or communication technique should be based on a *'unique basic model'* that consists of a basic entity type and a basic connector type. For instance, the widely known technique of ER-diagramming is based on the data-entity/relationship/data-entity basic model. Expressing similar basic models for I-BPM is the objective of the SPARTA Formalism meta-model.

Overall, we have identified seven basic entity types important for I-BPM: business process activity (Activity), activity flow (Flow), intended organizational state (State), underlying intention (Intention), actual organizational state (State^{-1}), new intention (Intention^{-1}) and new business process activity (Activity^{-1}). A combination of the above, results in six modeling primitives (cf. supra). The latter could be implemented using familiar, or less well-known modeling techniques. For instance, a Data-Flow Diagram (DFD), a Process Flowchart or an IDEF1 map are clearly implementations of the FAF modeling primitive; they represent a business process in terms of a logical flow of activities. Though it lies beyond the scope of this chapter to discuss the details of each Formalism construct, two central concepts deserve further clarification.

First, we repeatedly used the notion of *Intention* as a basic modeling variable. With the latter, we like to refer to the implicit and explicit assumptions and rationales that people assume for their working practice. Simply stated, they focus on the 'why?' questions underlying organizational action. For instance, an intentional statement of the form "... in order to identify typing errors" (INTENTION) might well constitute an intention underlying the existence of "a reviewed report" (STATE). Moreover, we suggest the use of systems diagrams to model intentional structures in a similar way, as is proposed by Ref. 19. As such, the +SIS construct refers to the identification of a reinforcing loop amongst a set of explicit and implicit intentions. The existence of a similar positive feedback loop explains why people stick to a specific working pattern. On the other hand the –SIS construct suggests the need to identify a balancing loop amongst a set of intentions. A similar negative feedback loop offsets ingrained thinking patterns and motivates a reconsideration of an existing working pattern. The integration of these semantic and syntactical elements enables us to assess the *dynamic complexity* in I-BPM decision situations.

A second important element of the SPARTA Formalism meta-model is the notion of the inverted version of a basic modeling variable. With the latter, we refer to any meaningful alternative to an original modeling statement. For instance, an intentional statement "... in order to divest myself of my responsibilities" ($INTENTION^{-1}$) might well be an inverted version of the original intention "in order to identify typing errors" (INTENTION) that underlies the existence of "a reviewed report" (STATE). Overall, inversion could vary from formulating a simple negation to a 'less mathematical' alternative of an original modeling statement. Essential is that the set of inverted entity types, integrated into modeling techniques, enables us to grasp the elements of *discontinuity* in I-BPM decision making situations. In essence they reflect the discontinuity with respect to an original representation.

While respecting the M.E.R.O.DE. modeling prescriptions, the figure below presents a conceptual object-relationship diagram for the overall SPARTA Formalism meta-model:

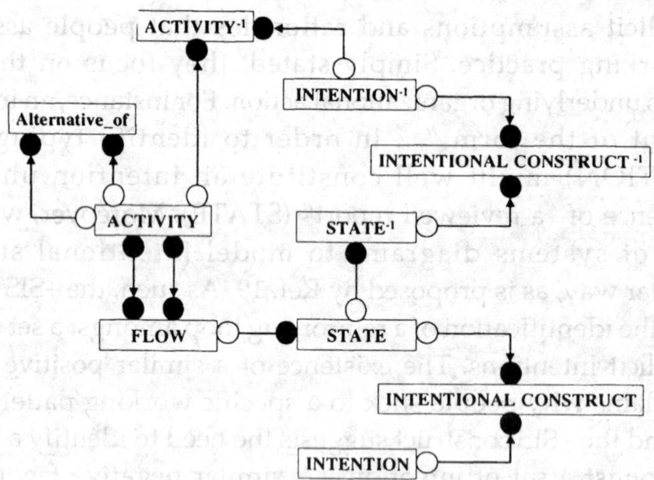

Figure 2 The SPARTA formalism meta-model

The box below provides an illustration of how a similar Formalism meta-model was 'instantiated' in a real-life banking case. The latter concerned an I-BPM project for the securities management business process. A simplified account of this 'business process story' is provided below:

> The moment a customer places (ACTIVITY) a securities purchase order (FLOW), the account manager sends (ACTIVITY) a hand-written order notification (FLOW) to the middle-office for customer cash position control (ACTIVITY) before sending an order validation (FLOW) to the back-office for final settlement of the transaction (ACTIVITY). The fact that the order notification forms arrive at the middle-office (STATE) was, amongst others, justified "because account managers should not deal with administrative control work" (INTENTION). The fact that account managers did not effectuate this type of control (STATE) however was offset by the fact that, in reality, they actually had real-time access to this type of customer information ($STATE^{-1}$). This new observation gained in importance "because it only takes a couple of seconds to verify customer cash positions" ($INTENTION^{-1}$). This insight resulted in the new working pattern that customer securities orders were directly entered into the system by the account manager ($ACTIVITY^{-1}$) for automatic cash position control.

In the above banking case, the ACTIVITY and FLOW constructs (cf. FAF) were presented and communicated along a flowchart model of the securities business process. The STATE and INTENTION constructs (cf. IS, ISI, SIS) were described and analyzed within a simple MS Excel spreadsheet form and with 'a type of' conceptual mapping technique, used during workshops. Finally, the alternative working pattern (AIA^{-1}) was formalized and discussed by means of a more textual 'model.'

6. The SPARTA Algorithm Meta-Concepts

In its turn, the SPARTA Algorithm inquires into the necessary decision making activities for I-BPM. We consider an Algorithm component to represent the activity of inquiring into the core Formalism meta-model. Decision making is about developing, inspecting and communicating the information contained within the formalism meta-objects. As such, whereas the SPARTA Formalism meta-model constructs define the type of information of business processes that is considered as important, the SPARTA Algorithm components define how this information is created and how it evolves over time during the I-BPM effort. Metaphorically speaking, the Algorithm components of decision making activities 'give life' to the Formalism meta-objects. Following the SPARTA reasoning, we distinguish between six different decision making activities for I-BPM: Observation, Introspection, Diversion, Discursion, Deracination and Conversion.

Each of the Algorithm decision making activities are primitives and can be implemented along different decision making techniques such as structured interviews, brainstorm sessions or group workshops. Also, depending on the type of I-BPM (BPR, TQM, streamlining, etc.), some Algorithm components gain or lose in importance. As such, the Discursion activity, having the objective of 'leaving no stone unturned,' will be more important in traditional BPR settings than is the case for a simple process automation effort. Even more, depending on the culture of the organization, the Algorithm components can vary in terms of formal rigor and procedural prescriptions. For instance, the Diversion activity, aiming at uncovering the implicit intentions[3] that underlie a specific working pattern, might well be organized in a series of structured workshops — while using techniques such as Nominal Groups — and be given the label of 'The Discovering Phase' in the overall project. In turn, the 'Conversion' activity, which aims at arriving at a consensus, might be organized along a set of open discussions together, while using a technique such as Force Field Analysis, and be given the label of 'The Validation Phase' in the overall project.

Following the logic underlying the SPARTA framework, the set of the above decision making activities constitutes a comprehensive whole; manifesting the emergent property of a double-loop learning cycle. In other words, the BPR Algorithm results in the creation of new knowledge, it transcends the traditional activity of merely describing a business process in infinite detail and justifying the status quo (i.e. first-loop learning concept).

We have integrated the SPARTA Algorithm meta-model concepts as 'information functions' that enact upon the Formalism meta-objects. In other words, from a meta-model perspective, we conceive, for instance, the Observation activity as a function, which will represent solicited information from its environment in terms of business process activities and flows:

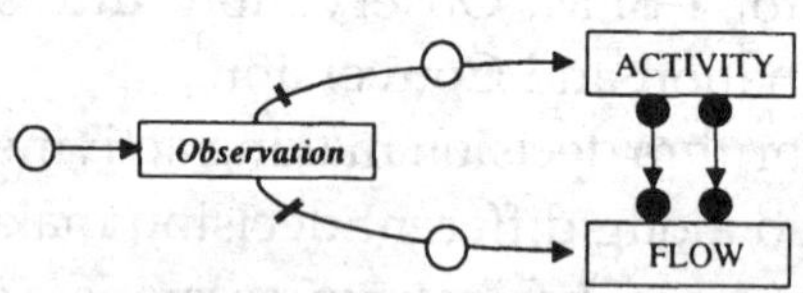

Figure 3 The SPARTA algorithm: meta-model concepts for the 'Observation' activity

[3]cf. 'why do we do what we do at all?'

The Observation activity as modeled above could be identified in the banking case as follows:

> From the moment the securities management business process had been identified for analysis, the initial step consisted in acquiring a first overall picture of what the business process looked like (i.e. the OBSERVATION activity). This decision making activity was labelled as 'the process description phase' in the overall I-BPM project. Furthermore, the activity had been organized along structured group interviews with a particular stress on open-ended questions about the logical process flow (e.g. "What are the most important activities you consider in this process?"). The objective of this phase was to get a quickmap picture of the business process while identifying the major business process steps and the ways in which they are interconnected (cf. instances of ACTIVITY and FLOW objects). As a result, multiple N:M relationships had been identified between instances of the ACTIVITY and the FLOW meta-objects. This quickmap served as the focal point for all members of the I-BPM project team and enabled them to arrive at a common definition of the business process before proceeding with further analysis (cf. INTROSPECTION, DIVERSION, etc.). Moreover, the interviews were organized in such a way as to avoid the danger of 'getting lost' in the infinite detail that might underlie each and every business process activity identified. Therefore, no stepwise refinement or 'functional decomposition,' similar to what is often done in IS projects, was allowed on the securities management business process quickmap.

7. The SPARTA Organism Meta-Concepts

The SPARTA Organism addresses the organizational roles to be fulfilled in I-BPM contexts. This dimension has traditionally not received the attention it deserves with respect to methodological support. Again, this was a result of the mechanistic and technology-oriented approach of classical BPR. Human activity was treated as simply another company resource to be scrutinized in business process analysis [16, 29]. A direct consequence of this evolution was that many BPR efforts failed due to demotivation, frustration and severe organizational resistance.

A related observation is that some early BPR modeling tools were intrinsically very interesting, but never gained a solid foothold in business practice, since their target audience did not possess the proper skills to handle the technique itself, nor to interpret business process models that resulted from its application.

Overall, the core motivation for integrating organizational issues into I-BPM methodologies is that it explicitly takes human aspects into consideration. This has always been highly problematic in business process management, and that is why it is often ignored. Not surprisingly, this evasion is one of the most often cited pitfalls advanced in the critical literature [1, 16, 30]. The SPARTA Organism deals with the so called 'people factor' up-front in a BPR exercise instead of considering it once the 'damage has been done.' The SPARTA Organism therefore is basically a frame of reference to address change management issues proactively, instead of reactively dealing with them once a business process solution is inflicted on the workforce.

Here too, the SPARTA Organism should be looked at as a system whereby its components are connected in such a way that they constitute a comprehensive whole. As suggested, we like to refer to this component using the concept of *a role*. In the first place, a role implies the notion of an actor or an agent. A second element is that a role is associated with the execution of an activity. Finally, an actor willing to execute an activity successfully should have the proper skills to do so. As such, there are three prerequisites to such a role: an actor, an activity and a skill set.[4] It is only when these three elements are present, that we can speak of a role.

What we envisage with the SPARTA Organism dimension is having the ability to manage the 'intellectual capital' within the context of I-BPM. Therefore, we should be able to inquire into the set of skills and actors that are present in an organization, and to apply them to various I-BPM efforts. This will provide us with a means to assess the (intrinsic)

[4]As an illustration, we could conceive the role of a policeman as a person x (actor) that has a thorough knowledge of traffic rules (skill) in order to intervene successfully at the site of a car accident (activity).

learning capability of an organization and take appropriate action. We should be able to assess whether a specific organization, with an existing set of actors and skills, is capable to assume the roles that are important in, for instance, a reengineering project. I-BPM is highly context sensitive and we want to assess the organizational ability to pursue with the effort. Clearly, a similar understanding of the SPARTA Organism necessitates the embedding of sophisticated skill and human resource management facilities as basic elements of an I-BPM methodology or tool.

Again, the roles indicated above are generic and several implementations can be observed in practice. For instance, the role of the 'Troubleshooter' to generate a creative tension or a degree of conflict in a business process study could be taken up by an external consultant for obvious political reasons. In particular, we would like to stress the importance of the 'Negotiator' role as the servomechanistic element in the SPARTA Organism. The basic responsibility of this role is to build a minimum critical mass of stakeholders that consider a particular reengineering blueprint as a worthwhile endeavor. The objective is to create the needed momentum to introduce organizational change and simultaneously anticipate the degree of organizational resistance. Clearly, in its implemented form, the 'Negotiator' encompasses major facilitating skills to mediate between the different parties (i.e. workforce and executive team). In essence, the role is to identify and build a 'winning coalition' as has been referred to in the socio-political school of Organization Theory.

Considering the importance attached to the role concept, we have deliberately integrated its constituent parts as core meta-model objects. As such, a specific role can be seen as a function that inquires into the set of skills and actors, and generates the sufficient input that triggers a SPARTA Algorithm component. The latter in its turn 'freezes' the information into a business process model. A representative implementation for the 'Reporter' role is provided as shown:

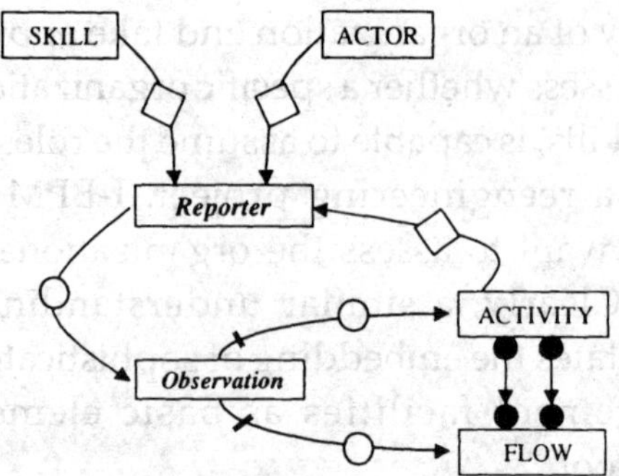

Figure 4 The SPARTA organism: meta-model concepts for the reporter role

Again, the above meta-model concepts were identified in the banking case:

> External consultants explained to top management the objective of the Observation activity (cf. ACTIVITY) that was labelled as 'the process description phase.' Furthermore, a request was made to organize a set of structured group interviews with persons that were able to provide an overall and 'objective' picture of the securities management business process (cf. REPORTER role). Basically, various process participants, including internal process customers (cf. ACTOR instances) were identified to participate. A couple of years of experience, preferably in various departments of the bank, as well as an outspoken ability to communicate freely and an ability to provide a structured view on working practices (cf. SKILL instances), formed the focus for the selection of these interview participants.

Overall, the connected set of roles within the BPR transformation process, again, makes out a whole that manifests the emergent property of a team or rather what has been referred to as a 'Self-Regulating Team (SRT)' [31]. Johnson *et al* argue that SRTs are "*the means to make the processes of an organization self-regulating.*" Related terms such as 'venture teams' or 'change teams' can be found in the BPR literature [32, 33].

8. Discussion: Applying the Sparta Logic at Different Levels

The SPARTA framework as presented in this chapter forms a platform on which to discuss and integrate methodological developments for I-BPM. However, once the principles behind SPARTA are understood, it can be used as a powerful tool to structure a discussion on I-BPM at other conceptual levels. Currently, the SPARTA logic proves to be applicable to any situation where the element of 'learning at the level of a process' is present.

In the first place, we could apply the framework as a learning instrument at the level of a single business process. Also in this situation, the execution of a business process thrives on a set of representation and communication tools (i.e. document forms, data files, procedures, memos, spreadsheets, etc.), a set of activities (i.e. control, copy, verify, classify, phone, etc.) and a set of roles (i.e. a process owner, a supervisor, a case manager, etc.).

A similar discussion could be set up at the aggregated level of all business processes of a particular industry. Here, a set of generic models of business processes could be defined in a similar way, as has been done for industry-specific ISO 9000 process frameworks. A set of roles, at the level of the industry, could be identified to participate in this discussion (e.g. labor unions as a servomechanism, industry associations as 'reporters,' consumer groups as 'trouble-shooters,' etc.).

Still another level of conceptualization is to consider SPARTA as a paradigm building instrument amongst business process academics and practitioners. Arriving at a business process paradigm is a process equally characterized by elements of dialogue and discussion. A new concept challenges the existent rhetoric to arrive at a consensus on theories and concepts. Again different roles are needed to succeed in this effort (cf. different schools of thought) as well as proper communication vehicles (cf. scientific journals, conferences, axioms, frameworks, etc.).

Finally, a less straightforward application level for SPARTA could be considered at the level of the I-BPM decision making process itself. Applying SPARTA recursively would involve a (re)consideration of I-BPM itself as a business process. The SPARTA logic applied in this situation ultimately should result in yet another form of learning, which is referred to as 'triple-loop' learning.

Clearly, many other levels could be considered to develop the business process phenomenon. We could even consider SPARTA at the level of the individual mindset, to develop 'personal mastery' as suggested by Ref. 19. Overall, our objective has been to demonstrate the integrative character of the framework. Our message is that the viability of the 'business process discipline' thrives on synthesis and integration rather than on analysis and segregation of concepts and disciplines.

References

1. S. Drew, BPR in financial services: factors for success, *Long Range Planning* **27**(5), (1994) 25–41.
2. G. Hall, J. Rosenthal and J. Wade, How to make reengineering really work, *Harvard Business Review*, November-December 1993, 119–131.
3. D. Holland and S. Kumar, Getting past the obstacles to successful reengineering, *Business Horizons*, May-June 1995, 79–85.
4. E. V. Martinez, Successful reengineering demands IS/business partnerships, *Sloan Management Review*, Summer 1995, 51–60.
5. I. Turner, How to re-engineer successfully, *Manager Update* **6**(3), (1995) 1–7.
6. I. Turner, Business process reengineering I, *Manager Update* **6**(2), (1994) 1–9.
7. J. Peppard, Broadening visions of business process reengineering, *Omega* **24**(3), (1996) 255–270.
8. V. Grover, J. T. C. Teng and K. D. Fiedler, Information technology enabled business process reengineering: an integrated planning framework, *Omega* **21**(4), (1993) 433–447.

9. P. Harmon, Business process reengineering with objects — Part II, *Object-Oriented Strategies* **5**(1), (1995) 1–13.
10. J. C. Henderson and N. Venkatraman, Strategic alignment: leveraging information technology for transforming organizations, *IBM Systems Journal* **32**(1), (1993) 4–16.
11. A. E. M. Khalil, Implications for the role of information systems in a business process reengineering environment, *Information Resources Management Journal*, Winter 1997, 36–43.
12. D. L. Schnitt, Reengineering the organization using information technology, *Journal of Systems Management*, January 1993, 14–20, 41, 42.
13. C. Avgerou, T. Cornford and A. Poulymenakou, The challenge of BPR to the information systems profession, *New Technology, Work and Employment* **10**(2), (1995) 132–141.
14. R. Coombs and R. Hull, BPR as 'IT-enabled organizational change': an assessment, *New Technology Work and Employment* **10**(2), (1995) `121–131.
15. D. Stoddard, S. Jarvenpaa and M. Littlejohn, The reality of business reengineering: Pacific Bell's centrex provisioning process, *California Management Review* **38**(3), Spring 1996, 57–76.
16. H. Willmott, The odd couple?: re-engineering business processes; managing human relations, *New Technology, Work and Employment* **10**(2), (1995) 89–98.
17. J. A. Taylor and H. Williams, The transformation game: IS and process innovation in organizations, *New Technology, Work & Employment* **9**(1), (1994) 54–65.
18. A. Bryant and D. Chan, Goal directed development; confronting organizational legacy, *Proceedings of the Sixth Annual Business Information Technology (BIT) Conference*, Manchester Metropolitan University, Manchester, 7/11/1996, pp. 143–154.
19. P. Senge, *The Fifth Discipline; The Art and Practice of the Learning Organization* (Doubleday, New York, 1990).
20. R. L. Ackoff, *Redesigning the Future: A Systems Approach to Societal Problems* (John Wiley and Sons, New York, 1974).
21. L. von Bertalanffy, *General Systems Theory: Foundation, Development, Application* (George Braziller, New York, 1973).
22. P. Checkland and J. Scholes, *Soft Systems Methodology in Action* (John Wiley & Sons, New York, 1990).

23. J. Vanhoenacker, A. Bryant and G. Dedene, The BPR holon; a framework for (re)orienting methodological developments for BPR, *Proceedings of the Fifth World Conference on Systemics, Cybernetics and Informatics (SCI'97)*, Caracas, Venezuela, July 1997.
24. J. Vanhoenacker, A. Bryant and G. Dedene, Rethinking BPR methodologies; an alternative framework, *Proceedings of the BPR'97 Europe Conference*, London, June 1997.
25. G. Dedene and M. Snoeck, M.E.R.O.DE: a model-driven entity-relationship object-oriented development method, *ACM SIGSOFT Software Engineering Notes* **13**(3), (1994) 51–61.
26. M. Verhelst, Objectgerichte systeemontwikkeling; een praktische aanpak met JSD en M.E.R.O.DE, (in Dutch) (Kluwer, Deventer, 1992).
27. G. L. Lohse, D. Min and J. R. Olsen, Cognitive evaluation of system representation diagrams, *Information & Management* **29** (1995) 79–94.
28. J. A. Zachman, A framework for information systems architecture, *IBM Systems Journal* **26**(3), (1987) 276–292.
29. C. Grey and N. Mitev, Reengineering organizations: a critical appraisal, *Personnel Review* **24**(1), (1995) 6–18.
30. A. Ascari, M. Rock and S. Dutta, Reengineering and organizational change: lessons from a comparative analysis of company experiences, *European Management Journal* **13**(1), (1995) 1–30.
31. L. Johnson and M. Stergiou, The necessary architecture of self-regulating teams, *Proceedings of the ME-SELA'97 Conference* (1997) 93–98.
32. D. C. Andrews and S. K. Stalick, *Business Reengineering, The Survival Guide* (Prentice-Hall, Englewood Cliffs, 1994).
33. D. P. Petrozzo and J. C. Stepper, *Successful Reengineering* (Van Nostrand Reinhold, New York, 1994).

Chapter 5

BPR-Enabled Systems Engineering

LESLIE JOHNSON
Information Systems Engineering Group,
Computing Laboratory, University of Kent, Canterbury,
Kent, CT2 7NF, England
E-mail: L.Johnson@ukc.ac.uk

MARIA STERGIOU
Information Systems Engineering Group,
Computing Laboratory, University of Kent, Canterbury,
Kent, CT2 7NF, England
E-mail: M.Stergiou@ukc.ac.uk

As traditional management techniques were no longer appropriate in the changing business environment, companies employed Business Process Reengineering (BPR) to achieve elevated business performance. Similarly, as traditional systems development approaches delivered disappointing results, system developers experimented with other models, including Evolutionary Delivery and Evolutionary Development, in order to enable successful technology exploitation by businesses. Both these business and systems initiatives embrace elements of cultural change, management flexibility, empowerment, organizational readiness, and technology introduction in a changing environment. We show how the management of a BPR project allows us to integrate Evolutionary Delivery and Evolutionary Development into the organizational transformation project. And by these means, we show how BPR can enable Systems Engineering.

1. Introduction

The world is changing greatly from day to day and new elements are added to an already long list of considerations any company should address when developing its strategic objectives [1]. Some of these elements are new to the current business environment (e.g. sophistication of customer, people demanding fulfillment and personal meaning at work, green issues, collapse of middle management) and some already existed but have recently intensified (e.g. the fierce competition, increasing importance of business ethics and the lack of these in some businesses, the move away from unitary organizations toward federal, franchising and networking models, the 'global village,' business ethics).

Throughout the eighties, the above mentioned elements in the business world, questioned traditional management behavior and practices. This dynamic business environment called for refocusing on management thinking and as a result, management 'gurus' around the world came up with management tools and behaviors that would qualify a company to survive and successfully compete in the new business era. Concepts like Total Quality Management (TQM), Just-In-Time (JIT), Downsizing, Business Process Reengineering (BPR), emerged; their purpose was formulated, and a 'methodology' was quickly attached to them.

Given the inherent complexity of Information Technology (IT), practitioners tried to develop new approaches of Systems Engineering in order to instill discipline into IT projects and make them more manageable. But in the rapidly changing business environment, IT still failed to deliver expected results. Hammer [2] gives two reasons for the disappointing results. The first reason is that companies tend to use technology to mechanise old, and possibly cumbersome, ways of doing business that have already proven inadequate. The second reason is that most IT applications were built applying traditional step-by-step system development methodologies. IT people attempted to address the inherent complexity of IT by providing solutions cut out for a stable environment. The developed methodologies assumed a stable environment and a great deal of creative intelligence was invested to bypass the inflexibility of methodologies. Such methodologies delivered systems that failed to meet the needs of both senior management and end users alike since they were only involved when the final system was delivered [3].

Step-by-step system methodologies were developed in an output-driven process. This meant that there was no conceptual room in the methodology to accommodate changing requirements discovered in the development process. As a result, these changing requirements could neither be captured in the development process nor addressed by the monolithic system delivered. Such methodologies failed to acknowledge that business requirements continue to evolve during the systems analysis, design (and maintenance) phases [4].

It is recognized that the more stable the requirements of a system the more feasible their successful implementation will be. In the past, Systems Engineering processes urged such stability; this is not possible now. Business requirements evolve continuously and BPR calls for the transformation of the application of technology in general and Systems Engineering specifically. Thus, applying Systems Engineering methodologies to BPR is questionable [5]; instead, applying BPR principles to Systems Engineering can be altogether more successful.

1.1. How do we capture evolving systems requirements?

As traditional systems development approaches deliver disappointing results, system developers experiment with new methodologies that promise to enable successful technology exploitation by businesses. Any methodology that aims to cater for evolving systems requirements must:

- Fit the dynamic business environment by providing ways of managing the development of systems that are quick, deployable, easily defined, executed and improved, not difficult, slow or bureaucratic.
- Allow developers to 'own' the process of system development (and in effect of organizational transformation) rather than have it imposed by outsiders (books, gurus, etc.).
- Be scalable and applicable to any situation so, as no method is a silver bullet, developers need to customize the methodologies to suit individual circumstances.
- Incorporate feedback loops built in the system development process for the sole purpose of evaluation and learning purposes — not for control.

It is our belief that meta-models have these characteristics. We will be illustrating this through Evolutionary Delivery, Evolutionary Development and BPR.

2. Evolutionary Delivery and Evolutionary Development

One of the main objectives of Systems Engineering[1] is to assure systems quality throughout the working life of the system which includes evolving the system as the requirements evolve. We present two methodologies that claim to address and cater for the difficulties of developing responsive systems: Evolutionary Delivery and Evolutionary Development.

---

[1]Wymore (1993) defines Systems Engineering as "the intellectual, academic, and professional discipline the principal concern of which is the responsibility to ensure that all requirements for a bioware/hardware/software system are satisfied through the lifecycle of the system" [10]. According to the Military Standard, the Systems Engineering process is a "logical consequence of activities and decisions transforming an operational need into a description of system performance parameters and a preferred system configuration" [11].

2.1. *Evolutionary delivery*

Evolutionary Delivery is a software development methodology based on the following simple principle [6]: Deliver something to a real end user on-site; measure the added value to the user in all critical dimensions; adjust both design and objectives based on the end users' feedback.

The complete project is divided up into potential steps. The steps with the highest ratio of user-value to development-cost are selected for early implementation (Fig. 1). In other words, the steps are prioritized based on the minimum development effort that delivers the highest payoff to the end users. When the feedback from the implemented step(s) is received then objectives, design, user-value and cost are re-appraised and adjusted if necessary.

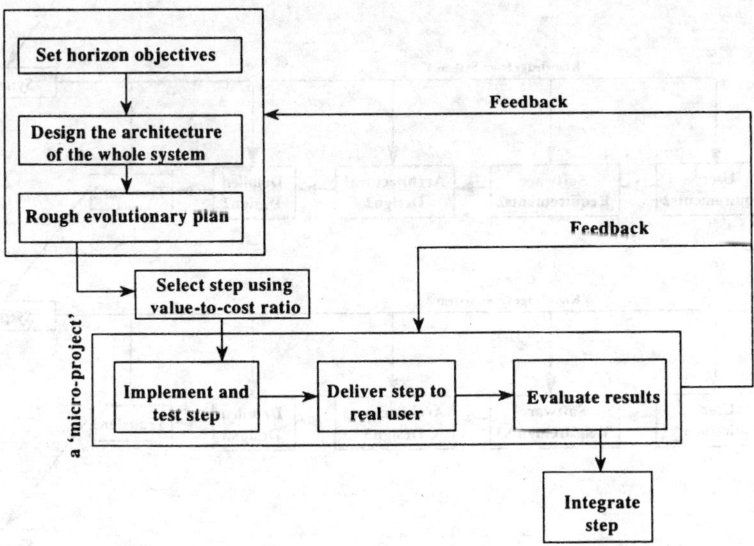

Figure 1 Evolutionary Delivery. Adapted from T. Gilb and S. Finzi, Principles of Software Engineering Management. Addison-Wesley, Wokingham, 1988

With Evolutionary Delivery the project evolves through steps which are continuously adjusted to meet the changing requirements of the end users.

2.2. *Evolutionary development*

Evolutionary Development is a software development methodology. The objective of this methodology is to deliver a flexible and expandable core system. When requirements change during the system development process, a modified system that fulfils these requirements can be designed and developed with minimum time and effort (see Fig. 2).

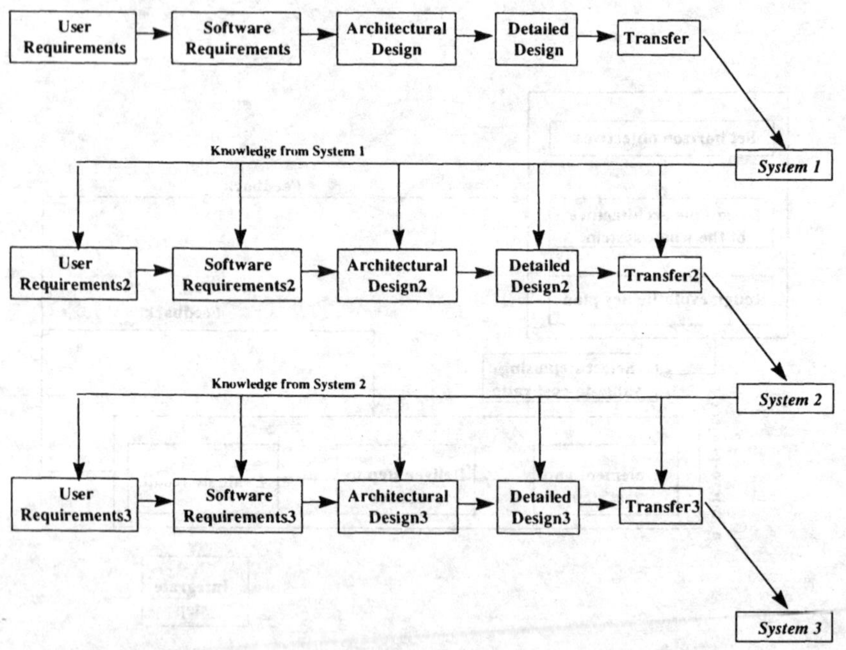

Figure 2 Evolutionary Development. Adapted from R. Barillere and C. Esciihuela, OOR&D Day, CERN, Geneva, November 3, 1995

The underlying principle is to design systems that are easily and quickly modified in the light of emerging requirements. The goal is to move from the design and implementation of static systems to the development of evolvable application families [7].

In Evolutionary Development, system 'evolution' can take many forms, from accommodating a quick fix to a moderate or full upgrade to a complete customization to particular business requirement. The aim is to develop each evolved system by investing minimum resources.

2.3. *Evolutionary delivery and evolutionary development are not methodologies*

The origins of both Evolutionary Development and Evolutionary Delivery are in the information systems world. They are both presented as methodologies. Their 'evolutionary' attribute makes them applicable to the constantly changing business environment, as it is difficult to both finalize a set of requirements and progress sequentially to its delivery.

In our opinion, Evolutionary Development and Evolutionary Delivery are inadequately presented as methodologies. They are both based on underlying principles rather than step-by-step approaches. Principles (i.e. guiding rules) outline what is to be achieved — not how. They are thus not best thought as methodologies — both are approaches to formulating systems development strategy.

2.4. *The evolutionary approach to strategy*

Both Evolutionary Delivery and Evolutionary Development address the necessity to capture evolving requirements into the system development process. However, their target is different; Evolutionary Delivery aims at the end user requirements and Evolutionary Development aims at the company requirements (see Table 1).

Table 1 Evaluation criteria for evolutionary delivery and evolutionary development

Evolutionary delivery	Evolutionary development
Testing procedures	Reviews
System testing to meet users' objectives	System review to meet the company's objectives (vision, mission statement, etc.)
"Deliver to the users what they asked for"	"Deliver to the company what it asked for" (and as this changed regularly, perform a continuous system development process)

Combined, Evolutionary Delivery and Evolutionary Development address the range of evolving requirements across the organizational spectrum.

3. What is BPR?

BPR is the fundamental rethink and radical redesign of business processes to achieve dramatic improvements in critical contemporary measures of performance, such as cost, quality, service, and speed [8]. In this section we show that BPR does not conceptually belong to the category of methodologies.

3.1. BPR is not a cookbook methodology

Hammer's famous statement, 'Don't automate, obliterate' (see Ref. 7 above) has one underlying message: there is no cookbook approach, no 10-steps-to-success plan, no manual for BPR. The people that cite, address, or deploy BPR as yet another management technique have misunderstood the real value of it. BPR is not like TQM, JIT, Downsizing, or any other management tool of our century.

All cookbook methodologies have inherent faults, in-built shortcomings: they have a narrow focus as they only emphasize some elements of a business and provide the silver bullet for their best performance. TQM emphasized quality of product/service and ways to achieve it. JIT focused on minimizing non-necessary activities in a customer-supplier relationship and ways to achieve it. BPR's focus should be wider than that; BPR potentially addresses all elements of a business but it does not prescribe any pre-specified ways to achieve their best performance. It only offers guidelines, heuristics, and some tools and techniques; the creative design and programme of change are provided by the practitioner.

So it is clear that BPR is not a cookbook methodology and this is why it appears to Hammer that all you can do is start with a clean sheet of paper. We agree with Hammer that BPR is not a cookbook methodology and hence any attempt to import Systems Engineering methodologies (particularly traditional ones) to BPR is bound to undermine the spirit of BPR. In our opinion, BPR is best thought of as an alternative perspective to formulating strategy showing that the organization has a clear vision on why and in what ways it should be reengineered.

Practitioners should have clear principles of how organizational change is aligned to the organization's vision and that all the tools/techniques/methodologies are the means toward this end and not ends in themselves. BPR is not TQM, JIT, downsizing, flattening the hierarchy, etc.; none of these are necessary, none of these are sufficient, although any one of these could figure in the creative response to the vision of an organization.

Thus, we claim that BPR is not best thought as a yet another methodology but rather as an approach to business strategy; it offers an alternative perspective to formulating business strategy.

4. Systems Engineering Meets BPR

It is generally understood that IT must support strategy, people and processes. Further, IT is considered to be a prime enabler of organizational transformation. Despite the growth of end user computing and the advent of BPR, software development methodologies remained rooted in the conceptual mental set of traditional computing.

Although the business vision is set, the myriad of consequential system changes are not a direct consequence of the business vision. These changes do not follow any particular cookbook pattern as they depend on the contingent features of the environment a business operates in.

A clean sheet approach would imply that there is no navigational guidance to challenge the evolving business, and, in effect, the systems requirements posed. Not only do we have heuristics, past experiences and folk memory, we already can distill a set of principles which can be used to guide us through organizational change and systems development.

We believe that BPR gives a new mental set and therefore new possibilities to Systems Engineering. The way to insure that software is aligned to business strategy is that the IT supporting the associated business processes is derived from the same business model. A business model is wider than the IT model as it embraces systems that cater for, among other business elements, personnel, finance, reward systems, and performance measurements.

4.1. *The common challenges of BPR, evolutionary delivery and evolutionary development*

It is clear that Evolutionary Delivery and Evolutionary Development, although motivated by software engineering concerns, are potentially more responsive to the organization's interests. If their strategic apex is driven by strategic needs, their computational base can more easily be aligned to business strategy. BPR is the most mature candidate for aligning strategy, people and processes. Therefore we suggest that some form of BPR is the appropriate framework for the strategic apex of system development methodologies.

To integrate Evolutionary Delivery, Evolutionary Development and BPR, we propose the construction of a meta-model of systems development.

4.2. What is a meta-model?

We consider a systems development methodology to be a practice that offers an integration of a number of tools with a number of techniques for the application of these tools. Underpinning the tools is a 'philosophy' (or a set of principles) which defends them by arguing that they realize certain qualities in a system developed and they facilitate or enhance the development process.

A meta-model of a systems development methodology is a high-level model in which the activity prescribed is that of deciding on the most appropriate approach to adopt at the top level at specific points in the development process. Deciding on an approach could entail selecting a particular model for part of the development process [9].

A meta-model accepts that a system is in a state of evolution without presupposing a particular change pattern. That is important if methods are to be linked to solve a particular problem.

4.3. ED^2, as a meta-model of BPR, is a methodology

In this chapter, we combine the principles of Evolutionary Delivery, Evolutionary Development and BPR to render ED^2 as an approach to shaping and delivering an integrated business and systems strategy. ED^2 is a meta-model of both BPR and software development as it integrates the two into a company-wide effort to sustain elevated business performance.

ED^2 is not a straightforward combination of principles; it is rather the framework through which the system development process will benefit from a strategic pull from BPR. Under ED^2, initiatives like Evolutionary Delivery and Evolutionary Development will be enabled and successfully implemented. Further, BPR, when integrated with software development methodologies, will become a systematic approach to organizational transformation.

The reality is that BPR requires its own solution strategy in each situation. This is why Hammer proposes to start with a clean slate. What we need is a model that controls but is not prescriptive. ED^2 is such a model. It is a versatile and more flexible system development approach because it:

- exploits a full repertoire of known technical and managerial methods,
- provides a mechanism that enables a sub-set of these methods to be linked easily into an appropriate solution strategy for any given problem, and
- can respond to new problems and new methods as they emerge.

ED^2 is called a meta-model because it incorporates and uses other models. It caters for system evolution, planning, process management and technical matters. The critical success factors of ED^2 are consistent with the ones of BPR.

4.4. *What is the value of ED^2?*

ED^2 would be required in all those circumstances where you have modern decentralised computing and related organizational transformation. It aims to develop a dynamic system, deliver it to real users and make them the point of reference when measuring the added value of the system (Fig. 3).

The orientation of ED^2 is the customer. From the notion of delivering value to an external customer, we get the notion of business process.

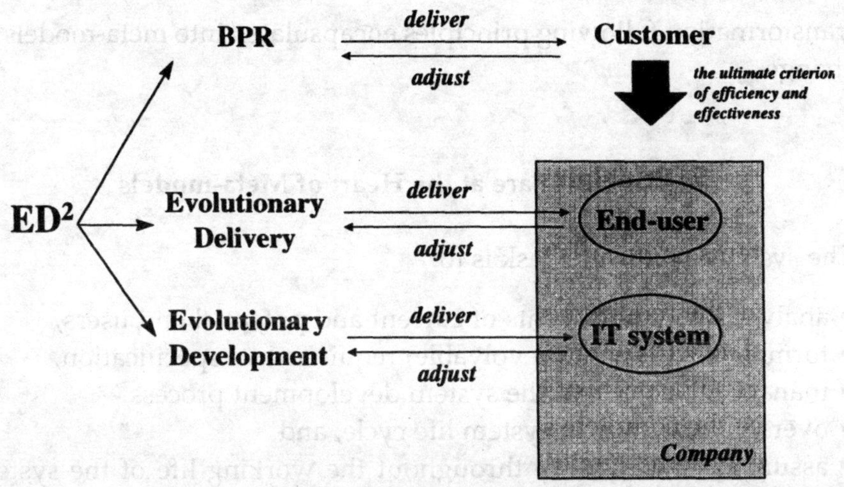

Figure 3 The ED² model

Within a business process, we have end users that are the internal customers for software support. The software can be evaluated from an internal perspective ("how does it support the end user?") and an external perspective ("does using this software add value to the business process and its external customers?").

By applying Evolutionary Delivery principles we aim to deliver something of value to the end user. The evolutionary character of Evolutionary Delivery allows us to adjust our system engineering process to fit the changing user requirements. Similarly, by applying Evolutionary Development principles we aim to deliver something of value to the company. The evolutionary character of Evolutionary Development allows us to adjust our system engineering process to fit the changing company requirements. BPR principles then become the vehicle with which successful implementation of Evolutionary Delivery and Evolutionary Development projects is achieved. BPR enables company requirements, and subsequently end-user requirements, to evolve. In the next section we show how BPR enables the system engineer to achieve successful organizational transformation following principles encapsulated into meta-models of change.

5. Principles are at the Heart of Meta-models

The systems engineer's task is to:

- analyze the requirements of current and potential end users,
- formulate a (dynamic, evolvable) requirements specification,
- manage all aspects of the system development process,
- oversee the complete system life cycle, and
- assure systems quality throughout the working life of the system which includes evolving the system as the requirements evolve.

As these are principles rather than methodologies, the Systems Engineer can benefit from the ED^2 meta-model. S/he can employ any tool, technique, or methodology (see Table 2), as long as the principle required is followed and the desired deliverables achieved.

A meta-model that does not restrict the Systems Engineer to any particular course of action but rather allows the project all the flexibility to develop is a key element of any successful Systems Engineering project. Meta-models are models that show you what is to be achieved, not how. You can use any methodology but with solid principles on where a methodology should lead you.

For example, an organization may decide that it fits its vision for closer links with its suppliers to introduce a new purchasing system. This purchasing system will support the purchasing process which cuts across organizational departments (and boundaries) and will deliver a high quality service to both the organization and its suppliers. IT will be employed to support this new system.

The principles (i.e. what is to be achieved) would include:

- delivering added value to the customer of the redesigned process (possibly achieved through BPR, work study, etc.),

Table 2 Principles outline what is to be achieved — not how

Principle	Tool, technique, etc.
Deliver something to a real end user	Evolutionary Delivery, etc.
Measure the added value to the user in all critical dimensions	
Adjust both design and objectives based on observed realities	
Replace the old system with a new one that satisfies the new requirements as quickly as possible	Evolutionary Development, etc.
All redesigned processes have the 'customer' as the recipient and determinant of the added value of the redesigned processes	BPR, etc.
Plan the contents of each version based on the results of previous version	Evaluation management, project management, CPM/PERT/GANTT/etc.
Divide up a large project into a series of smaller projects, each of which delivers increased functionality at short intervals ...	ROI, cost/benefit analysis, value-to-cost ratio, etc.
... this implies a series of shorter timescales, over which it is easier to forecast the impacts of changes and also minimize the risks of uncertainty	Change management, risk management, etc.
Involve end users (= internal + external customers)	Quality circles, interviews, etc.
Effective communication amongst management — end users — application developers — customers	Management commitment, etc.
Organizational culture that encourages teamwork, empowerment and development	Empowerment, team management, etc.

- involving the customers, internal and external, to the redesign of the process (possibly achieved through quality circles, interviews, knowledge elicitation, questionnaires, etc.),
- allowing the system to incorporate new organizational requirements as they evolve (possibly achieved through Evolutionary Development, etc.), and
- building the new system incrementally with each increment directed and justified by the end users (possibly achieved through prototyping, Evolutionary Delivery, etc.).

This list of principles is by no means exhaustive; neither is the list of tools and techniques that could deliver each principle; we highlight a pattern for principle-centered meta-models. Further research on a taxonomy of principles and supporting tools and techniques would lead to a theoretical framework of such meta-models.

6. Summary and Conclusions

In this chapter we have emphasized how BPR is not a cookbook approach. Therefore, traditional Systems Engineering methodologies cannot be imported to it or used as a basis for flexible systems design. The framework for integrating BPR and IT would be through meta-models that are based on principles and allow use of non-prescribed tools and techniques.

ED^2 is an example of one such meta-model

- where BPR is used to realise a corporate vision,
- where people working in business processes are supported by technology whose functionality is delivered in an evolutionary way, and
- where the system software is developed through evolutionary means.

ED^2 captures evolving system requirements in a way that fits the dynamic business environment, allows developers to own the system development process, is scalable and applicable to any problem situation, and its feedback loops facilitate evaluation and learning — not control.

A key concept in any meta-model is a set of principles that guide evolution. A principle-centered meta-model allows Systems Engineering to meet the challenges of systems development in uncertain environments. ED^2 — as a meta-model of both business and systems development methodologies — is meeting our need for a systematic approach to organizational transformation and software development whilst largely preserving our investment in the traditional tools and techniques of software development methodologies.

References

1. M. Pedler, J. Burgoyne and T. Boydell, *The Learning Company: A Strategy for Sustainable Development* (McGraw-Hill, Berkshire, 1991).
2. M. Hammer, Reengineering work: don't automate, obliterate, *Harvard Business Review*, July-August (1990).
3. D. E. Avison and G. Fitzgerald, *Information Systems Development: Methodologies, Techniques and Tools* (McGraw-Hill, Berkshire, 1995).
4. A. Kuryla, *Iterative Application Development: An Evolutionary Strategy for the 90s* (Open Insight White Papers, 1997).
5. J. Vanhoenacker, A. Bryant and G. Dedene, The 'BPR holon'; a framework for (re) orientating methodological developments for BPR, in *Proceedings of SCI'97 World Multiconference on Systemics, Cybernetics, and Informatics*, N. Callaos, C. M. Khoong and E. Cohen (eds.) (Caracas, 1997).
6. T. Gilb and S. Finzi, *Principles of Software Engineering Management* (Addison-Wesley, Wokingham, 1988).
7. N. Williams, *Evolutionary Development* (On line), Available at: http://siris.sund.ac.uk/~calnwi/html/swproto/evdev.html (1995).
8. M. Hammer, Reengineering work: don't automate, obliterate, *Harvard Business Review*, July-August (1990).
9. G. H. Galal and L. Johnson, *KBS Methodologies: Principles and Mis-conceptions* (Technical Report, Department of Computer Science, University of Brunel, Middlesex, 1993).

10. E. D. Dean, *Systems Engineering from the Perspective of Competitive Advantage* (On-line), Available at: http://akao.larc.nasa.gov/dfc/syseng.htm (last modified 09/04/97).
11. *Military Standard 499B: An Overview* (On-line), Available at: http://www.incose.org/lib/sebib.html (last modified 05/01/97).

Chapter 6

A Simulation-Based BPR Support System for Supply Chain Management

SHIGEKI UMEDA
Musashi University, 1-26 Toyotama-kami Nerima, Tokyo 176, Japan
E-mail: shigeki@cc.musashi.ac.jp

ALBERT JONES
National Institute of Standards and Technology,
Met 220 A127, Gaithersburg,
MD 20899-001 USA
E-mail: jonesa@cme.nist.gov

Modern manufacturing enterprises must collaborate with a large number of suppliers to design and produce their products. Management of these supply chains is crucial. This chapter proposes a simulation-based, supply chain management system, which supports the implementation of Business Process Reengineering (BPR) in an integrated system environment. The scope of the BPR includes management processes for production and operations within the supply chain. This chapter describes the process analysis, models, and simulation methodologies. It also discusses a supply chain integration methodology.

1. Introduction

Global supply chains are responsible for the manufacture of modern, complex products such as automobiles, airplanes and computers. Each member of the chain is required to cooperate with other business partners, including vendors, retailers, and distributors. This forces enterprises to continually review their business strategies, their corporate procedures, and their fabrication processes. This, in turn, can lead to fundamental decisions regarding internal management practices, which must be made in collaboration with business partners. Examples of such decisions include a change in business practices, the introduction of a new production process, a modification to the organizational structure, additional performance measures, and access to enterprise information systems. In making these decisions, each enterprise management system must take into account the goals and requirements of the target supply chain. These goals and requirements are set by the Supply Chain Management (SCM) system, which is responsible for the overall management of logistics within the chain.

SCM is currently one area that has received a great deal of attention in the worldwide business community. In the United States alone, the average manufacturing firm incurs logistics costs that account for approximately 30% of the cost of goods sold [1]. With numbers of this magnitude, the potential saving from a reduction in these costs cannot be ignored. Such reductions can increase company profitability. The Yankee Group, a Boston-based consulting firm, did a study of 1,000 European firms. The study showed that supply-chain costs, which are included in the logistics costs, are estimated at 10% of the revenues of most companies. The study further showed that some leading companies have logistics costs that are more than 36% below the average. Those companies realized nearly a 4% increase in net profit margin [2]. Therefore, the development of strategies and software that can reduce logistics costs, and improve the overall performance of the supply chain, can impact profitability.

Some of the earliest attempts to reduce supply chain logistics costs were undertaken by the apparel industry. Industry studies showed (1) that the time to go from raw material to finished goods was 66 weeks, and (2) that 40 weeks of that time were spent in warehouses or in transit. A concept called Quick Response Manufacturing (QRM) was used to address this problem [3]. QRM incorporates marketing information on promotion, discounts, and forecasts into the manufacturing and distribution plan across the entire chain. It is, therefore, a partnership in which retailers and suppliers work together to respond more quickly to customer demands by sharing information. That sharing is based on the Universal Product Code and Electronic Data Interchange (EDI) standards. Using these standards, retailers began to install Point-Of-Sales (POS) systems to transfer sales information electronically to distributors and manufacturers.

In 1992, the Efficient Consumer Response (ECR) Working group ran an industry task force on logistics in the grocery industry. The objective of this group was to identify opportunities to make the grocery supply chain more competitive [4]. There were two main results of this study. First, the group identified a set of best practices that, if implemented, could improve overall performance of the supply chain substantially. The working group projected an overall reduction in supply chain inventory of 37% leading to cost reductions in the range of $24 billion to $30 billion. Second, they espoused the concept of Continuous Replenishment (CR). CR is a move away from the conventional *push* strategy for controlling inventory to a *pull* strategy to put products onto grocery shelves based on consumer demand [5]. The implementation of this pull strategy requires retailers to forward point-of-purchase transactions to the manufacturer electronically. The manufacturer can then keep the retailer replenished and balanced, in a just-in-time manner [6].

Hammer and Champy [7], and Porter [8] have popularized the use of Business Process Reengineering (BPR) as a way addressing the logistics problems of a supply chain. It is easy to see that, as management philosophies, BPR and SCM have a great deal in common. Specifically, both approaches analyze the value-added implications of all business-related activities. Evans *et al* discussed the similarities between BPR and SCM more rigorously [9]. They classified SCM planning problems into three hierarchical levels: strategic, tactical, and operational. They claimed that the distinguishing characteristic of these three levels is the time horizon — strategic planning has the longest and operational planning has the shortest [1]. The authors showed that the methodologies of BPR are effective for solving strategic planning problems. In Berry *et al*, some of the same authors describe the use of BPR to address strategic planning problems within an electronic products supply chain [10].

The use of BPR as an approach to implement SCM requires the identification of all value-added activities. O'Sullivan and Geringer [11] present an important concept in the SCM, the notion of a natural versus contrived value chain. The natural value chain is "a conceptual ideal of the necessary value chain activities," while a contrived value chain is "an imperfect implementation of the natural value chain." The authors outlined an approach for defining the natural value chain and stress the importance of keeping this natural chain in mind when reengineering the actual, 'contrived chain.' BPR is said to be a method to reform 'Contrived value chain' to 'Natural value chain.'

It is quite common for an individual company to be a member of several supply chains, concurrently. Each time a company joins a new chain, it must determine if its current management system suits the specific needs of the new chain. Changes may be needed in both its strategic business management practices and its performance measures. Different methods may be needed to evaluate new product introduction, to examine required organizational changes, and to modify existing information systems. This chapter proposes Business Process Reengineering (BPR) models, together with simulation models, to address many of these changes. Companies can use BPR models to recognize critical problem areas, and simulation to measure the impact of possible changes in those areas [12]. The chapter includes a description of the process analysis, models, simulation methodologies, and a supply chain integration methodology.

2. Business Process Models for Supply Chain Management

Every major manufacturing company goes through a 'strategic planning' process on a regular basis. Strategic planning considers issues such as the way the company does business, the organizational structure, business management practices, performance measures, and the information system [13]. Strategic planning must also be done at the supply chain level. There, it occurs in three macro-scale stages: procurement, production, and distribution. Each of these stages may be implemented in facilities from different companies simultaneously. This implies that the supply chain for a particular product frequently crosses both functional and corporate boundaries. The implication of this is, as Fawcett points out [14], that knowledge of value-added activities gets distributed in such a way that no one has a complete picture of activities in the chain. Consequently, models to analyze strategic planning for the supply chain must be able to represent the business processes within each company in the chain. They must also capture constraints needed to coordinate activities across those companies [14].

We propose a network of models representing business processes and information flows among those processes. Each of these models is composed of a set of functional activities (the business processes) and relationships among them. While there are many activities in each supplier company, we believe that there is a collection of activities common to all suppliers (see Fig. 1). This common set of activities forms the basis for a coherent production and operations management plan for the supply chain. Each individual activity can have its own internal decomposition. Eventually this decomposition will end with a sequence of primitive processes or actions. A primitive action consumes both time and some combination of information and material resources. This

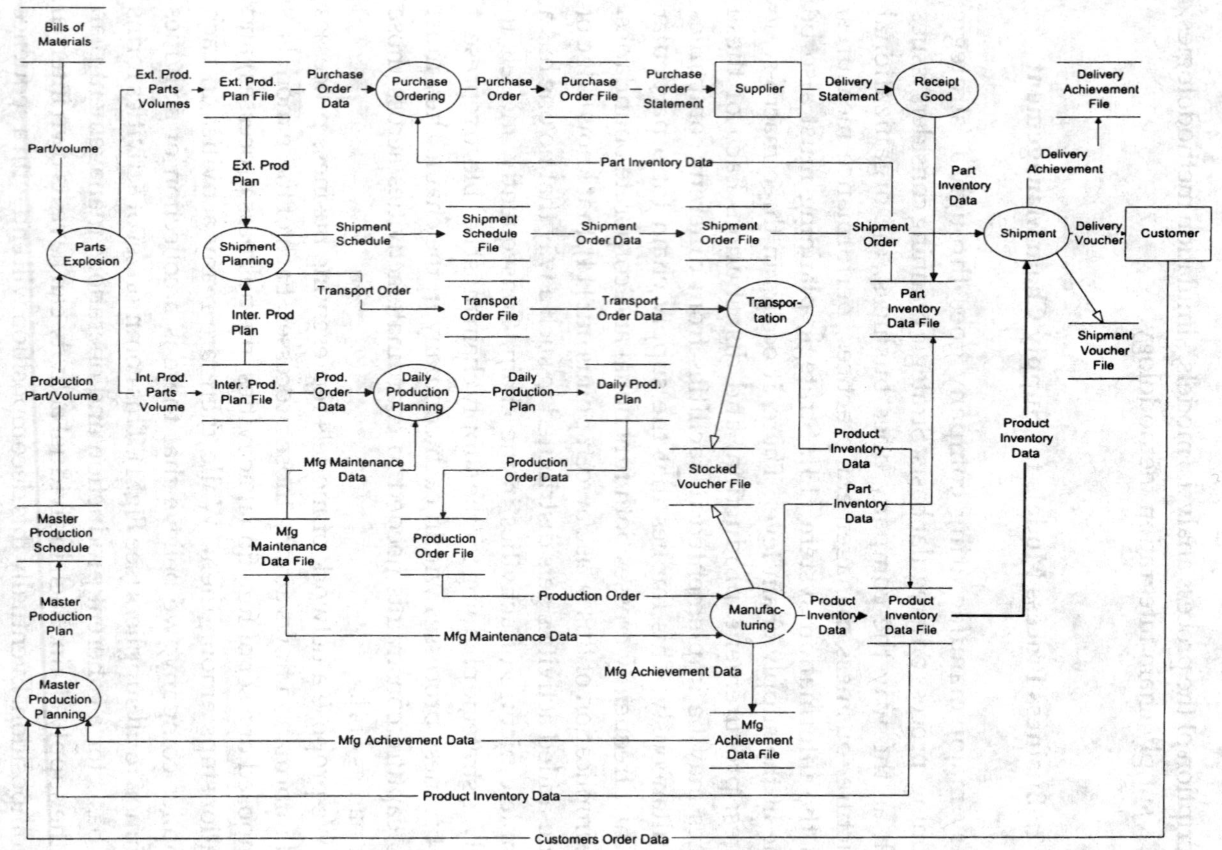

Figure 1 Strategic level business process model at a single company

is so because all business activities get materials and/or information, process them to add value, and make them available for use by the next process. Some examples are: generate, dispose, assemble, branch, batch, unbatch, merge, split, join, transform, copy, assign, seize resources, and release resources.

Figure 1 shows the business process model at the strategic level operations of supply chain. The modeling notation of this is equivalent to 'data-flow model' of OMT method. The circular nodes and the rectangular nodes represent business processes and actors, respectively. The node described by parallel lines represents a data store (for example, a database). Each individual arc corresponds to the 'information class,' which is defined in class hierarchy models. These models describe the timing requirement of information transfer within and across factories. Some information can be stored in a relational or object database with specific pieces transmitted in response to specific queries. Some information must be stored and transmitted using messages in 'real-time.' These requirements give a solution to the questions regarding storage options. These determinations can also specify the details of file formats, database structures, and message protocols.

The information that flows between these activities is tightly coupled with the descriptions of the business process models. We have developed formal models for this information using OMT methodology [15]. These models describe individual flows as entities (objects) with complete and detailed definitions. They also identify all of the relationships that exist among these entities. The modeling method used here is based on our previous research [16, 17]. The concrete procedures are summarized as follows:

1. Extract 'instances' of information objects in manufacturing enterprises: These instances are the documents that flow among individual business process activities (see Fig. 2).
2. Abstract the above 'instances' to define a class hierarchy model: In this process, the relations among the instances are the important keys to define 'class.' Based on concepts such as super-type,

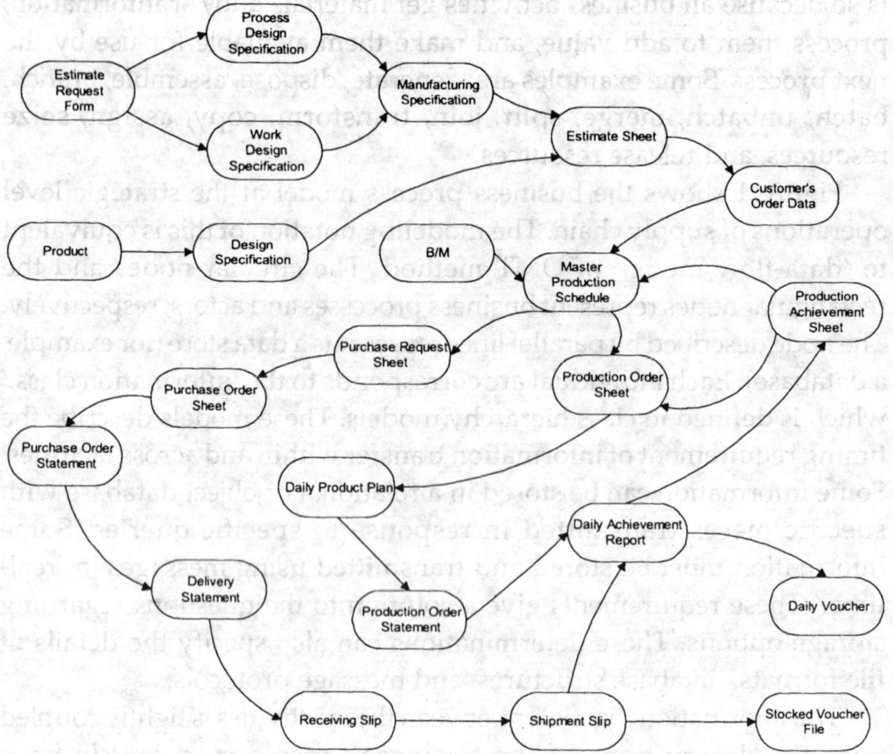

Figure 2 Business document flow analysis

sub-type, and relevance, these instances are classified into several groups. The objects that own the same attribute belong to the same 'class.'

3. Adjust the relations among the sub-classes to define a framework of business process.

3. Virtual Supply Chain System

The business process model for the supply chain is a hierarchical network of the models identical to the one shown in Fig. 1. The business processes shown in Fig. 1 can be divided into two groups. The first group includes parts explosion, master production scheduling, shipment planning, purchase ordering, and daily production planning. These generate and use information only. The second group includes transportation, manufacturing, receipt, and shipment. These processes use both information and materials. Our virtual supply chain system must include dynamic models of both types of processes at both the supply chain level and the individual company level.

To reduce logistics costs and improve performance across the entire chain, we must integrate the individual business models into a single system. This will allow a process at an individual company to exchange information and share resources with other processes in the same company, or with related processes at other companies. To accomplish this, we must define neutral specifications for all information shared across the network, and mechanisms for exchanging that information. These mechanisms must take into account the size of the information exchanged and the frequency of the required transfers. Furthermore, they must preserve the autonomous nature of the individual companies, who have their own unique manufacturing capabilities, information capabilities, and system resources, and the distributed nature of the chain, which arises because of the loose connections among those companies.

3.1. *Hierarchically-structured simulation model*

To implement this network structure, we propose a hierarchical, simulation-based system, called 'Virtual Supply Chain Management System (VSCMS).' The tasks of the simulation are to simulate (1) the business processes at the chain level, (2) the business processes at individual suppliers (factories), and (3) the transactions within the manufacturing cells in each factory. These simulations provide insight into multiple levels of activities in the chain required to meet the production orders and daily schedules. These are stored as simulation logs, which are accessible by the decision makers across the chain.

These three levels of simulation form a hierarchical structure. The top layer is the 'Chain' simulation. It is composed of the objects representing individual suppliers such as vendor's factories, warehouses, distributors, and so on. These objects are controlled by 'Virtual Suppliers Manager' (VSM) (see Sec. 3.2). The middle layer contains the 'Factory' simulations. Each such simulation is a high-level model of information and material flow through the factory. The bottom layer contains what we call, 'Cell' simulations, which model processing of materials through equipment like NC machines, or robots, and coordinate measuring machines. Taken together, these simulations correspond to the SCM hierarchical layers: 'Strategic,' 'Tactical,' and 'Operational' (Fig. 3).

The 'Chain' simulation handles the highest level interactions between the factories that make up the chain. The underlying model consists of a network of suppliers linked together by global transportation facilities. The 'Chain' simulation connects suppliers in either a 'PUSH' mode or 'PULL' mode. When 'PUSH' mode is chosen, the supplier factory works on the orders generated in VSM, and when 'PULL' mode is chosen, the supplier factory works on the orders generated by their downstream factories. Our model allows for both. Therefore, we call it a 'Hybrid PUSH-PULL' system.

A set of rules and mechanisms must be developed to control the transfer of materials in the simulation (At this level, the transfer means the long distance transportation by trucks, rails, boats, or planes.). These rules and mechanisms comprise what we call the 'Chain-level Logistics model.' This model includes order planning, warehouse operation planning, transportation planning, and inventory planning among them.

'Factory' simulations handle the factory level interactions in the chain including warehouses, retailers, and distributors. The underlying model for these simulations consists of a network of processes linked

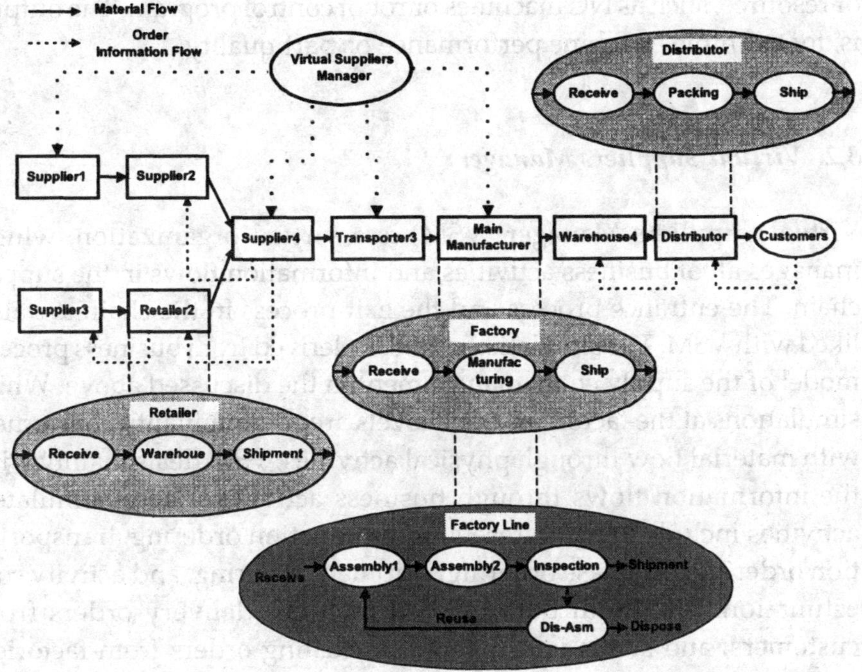

Figure 3 Hierarchical structured simulation model

to each other by the factory transportation facilities. Factories typically include more than one material processing line. These lines include multiple manufacturing cells, parts buffers, material removal processes, inspection process shipment processes, and factory transportation devices (such as conveyors). These simulation models are similar to the traditional discrete-event, manufacturing line simulation, with two major differences. First, the arrival process is controlled by the hybrid, push-pull strategy described above. Second, the flow of materials through the factory is controlled by the scheduler and not by the simulator.

'Cell' layer's simulations are usually control logic simulations. The input is the physical transaction control rules of a particular machine or resource, such as NC machines or robot control program. The output is, for example, machine performance or part quality.

3.2. *Virtual Suppliers Manager*

Virtual Suppliers Manager (VSM) is a virtual organization, which manages all of business activities and information flows in the supply chain. The entrance process and the exit process in the chain are also liked with VSM. The simulation model is derived from business process model of the supply chain management in the discussed above. While simulations at the factory and cell levels are predominantly concerned with material flow through physical activities, VSM deals mainly with the information flows through business activities. These simulated activities include demand receiving, production ordering, transportation ordering, purchase ordering, shipment ordering, and activity cost estimation. The input data to VSM includes delivery orders from customers, and status information on existing orders from factories. The outputs are the orders to the individual suppliers' factories, warehouses, transporters, and distributors. That is, it sends orders for production, transportation, purchase, and shipment to the individual suppliers in the chain.

As stated, the main job of VSM is to provide individual suppliers with production orders according to the 'PUSH' ordering mechanism. Therefore, some processes of VSM are linked with individual factory schedulers that schedule the activities needed to fill those production orders. The details of this scenario can be described as follows:

1. It predicts customers' demand volume in the next phased term by using the past log data of demand and production, and builds 'Master Production Schedule' (MPS). MPS is an anticipated build schedule for those items assigned to the master scheduler. The master scheduler maintains this schedule, and in turn, it becomes a set of planning numbers that drives material requirements planning.

2. It calculates the each part volume required in individual factory. It represents what the company plans to produce expressed in specific configuration, quantities, and dates. This stage is the simulation of the part explosion using a BOM (Bill Of Material) table. In this mechanism, the synchronization of suppliers is performed in schedule-driven. At this time, it uses the suppliers/part table, which shows parts name and its supplier.
3. It gives the production orders to individual suppliers. The order information transaction flows from VSM to suppliers, and the materials flow from up-stream factory to downstream factory.

Although the master production schedule is not a sales forecast that represents a statement of demand, it must take into account the forecast, the production plan, and other important considerations such as backlog, availability of material, availability of resource capacity, and management policies and goals. In other words, this process is a typical prediction-based planning. In a sense, the VSM plays a role of prime contractor for the supply chain.

3.3. *More on push versus pull systems*

We have described the major function of the VSM as the generation of orders for the members of the chain. This is tightly tied to the concept of a 'PUSH' system. We have also stated that some members of the chain may interact according to a 'PULL' system. A typical 'PULL' system is a Kanban system [16]. Each station has a collection of input and output buffers. A station will pull inventory from up-stream stations whenever its input buffer becomes too low. A station will receive a request for new production orders when the inventory level in its output buffer is too low. In our case, the prime contractor will pull inventory from suppliers whenever it is needed. The 'PULL' system can be defined as a buffer-driven system. This scenario can also be extended to a supply chain environment. Part suppliers or distributors individually define the replenishment point on the inventories. When the input material volume becomes lower than the predefined stock level, the suppliers independently make orders to their up-stream suppliers. The up-stream suppliers who received the orders generate their own production orders. Materials flow from up-stream to downstream, while the order information transactions flow from downstream to up-stream.

In practical production management, some particular supplier's factories receive production orders not from the central control system (VSM) but from their downstream's factory directly. In other words, some suppliers' factories or field warehouses use replenishment points to control input part inventories. When the volume of input parts goes below the predefined replenishment point, the factory independently publishes production orders of a fixed volume. These suppliers re-stock inventory whenever it becomes too low. We define this scenario as 'hybrid PUSH-PULL' system.

VSM provides such a 'hybrid PUSH-PULL' system environment to represent manufacturing logistics in a supply chain. This facility can give a good solution to the 'PULL factory selection problem', which is often difficult to implement. The solution impacts not only material flow, as we have seen, but also the information flow (and the communications infrastructure needed to support that flow) between the prime contractor and suppliers.

3.4. Business process planning using VSM

VSM is a business process simulation to support supply chain managers in their job of designing and reengineering the makeup and behavior of the chain. VSM simulations enable designers and analysts to observe the information and material flows in their entirety. This business process simulation provides estimates for both order completions and supplier behavior. Such estimates help managers make decisions regarding a redesign or reengineering of the chain. When a problem is detected, managers can simulate various business scenarios to find a cause for the problem. When solutions are proposed to eliminate the problem, managers can simulate their impact to determine if they really work. After each simulation is run, managers can examine the outputs to find out why the proposed solution did or did not work. Finally, managers can use the results to pick the best of the proposed solutions.

This combination of BPR and simulation within the VSM enables managers to gain insight that will help them control the operation of the chain. The insight and the process analysis will help to identify areas that need reengineering and to predict the quantitative impact of reengineering efforts. The managers of the suppliers could use this same approach to evaluate changes to their organizational structure, business processes, and the policies and methods by which those processes are implemented. This type of reengineering emphasizes the overall improvement of a process based on its quality, cost, and efficiency. If it is not done on a regular basis, the damage to the company, and to the supply chain, can be huge.

Figure 2 includes all of the modeling primitives of the business process flows that generate process orders (manufacturing orders, shipment orders, etc.) to individual factories. These are critical to understanding the potential impact when the structure is changed. The examples are:

1. Suppose that all of factories in the chain use a common database for purchase ordering processes, what impacts occur on total lead time in the chain?
2. Suppose that two processes of internal and external production planning are linked together, what impacts occur on the total productivity in the chain?
3. Suppose that all factories and distributors work on PULL-mode, all of planning processes will be extremely simplified. While, all factories always keep balanced inventory, and require distributed inventory management system. Which is better?

4. Toward the Integrated Supply Chain

4.1. Decision-making processes in SCM

In addition to the strategic problems described above, the aforementioned simulation models will be an important part of methodologies to solve tactical optimization problems related to production planning, scheduling, and operational optimization problems related to control. Examples include:

- Which material is the best to choose for various products?
- Which supplier is the best to produce and distribute?
- Where and how many inventories should be stored?
- What workload should be handled by each supplier?
- How much production capacity do suppliers need to meet demand?
- When and what suppliers should produce and associated due dates.
- When and how much volume of products or component parts should be transported.
- The determination of number, location, capacity, and type of manufacturing plants and warehouses to be used.
- The set of suppliers to be selected.
- The transportation channels to be used.
- The amount of raw materials and products to ship among suppliers, plants, warehouses, and customers.
- The amount of raw materials, intermediate products, and finished goods to hold at various locations in inventory.

Typically, the formulation of these optimization problems has an objective function that includes several performance measures such as cost, lead-time, highest utilization of resources, throughput performance, and due date. Generally, this kind of problem formulation is classified as NP-complete. This means that optimal solutions will be hard to find [25]. Some researchers have attempted to solve some of these problems (location, selection, and configuration of the suppliers-distributors network, for example) by using Mixed Integer

Programming (MIP) [26]. We do not believe that such traditional mathematical programming methods can capture the details of these highly dynamic, stochastic problems. We are pursuing hybrid techniques that combine mathematical programming, artificial intelligence, and simulations to guide the search for sub-optimal solutions quickly.

4.2. Sharing data across the chain

The VSM uses customer order data and production status data from all suppliers in the chain to make its decisions. Factory simulations require production order data from the VSM, and production status data from other suppliers. Consequently, the successful management of the supply chain requires (1) neutral specifications for all shared information, and (2) mechanisms for the electronic exchange of that information in a timely, transparent manner. To address these issues, we have begun the development of a virtual supply chain testbed. The initial design of this testbed has been completed, and the construction has commenced. The product being manufactured in this virtual supply chain is a personal computer. The initial members of the chain are the National Institute of Standards and Technology in the United States, and Musashi University in Japan. All functions and business processes within the chain are simulated on computers at one of the member sites.

Information management within the testbed will be carried out using three data driver sub-systems.

1. The **Production Data Driver** receives tactical operational data from suppliers and translates it to meet the format specifications of the target software applications (simulator and optimizer). Most of these are commercial, operations management applications.
2. The **Demand Data Driver** receives demands data from retailers or distributors. The data is used as input parameters for simulators and optimizers, and to update demand prediction.

3. The **Communication Server** provides the data access methods and utilities, which the above drivers use.

One of the keys to the successful implementation is the timely and accurate exchange of information across the software applications in the system. Three barriers must be overcome:

1. **Data security problem**: The companies participating in a particular supply chain are independent and frequently compete against one another. They may not want to share information with their competitors, so security control will be a significant issue in such an environment.
2. **Application interface problem**: Each company has a different set of software applications and business practices. The information produced by the software in one company cannot be processed directly by the software in another company.
3. **Semantics problem**: Two applications cannot process each other's data because they do not understand the internal organization of each other's data.

The solution to these problems requires (1) the development of formal data flow and information models, (2) a collection of standard interface protocols, and (3) a networking technology that is cost-effective, reliable, and hardware independent. In the testbed system implementation, we are examining the following four methods.

- WWW — The World Wide Web encapsulates communications protocols to organize and access data across the Internet [18].
- PART 21 — An international standard that provides a standard physical file structure that is easily produced and consumed by multiple applications [19].
- CORBA — The Common Request Object Broker allows applications to use each other's resources by supporting message calls between objects through a network [20]. IDL is a language to define application interface.

- EDI — Electronic Data Interchange provides a collection of forms for the electronic exchange of a variety of business and manufacturing data [21].

4.3. A system architecture for SCM

As discussed above, we are constructing a virtual supply chain testbed to investigate integration, business process reengineering, and decision support issues related to Supply Chain Management. The proposed system is based on a collection of hierarchical, simulation models integrated with other manufacturing applications software. The system focuses on both BPR and DSS for production and operations management within the supply chain. Since suppliers can be distributed across the globe, communicating information and transporting material can be costly and time-consuming. Therefore, the proposed architecture must support communication protocols to allow worldwide information transfer through the Internet. The main modules in this architecture are (see Fig. 4). We have just begun the design and implementation of these modules.

- Simulation kernel (including simulation models libraries)
- Supply-chain Management Data Server
- Production Management Decision Support
- Suppliers Management Knowledge Data Base

5. Concluding Remarks

Every enterprise system implementation must go through the following cycle repeatedly: (1) Decide on business goals; (2) Design the business processes and systems to meet those goals; (3) Implement the processes and systems; and (4) Measure the performance of the processes and systems. To be successful, powerful support software systems are

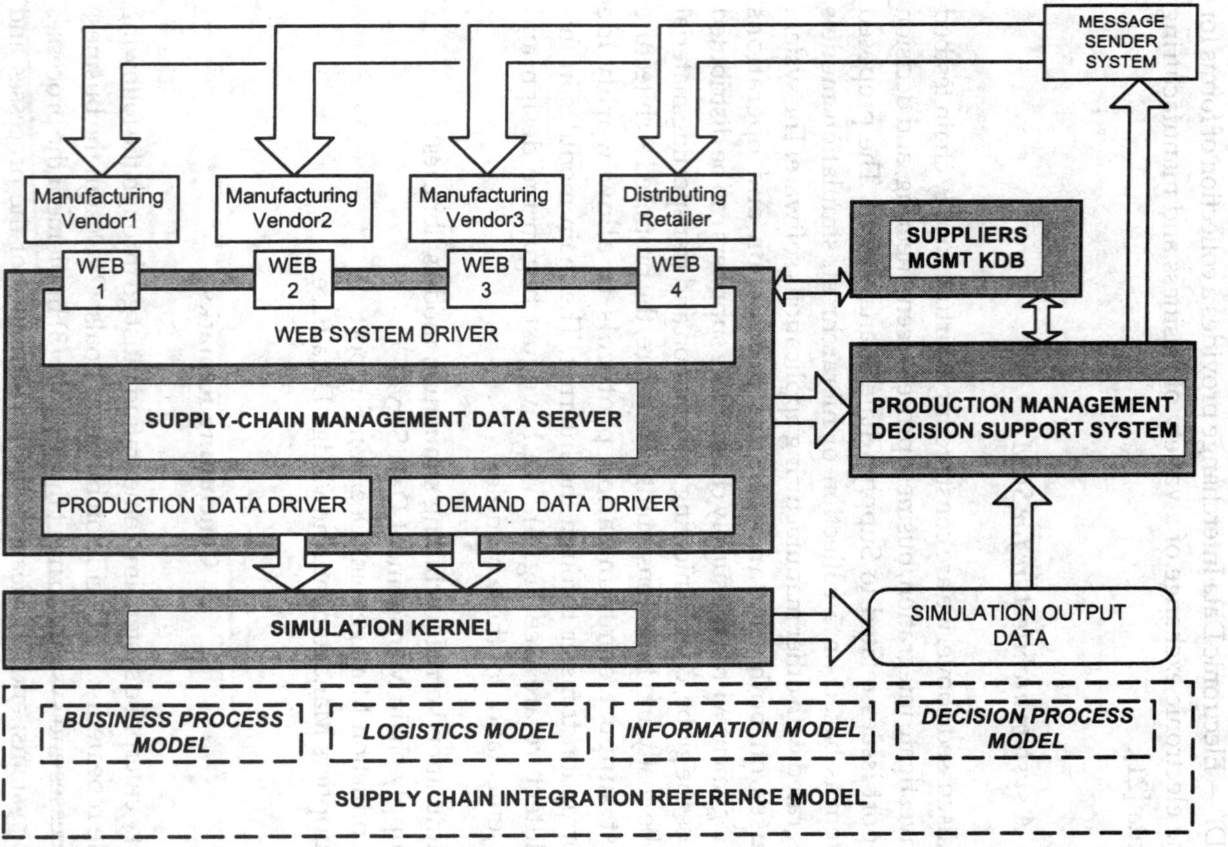

Figure 4 System architecture of virtual supply chain management system

needed at each of these stages. If the results of each stage can be estimated before moving to the next stage, the chances for success will be greatly improved.

A supply chain can be viewed as a special kind of enterprise. This chapter has proposed a virtual supply chain testbed as a way of developing software to support this cycle for a supply chain. The goal is the management of the suppliers that make up the chain. The objectives of the integration testbed are:

1. The system implementation to synchronize operations to changing demands.
2. A thorough understanding of the business processes and BPR practices at these suppliers.
3. Performance prediction of the supply chain system.

Among them, the increased demand may have a significant impact on the supply chain because it creates a disturbance that can ripple through the entire supply chain [22]. For instance, a sale or promotion can increase demand from the distributor back to prime contractor. This will have little effect if the prime has enough stock. When the increase in demand exceeds available inventory, this cam impact other links in the supply chain. This is especially significant at two extreme situations:

- When the demand increase due to the promotion strains the supply chain's capability to produce at the new level. The temporary increase in demand may be met through building inventory in slack periods or by activities such as overtime production.
- When predictions of the impact of the promotion activity are inaccurate. For instance, a retail-advertising program is expected to increase demand by 5% for three weeks, and instead prompts a 10% increase. This unplanned demand forces the chain react in the short term to provide product.

The strength of simulation-based system proposed above is its ability to analyze and diagnose dynamic behaviors such at this [23].

The integration of these simulations with optimization techniques will be useful to synchronize processes inside each company in the chain and to monitor business processes across the chain, so as to achieve the shortest total business lead-time. If successful, we will be able to realize the reduction in total lead-time prophesied in the literature [24].

References

1. R. H. Ballou, *Business Logistics Management* 3rd edn. (Prentice-Hall, Englewood Cliff, NJ, 1992).
2. T. Davis, Effective supply chain management, *Sloan Management Review* **34/4** (1993) 35–46.
3. T. Mullin, A new frontier, *Stores*, July, 1994 .
4. Kurt Salmon Associates, Inc., Efficient consumer response: enhancing consumer value in the grocery industry, *Food Marketing Institute*, January, 1993.
5. The ECR performance measures operating committee, performance measurement, applying value chain analysis to the grocery industry, Joint Industry Project on Efficient Consumer Response, 1994.
6. M. Garry, Is there life after CRP? *Progressive Grocer*, September, 1994.
7. M. Hammer and J. Champy, *Reengineering the Corporation: A Manifesto for Business Revolution* (Harper Business, 1993).
8. M. E. Porter, *Competitive Advantage: Creating and Sustaining Superior Performance* (Collier Macmillan, New York, 1995).
9. G. N. Evans, D. R. Towill and M. M. Naim, Business process reengineering the supply chain, *International Journal of Production Planning and Control* **6/3** (1995) 227–237.
10. J. Berry, M. M. Naim and D. R. Towill, Business process reengineering of an electronic products supply chain, *IEE Proceedings — Science, Measurement and Technology* **142/5** (1995) 395–403.
11. L. O'Sullivan and J. M. Geringer, Harnessing the power of your value chain, *Long Range Planning* **26/2** (1993) 59–68.
12. S. Craspar and C. Gray. Manufacturing the demand and supply chain: how to make the customer-supplier partnerships of the future work today, *APICS 1995 International Conference Proceedings*, October 1995.

13. T. A. Stewart, Reengineering: the hot new managing tool, *Fortune* (August 23), 40–45.
14. S. E. Fawcett, Using strategic assessment to increase the value-added capabilities of manufacturing and logistics, *Production and Inventory Management Journal* (2nd Quarter 1995) 33–37.
15. G. Booch, *Object-Oriented Analysis and Design*, 2nd edn. (Benjamin/Cummings Pub. Inc., San Jose, 1994).
16. S. Umeda, A reference model for manufacturing enterprise system by using OMT method, *ACM SIGGROUP Bulletin* **8**(1), (1997) 54–57.
17. S. Umeda, An object-oriented system model for manufacturing enterprise information system *Proceedings of APMS, IFIP WG5.7* (1996) 395–400.
18. T. Berners-Lee and R. Cailliau, A. Luotonen, H. Frystyk Nielsen, and A. Secret, The World-Wide Web, *Communications. ACM* **37**(8), (1994).
19. ISO/IS 10303-21, Industrial automation systems and integration — product data representation and exchange — Part 21: Clear text encoding of exchange structure, ISO, 1 rue de Varambe, Case Postale 56, CH-1211 Geneva, Switzerland (1994).
20. OMG, The common object request broker: architecture and specification ver. 2.0 (1995).
21. S. Banerjee, EDI: characteristics of users and no-users, *Information & Management* **26** (1994) 65–74.
22. C. Hadavi, Tightening the supply chain using real-time information, *APICS — The Performance Advantage*, January,1996
23. Z. Mahmut Parlar and K. Weng, Designing a firm's coordinated manufacturing and supply decision with short product life cycles, *Management Science* **43**(10), (1977) 1329–1344.
24. D. C. Andrews and S. K. Stalick, *Business Reengineering* (Yourdon Press, 1994).
25. A. M. Geoffrion and G. W. Grave, Multicommodity distribution system design by Benders Decomposition, *Management Science* **20/5** (1974) 822–844 .
26. M. A. Cohen and H. L. Lee, Strategic analysis of integrated production — distribution systems: models and methods, *Operations Research* **36/2** (1988) 216–228.

Chapter 7

Process Design with Reference Process Building Blocks

FREIMUT BODENDORF, KLAUS LANG and WOLFGANG TAUMANN

Department of Information Systems,
University of Erlangen-Nuremberg,
90403 Nuremberg, Germany
E-mail: bodendorf@wiso.uni-erlangen.de

Business processes have been widely accepted as the key factors in designing organizational structures. Tools and methods that support process design are limited to abstract design principles, general handbooks or rigid reference models and are therefore insufficient. This paper provides a theoretical foundation for using reusable Process Building Blocks to design organizational processes. In this novel approach to Process Design, enterprises can design their processes by selecting, combining and customizing Reference Process Building Blocks (RPBs) provided by a library. RPBs represent design patterns and Best Practices for the organizational design and IT-support of business processes.

1. Introduction

Business processes are becoming increasingly a central issue for enterprise modeling. However, tools and methods that support core activity process modeling are inadequate. For the organizational design and IT-enablement of processes, two approaches are currently in use:

1.1. *Conventional approach*

The starting point in the conventional approach is a thorough view of the AS-IS state of the process followed by an in-depth analysis. The diagnosis of the deficiencies in the process provides the basis for the organizational redesign and IT-enablement. Alternatively, the search for design solutions on a 'greenfield site' without a detailed process analysis can create breakthrough results. Performing process design in this way can be compared with producing tailor-made goods, which often leads to high costs, low productivity and disappointing results. The key problem is a lack of methods and tools providing reusable process know-how, so that in most cases process design starts 'from scratch.'

1.2. *Reference process model approach*

The main idea of this approach is to use proposed design patterns of processes that are defined as Reference Process Models [1, 2]. Problems with mapping entire business processes as reference models are presented by the high complexity and limited insight, reflected by the process model as well as the inability to show alternatives within the model. Another critical aspect of Reference Process Models is that the organizational process and IT-support are not modeled simultaneously. In addition, Reference Process

Models concentrate on selected branches which narrows the range of use.

Two further approaches in designing business processes are currently being considered and have not been put to practice yet:

1.3. Skeleton approach

The Skeleton approach discusses aspects of supporting the reuse of software components. The idea of utilizing macro structures which are refined according to the requirements of the enterprise is transferred to the field of process design. Depicting processes which rely on the Skeleton approach opens up a large range of design possibilities but still stands in need of supporting tools.

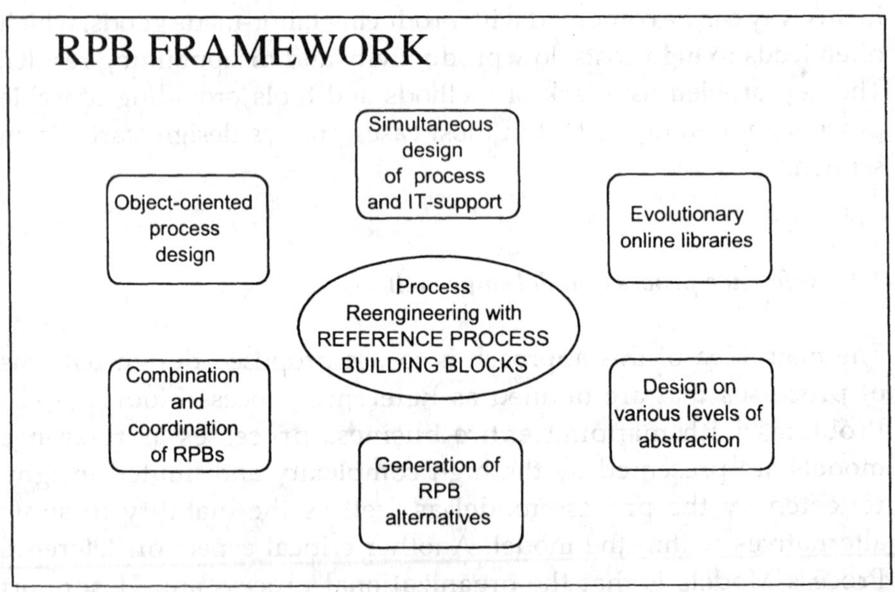

Figure 1 RPB framework

1.4. Reference process building block approach

This novel approach focuses on improving the quality of process design by utilizing reusable Reference Process Building Blocks (RPBs). RPBs represent *design patterns* and *best practices* for the organizational design and IT-support of business processes. With this innovative approach, enterprises can design individual process models by selecting, combining and customizing RPBs provided by an electronic library.

2. RPB Approach

The basic approach consists in designing business processes by combining reusable, abstract Process Building Blocks. The main characteristic of this methodology is the simultaneous design of process and IT-support, which is accomplished by embodying both aspects coexistent in the form of integrated process solutions and design patterns. Due to the strong interdependencies of process design and IT support, simultaneous design efforts have been recommended for Business Process Reengineering [3]. Further, RPBs represent Best Practices of how processes can be performed and are modeled on varying levels of abstraction.

The modeling of RPBs focuses the utilization of innovative IT as enabler together with the generation of new coordination mechanisms for combining RPBs to create innovative process solutions. RPBs that manifest the process solutions are stored in electronic libraries.

The business processes are designed by selecting and combining alternative RPBs provided by the library. In a next step, the modeled 'process chain' composed of the combined RPBs is customized and adapted to the specific demands of the enterprise supported by object-oriented mechanisms.

3. RPB Model

Every RPB consists of a standardized structure with defined basic properties (see Fig. 2). These basic properties make up the fundamental attribute classes of the *object RPB*. Each attribute class includes single attributes that describe the object RPB in order to meet the needs of the process design effort. These single attributes are the key elements of the RPB Model and will be referred to as *basic attributes*.

3.1. Coordination attributes

The attribute class *Identification* includes a definite identifier as well as a description of the RPB. The *Coordination Code (COORD)* describes the

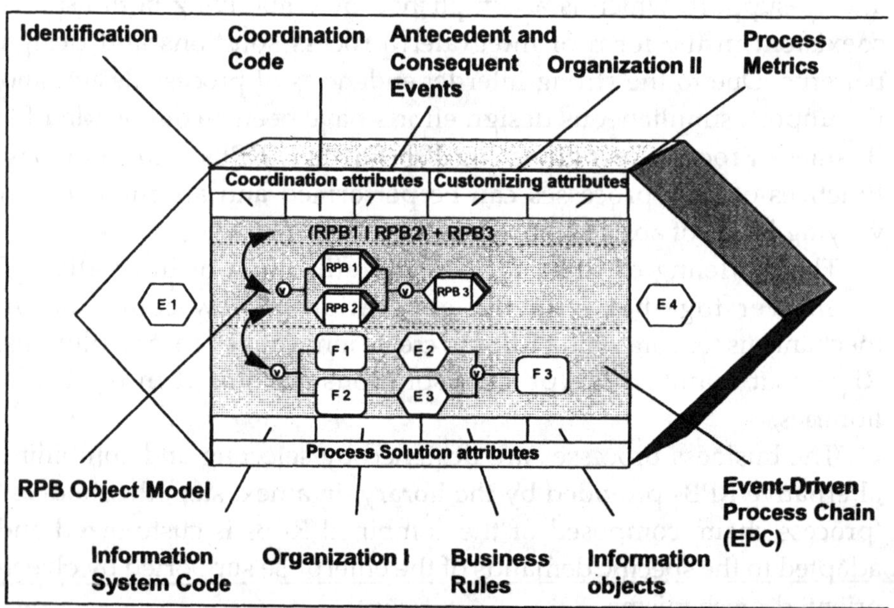

Figure 2 Reference process building block (RPB)

decomposed RPB chain in semi-formal terms. In this way the COORD provides a semi-formal representation of the relationships between the various RPB layers that constitute the RPB library, thus supporting the navigation inside the RPB library. The COORD formalism is based on an easy grammar [4].

Antecedent and Consequent Events represent the interfaces of an RPB and are modeled for the purpose of connecting RPBs in a proper way.

3.2. *Process solution attributes*

The *Information System Code (ISC)* shows the IT-systems and the way they support the RPBs. The choice and application of organizational units that will be responsible for performing the RPBs are stored in the attribute class *Organization I*. The key ideas for process solutions can often be found within methods or principles. These ideas can seem meaningless in isolation, but can, however, create breakthrough process solutions when used to generate new process scenarios. We will refer to these sort of key ideas as *Business Rules*. Lastly, the information objects needed for process design belong to the attribute class *Information Objects*.

3.3. *Customizing attributes*

When customizing arranged RPB chains, empty attribute values can be filled, and attribute values can be modified. In addition, new attributes may be specified which can be filled during the customizing process. An example of these customizing attributes are attributes which specify the individual organization of the process, e.g. the name of the process owner. Another example are process metrics which can be filled on an ongoing basis to support process controlling and continuous improvement efforts.

Table 1 Attributes of an RPB

Attribute category	Attribute class	Attributes	Description
coordination attributes	identification	identifier	short definite key (primary key)
		RPB designation	activity and object-reference of the RPB
		process solution	description of the key elements of the process solution in free-form text
		version number	current version number
	coordination code (COORD)	COORD	process description in semi-formal terms
	antecedent and consequent events	antecedent event	defined starting event of an RPB
		consequent event	defined ending event of an RPB
process solution attributes	information system code (ISC)	application systems	e.g. workflow management system
		help/support systems	e.g. electronic time scheduler
		level of IT-support	manual | partly automated | automated
		integration to other applications	e.g. customer information system
		information storage	e.g. tape | hard disc | disc | chip-card | CD-ROM | paper

Table 1 (*Continued*)

Attribute category	Attribute class	Attributes	Description
		hardware components	e.g. touch-activated screen
		carrier techniques	e.g. wired ∣ wireless ∣ paper transport
		communication systems	e.g. telephone ∣ fax ∣ email ∣ video-conferencing
	organization I (ORG I)	organizational category	e.g. customer ∣ supplier
		division of labor	case worker ∣ case team
	business rules	business rules	e.g. yield management
	information objects (IO)	input-IO	e.g. customer name
		output-IO	e.g. credit standing
customizing attributes	organization II (ORG II)	organization unit	e.g. customer care department
		superior organization unit	
		process owner	responsible person
	process metrics	lead time	total time over run time, wait time, and transport time
		run time	time for running
		wait time	time for waiting
		transport time	time for transporting

4. RPB Categories

The RPB framework distinguishes between two main categories of RPBs:

4.1. *Generic RPBs*

These RPBs are modeled on a high level of abstraction and do not relate to any specific domain (i.e. specific process types or branches). They include generic process solutions and design patterns and offer the highest level of reusability within all categories of the RPBs. Examples, on an elementary level, are 'collecting information' and 'transmitting information.'

4.2. *Domain RPBs*

Domain RPBs refer to a specific field of interest, i.e. a certain process type or branch. An example of a domain RPB is 'acquiring billing data through electronic voice recognition.'

Additionally, generic and domain RPBs are separated into general RPBs and process solution RPBs.

4.3. *General RPBs*

General RPBs are specified only by their coordination attributes. By combining general RPBs, templates are created which constitute the structure of RPB libraries.

4.4. *Process solution RPBs*

Process solution RPBs add a process solution to the coordination attributes, which is expressed in their process solution attributes as application systems, business rules, etc. They are of major importance for the process design effort as they embody the essential process know-how.

Moreover, general RPBs — as well as process solution RPBs — can be classified according to the object they refer to, i.e. the object they basically deal with, e.g. the object 'customer information.' The *object-reference* determines the core activity along with the process solution of an RPB.

Of primary interest within the RPB framework are *generic RPBs* which include process solutions (*process solution RPBs*) and do not refer to a specific object (*without object-reference*). They embody key ideas and design solutions that can be applied to a wide range of uses. Moreover, they are an important basis upon which domain RPBs can be developed. Generic RPBs are provided on various levels of abstraction relying on a basis taxonomy. The following example will illustrate the notion of generic RPBs with process solution and without object-reference. On an elementary level of abstraction the generic RPB 'collecting information' is offered in tandem with process solutions as:

- manual collection of information by using touch-activated screens
- partly automatic collection of information with product code scanners
- automatic collection of information through the use of smart-cards

Specialization and inheritance mechanisms support the development of domain RPBs, e.g. the RPB 'collecting orders with a touch-activated screen.'

5. Software Tool for the RPB Approach

For implementation of the RPB approach the ARIS Toolset (software tool for process modeling) is taken as a basis. Its functionality for editing and visualizing RPBs is applied to represent and manipulate RPBs diagrammatically. For storage and administration of RPB attributes a relational database is built up using the database system Microsoft Access. This database helps to handle the information load and provides direct and fast information retrieval.

The RPB descriptions stored in the database system are transferred to the ARIS-Toolset by an interface module. The separation of RPB data storage (Microsoft Access) and RPB handling (ARIS-Toolset) has important advantages:

- RPB libraries are independent of the ARIS-Toolset. Any modeling software tool is able to use the RPB descriptions by providing a specific interface module.
- RPB specific functions can be realized with the program language of Microsoft Access (e.g. methods for coordination and combination of RPBs).

Several libraries with a considerable number of RPBs have been developed with this software environment.

6. Conclusion

The RPB framework intends to improve the design of organizational processes and IT-support. The innovative approach is to provide RPBs which represent integrated Process Solutions. This enables the immediate and easy use of Best Practices in designing business processes, which leads to lower costs, less time consumption and a higher quality of the process design effort. The RPB methodology can be of fundamental help for all who rely on efficient tools for designing processes, e.g. consulting firms. Furthermore, the method can influence the research in designing organizational structures.

Using RPBs promises essential advantages in contrast to conventional tools. The possibility of systematically combining and customizing RPB chains by selecting from alternative RPBs offers a high flexibility in finding process solutions that will suit the individual needs best, e.g. in contrast to the considerable inflexible nature of fixed

Reference Process Models. Another difference to more common tools is that process solutions of RPB integrate the interdependencies of process and IT-support. Moreover, RPBs have the capability to express the nested, layered quality that characterizes many kinds of organizational processes which widens the range of use.

The easy way of arranging and rearranging RPBs that embody ideas for the innovative utilization of IT as well as novel coordination mechanisms opens up a wide range of ways to explore innovative process solutions. By systematically evaluating new ways of performing processes with the RPB methodology, enterprises can gain substantial competitive advantages.

In the future you can imagine markets for RPBs established for various branches. In this vision, RPBs can be thought of being traded among different branches as well as being sold from professional RPB designers.

References

1. T. W. Malone, K. Crowston, J. Lee and B. Pentland, Tools for inventing organizations: towards a handbook of organizational processes, in *Proceedings of the Second Workshop on Enabling Technologies Infrastructure for Collaborative Enterprises* (Los Almitos, 1993) pp. 72–82.
2. A.-W. Scheer, *Wirtschaftsinformatik — Referenzmodelle für industrielle Geschäftsprozesse* (Springer, Berlin, 1994).
3. O. Petrovic, MIASOI: Ein Modell der iterativen Abstimmung von Strategie, Organization und Informationstechnologie, in *Geschäftsprozeß management* O. C. Krickl (ed.) (Heidelberg, 1994).
4. K. Lang, W. Taumann and F. Bodendorf, Business process reengineering with reusable reference process building blocks, in B. Scholz-Reiter and E. Stickel, *Business Process Modelling* (Springer, Berlin, 1996) pp. 265–290.
5. K. Crowston, A taxonomy of organizational dependencies and coordination mechanisms, *Working Paper,* The University of Michigan, School of Business Administration (Tappan, 1994).

6. T. H. Davenport and J. E. Short, The new industrial engineering: information technology and business process redesign, *Sloan Management Review* **4** (1990) 11–27.
7. M. Hammer and J. Champy, *Reengineering the Corporation* (New York, 1993).
8. M. Hammer and S. A. Stanton, *The Reengineering Revolution — A Handbook* (New York, 1995).
9. IDS Prof. Scheer (ed.), ARIS-Methodenhandbuch, Buch 5, Release 3.0 (Saarbrücken, 1995).
10. H. R. Jorysz and F. B. Vernadat, CIMOSA Part 1: total enterprise modelling and function view, *International Journal of Computer Integrated Manufacturing* **3–4** (1990) 144–156.
11. R. B. Kaplan and L. Murdock, Core process redesign, *The McKinsey Quarterly* **2** (1990).
12. G. Keller and St. Meinhardt, SAP R/3-Analyzer: Optimierung von Geschäftsprozessen auf Basis des R/3-Referenzmodells. SAP AG, (Walldorf, 1994).
13. T. W. Malone and K. Crowston, Toward an interdisciplinary theory of coordination, *Working Paper*, Center for Coordination Science, Sloan School of Management, Massachusetts Institute of Technology (Cambridge, 1990).
14. B. T. Pentland, Process grammars: a generative approach to process redesign, *Working Paper*, University of California (Los Angeles, 1994).
15. M. G. Wyner and J. Lee, Applying specialization to process models, *Working Paper*, Center for Coordination Science, Sloan School of Management, Massachusetts Institute of Technology (Cambridge, 1995).

Chapter 8

Diagnosing Process Design: A Formal Approach*

PEDRO RAMOS
Department of Informatics,
Instituto Superior das Ciências do Trabalho e da Empresa (ISCTE),
1600 Lisboa, Portugal
E-mail: Pedro.Ramos@iscte.pt

JOSÉ LUIZ FIADEIRO
Department of Informatics, Faculty of Sciences,
University of Lisbon 1700 Lisboa, Portugal
E-mail: llf@di.fc.ul.pt

Computational tools that support process design have been widely used in Business Process Reengineering. In order to assist the designer, they use information about the organization (structure, tasks, documents, etc.). However, knowledge and inference about the expected behavior of processes have not been supported to the same extent. In this chapter we redress this situation by showing how the compliance of a process design with respect to organizational rules can be formally analyzed using techniques from artificial intelligence and computer science. Based on these formalisms we have built a software tool that detects incorrect and incomplete designs of organizational process, and helps the designer to decide between alternative choices.

*This work was partially supported by the contract PSCH/OGE/1038/95 and UNIDE/ISCTE.

1. Introduction

Computational tools that support process design have been widely used in Business Process Reengineering (BPR) [1, 2, 3]. In order to assist the designer, they use information about the organization (structure, tasks, documents, etc.). However, knowledge and inference about the expected behavior of processes have not been supported. As Michael Earl and Bushra Khan [4] discussed, knowledge (they call it prescription of rules) can be used in the (re)design of structured process.

In this chapter we present a framework to help the designer to make better designs of structured processes, using general rules (principles) that the organization believes a design must comply with.

It is not very common to use formal techniques in organizational domains, namely in BPR. However, formal approaches usually provide a solid and rich framework to describe the core concepts and relations between them. Formal languages are universal and notably rich and flexible. With them, it is possible to conceptually analyze relations between concepts and insure the correctness of the conclusions we draw.

In the chapter we show how the compliance of a process design with respect to organizational rules can be formally analyzed using techniques from artificial intelligence and computer science (namely, Theory of Diagnosis and Deontic Logic). These techniques have been implemented in a software tool that detects incorrect and incomplete designs, and helps the designer to decide between alternative choices. In the chapter, we use the control rules for accounting procedures compiled by Chen & Lee [5].

The main contribution of the chapter is that it shows that the classic Theory of Diagnosis can be easily extended in order to be used for organizational process aided design, and propose a formal language to describe the organization, the process and the principles within the same framework.

In Sec. 2, a general description of the framework is presented. In Sec. 3, we present an example of an Order Delivering Process. This example will be used throughout almost all of the chapter. In Sec. 4, we introduce the classical theory of diagnosis (showing how it can be changed in order to be applied to the domain of process design) and a formal deontic language suitable for our framework. In Sec. 5, we show how the formal approaches of Sec. 4 are combined in our Deontic Framework for Diagnosis of Organizational Process Design (DDD).

2. Framework

The main goal of the framework presented in this chapter is to help the designer to make better process designs, using general rules (principles) that the organization believes a design must comply with. The framework supplies different features like the detection of incorrect and incomplete designs, and the capacity to help the designer to deal with alternative choices (namely with conflicting rules). The main components of the framework are:

Organizational structure — a set of structural concepts that characterize a specific organization, e.g. *agents, tasks, hierarchies*. These concepts are independent of the processes. They describe the fixed components over which the processes 'flow.'

Process description — description of the process design. The description is made with typical primitives used in organizational process, e.g. *assign, output-to-task*.

General organizational knowledge — definitions (e.g. *available, informed*) and rules (e.g. *if a task is assigned to a collective agent, the task is assigned to all the members of the collective agent*) common to all organizations.

Principles — general rules that characterize the ideal behavior of an organization. Each organization decides which rules should be used. Usually the rules that guide the design are general rules (e.g. "*no employee can be assigned to a control task if the decision to control is assigned to an agent up in the hierarchy*"). We are interested in forms of diagnoses of the process design that report violations of such principles.

With the framework the user must design a process (using a diagrammatic language), specify general principles and describe the structure of the organization. The translation from a diagrammatic language to a textual formal language is one step of the diagnosis procedure. We choose to adopt a declarative formal language because we want to use formal deduction methods in the diagnosis procedure. The interaction between the software tool and the user is crucial. The diagnosis procedure can be executed at any time during the design. As a result of running the diagnosis procedure the user is informed of the 'mistakes' he has done so far and what is left to do.

3. Example — Order Delivering Process

In order to better understand diagnosis in organizational process design, we present an example of an Order Delivering Process. This example is adapted from Chen & Lee [5]. The same authors have also compiled all the general accounting rules used in it. The example will be used throughout the chapter. To avoid frauds in organizational accounting procedures some control rules are often used. Consider the process design in Fig. 1.

The process is as follows: the stock manager receives an order (from a salesman, for example), fills up an Internal Delivering Order (Fu-IDO) and sends it to the Warehouse which has to fill up an Outgoing Del. Order (Fu-ODO); after filling the Outgoing Delivering Order (ODO) the Warehouse sends it to the client together with the goods. After receiving the same order, the Accounting Department fills up the Invoice and stores it in the Invoice File. With this design, a fraud might occur involving, for example, the Stock Manager and the Warehouse (they can retrieve more goods from the warehouse than the amount considered in the invoice).

The following five rules exemplify some concerns of the organization about potential frauds (the rules assume that there are control tasks that control operational tasks):

Rule 1: *"When a control task exists, it must be furnished with the supporting documents";*
Rule 2: *"If a control task uses a supporting document, the supporting document should be transferred directly from the task that produces the supporting document";*
Rule 3: *"A control task and the operating task it intends to control should be segregated into two different agents";*
Rule 4: *"The position assigned with a control task cannot be lower in the formal power hierarchy than the position of the operating task to be controlled";*
Rule 5: *"The agent in charge of a control task should be socially detached from the agent responsible for the corresponding operational task."*

Consider also the following specific rule and the organization structure presented in Table 1:

Rule 6: *"Only one employee who has worked for at least three years in the organization can be the Warehouse Manager."*

In Fig. 2, the same order delivering process is (re)designed in order to fulfil the rules. The process is as follows: the stock manager (John) receives an order, fills up an IDO and sends it to the Stock/Invoice Controller (Phil) assigned to task Verify Internal Delivering Order (Ve-IDO); after receiving the same order the Accounting Department (Ann) fills up the Invoice and sends it to the Stock/Invoice Controller;

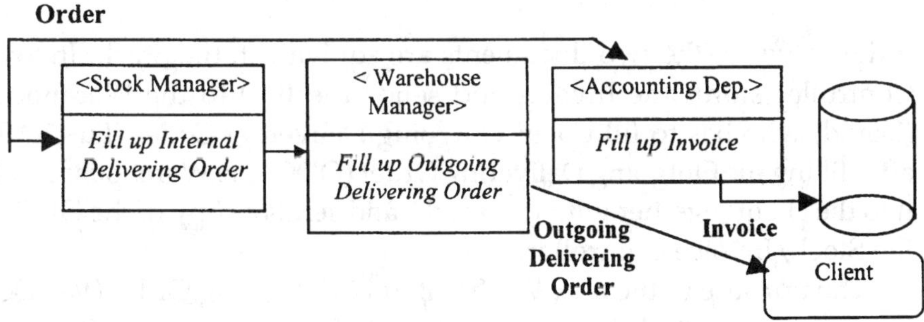

Figure 1 Example of an Order Delivering Process that allows fraud

Table 1 Organization structure

Organization Structure
Agents: John, Ann, Phil, Paul, David *Roles*: Stock Mng, Warehouse Mng., Accounting Department Mng., Stock/Invoice Controller Phil is hierarchically superior than John; John is hierarchically superior than Paul David and Paul are socially close; Only David and Paul work for more than three years in the organization.

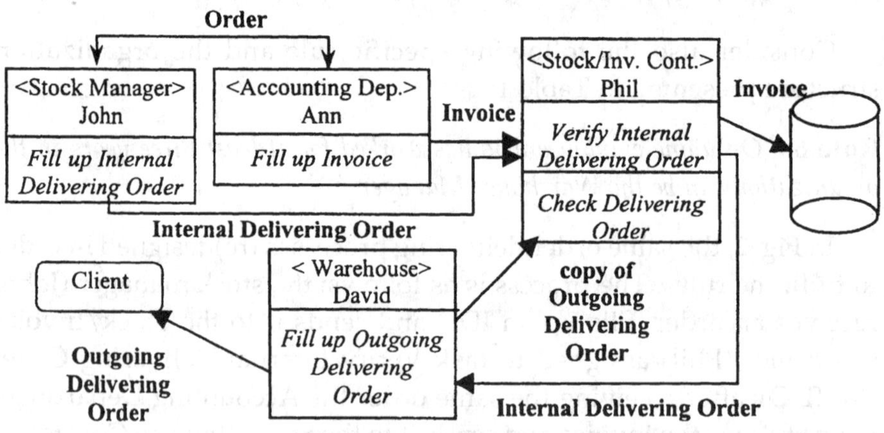

Figure 2 Example of an ideal Order Delivering Process

if the values of the two documents are equivalent, the Stock/Invoice Controller stores the Invoice and sends the IDO to the Warehouse (David) who has to fill up an Outgoing Delivering Order (Fu-ODO); after filling the Outgoing Delivering Order (ODO) the Warehouse sends it to the client together with the goods, and sends a copy of the ODO to the Stock/Invoice Controller.

The purpose of the task Verify Internal Delivering Order (Ve-IDO) is to control the task Fill up an Internal Delivering Order (Fu-IDO), that is done by using the supporting documents Invoice and IDO. The purpose of the task Check Delivering Order (Ck-DO) is to control the task Fu-IDO, that is done by using the supporting documents copy-ODO and IDO. The role of the Stock/Invoice Controller is to prevent frauds.

As it can be easily checked, all the rules are fulfilled, for example, rule 4 is fulfilled because Phil is hierarchically superior to John. Given the previous design (Fig. 2) a diagnosis framework should report that there are no violations in the design.

Scenario 1: Consider now an incomplete attempt to design an Order Delivering Process where (i) no one is assigned yet to Fu-ODO (Warehouse Manager); (ii) David is the Stock/Invoice Controller; (iii) instead of sending the invoice to the Stock/Invoice Controller, Ann stores it in the Invoice file; (iv) the copy of the ODO is not sent to anyone yet.

Some situations are unambiguous: rule 4 is fulfilled because Phil is hierarchically superior to John; rule 2 is violated because the Invoice is not transferred directly to the Stock/Invoice Controller. Other situations require a more deep analysis:

(i) How should a diagnosis report the impossibility to fulfil simultaneously rules 3, 5 and 6 in what regards the assignment of the task *Fill up Outgoing Delivering Order* (notice that given rule 6 only David and Paul can be assigned, but given rules 5 and 3 Paul should not be assigned and David should also not be assigned)? Is the impossibility a consequence of previous design choices made by the designer, or does it remain whatever choices are made by the designer?

(ii) Should a diagnosis report that rule 5 can also be violated because the designer has not yet assigned anyone to the task *Fill up Outgoing Delivering Order* (it is possible to assign Paul to the task, but that will be a violation of the rule because David and Paul are socially close)? Or should we consider that a diagnosis must not report that situation because there is no violation yet?

(iii) Should the designer 'prove' that David and John are not socially close (in order to ensure that rule 5 is not violated)?

In the next sections we show how formal approaches to diagnosis and reasoning can provide a precise way to answer these questions.

4. Formal Contributions to the Diagnosis of Process Design

It is not very common to use formal techniques in organizational domains, namely in BPR. However, formal approaches usually provide a solid and rich framework to describe the core concepts and relations between them. Moreover, when we want to have a deductive system (i.e. to derive conclusions based on given information, such as the detection of potential frauds given a process design) it is very important to be certain about the correctness of the conclusions. Software tools are usually the final goal, but they are not expressive enough to provide the kind of analysis described above. Formal languages (like logic) are universal and notably rich and flexible. With them, it is possible to conceptually analyze relationships between concepts and insure the correctness of the conclusions we draw. If a software tool implementation is based on a formal language, it is possible to discuss the approach at a higher level of abstraction, without having to know the details of the implementation.

4.1. Theory of diagnosis

In the framework proposed by Chen & Lee [5] for the evaluation of internal accounting control procedures, the idea of having general rules guiding organizational diagnosis is already present. However, this framework is not supported by a theory of diagnosis. For instance, situations (i) and (ii) described in III are partially answered by the theory of diagnosis, and are not answered by Chen's framework. In this section we briefly introduce the classical Theory of Diagnosis and show how it can be extended in order to be used for the diagnosis of process design.

4.1.1. Model Based Reasoning approach to diagnosis

The Model Based Reasoning (MBR) approach to diagnosis has been studied for several years (for a survey of the topic see Ref. 6). Numerous applications have been built, most of all for diagnosis of physical devices. The basic paradigm is the interaction between prediction and observation. If a discrepancy between the output of the system (given a particular input) and the prediction is found, the diagnosis procedure will search for malfunctions in the components of the system (the correction of the model is assumed).

The contribution of Reiter to the theory of diagnosis has become a standard in the field of diagnosis theory. His 'Consistency-Based Approach' [7] is the first one to formalize the MBR approach to diagnosis. The main goal is to eliminate system inconsistency, identifying the minimal set of abnormal components that is responsible for the inconsistency. An abnormal component (AB(c)) is a component that, given a specific input, does not produce the expected output.

Reiter Diagnosis — ***Given*** a system (SD, COMP, OBS) where SD is the system description, COMP is the set of components of the system, and OBS are the observations, a diagnosis is a minimal set $\Delta \subseteq \text{COMP}$ such that:

$$\text{SD} \cup \text{OBS} \cup \{\text{AB}(c) \mid c \in \Delta\} \cup \{\neg\text{AB}(c) \mid c \in \text{COMP} - \Delta\} \text{ is consistent} \tag{1}$$

In the definition, ¬ means not. This definition is based on the Principle of Parsimony, according to which a diagnosis is a conjecture that some minimal set of components is faulty.

In order to illustrate the definition consider a situation where someone tries to save a file in a floppy disk and receives an error message saying that it is not possible to save the file because there is a problem in the drive. There are several possible explanations for the error message: the floppy disk is damaged, the drive is damaged, the mainboard is damaged, the driver is not correctly installed, etc. The explanation can be just one of those, but it is also possible that all the components are damaged.

What the diagnosis definition tells us is that it is not rational to assume that all components are damaged if it is possible that only one damaged component explains the error (principle of parsimony). More formally, the diagnosis $\Delta = \{AB(\text{floppy disk})\}$ means that it is consistent to assume that the floppy disk is damaged and all the other components are not damaged ($\neg AB(\text{drive})$ and $\neg AB(\text{mainboard})$ ...). It is also possible to assume that the floppy disk and the drive are damaged ($\Delta = \{AB(\text{floppy disk}), AB(\text{drive})\}$) and the others not, but since this is not a minimal set, it is not a diagnosis, according to Reiter's definitions.

Let us consider that if the mainboard is damaged, it is also not possible to write in the hard disk. Consider also that the user managed to save the file in the hard disk. Now all diagnoses that assume that the mainboard is damaged AB(mainboard) are not consistent. There remain three alternative diagnoses (three consistent minimal sets): $\Delta_1 = \{AB(\text{floppy disk})\}$; $\Delta_2 = \{AB(\text{drive})\}$; $\Delta_3 = \{AB(\text{drive installation})\}$.

MBR can also be applied to diagnosis of process design. The role of symptoms (evidence of malfunctioning) is crucial in the MBR approach because it guides the diagnosis. However, there are situations in which, even if it is not possible to detect the malfunctioning of a system, a preventive diagnosis is recommended. Process design diagnosis is one such situation.

In process design diagnosis, the Organization Structure is the input of the system. The System Description corresponds to the Process Design, together with the General Organizational Knowledge. The components are the parts of the design that are in the scope of the rules. Rules are used to check for abnormalities (violations) of the components. Assuming the fulfilment of the rules there is nothing to be predicted. This happens because there is not a real output that can be observed. Evidence of malfunction appears later when the process runs in the organization. However, in order to insure that the process design fulfils the rules, a preventive diagnosis is needed.

4.1.2. Model Based Reasoning approach to diagnosis of process design

Consider the example presented in Sec. 3. Given the organization structure and the general organizational knowledge, it can be deduced that, in a correct design, the following specific rules (particular cases of the general rules), among others, must be followed (*task-output-input-task (Task1, Output1, Task2)* means that the output Output1 of task Task1 goes to task Task2):

R1: ¬(assign (Fu-IDO, Phil) and assign(Ver-IDO, John));
R2: task-output-input-task(Fu-Invoive, Invoice, Fu-IDO);
R3: task-output-input-task(Fu-ODO, Copy-ODO, Ck-DO).

Given scenario 1, namely the assignment of Ve-IDO to David, the designer must insure that:

R4: ¬assign(Fu-ODO, David);
R5: ¬assign(Fu-ODO, Paul).

It is not consistent to assume that the empty set ($\Delta_1 = \{ \}$) is a diagnosis. If that is assumed, it means that all rules are fulfilled, namely R2 (*task-output-input-task(Fu-Invoive, Invoice, Fu-IDO)*), which is inconsistent with scenario 1. However, it is consistent to assume that $\Delta_2 = \{R2\}$ is a diagnosis. If we consider that an abnormal behavior of one rule is its negation (AB(R2) = ¬R2), a diagnosis $\Delta_2 = \{R2\}$ means that there is no inconsistency between the design and the following assumptions (R1, R3, R4, R5 fulfilled and R2 not fulfilled):

¬(assign(Fu-IDO, Phil) and assign(Ver-IDO, John));
¬(task-output-input-task(Fu-Invoive, Invoice, Fu-IDO));
task-output-input-task(Fu-ODO, Copy-ODO, Ck-DO);
¬assign(Fu-ODO, David);
¬assign(Fu-ODO, Paul).

The design does not say that *¬assign(Fu-ODO, Paul)*, but it also does not say either *assign(Fu-ODO, Paul)*, so, it is possible to assume that there is no violation of the rule. Any set that contains the violation of R1 (*assign(Fu-IDO,Phil)* and *assign(Ver-IDO, John)*) cannot be a diagnosis because it is inconsistent with the fact (represented in the design) that ¬(*assign(Fu-IDO, Phil)* and *assign(Ver-IDO, John)*).

The previous example shows that Model Based Reasoning Diagnosis (Eq. (1)) can be used in process design domain:

Process Design Diagnosis — Given a system (ORG, PD, RL) where ORG is the organization structure and general organizational knowledge, PD is the process design, and RL are the rules (principles), a diagnosis is a minimal set $\Delta \subseteq$ RL such that (equivalent to Eq. (1)):

$$\mathrm{ORG} \cup \mathrm{PD} \cup \{\neg(r) \mid r \in \Delta\} \cup \{r \mid r \in \mathrm{RL} - \Delta\} \text{ is consistent} \quad (2)$$

Now we show how MBR deals with the questions of Sec. 3:

4.1.2.1. Implicit and explicit violations and conflicting rules

In question (i) (Sec. 3) we said that a diagnosis should report the impossibility to fulfil several rules simultaneously. Consider the four following specific rules and scenario 1:

R1: assign(Fu-ODO,Paul) or assign(Fu-ODO, David);
R2: ¬assign(Fu-ODO, David);
R3: ¬assign(Fu-ODO, Paul);
R4: task-output-input-task(Fu-Invoice, Invoice, Fu-IDO).

It is impossible to fulfil simultaneously R1, R2 and R3 (R4 is already violated). Indeed, Eq. (2) gives us three alternative diagnosis): Δ_1 = {R1, R4}; Δ_2 = {R2, R4}; Δ_3 = {R3, R4}. In every diagnosis R4 is violated, and there is no diagnosis where R1, R2 and R3 are simultaneously fulfilled (i.e. Δ_4 = {R4} is not a diagnosis). The set {R1, R2, R3} is called an Implicit Violation Set. Formally, we have,

Implicit Violation Set — IVΔ_i is an Implicit Violation Set iff IVΔ_i is a minimal set such that

$$\text{IV}\Delta_i \subseteq \text{RL and ORG} \cup \text{PD} \cup \{\text{r} \mid \text{r} \in \text{IV}\Delta_i\} \text{ is inconsistent}. \quad (3)$$

Informally, it is not possible to fulfil all the rules related to the violations in $\text{IV}\Delta_i$ (at least one violation will occur). This definition corresponds to Reiter's definition of Conflict Set.

For a particular process description it is possible to have several implicit violation sets. We call V_k an Implicit Violation iff there exists one $\text{IV}\Delta_i$ such that $V_k \in \text{IV}\Delta_i$.

$$\textit{Explicit Violation} - V_k \text{ is an Explicit Violation iff } \{V_k\} \text{ is an implicit violation set} \quad (4)$$

Informally, if V_k is an Explicit Violation then the rule related with V_k is always violated unless the designer changes the design (R4 is explicitly violated).

As mentioned in question (i) (Sec. 3), it is not sufficient to alert the designer that it is impossible to simultaneously fulfil R1, R2 and R3 (i.e. deduce that {R1, R2, R3} is an Implicit Violation Set). It is important to know if that impossibility is a consequence of previous design choices made by the designer or the impossibility remains whatever the designer does (i.e. it results from a conflict between the rules).

A conflict between rules occurs when, whatever options the designer takes, it is impossible to fulfil those rules together (in the example there are not conflicting rules; in Fig. 2 all rules are fulfilled).

Conflicting Rules — $\text{CO}\Delta_i$ is a Conflicting Rule Set iff $\text{CO}\Delta_i$ is a minimal set such that

$$\text{CO}\Delta_i \subseteq \text{RL and ORG} \cup \{\text{r} \mid \text{r} \in \text{CO}\Delta_i\} \text{ is inconsistent}. \quad (5)$$

Notice that all conflicting rule sets are implicit violation sets. The only difference between definition 3 and 5 is that in Eq. (5) we leave out the process design (the rules are inconsistent with the organization, whatever the design).

MBR is powerful enough to deal with question (i). We only need to extend MBR with definition 5 in order to obtain the desired results. As it will be presented in the next section, question (ii) illustrates the insufficiency of MBR to deal with diagnosis of process design.

4.1.2.2. Benevolent and exigent diagnosis

Let us consider that in Fig. 2 the designer assigns the task *Verify Internal Delivering Order* to Phil (*assign(Ver-IDO, Phil)*), instead of assigning it to David (notice that, with that decision, the Implicit Violation Set of the previous section disappears). As a consequence of the general rule 4 (Sec. 3), Paul should not be assigned to the task *Fill Up Outgoing Delivering Order* (*¬assign(Paul, Fu-ODO)*). Since the designer has not yet assigned anyone to the task Ver-IDO, there is not a violation yet, but the violation can occur if Paul is assigned.

In spite of not knowing anything about the fulfilment of that rule, a MBR approach based on the Parsimony Principle 'accepts' that situation (that is, a diagnosis will not report that rule). That happens because there is no evidence of the violation of the rule. The Parsimony Principle follows the rule 'innocent until proven guilty.'

If it is really important that the task is not assigned to Paul, a design that does not commit himself with that assignment must be avoided. Indeed, if the rule is not enforced, it is possible that, during the implementation of the process in the organization, the task is assigned to Paul. To avoid this undesired situation, the diagnosis should alert to the 'incompleteness' of the design. When it is important to ensure that all rules are fulfilled, and not only detect violation of rules, the Parsimony Principle is much too *benevolent* (it is like the assumption of the fulfilment of rules in the absence of information). In that case, one approach based only on minimal diagnosis is not adequate and an *exigent* diagnosis (where unfulfilled rules are detected, i.e. 'guilty until proven innocent') is more suitable.

To deal with the notions of benevolent and exigent diagnoses, we do not consider the Parsimony Principle to be a built-in feature of diagnosis, but an extra logical principle that can be applied or not. We choose to have a more general and independent diagnosis definition (Potential Diagnosis) over which principles, like the Parsimony Principle, can be applied.

Underlying the notion of exigent diagnosis we are considering a different principle (opposite to the Principle of Parsimony): a diagnosis is a conjecture that a maximal set of rules can be violated. In order to capture the notion of exigent diagnosis, a computation of maximal sets is required. In Fig. 3 we illustrate the kind of useful information that can be presented during the design.

Consider the six following specific rules and scenario 1:

R1: assign(Fu-ODO, Paul) or assign(Fu-ODO, David);
R2: ¬assign(Fu-ODO, David);
R3: ¬assign(Fu-ODO, Paul);
R4: task-output-input-task(Fu-Invoive, Invoice, Fu-IDO);
R5: ¬(assign(Fu-IDO, Phil) and assign(Ver-IDO, John));
R6: task-output-input-task(Fu-ODO, Copy-ODO, Ck-DO).

Each set in the tree represents one consistent set of violated rules. V_i means violation of rule R_i (for example, $\{V_2, V_4\}$ means that it is consistent to assume the violations *assign*(Fu-ODO, David) and ¬*task-output-input-task (Fu-Invoive, Invoice, Fu-IDO)*, and the fulfilment of rules R1, R3, R5 and R6). All consistent sets of violated rules are considered in the figure. The sets are ordered by set inclusion.

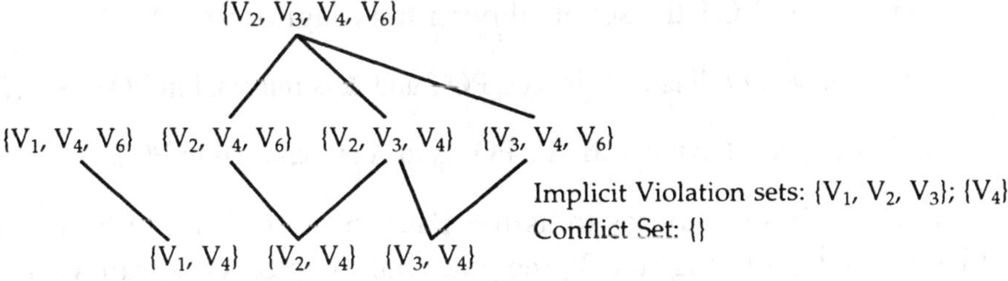

Figure 3 Consistent violation sets

The three minimal sets are the only three diagnoses according to Eq. (2). In order to capture the so-called Exigent diagnosis, the maximal set is required. Indeed the sets {V_2, V_3, V_4, V_6} and {V_1, V_4, V_6} must be understood as the 'work to be done,' that is, all the rules that are not yet fulfilled, but ought to be. Given the two exigent diagnosis, the user knows that it must fulfil rules 4 and 6, and must also fulfil rules 2 and 3 or, alternatively, rule 1 (notice that is not possible to violate simultaneously rules 1, 2 and 3. That is the reason for having two exigent diagnosis). Notice that rule 5 (already fulfilled) does not appear in any set, and rule 6 (not violated or fulfilled yet) does not appear in minimal sets).

Given the entire diagram, the designer has a clear picture of what should be done and what 'mistakes' have been done so far. If we do not consider the possibility to change previous design decisions, and assuming that RL does not change, the designer knows that, whatever is done, any diagnosis will always be in the original diagram.

All consistent sets of violations (all sets of the tree) are Potential Diagnoses, minimal sets are Benevolent Diagnoses and maximal sets are Exigent Diagnoses. Formally,

Potential Diagnosis — Given a system (ORG, PD, RL) where ORG is the organization structure and general organizational knowledge, PD is the process design, and RL are the rules, Δ is a potential diagnosis iff $\Delta \subseteq$ RL and:

$$\text{ORG} \cup \text{PD} \cup \{\neg(\text{r}) \mid \text{r} \in \Delta\} \cup \{\text{r} \mid \text{r} \in \text{RL} - \Delta\} \text{ is consistent}. \qquad (6)$$

Considering POT the set of all potential diagnoses:

$$\Delta \text{ is a } \textit{benevolent} \text{ diagnosis iff } \Delta \in \text{POT and } \Delta \text{ is minimal in POT}. \qquad (7)$$

$$\Delta \text{ is a } \textit{exigent} \text{ diagnosis iff } \Delta \in \text{POT and } \Delta \text{ is maximal in POT}. \qquad (8)$$

If the designer chooses to assign Paul to the task Fu-ODO (fulfil rules 1 and 2, violating rule 3), the potential diagnosis diagram will be as presented in Fig. 4.

$\{V_3, V_4, V_6\}$

Implicit Violation sets: $\{V_3\}$; $\{V_4\}$

$\{V_3, V_4\}$

Figure 4 Potential diagnoses after fulfilling rules R1 and R2

With the introduction of the notions of Potential, Benevolent and Exigent Diagnosis we show how the Theory of Diagnosis can be reformulated in order to answer question (ii) of Sec. 3. Question (iii) raises a different problem. As it will become clear in the next section, that question is related with the representation and interpretation of the rules.

4.2. Formal logic

In previous sections we presented a diagnosis-based approach to aid process design. We must now define how that approach can be supported. Namely, we have to show how to represent the rules and how to detect violations. As mentioned in the beginning of Sec. 4.1, we want to use formal deduction within the diagnosis procedure. Formal logic is a rich and flexible language, suitable to represent and analyze relations between concepts, and to infer correct conclusions.

It is not our purpose to present a full description of the logic we developed (L_{DD}, language for deontic diagnosis) for the diagnosis of process design [8, 9]. However, a brief description is required in order to enhance some characteristics of the framework we have built.

An applicational logic to diagnosis is introduced by Tan & Torre [10]. They use Deontic Logic, one well-known kind of formal logic. For several reasons that we do not present here, their logic is not suitable enough to deal with the kind of diagnosis we want (namely, exigent diagnosis). However, since Deontic Logic provides an intuitive and natural way to represent the kind of rules that arise in process design, we have chosen to use it, but in a more appropriate way (for a comparison between our logic and Tan & Torre logic, the following paper is recommended [9].

Deontic Logic (DL) is based on the concept of obligation. The notion of obligation can be used to explicitly represent ideal situations. For example, when we say that a designer must insure that *¬assign(Fu-ODO, David)*, we are saying that: in order to ensure that an ideal design is made, the designer is 'obliged' to *¬assign(Fu-ODO, David)*. In DL obligations are represented with the O operator: O(*¬assign(Fu-ODO, David)*). With this operator, ideal and actual situations can coexist, even when ideal situations do not occur. For example, it is possible to have simultaneously O(*¬assign(Fu-ODO, David)*) and *assign(Fu-ODO, David)*. When such a situation occurs we say that the obligation is violated.

DL has been applied to several domains, for example: agent's responsibility within organizations [11], confidentiality in databases [12] and security in computer systems [13]. Here we show how deontic logic can be easily used in aided process design.

4.2.1. Conditional obligations

Most of the rules that guide the design of a process are better represented in a conditional way (for example, *"If one person is lower in the formal power hierarchy than another person* [condition] *then the first one cannot control the second"*). We consider that a conditional obligation has two components: the *design action* that indicates what the designer should do, and the *context* (condition) that describes the situation in which the *design action* should be done. That distinction is crucial in our approach.

Conditional obligations are represented with Von Wright's dyadic operator O[_/_] [14]. The obligation O[p/q] should be read as "if the context q is the case, there is an obligation to perform the action p." An unconditional obligation O[p/True] is abbreviated to O[p].

4.2.2. Structural and design concepts

In our approach to process design in organizations, two types of concepts are considered: Structural and Design concepts. *Structural concepts* represent the organization structure, i.e. what is fixed in the organization and cannot be changed as a consequence of a process (re)design. For example: ability, existing tasks, kinds of tasks, employees. *Design concepts* are those that can be manipulated by the person that designs the process. They can be understood as 'design actions.' For example: assign tasks to agents, redirect outputs.

We assume that it makes no sense to have obligations according to which a process designer has to act over the structure of the organization. It follows from that assumption that, whatever the context might be, any obligation where the action is represented by a structural concept is not a valid one. For example, the rule *if the task Approve Budget is assigned to John, John must be the Head of Department (HD)* can only be valid if it is interpreted as a restriction upon the action of assigning task *Approve Budget* to *John*, and not, as an obligation to decide that *John* is the *Head of Department* if the task is assigned to *John* (being the Head of Department is a structural concept).

4.2.3. Detachment

In what concerns the detachment of the condition in a conditional obligation (remove the condition in order to obtain an unconditional obligation), we follow the approach of Carmo and Jones [15]. In their approach, the condition can only be detached if (among other restrictions) the condition represents a fixed situation.

In our approach, fixed situations correspond to structural characteristics of an organization. Indeed, when the condition of an obligation is a structural concept and the condition holds, the detachment can be made. For example, consider the rule: *if John is the HD he should be assigned to the task Approve Budget*. If John is the HD, whatever the designer does, John will always still the HD and the designer should assign him the task Approve Budget. Notice that design decisions are not fixed. All that is designed can be undone until the design is not ended.

4.2.4. Conditional obligations in an exigent diagnosis

As mentioned in Sec. 4.1.2, an exigent diagnosis does not only detect violations of obligations, but also reports obligations that are not yet fulfilled. Given the definition of exigent diagnosis (Eq. (8)), it is consistent to assume that a conditional obligation can be violated (i.e. be a member of an exigent diagnosis), even if the condition and the action are unknown (it is not possible to infer if they are true or false). However, in our view, a diagnosis should not report all conditional obligations that can be violated. The next two examples illustrate the kind of conditional obligations that should be considered in an exigent diagnosis. The second example answers the question (iii) we raised in Sec. 3.

Consider again the following rule: *if the task Approve Budget is assigned to the HD, the HD cannot be assigned to the task Prepare Budget.* If, in the design, the tasks Approve Budget and Prepare Budget are not assigned to anyone yet, we do not consider that an exigent diagnosis should report the unfulfilment of that obligation (it would be an extremely exigent diagnosis). However, if the task Prepare Budget is assigned to the HD, we believe that, even if the designer has not made any commitment with respect to the task Approve Budget, an exigent diagnosis should report that situation (i.e. from the design it should be deduced that the condition does not hold).

However, it is not always the case that a decision not to execute an action (when the truth value of the condition is unknown) should be reported in an exigent diagnosis. Consider the following rule: *if John is assigned to the task Prepare Budget and he is socially close to Ann, Ann cannot be assigned to the task Approve Budget.* Suppose the designer assigned Ann to the task Approve Budget and John to the task Prepare Budget. Consider also that we do not know if Ann and John are socially close, and that 'socially close' is a structural concept (it is 'fixed'). If that situation is reported in an exigent diagnosis it means that the designer should assume that Ann and John are not socially close. However, as it was said before, since the designer should not act in the organization structure, he cannot be obliged to enforce anything on the social lives of Ann and John.

A conditional obligation should only be considered in an exigent diagnosis if (i) the condition is true or (ii) the action is not performed and the condition is not fixed. From now on, all obligations that can be considered in a diagnosis (exigent or not) will be called *Applicable Obligations.*

4.2.5. Conflicting obligations

In Sec. 4.1.2.2, we mentioned that the framework should help the designer to make decisions when there are implicit violation sets or conflicting sets. In those situations, the designer must choose between the fulfilment of one obligation and the fulfilment of other obligation(s). Castañeda's proposal [16] for handling conflicting obligations seems to be suitable for our approach. The general idea is to accept conflicts and have a supra-normative system that tells which obligation prevails whenever a conflict is detected.

Considering the amount of obligations that can rule a design, it is preferable to allow the organization to express the preferences in terms of sets of obligations. Grouping obligations in different normative systems seems to be a suitable approach. Since conflicts can occur in real situations, the language must allow conflicts between normative systems. Due to space limitation we do not present here the details of our proposal. For detailed informations see Ref. 8.

5. Deontic Diagnosis in Organizational Process Design

Given the proposed extension to the MBR approach to diagnosis and the L_{DD} language, we can now present our Deontic Framework for Diagnosis in Organizational Process Design (DDD).

Considering that OB is the set of obligations:

Applicable Obligations Set: $AOS = \{O[\alpha/\beta] \mid OB \cup ORG \cup PD$ $(O[\alpha/\beta] \wedge \beta)$ (all obligations where the condition is true, that definition is only possible because in the language we have the following schema $O[p/q] \wedge \neg struct(q) \rightarrow O[\neg q/\neg p]$).

Violation: $Viol\ [\alpha/\beta] = abv\ (O[\alpha/\beta] \wedge \beta \wedge \neg\alpha)$ (one obligation is violated if the condition is true and the action is not performed).

Violation Set: $VS = \{Viol\ [\alpha/\beta] \mid O\ [\alpha/\beta] \in AOS\}$ (only violations of applicable obligations will be checked).

Potential Diagnosis — considering that OB is the set of obligations ORG the description of an organization, PD a process description and VL the set of all violations, Δ' is a potential diagnosis iff $\Delta' \subseteq VS$ and

$$ORG \cup PD \cup OB \cup \Delta' \cup \{\neg Viol[\alpha/\beta] \mid Viol[\alpha/\beta] \in VS - \Delta'\} \text{ is consistent}. \tag{9}$$

The definition of Benevolent and Exigent diagnosis is the same as presented in Sec. 4.1.2 (Eq. (7) and Eq. (8)).

Implicit Violation Set — $IV\Delta_i$ is an Implicit Violation Set iff $IV\Delta_i$ is a minimal set such that $IV\Delta_i \subseteq VS$ and

$$ORG \cup PD \cup OB \cup \{\neg Viol[\alpha/\beta] \mid Viol[\alpha/\beta] \in IV\Delta_i\} \text{ is inconsistent}. \tag{10}$$

Conflicting Obligation Set — $CO\Delta_i$ is an Conflicting Obligation Set iff $CO\Delta_i$ is a minimal set such that $CO\Delta_i \subseteq VS$ and

$$ORG \cup OB \cup \{\neg Viol[\alpha/\beta] \mid Viol[\alpha/\beta] \in CO\Delta_i\} \text{ is inconsistent}. \tag{11}$$

6. Implementation

We have implemented a framework in Prolog. Prolog (Programming in Logic) is a very powerful computational language, appropriate to develop applications based on logic. Most of the logic properties (correctness, for example) are almost automatically guaranteed by Prolog. The framework allows the user to describe the organization structure, the general organizational knowledge, the principles and the process design. The diagnosis is automatically made.

7. Conclusions

The compliance of a process design with respect to organizational rules has been formally analyzed using techniques from artificial intelligence and computer science: Theory of Diagnosis and Deontic Logic. Organizational theory, and particularly BPR, can be highly enriched with formal approaches. Formal languages are universal and notably rich and flexible. With them, it is possible to conceptually analyze relations between concepts and insure the correctness of the conclusions we draw. We have extended those formal approaches in order to build a framework applied to the domain of process design.

A flexible and easy interaction between the software tool and the user is crucial. In future versions, we intend to supply a diagrammatic language for the designing of processes. Until now we only used control rules for accounting procedures. In future, the framework needs to be tested with different rules.

References

1. G. Lyons, Application of information technology in the redesign and implementation of business processes, *Proceedings of the IFIP TC5/WG5.7 Working Conference on Reengineering the Enterprise* (Galway, Ireland, 1995).

2. K. W. Lyons and M. R. Duffey, Requirements, methods and research issues for modeling the product realization process, *Proceedings of the IFIP TC5/WG5.7 Working Conference on Reengineering the Enterprise* (Galway, Ireland, 1995).
3. D. Berkeley, P. Humphreys and F. Quek, Dynamic process modeling for organizational systems supported by SASOS, *Proceedings of the Third International Working Conference on Dynamic Modeling of Information Systems* (Noodrwijkerhout, Netherlands, June 1992).
4. M. Earl and B. Khan, How new is business process redesign?, *European Management Journal* **12**(1), March 1994.
5. K.-T. Chen and R. Lee, Schematic evaluation of internal accounting control systems, Research Monograph No. RM-1992-08-01, Euridis, Erasmus University Research Institute for Decision and Information Systems, 1992.
6. R. Davis and W. Hamscher, Model based reasoning: Troubleshooting, in *Exploring Artificial Intelligence: Survey Talks from the National Conferences on Artificial Intelligence,* H. E. Shrobe (ed.) (Morgan Kaufmann, 1988) pp. 297–346.
7. R. Reiter, A theory of diagnosis from first principles, *Artificial Intelligence* **32** (1987) 57–95.
8. P. Ramos and J. L. Fiadeiro, A deontic logic for diagnosis of organizational process design, *Fourth International Workshop on Deontic Logic in Computer Science (DEON'98)* Bologna, Italy, 1998.
9. L. V. der Torre, P. Ramos, Y.-H. Tan, J. L. Fiadeiro and J. Luiz, The role of diagnosis and decision theory in normative reasoning, *Model Age, 4th Workshop 'Formal Models of Agents'* Italy, 1997.
10. Y.-H. Tan and L. V. der Torre, Representing deontic reasoning in a diagnostic framework, *ILCP'94 Workshop on Legal Applications of Logic Programming,* Genova, Italy, 1994.
11. F. Santos and J. Carmo, Indirect action, influence and responsibility, in *Deontic Logic, Agency and Normative Systems,* M. Brown and J. Carmo (eds.) (Springer, 1996) pp. 194–215.
12. F. Cuppens and R. Demolombe, A deontic logic for reasoning about confidentiality, in *Deontic Logic, Agency and Normative Systems* M. Brown and J. Carmo (eds.) (Springer, 1996) pp. 66–80.
13. A. Jones and M. Sergot, On the characterization of law and computer systems: the normative systems perspective, in *Deontic Logic in Computer*

Science, J.-J. Ch. Meyer and R. J. Wieringa (eds.) (John Wiley & Sons, 1993) pp. 275–305.

14. G. H. Von Wright, Deontic logic and the theory of conditions, in *Deontic Logic: Introductory and Systematic Readings*, R. Hilpinen (ed.) (1971) pp. 159–177.
15. J. Carmo and A. Jones, A new approach to contrary-to-duty obligations, accepted for publication in *Defeasible Deontic Logic* **I**, D. Dute (ed.) Synthese Library, 1996.
16. H.-N. Castañeda, The paradoxes of deontic logic: the simplest solution to all of them in one fell swoop, in *New Studies in Deontic Logic*, Hilpinem, (1981).

Chapter 9

Questioning the Unit of Analysis in BPR

JAAKKO VIRKKUNEN
Center for Activity Theory and Developmental Work Research, University of Helsinki, Helsinki, FIN-00560, Finland
E-mail: jaakko.virkkunen@helsinki.fi

KARI KUUTTI
Department Information Processing Science. University of Oulu, Oulu, FIN-90570, Finland
E-mail: kuutti@rieska.oulu.fi

We criticize BPR as being radical only in relation to the way of doing things but not in relation to what and why things are done. This conservatism is related to the use of 'process' as a unit of analysis and development in organizational change. We propose another unit called an 'activity system,' which is based on the cultural historical activity theory. This unit helps the concrete analysis of the needs and possibilities of reinterpreting the object and purpose of the activity. The new interpretation can be made a part of practice by changing the actors' relation to the object of their activity with the help of IT. After characterising the key elements and problems of BPR, we present the main principles of cultural historical theory of activity, the concepts of activity system, expansive transition and remediation. We then show how these concepts can be used to realize organizational transformations and give a case example of the use of these conceptual tools.

1. The Doctrine of Business Process Reengineering

The essence of BPR: Business Process Reengineering is one of the most widely discussed and practiced management phenomena of the 1990s. The origins of BPR when defined as "the analysis and design of work flows and processes within and between organizations" [1], and as "the use of information technology to radically redesign business processes" [2] is traced by the majority of writers [3] to an article by Michael Hammer in 1990 in the *Harvard Business Review* [2]. This article claimed that as business processes had never originally been explicitly designed, and IT had often been used merely to automate these inefficient processes, improvement schemes were likely to be sub-optimal and could not deliver the required improvements.

Earl and Khan [4] summarize the features they found common across all the reengineering activities they had observed: "Focusing on processes, seeking radical, transformational performance improvements, and embracing information technology in combination add up to a new recipe which seems to work for some organizations ..." (p. 29). Despite the diversity of approaches there would seem to be a level of agreement on these three basic factors of BPR.

BPR seems to offer a solution to some important management problems. The match between the problem and the solution is, however, not clear. In many cases, BPR has not delivered its promises. We think one important reason for this is the inadequacy of the key concept of BPR, i.e. the concept of 'process' as a tool for analyzing and developing organization. We suggest that another unit of analysis, namely 'activity system,' could better fulfill the demands of organizational analysis and illustrate how some of the problems plaguing BPR can be alleviated using this unit of analysis.

Problems with BPR: Some authors question what constitutes BPR and what, if anything, it has to offer. Criticisms are leveled at the lack of any implementation methodology and the inability of the approach to come up with anything new [5]: the idea of process thinking, the urgent need for radical organizational change and the transformational potential of IT are not particularly original. Neither is the idea of a fresh start, which BPR emphasizes, new. It has been a central, recurring theme in the thinking of industrial engineers from the beginning of the century [3] [6]. Davenport and Short [1] explicitly present BPR as an extension of traditional Industrial Engineering whose roots lie in F. W. Taylor's principles of scientific management. The tensions and contradictions within the field of BPR recapitulate the earlier debates about Industrial Engineering and reflect BPR's paradoxical relation to its roots. Debates are constant on the scale of change involved, on the role played by information technology in the process, and the degree of worker empowerment, splitting the BPR movement into several camps.

According to Hammer and Champy [7] reengineering involves 'fundamental' change based on a reappraisal of ways of achieving the desired outputs. For them the radical change in BPR means "discarding [existing processes] and replacing them with entirely new ones" so as to achieve a "quantum leap" in performance. It "is about beginning again with a clean sheet of paper ... with no assumptions and no givens ... It means disregarding all existing structures and procedures and inventing completely new ways of accomplishing work ... Tradition counts for nothing. Reengineering is the new beginning." [3, p. 367].

In closer look, the target of BPR's offensive against existing structures is the functional organization, typical to mass production, which is based more on specialties than clients and products. According to Davenport [8], given that existing approaches are so functionally based no amount of incremental change could ever yield the required 'interdependence' (p. 4). Paradoxically, BPR uses the other central concept of mass production: the 'process' to build a vision of an alternative way of organizing activities.

BPR's insistence upon radical change has, however, been challenged. The argument to throw away all existing processes, ignores the fact that 'processes' have histories [4, p. 3]. Clean slate change, as advocated by Hammer and Champy, "disregarding all existing structures and procedures," ignores the historical nature of work processes. Radical and incremental change are perhaps not real alternatives: "Notwithstanding evidence that suggests radical improvements can be achieved through incremental change [9], it appears to be almost self evident that periods of change need to be followed by periods of relative stability during which time the change is being put into effect" [5, p. 4]. Incremental changes are needed after a radical change and in situations where radical change is either "unnecessary or foolhardy" [5, p. 16].

Tensions are also evident in the discussions on the extent of empowerment and the need for executive leadership. Hammer and Champy [7] argue that "processes cannot be reengineered without empowering process workers" and that this empowerment is an essential feature of the reengineered corporation. Yet, concurrent with this belief in empowerment, they state that reengineering is "always born in the executive suite." Davenport and Short [1] are also very clear that reengineering is a top-down process which requires strong direction from senior management.

Jones [3], however, questions the compatibility of empowerment with an executive-led and -controlled process. In fact, discussions on 'empowerment' and the implication of flexibility seem somewhat problematic within this rational analytical approach. One can ask how much a process deliberately redesigned by senior executives leaves room for local change and individual interpretation [5, p. 6].

There are also two quite opposing viewpoints as to the strategic impact of information technology: one, suggesting that the changes IT can bring about are profound and overwhelmingly beneficial; the other, pointing out the disappointing results following even quite massive investments in IT [10, p. 2].

While the importance of IT is by most writers virtually unquestioned, most of them also recognize that IT alone does not bring about process change. "... there is a danger in viewing IT as *the* solution to problems of organizational inefficiency and ineffectiveness ... Certainly, IS/IT may well have a key role to play, but it will be but one aspect of the whole change process" [3]. While it is important that our attention is refocused from the IT-induced business change, it is equally important that IT and IS are not left out of the equation. [4, p. 28].

From process reengineering to organizational change: Several authors have felt a need to "... bring business process reengineering a step beyond reorganization of business processes and make it a process of organizational change." [11] Earl and Khan [4] suggest the use of Leavitt's [12] model of approaches to organizational change (Fig. 1) here presented in the form amended by Davis and Olson [14]. Galliers [5] also sees that Leavitt's model could capture the 'holistic' vision needed to realize organizational change successfully (p. 7). He argues that any assessment needs to take not only process and technology into account, but also should understand the cultural context in which the change is implemented. Leavitt's diamond illustrates that any change in process impacts all other aspects in the socio-technical system. Leavitt's model has also been the core framework of the large research program on the 'Corporation in the 1990s' conducted in MIT [13].

Leavitt's model directs attention to aspects of organizational change that critical reviewers of BPR have found to be missing from the 'plain' process concept. The model, however, is basically only a list of interdependent aspects of activity, without any indication as to what the nature of the dependencies might actually be. That is why the model's analytic power is rather weak. It can serve as a reminder of

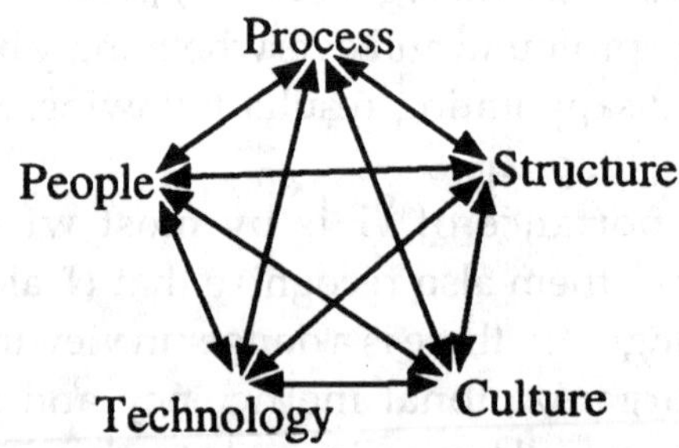

Figure 1 Amended version of Leavitt's 'diamond'

the different aspects of the change process, but not as an analytic tool to specify the needs and possibilities of change in a concrete situation.

We think that Leavitt's model completely misses the most central element of organizational change, and BPR's process concept puts it into too peripheral a role. We call that element 'the object of the activity.' In every process something ideal or material is being processed, something is constructed to meet the needs of the clients. This something is the object of the activity.

The central issue in organizational transformation is not in the first place the radical reengineering of a process, but an expansive reinterpretation of the object of the activity including the value produced to the clients and the society in general. By reinterpretation of the object of activity we do not mean a purely intellectual exercise, but also an altered relationship between the actors and the object of their activity. This kind of change in the practical relationship to the object is possible through the development of tools and instruments that mediate the actors' relationship to the object of their activity. IT can have a central role in this kind of expansive remediation.

Hammer & Champy [7] do not explicitly exclude the change of the 'desired output,' but they are not interested in it. In our view, the BPR is radical as regards the way the outcome is produced, but conservative in relation to what is produced and why. It takes the object and the outcome of the activity as given. The potentials of IT lie, however, not only in doing the old things in a new way, but in doing new things.

The idea of a radical, once and for all reengineering procedure seems to us to be reminiscent of the times of mass-production in which both the process and the product are standardized and developed seldom, to endure for long lengths of time. This view of the development process does not meet the requirements of a modern flexible and customized production in which the output is a large bunch of versions of a product or customized solutions that are constantly developed. In this kind of mass customized production [15], the focus is in recognizing the different needs of individual customers and the available resources to help the customers, that is, the object of the activity, rather than the internal processes. Instead of reengineering the processes radically every now and then, the processes have to be constantly developed.

How, then, should the unit of organizational analysis be conceptualized to include the object of activity in it? Cultural Historical Activity Theory (CHAT), which builds upon the concept of object oriented activity, can give one answer. In the next section we review this theory briefly.

2. Cultural Historical Activity Theory and the Concept of Activity System

CHAT is a framework used in studying human practices as historically developing societal systems. It has its roots in Russian cultural-historical psychology, where it was suggested that isolated individual actions are too small a unit for understanding human development and thinking, and that these should be seen in the context of the culturally formed activities in which the individuals are taking part. During the 1980s, Y. Engeström and his co-workers developed, on the basis of this theoretical idea, a practical approach for analyzing and developing different work practices [16, 17].

The CHAT is based on four basic principles. (1) Cultural mediation of human activity: Man's relations to the objects of their environment are mediated by cultural artifacts such as concepts, tools, etc. (2) Historicity: The forms of human activity develop historically as new types of mediating artifacts are invented. (3) Object orientedness: Human activity is always oriented to some ideal or material object which is transformed in the activity. There cannot be an activity, for instance of healing without patients that need to be healed, or an activity of constructing without places to build on, building materials and an idea of the house to be built. The objects of activity are culturally constructed. The object and outcome of a historically formed activity is its motive.

The fourth principle is the hierarchic structure of activities. A collective activity is always realized through individuals' coordinated actions that are goal-directed and conscious. The coordination of the individuals' actions is created by the historically evolved division of labor and the rules of the community of those taking part in the same activity. The individuals' actions are realized through psychologically and/or technically-automated operations that are the smallest components of activity. The operations needed to realize an action (and to attain its goal) depend on circumstances. A process, in the sense the concept is used in BPR, can be interpreted as a coordinated chain of different individuals' actions. When technology develops, more and more of the operations needed to realize an action are delegated to the tools, and the individuals' actions can comprise large processes.

Each individual taking part in the activity sees the object of the activity in a different way depending on his or her position in the division of labor and the intellectual and practical tools available to him or her. In the model of the activity system presented below, activity is depicted from the point of view of one subject. The subject takes part in the transformation of the object of the activity using specific tools, according to historically formed division of labor and rules (Fig. 2).

The lines in the model depict the many mediated interactions in an activity. The object of a common activity is never definite and finite, as are the goals of individual actions. The object of an activity can rather be seen as a horizon of possibilities. The conception of the object of the activity develops during the history of the activity.

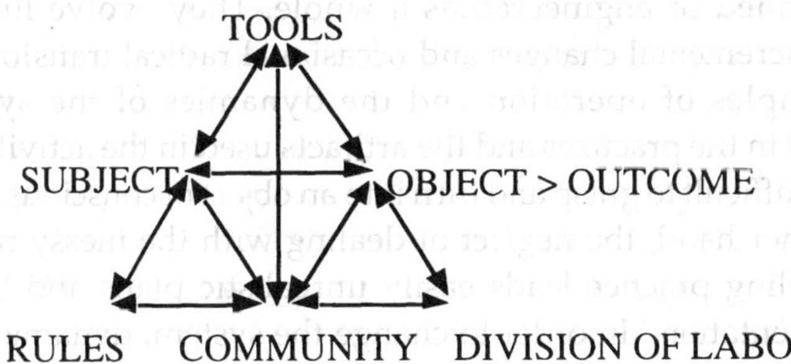

Figure 2 A model of activity system [16, p. 78]

It is not postulated that participants of an activity share the same goals. On the contrary, the object and outcome of the common activity is constantly renegotiated in the activity between the different parties taking part to the activity and between the different interests connected to it. Even if the participants have different goals, they all share, however, partly the object of their activity and its problems.

Because activities are embedded in culturally formed settings and use certain cultural artifacts as mediators, they are relatively stable, long-standing formations. Nevertheless, the elements of the activity change both incrementally and abruptly. Remnants of older phases of the activity are often embedded in the activity system. The present form of the activity and the causes of problems and disturbances in it can only be understood by analyzing the history of the activity.

There are normally many activity systems in an organization and usually people participate in more than one of these. Activity systems are functionally linked to other activity systems and form networks of activity systems. For an activity system, there is, for instance, a client activity that uses the output of the activity and an activity system that produces tools for that activity.

3. Remediation of the Object of the Activity

The cycle of expansive transition of an activity: Activity systems are never planned or engineered as a whole. They evolve historically through incremental changes and occasional radical transformations. The principles of operation and the dynamics of the system are embedded in the practices and the artifacts used in the activity and are therefore difficult to grasp and turn into an object of conscious planning. On the other hand, the neglect of dealing with the messy realities of the prevailing practice leads easily unrealistic plans and 'problems of implementation.' In order to change the system, dynamic forces of change have to be found in the present practice. Instead of obliterating all the existing cultural mediators, we have to make those taking part in the activity conscious of the roots, the content and possible inadequacy of the old ways of thinking and acting by studying the activity. This helps those involved to surpass the old ways and to create a new form of the activity. This process of analyzing and transforming the activity can be guided with the following model of the cycle of expansive development of an activity [16, p. 189].

According to CHAT, the forces of change in an activity are created by inner tensions and contradictions within the system. There are five different types of contradictions within the system. First, in all activities there is a constant tension between the benefits and the costs of the different components of the activity. This tension leads to a constant search for incremental improvements.

Second, internal and external influences may change some of the elements of the activity to the extent that a mismatch between the elements is created. The first indication of a developing contradiction between the elements of the activity system is an increasing amount of value conflicts and dilemmas in the daily work. The chance process begins by identifying and bringing these to common discussion. The problems of daily work create a need state in which there is increasing dissatisfaction with the current practice but not necessarily a clear picture of what is wrong with it. This dissatisfaction can be turned into a motive to change the activity system.

If the contradictions between the elements of the activity system are further aggravated, the actors experience the situation as incompatible, as having paradoxical demands or even as a double-bind situation with only unacceptable choices left to choose from. Analyzing together the development of the activity and the nature of daily disturbances, ruptures and attempts to do things better, reveals to those taking part in the activity the potential double-bind situations.

The double-bind situation, or its anticipation, initiates a search process. The members of the community of the activity begin to search for a solution to the contradiction by questioning the traditional interpretation of the object of the activity, its tools, rules and division of labor. They search for and construct new mediators for the activity.

The remediation of the object of the activity is often made possible by a 'given new,' an analogy or example taken from another context.

The change in practice begins when some new mediators of the work are introduced, new tools are implemented, new rules or changes to the division of labor are applied. In this phase of the development of the activity system, two sets of mediators compete and crash against each other. The dynamic forces of change in this phase arise from the need to surpass the conflicts between the old and new forms of acting. Many small innovations are needed to overcome these contradictions.

The new form of the activity gradually takes over and becomes the prevailing practice which is eventually consolidated with formal statements and rules. In this phase, the fifth type of contradictions arises. The changed form of the activity is not compatible with the requirements of the surrounding activities. The contradictions between the activity and the surrounding activities begin to form the content and dynamics of the change process.

In the next section we will describe a cycle of expansive development in a regional labor protection unit. The creation of the new conception of the object of the corresponding work activity and a new instrument had a central role in the process.

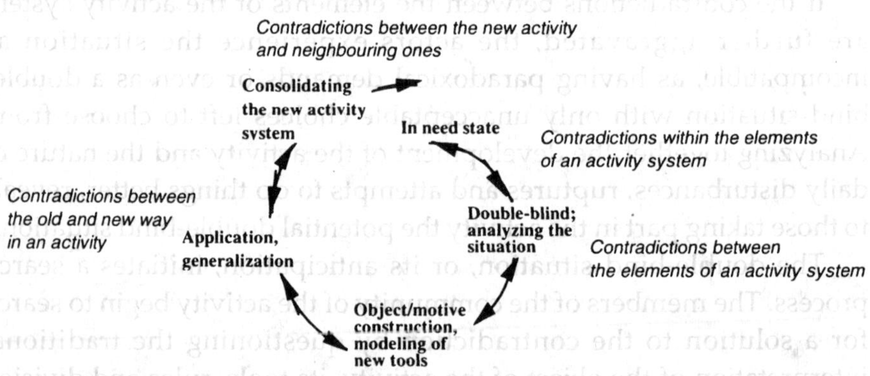

Figure 3 The cycle of expansive development of an activity

A case of expansive transition: The enforcement of labor protection legislation in Finland is in the hands of 11 district authorities of labor protection. The main form of activity of the labor protection districts is the inspection of working premises, which is done by labor protection inspectors. The object of their work is to insure that the labor protection regulations are being observed in workplaces and to advise organizations on improvements of working conditions and safety. Inspectors give instructions aimed at eliminating defects and hazards. If this is insufficient, they can order the employer to remedy the defect within a given period of time, under threat of a fine if necessary. In extreme cases an inspector can demand that work in a specific site or with a specific machine or method be discontinued.

From the 1980s on, there was a growing awareness among inspectors that it is not possible to get an overall diagnostic picture of the safety situation in the work places and to have influence with the real causes of safety hazards by making surveys in work premises. A national project was launched in 1989 to develop the inspectors' work forms. At the beginning of the project, an analysis of the development of labor inspectors' work was made in order to identify the inner contradictions of the inspectors' activity system.

The analysis revealed that the object of the inspectors' work activity, the work places to be inspected and the labor safety hazards in them, had changed remarkably. The inspectors' tools had not developed to meet the new challenges and the prevailing division of labor had become inadequate. The analysis of the history of the present form of the activity had several effects. First, a model of the inspectors' activity system and its inner contradictions was created (Fig. 4). Second, the inspectors began to look critically at their practices, and third, a hypothesis was made about the possibilities of overcoming the contradictions in the present practice. The analysis of contradictions was verified by videotaping ten real inspections and analyzing the causes of disturbances observed in these. Many of these could be explained by the inner contradictions found in the historical analysis.

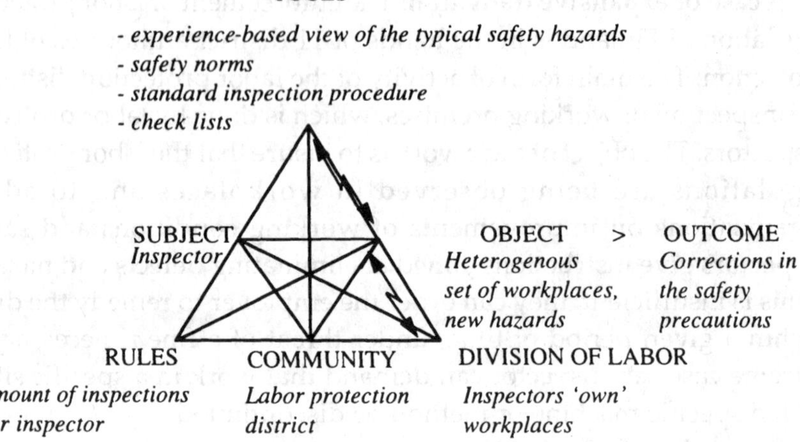

Figure 4 Model of labor protection inspectors' old activity system and its inner contradictions

To overcome the inner contradictions of the old activity system a new instrument was needed which would allow the inspectors to identify important general safety problems, analyze their causes and plan an intervention to change the situation. These larger objects of work would be worked out by teams of inspectors set flexibly according to a general analysis of the most urgent safety problem areas. The new instrument, a 'System for Depicting the Field of Activity' (SDFA) was developed in the Uusimaa labor protection district. It was a simple information system, realized with the Excel spreadsheet program, collecting together the statistical indicators about the status of occupational health in the district's area, and the experiences and records from the inspectors' own work.

The use of the common SDFA tool led in the Uusimaa District of Labor Protection to a new form of labor protection inspection activity (Fig. 5). The object of the activity was now an identified, common, important labor safety problem instead of a fixed set of work places.

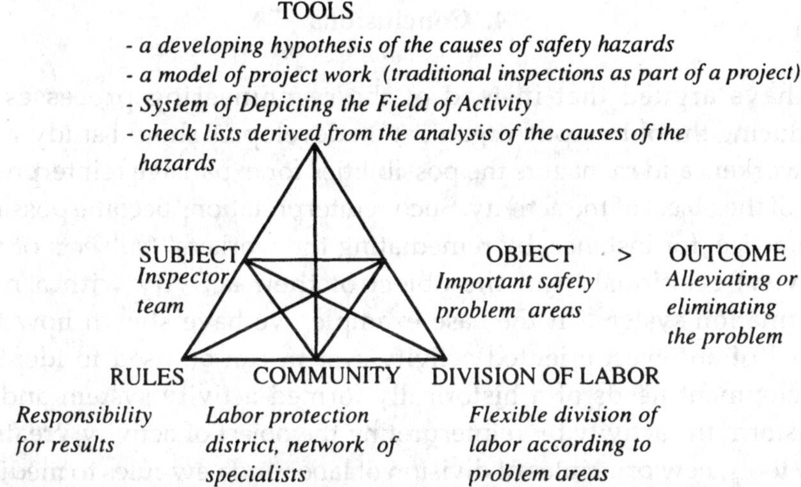

Figure 5 Model of labor protection inspectors' new activity system

The head of the district formed inspector teams according to the needs revealed by the information that was gathered and the analyses that were made in the inspection projects. Each team planned its work according to the special character of the object of its activity although many standard elements of the traditional inspection process were used. Thus the organizational structure and the processes were now continuously adapted to the changes in the field whenever such are identified using the SDFA tool. The SDFA became instrument to identify and describe the object of the inspector team's work both for the teams and for the management. The constant analysis of the causes of hazards and the testing of hypotheses led the inspectors to develop and sharpen their tools of labor protection.

The new inspector teams could not be managed according to the old division of the management's work because the teams crossed the boundaries of the existing organizational units. To overcome these problems the management of the district was reorganized. This change consolidated the inspectors' new way of working.

4. Conclusions

We have argued that instead of the reengineering processes of producing the old output, organization developers should study with the workers and managers the possibilities for expansive reinterpretation of the object of the activity. Such reinterpretations become possible in practice, for instance, by remediating the workers' (subjects of the activity) relationship to the object of their activity with a new information system. In the case example, we have shown how the model of an object-oriented activity system can be used to identify development needs of a historically formed activity system and to transform the activity by reinterpreting the object of activity, creating new tools, new principles of division of labor and new rules to mediate subjects relation to the object of the activity.

'Process' is not an adequate unit of analysis for creating expansive transitions because it does not help identify the concrete need and possibilities for development, and problematize the prevailing conception of the object of the activity. Also, it can be used only to depict routine processes, but not activities in which the process changes much. The 'reengineering' of a process may be a natural concomitant of the reinterpretation and remediation of the object of the activity with the help of new concepts and tools, but reengineering, as such, does not lead to new ideas about what the activity produces and why.

In BPR literature, the greatest emphasis has been put on applications rationalizing and coordinating the work processes, such as workflow systems. Our experience has shown, however, that another class of applications can be even more vital to success: namely systems that make the object of work more visible and comprehensible and, thus, enable reflection on it. In the expansive cycle of the case the SDFA tool had a crucial role in the formation of a new conception of the new object of work. Such systems are familiar outside of BPR literature [18].

We believe that returning to the systems analysis or the sociotechnical design is not the answer. The problem is not that BPR neglects the 'social system' but that it neglects the object of the activity and the clients' changing needs which the object is meant to meet.

References

1. T. H. Davenport and J. E. Short, The new industrial engineering: information technology and business process redesign, *Sloan Management Review* **31**(4), (1990) 11–27.
2. M. Hammer, Reengineering work: don't automate, obliterate, *Harvard Business Review*, July-August 1990, 104–112.
3. M. Jones, Don't emancipate, exaggerate: rhetoric, reality and reengineering, in R. Baskerville, S. Smithson, O. Ngwenyama and J. I. DeGross (eds.), *Transforming Organizations with Information Technology (A-49)* (Elsevier Science, Amsterdam, 1994) pp. 357–378.
4. M. Earl and B. Khan, How new is business process redesign?, *European Management Journal* **12**(1), 20–30.
5. R. D. Galliers, *IT and Organizational Change: Where does BPR fit in?* (Warwick Business School, University of Warwick, 1994).
6. W. E. Akin, *Technocracy and the American Dream. The Technocrat Movement*, London (University of California Press, London, 1977) pp. 1900–1941.
7. M. Hammer and J. Champy, Reengineering the corporation. A manifesto for business revolution (Nicholas Brealey Publishing, London, 1993).
8. T. H. Davenport, Process innovation: reengineering work through information technology (Harvard Business School Press, Boston, 1993)
9. J. A. Senn, The myths of strategic systems: what defines a true competitive advantage?, *Journal of Information Systems Management*, Summer 1992, 7–12.
10. R. D. Galliers, Information systems, operational research and business reengineering, *International Transactions on Operational Research* **1**(2), (1994) 1–9.
11. W. Baets, The corporate mind-set as a precursor for business process (reengineering: about knowledge, perceptions and learning), in W. Baets, and R. Galliers (eds.), *Proceedings of the Conference on Information Technology and Organizational Change*, Nijenrode University, Breuklen, The Netherlands, April 1994.

12. H. Leavitt, *Applied Organization Change in Industry: Structural, Technical and Human Approaches* (Wiley, New York, 1964).
13. M. S. Scott Morton (ed.), *The Corporation of the 1990's. Information Technology and Organizational Transformation* (Oxford University Press, New York, 1991).
14. G. B. Davis and M. H. Olson, *Management Information Systems: Conceptual Foundations, Structure and Development* (2nd edition), (McGraw-Hill, New York, 1984).
15. J. B. Pine II, *Mass Customization. The New Frontier in Business Competition* (Harvard Business School Press, Boston, 1993).
16. Y. Engeström, *Learning by Expanding* (Orienta-Konsultit Oy, Helsinki, 1987).
17. M. Cole and Y. Engeström, A Cultural-historical approach to distributed cognition, in G. Salomon (ed.), *Distributed Cognitions. Psychological and Educational Considerations* (Cambridge University Press, Combridge 1993) pp. 1–46.
18. A. P. De Geus, Planning as learning, *Harvard Business Review*, March-April 1988, 70–74.

Chapter 10

Electronic Commerce and Organizational Transformation

KAIYIN HUANG
Business Alliance Services International Company,
Witbreuksweg 397-303
7522 ZA Enschede, The Netherlands
E-mail: Huang.K@usa.net

The development of electronic commerce offers a promising way for businesses to meet challenges of the ever-changing market. It induces and enables organizations to redesign their business processes and organizational structures to meet the new business requirements. The gains from technology development alone are elusive. To reap the real benefits from electronic commerce, we need to tackle the more challenging but potentially more rewarding problems of improving the conduct of business. Electronic commerce always puts business process reengineering on the strategic agenda.

A norm-oriented approach enables us to differentiate the substantive, productivity-related activities from the bureaucratic procedures. The substantive activities form the stable kernel of the business functions that must be preserved through any changes to the bureaucratic procedures. In this way, we encourage organizations to devote most of its energy to the substantive kernel, while necessary redesign of business processes can be carried out systematically. Hammer, the champion of reengineering, gave a number of precepts which the process should aim to achieve, but he proposed no methods of diagnosis and redesign. We demonstrate how our approach leads to Hammer's precepts being satisfied.

1. Introduction

Today's technology connects every part of the world. Organizations can connect directly to customers and trading partners through the internet, value added networks, and EDI. Internal computer applications can be interconnected with client-server, groupware; and intranet tools are used to distribute data, processes, and user interfaces to make possible the widest use of all organizational hardware. However, technology alone does not insure a successful business. Business is intrinsically a human information function. It relies on people, organizations, and our society. The challenges of electronic commerce (EC) come not only from technology, but also from how the human information function is carried out.

In his report on the development of EDI in the European scheme, Weltevreden [1] states that "Of the problems to be solved when EDI is established in a firm, whether private or public, 25% are of a technological nature. The remaining 75% relate to management techniques." The management of a company based on the circulation of paper documents is very different from one based on the exchange of electronic messages. Hedberg [2] reports that organizational structures are clearly changing for both competitive and managerial reasons. Business organizations and information technology architectures are coming closer together or even merging. Earl [3] studied 21 UK companies and identified five different approaches to strategic information systems planning: business-led, method-driven, administrative, technological and organizational approaches. He reported that those companies which have adopted the organizational way of developing information systems achieved very successful projects, the key words being integration, interaction and learning. Reponen [4] argues that competitive advantage is achieved through a good understanding and a good management of the whole information system, and not only from the competitive IT applications. Although EC is initiated in many companies by simply focusing on automating existing processes to increase operational efficiency and replace paper to reduce costs and improve accuracy, the benefits from IT development are marginal if only superimposed on existing organizational conditions (especially strategies, structures, processes, and culture). The benefits accrue in those cases where investments in IT functionality accompany corresponding changes in organizational characteristics [5].

Many attempts for EC failed because the projects were too narrowly defined and they have little impact on overall performance; there is often a lack of performance-tracking mechanism to monitor the effect of applying EC technologies to business processes; and EC is often applied to processes that do not create value. To lead to competitive advantage, EC has to be fully integrated with the core business. It requires business process reengineering (BPR) and reorganization to improve the business effectiveness, and reengineering sales, marketing, and coordination to create new demands, new distribution channels and new products.

The different viewpoints toward EC reflect on how information systems are designed and how they function. The usual method for boosting performance is through process rationalization and automation. This yields efficiency gains in the short term, but the biggest rewards may come in the long term from being able to do things differently, to improve the effectiveness through organizational reengineering. Michael Hammer has brought to the attention of the business community the potential for major organizational improvements through radical thinking. The title of his 1990 *Harvard Business Review* paper recommends: 'Don't Automate, Obliterate.'

To contend with a changing environment, organizational reengineering should be a continual and systematic process. Rethinking one's familiar business processes in order to do things differently is not easy. Hammer [6] provides six reengineering principles.

- Organize around outcomes, not tasks.
- Have those who use the output of the process perform the process.
- Subsume information-processing work into the real work that produces the information.

- Treat geographically dispersed resources as though they were centralized.
- Link parallel activities instead of integrating their results.
- Put the decision point where the work is performed, and build control into the process.

These are helpful and may be more so, given precise instruments of analysis. We must ask, therefore: Can we systematically search for greater effectiveness?

This chapter provides an affirmative answer by showing how the norm-oriented methods can be applied to reengineering. Getting the vision right is the single most important activity for successful organizational transformation. An organizational morphology helps us to distinguish the essential from the inessential activities in the firm — to find a pivot around which fundamental reengineering changes can safely be made. It encourages organizations to devote most of their energy to the substantive, productivity-related business activities, while necessary redesign of business processes can be carried out in a systematic way.

We illustrate our approach by applying it to the well-known mini-case of Ford and Mazda cited by Hammer [6]. This is sufficient to demonstrate the principal analysis techniques on a small scale. We should point out that the results of this kind of analysis of business issues can lead directly to the implementation of computer-based systems, using the concept of a Semantic Temporal DataBase (STDB) or the more sophisticated Normbase.

2. The Organizational Impacts of Electronic Commerce

Electronic commerce is an exercise of employing the computer-based, networked systems to conduct business according to certain socially agreed norms. Of course it involves technical considerations, e.g. how to communicate with external systems and how to integrate internal applications. However, the success of EC depends on how people use the technology correctly to serve their business objectives [7, 8].

For internal organizations, we mainly concern how EC can fit and best serve organization's goals, objectives and strategies; how culture, tradition and habit are influenced by the new kinds of transactions; what power and bureaucratic structures should be changed to meet the new requirements; how human relationships change; how to re-allocate authority and responsibility; how to improve the communication and coordination between staff; what kind of know-how and expertise are needed; what reward and sanction system should be introduced; and what work process have to be redesigned.

EC cannot be superimposed on business and organizations. The advantage from EC is gained by the way it is used, not by the technology itself. Just as Leyland [9] states for EDI: "Unless you have decided on the best way of using EDI for your business, you will not know whether the decision you are making is in your interests or not." If we want to reap the real benefits, we need to tackle the more challenging but potentially more rewarding problems of improving the conduct of business. These efforts are achieved through organizational reengineering.

For external organizations, EC has great impacts on market and business convention. EC should be implemented within the network of companies and their social context. The market must accept the new processes; trading partners must be ready to use EC technologies and adopt new processes; the EC technologies must be readily available and priced appropriately; the enterprises and consumers involved must be willing to change; and the legal systems have to provide protections for the new transactions. We have to handle these aspects properly in order to implement EC successfully.

The social context is the essential element for realising EC. Trading relationships, competition in the market place, logistic processes and business norms, etc. all need to adapt to the ever-changing environment. In this respect, legal systems, which are essential for a successful implementation of EC, are very slow to respond to the change of the new business practices. The conflict between security and flexibility of the transactions is not handled well by the current legal systems. This makes EC more risky than the conventional business.

Redesigning the logistic process and re-structuring the market place are the efforts to improve the social context. The role each party plays in the venture is being redefined. The conventional view of banking, vendor, retailer, or competitor and partner, etc. is no longer fixed in the current situation. The meanings of terms in use are changing from time to time, from place to place. Our systems need to meet this change. Such systems should be based on how we conduct business not on what technology in used [10].

While a technical approach to EC enables us to deal with problems of improving efficiency, or how to do business the same way but faster and cheaper, the human information function to EC helps us to tackle more elusive problems of effectiveness, or how to do business better in new ways. These are two aspects of an interrelated problem domain. We are relatively well practised at solving the efficiency problems, but we need to do more on the effectiveness aspects if we aim at a beneficial EC system.

3. The Practices of Organizational Transformation

How does EC induce and enable organizational changes? How do we carry out these changes? What problems occur in practice? A brief review on the practices of BPR will show us some helpful solutions.

3.1. Venkatraman's framework for business transformation

Venkatraman [5] presents a five-level framework of IT enabled business transformation. He describes each level's characteristics and offers guidelines for deriving maximal benefits. The framework is based on two dimensions: the range of IT's potential benefits and the degree of organizational transformation. The levels he presents are not conceptualized as stages of evolution because effective strategies do not follow any one prescribed model of evolutionary stages. Over time, higher levels may be necessary, depending on competitive pressures and the need to deliver greater value than competitors in the marketplace. During the implementation of EC we see this evolving toward higher levels.

- Level one — Localized Exploitation: leverage IT functionality within a business.
- Level two — Internal Integration: a more systematic attempt to leverage IT capabilities throughout the entire business process. This level involves two types of integration: technical interconnectivity and business process interdependence. Neither of them alone is sufficient.
- Level three — Business Process Redesign: IT functionality can significantly alter some of the business processes. The importance is to understand the rationale of the current business process — especially its strength and limitations. A careful analysis of the costs and benefits of the current design against a set of feasible options allows an organization to execute a coordinated plan for redesign.

Benefits from BPR are limited in scope if the processes are not extended outside the focal organization's boundary to identify options for redesigning relationships with the other organizations that participate in ultimately delivering value to the customer. Hence, two more levels:

- Level four — Business Network Redesign: redesign of the nature of exchange among multiple participants in a business network through effective deployment of IT capabilities. Strategy considerations include transaction processing, inventory movement, process linkage, knowledge leverage, or effective business network redesign.
- Level five — Business Scope Redefinition: IT influences business scope and the logic of business relationships within the extended

business network. Strategic concepts, such as economics of scale, product-line extension through vertical integration, and mergers and acquisitions that led to increased emphasis on vertical integration, are being replaced by newer concepts such as joint ventures, alliances and partnerships, and virtual business networks with a marked emphasis towards a more flexible and fluid corporate scope.

The core logic of organizational strategy involves the three higher levels of transformational framework with business processes designed (level three) to support the logic of business scope definition (level five) and the specific positions in the business network (level four). Companies should accompany the current strategic thrusts toward core competence and out-sourcing with a systematic approach to combine the critical competencies in a form acceptable to the customers.

3.2. *The problems of BPR in practice*

Venkatraman focuses on IT functionality that enable organizational changes. He does not address how such a transformation be carried out systematically. Many redesign projects failed because of the lack of structural approaches. Dietz [11] points out some problems of the conventional approaches for BPR:

- there is no method that distinguishes the central issue (the essential business activities) and the side issues (the supporting activities);
- the conventional methods and techniques cannot guarantee that the results are complete because of the lack of understanding of the business processes;
- the results are extremely difficult to maintain.

The prominent problem here is the understanding of how business is being conducted. Focusing on IT functionality alone does not prevent us from misplacing emphasis on less value-bidding activities. Only by attending to the human functions can we correctly focus on the real essential issues.

3.3. *Dietz's business model*

To deal with the problems, some business models are proposed to support the redesign by analyzing the business transactions, like internal and external orders. These transactions are essential in the sense that they lead to agreements between parties. The identification and registration of these transactions form a business model that is independent of IT and a particular firm.

Dietz [11] gives three abstraction levels of such a business model:

- The essential level: an organization is seen as a system of individuals with competence and responsibility (to achieve the organizational goals).
- The information level: the exchange of information between individuals and organizations.
- The document level: the realization of the information level, within this level the organization is considered as a system that produces, archives, transports and destroys documents.

The information level supports the essential level and the document level supports the information level. He claims that with the help of this principle it is possible in an innovation process to state what will be unaltered and what can be changed. In this way it is also possible to make clear distinctions between the redesign of the business processes and the redesign of the information systems.

3.4. *What is essential? — substantive versus semiological activities*

Dietz's business model has begun to touch on the point that we need to understand business by separating essential activities from supporting ones. The questions here are what are the essential activities of business? Is business a set of transactions? Can we be sure what is essential by focusing on business transactions? We use the following simple example to indicate the different focal points. Actions on the left side are substantive business activities, while those on the right side are passing messages about the activities on the left. The dichotomy reflects how information systems function: doing business or running bureaucracy.

Substantive activities	Message-passing activities
• stock of items	• inventory of items
• contract	• order & acceptance notes
• loads for shipment	• picking list
• expected delivery	• delivery ticket
• acceptance	• receipt

The difference reflects in two quite different ways of processing information: at the substantive or at the semiological levels. One can speak semiologically about how to handle documents and files. The processing rules for these sign tokens would tell what to do with them, such as raising a delivery ticket if we have suitable goods and putting the order into the back-order file if we have no stock for an item on the order. These rules deal with the manipulation of documents and the character strings on them. From this point of view, the information system can be seen as a paper-based system which can easily lead to a superficial bureaucracy.

Obviously, what is essential to business are those substantive, productivity-related activities (e.g. those listed on the left side above). These activities are what valuable and meaningful to business and they contribute directly to the business goals. If we want to improve the business effectiveness, we should base our system on these activities, to make sure they are carried out right. A norm-oriented approach enables us to specify the business rules at the substantive level. This way of abstracting the essential business norms from the superficial bureaucratic rules for paper-processing allows us to reengineer the business processes more easily.

4. A Norm-Oriented View of Reengineering

We acknowledge that the problems of BPR exist because the common practices of information system professionals rely on improper organizational theories and methods. Many people treat an information system as a computer-based system and struggle to fit IT into organizations. Such an approach lacks a theory and general structure that provides direct linkage between IT and the organization which IT serves. Very often we are lost in the complexity of the technicality but forget the actual need of the organizations.

We take the view that it is unwise to think of an information system as necessarily a computer-based system but far better to think of it as an organization. An organization (or a market as a whole) as a system of social norms is the real information system (Fig. 1). A computer-based system is only part of the information system, playing a limited role in an organization by capturing, storing, forwarding and processing the signals. Organized human behavior depends on a far richer form of communication than any machinery can account for. By analyzing the norms that govern human behavior, we can reveal precisely the information requirements for business as well as for computer systems development. Analyzing, designing, building and implementing an information system is the same as analyzing, designing, building and implementing a system of social norms. To redesign an organization is to redesign an information system. Redesigning an information system amounts to redesigning an organization. Such an approach is not based on technology that changes dramatically, but on the ways people conduct business which evolve and become relatively stable over a long period of time.

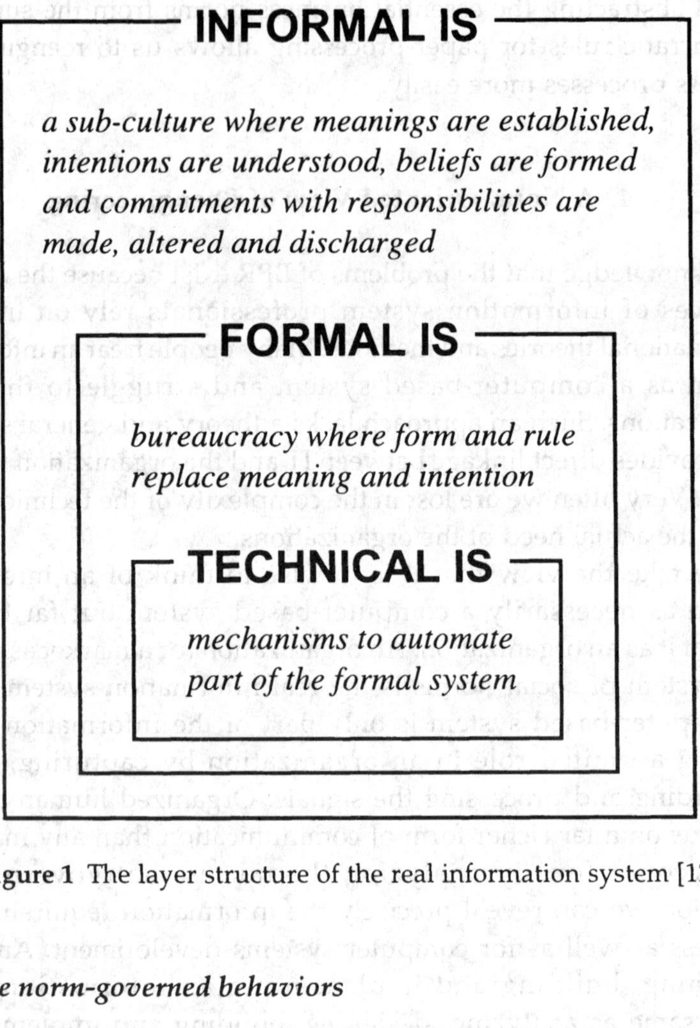

INFORMAL IS

a sub-culture where meanings are established, intentions are understood, beliefs are formed and commitments with responsibilities are made, altered and discharged

FORMAL IS

bureaucracy where form and rule replace meaning and intention

TECHNICAL IS

mechanisms to automate part of the formal system

Figure 1 The layer structure of the real information system [12]

4.1. The norm-governed behaviors

Conventional theories explain organizational behavior in terms of rather broad features such as the shape of the hierarchy of control and the proportions of operators, managers, administrators, professionals and so on (e.g. Ref. 13). The various contingencies molding the shape of an organization have been presented [14], among the most important are the relative costs of administered and market transactions [15, 16], or in terms of cultural influences [17–19]. The organizational semiotics help in understanding how the responsibilities and tasks derived from the organization's objectives are assigned to its constituent agents and how those agents collaborate [20].

Two essential elements make an organization alive — agents and their actions — which are coordinated through the norms they share. Norms establish a foundation of common understanding on which business can be conducted within and between organizations. These norms fall into three categories: *substantive, communication* and *control* [21].

The *substantive* norms govern the essential, productivity-related tasks of the organization and are the pivot around which a given institutional structure can be realigned. Obeying the substantive norms contributes directly to the attainment of the basic goals of the organization. They direct the actions which result in changes to the physical or social resources and to the environment, e.g. obtaining materials, making contracts, and so on.

Communication (message passing) is prescribed by the second type of norms. Messages pass from one agent to another in order to coordinate their substantive actions (e.g. to issue a task, to arrange a transport, etc.). Within a firm, for example, we coordinate the temporal and spatial use of resources by people who have no direct contact. Between organizations, messages such as inquiries, orders, invoices, reminders, etc., are sent to each other in order first, to establish legally binding contracts, and then, to coordinate the discharge of the contracts by the parties, their staff and their representatives. Business transactions fall into these norms.

The third type, the *control* norms, govern organizational behavior by imposing appropriate rewards and sanctions. Within an organization, the power of enforcement may be informal or it may be explicitly stipulated in rules and regulations. Between organizations, it may be generated by inter-firm agreements or contracts governed by law. But the power of enforcement both within and between organizations ultimately rests upon socially established norms within the business sector and by the wider cultural conventions. Formal control norms supplement the informal norms in cases where they are deemed insufficient to insure that every relevant agent acts properly in performing the substantive tasks.

Figure 2 shows a conceptual model of organization resulting from our organizational morphology. An organization as a norm-governed system **x** is composed of three subsystems: substantive **x**.s, message-passing **x**.m and control **x**.c. Each of them may be further divided in the same way in more detail, such as substantive message tasks x.m.s, messages about messages x.m.m, and control of messages x.m.c, until the level of detail is sufficient for the purposes of analysis.

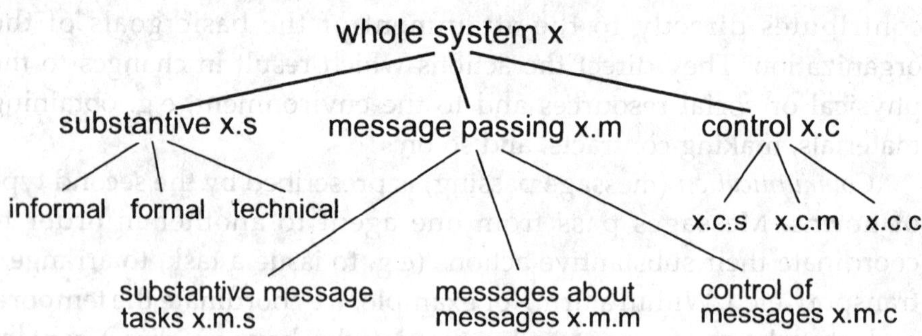

Figure 2 Organizational morphology model

4.2. *Identifying reengineering options*

Organizations, despite their diversity, display a basic, uniform morphology the understanding of which can help organizations to systematically identify reengineering options. Organizational Morphology and Semantic Analysis (introduced later), two of the norm-oriented methods, enable us to separate the stable kernel of substantive business tasks from the supporting semiological tasks and then, recursively to reveal a structure of *substantive, communication* and *control* activities which may be implemented one of three ways: *informally*, *bureaucratically*, or by *technical* means.

The substantive activities are the stable kernel of business functions. If one changes its substantive activities, it changes its business. Therefore, they must remain invariant throughout the reengineering changes. Although changes to the kernel are not ruled out but such innovations are more difficult to define and implement, we do not consider them here.

The communication and control activities may differ from one organization to another, from manager to manager, from time to time. They are subjected to change in order to carry out the substantive activities more efficiently and effectively in different situations.

A 'lean and healthy' organization should consume minimal resources in message-passing and control activities and direct most of its resources in building up the organizational platform for substantive activities. However, an 'unhealthy' or badly-designed organization will have to consume a great deal of its energy in building elaborate communication subsystems and have to rely largely on formal control subsystems. These two types of subsystems comprise large parts of typical bureaucratic infrastructures. The more elaborate these two subsystems are, the heavier the bureaucratic burden on the organization. They are the targets for organizational reengineering.

4.3. *Reengineering issues*

Problems of reengineering may be complex, but a simple semiotic framework [12] can be applied to partitioning a complex organizational structure and distinguishing six rather less complex, relatively independent problems:

- Social - norms of the organization and its environment
- Pragmatic - speech acts and the intentional communication of messages

- Semantic - relationships between signs (e.g.: data) and actions
- Syntactic - formal structures of signs (e.g.: programs and database)
- Empiric - properties of repeated signals (e.g.: error rates, redundancy etc.)
- Physical - hardware and human agents, their performance and economics

The classification of norms into substantive, communication and control kinds, helps us recognize some features of the social level:

- Social level - evaluative behavioral and cognitive norms belonging to the substantive kernel
- Pragmatics - norms governing sign-behavior for the communication of intentions
- Semantics - perceptual norms dealing with the relationships between signs (words etc.) and actions

These three levels are concerned with the business problems of how we want the organization to operate. The other three levels are concerned with technical issues which we only want to address once we have sorted out the business side.

Organizational morphology is concerned mainly with the human and social aspects of the information system: the semantics, pragmatics and the norms which constitute the social structure, while the technical aspects of syntactics, empirics and physical information resources can be specified as a by-product of designing the organizational system to solve business problems.

4.4. The process of designing an organization

By separating an essential, stable kernel from changeable communication and control activities, we can encourage organizations to systematically design 'lean and healthy' systems that devote most of their energy to the substantive activities (Fig. 3).

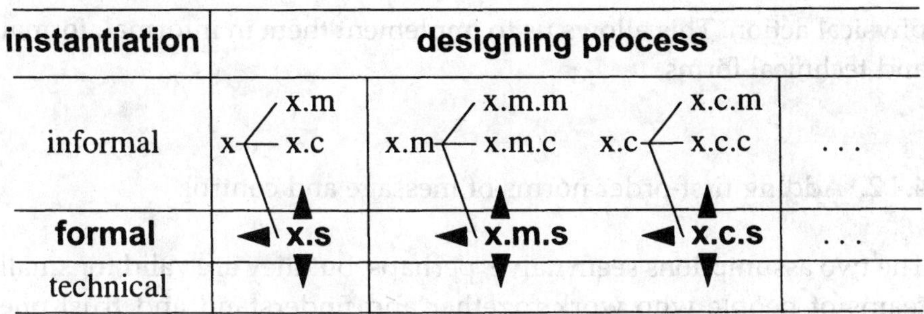

Figure 3 Design process for an organization

4.4.1. Expressing substantive tasks

We begin by working on the substantive norms and making use of two simple assumptions:

- everyone obeys all norms on all occasions — this excludes formalizing control norms;
- everyone always knows all the facts relevant to the norms to be obeyed — this excludes formalizing message norms.

These assumptions suggest an open and trusting group as an informal system **x**. In such a small team of committed members, who have been working together for a long time, there is no need to make any norms explicit. If we do so, it will probably be to spell out the details of how to perform some complex, new, substantive activities. We shall continue to rely upon the team's well-established, informal system to look after all communications and controls — after all, they know who to ask when they need anything and from whom they can obtain information, and, as for control, they can rely on their colleagues to do all that is expected of them.

Defining substantive norms (tasks) is the matter of expressing them in a formal system (e.g. semantic analysis introduced below). Ultimately all behavioral norms can be regarded as substantive, requiring some physical action. This allows us to implement them in informal, formal and technical forms.

4.4.2. Adding first-order norms of message and control

The two assumptions seem naive, perhaps, but they are valid for small teams of people who work together and understand and trust one another. If that is not the case, for example, considering the accessibility of agents to one another in larger, more complex organizations: people who need to coordinate their activities may be separated in different locations, or belong to different professions, or have different interests, in which barriers of communication exist [22], we can begin to lay down the class of first-order message norms **x.m** that will solve any serious communication problems. Similarly, if control needs to be exercised, we can add some first-order control norms **x.c**. This can only go as far as necessary.

By always making the two assumptions above, the same principle is applied here by relying on the informal system to take care of the messages about messages **x.m.m** and the control of messages **x.m.c**. We can alone focus on the substantive message tasks **x.m.s** and the substantive control tasks **x.c.s** and express them formally.

4.4.3. Deciding on implementation

At this point we can decide how to implement the first-order substantive norms **x.s** (maybe also assisted by considerations such as cost-effectiveness, technology availability, etc.). Implementing norms *informally* implies changing the organizational culture which management needs to handle properly for the transition to succeed. The *technical* implementation may involve automation facilities that require certain amounts of capital investment (Fig. 4). Both implementation options demand certain training and education of the members to adapt to a new situation. Implementation by *formal* procedures which people carry out is another option, especially in the short term, but it increases the level of bureaucracy and can often be costly in itself as well as displacing attention away from important business tasks. With the same principle we can also treat the x.m and x.c as second-order substantive norms **x.m.s** and **x.c.s** and decide how to implement them.

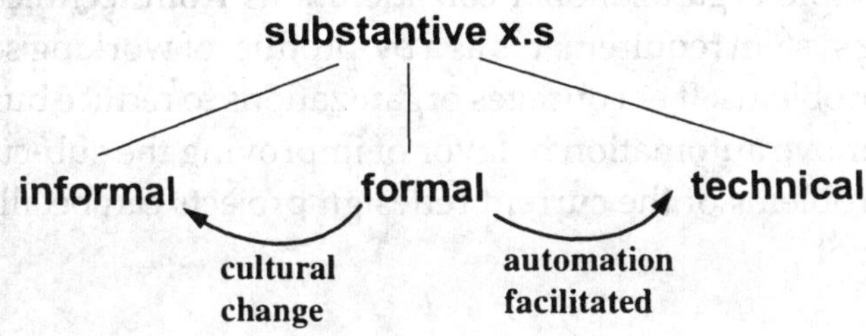

Figure 4 Implementation options

In most small organizations or teams, most norms are instantiated by an informal culture where openness and trust guarantee adequate communication and control. Bureaucracy tends to be induced where spatial, psychological, social and political barriers impede communication and raise suspicion. The efficiency and adaptability of organizations based on networks of small teams can be understood in this light because their informal mechanisms make expensive layers of explicit bureaucratic communication and control norms unnecessary. This shift from bureaucracy to lean, team-based manufacturing is well documented by Womack *et al* [23] in their book 'The machine that changed the world.'

4.4.4. Adding other norms if necessary

If we cannot always trust people to communicate and behave correctly, despite our effort with the new message and control norms, we can add norms about messages about messages **x.m.m**, control of messages **x.m.c**, messages about controls **x.c.m** and controls of controls **x.c.c**, which gives us a third-order analysis. This can go on as far as we need, but ultimately we always have to make the two assumptions.

The instantiation of norms reveals a layer structure of an information system that positions IT properly in an organization (Fig. 1). Such an approach naturally extends human activities to machinery. It enables us to decouple organizational considerations from technical ones by generating system requirements as a by-product of working solely upon business problems. It encourages organizations to reduce bureaucracy, even to remove automation in favor of improving the sub-culture. The existing problems of the current redesign projects can be alleviated or taken care of.

5. Systematic Business Reengineering

We are now ready to demonstrate how we carry out BPR systematically. In the space available in this chapter, we cannot go into the theory so we present the ideas using the mini-case that Hammer [6] tells, an anecdote concerning the Ford Motor Company which had acquired a share of Mazda in order to obtain organizational expertise. Ford managers explained to the visiting Mazda executives that they were aspiring to reduce the 500 staff in Accounts Payable to 400 using a more efficient computer system. Asking how many staff Mazda employed in Accounts Payable, they were astonished to learn the answer: 'five.' Let us see how this may happen.

5.1. The main steps of reengineering

Our analytical strategy is to move to an examination of reengineering strategy that can be carried out step by step for searching greater effectiveness.

- The first step is to identify the substantive elements of the problem domain — the aspects of the physical and social world that we want to know about, influence or even control. We formalize them by performing a Semantic Analysis of these concepts to create an ontology chart.
- To operate on these elements, the agents (always human individuals or groups), must communicate their intentions. This brings us to the pragmatic analysis which adds the essential speech acts to the ontology chart.
- Comparing this chart with the actual physical communication pattern, we can see many of the opportunities for increasing organizational effectiveness by reengineering.
- The precise details of how people in the organization should operate are now added by Norm Analysis in the forms of norms or allocations of responsibility to individual and group agents.
- The broad design of the implementation is achieved by specifying the informal-formal interface and then the human-computer interface.
- Now, knowing who handles the essential messages and knowing their meanings and the intentions behind them, we can deal with the technical aspects by designing syntax and codes (an aspect of empirics) and by adjusting the platform of technical resources.

This whole design process places business considerations first and technical considerations last.

5.2. *Modeling meaning and action in the kernel of the organization*

The kernel of the organizational system in the mini-case is concerned with making and discharging contracts for the supply of items to the right places as required by production departments. In this step of analysis for the purposes of organizational reengineering, we isolate the substantive kernel and represent the perceptual norms in the

Ontology Chart (Fig. 5) resulting from Semantic Analysis (the underlying theory is explained in Ref. 24). These are the companies, their departments, the contracts and the delivery of items at specified places located in the departments. The agents involved are Ford and its departments and the various suppliers. The structure captures the most basis aspects of the semantics of these terms.

To understand Fig. 5 you need to know that the arcs between the elements in the picture represent time constraints. *They are NOT cause-and-effect or sequence or flow relationships, NOR are they relationships between entities.* For example: to locate an item at a place, there must simultaneously exist an appropriate item and a place; a contract only exists if there exists a pair of companies and the contract has two parts (sets of norms or rules) giving the supply and payment conditions. (The dot on an arc indicates a whole/part relationship is involved.) A supply only occurs when an item is located at a designated place under the provisions of a contract. This product of analysis is totally different from the customary data modeling for computer systems design.

In the first place, one is often led to discover unexpected business problems. This mini-case is not rich in illustrations of this point but

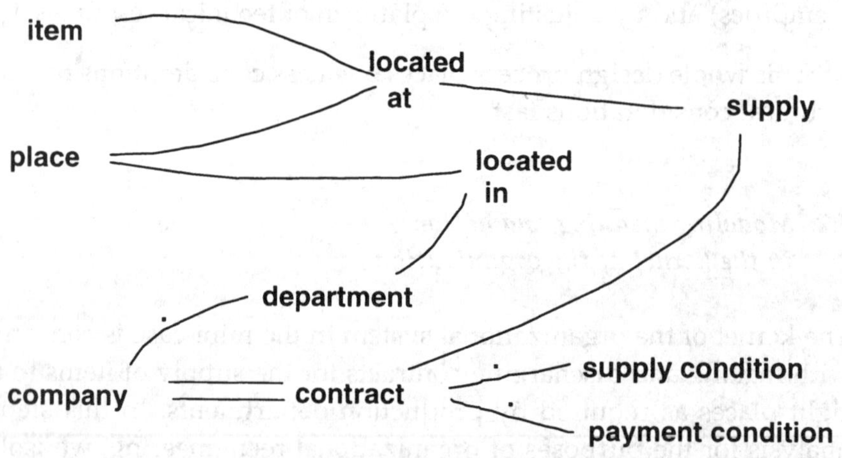

Figure 5 Part of a simple business map

one can see that a loose interpretation of the word 'supply' might fail to take into account the need for a contract to be involved. In the second place, an Ontology Chart tends to be of a much higher quality than a conventional data model (which it can replace) because there is less room for arbitrary choice of solution. This leads to a third advantage that the analysis is very stable, capable of evolving without any need to disturb the existing structure, and therefore the basis of systems that are easy to maintain. Moreover, the Ontology Chart can be implemented directly to create a semantic temporal database (STDB, introduced in Sec. 6).

5.3. *Adding essential pragmatic aspects*

The next step is to add the pragmatic features of the business. To get things to happen, the agents involved must communicate their intentions. The basic conversational pattern in our mini-case begins when a department makes a *request* within the company that the purchasing department make an *order* (actually another kind of request) to another company to supply some items at a certain place. If that company sends a message that it will *accept* the order, a contract starts its existence. The right goods delivered to the right place in conformity with the supply conditions of the contract, will justify the purchaser *accept*ing the supply. Note that 'accept' is used in two different senses. Under the terms of the contract, accepting the supply will give rise to a debt which the purchaser then pays. Each message passed in this conversation is a speech act, technically called an 'illocution' (the theory of speech acts was founded by Austin [25] and developed by Searle [26, 27] and subsequently). Every well-formed speech act must be performed by an agent using a meaningful sign. The intentional speech acts in this conversation can be added to the Ontology Chart (Fig. 6).

Notice that some of the arcs are now broken lines. Take the instance of supply - - - - - order. In this case the antecedent, supply, does not govern the existence of the order: the order has to be made some time

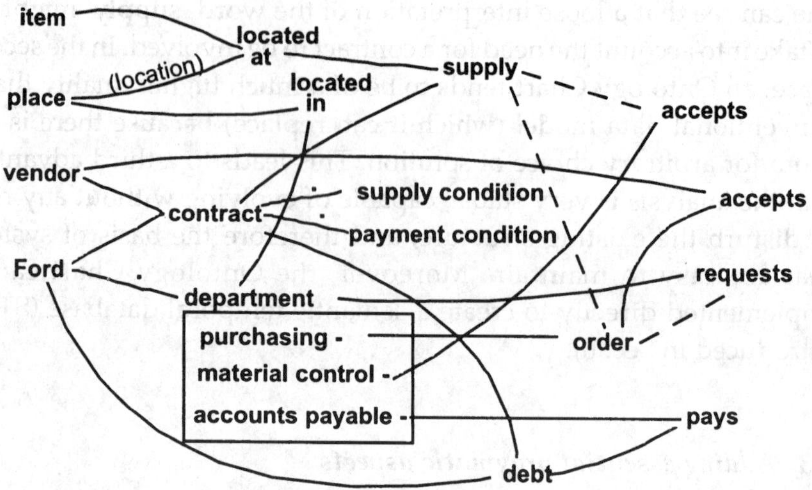

Figure 6 Substantive aspects and essential communication acts

before the supply so the constraint indicated by the solid line would not be justified. The actual antecedent for *order* is a sign representing the desired supply. The broken line links the illocution, *order*, not to the sign used by the communicating agent, the purchasing department, but the meaning of the sign. The reader can see how this works in the case of the other illocutions. Note the two uses of *accept*. In the case of accepting an order, the order has to be in existence still, and not withdrawn. In the case of accepting the supply, it is logically possible that the message indicating acceptance may not be made until after the goods have left the delivery point, hence the need for a broken line.

We have now added the pragmatic element to the analysis. These illocutions are just as much a part of the substantive kernel of the organization as the physical elements. Their functions are to create the expectations, commitments, beliefs and so on which comprise the relevant parts of the social world. We have now captured the irreducible core of this fragment of organization which would be the same for Mazda and Ford. We can use this essential part of the activities as a reference for comparing to the actual physical system and find out what are the differences.

5.4. Comparing with the actual physical system

Turning to examine the technical aspects of the information system, we see that Ford has quite a complicated paper-chase, shown in Fig. 7. There are distinguishable functions performed by separate departments: Manufacturing departments, Purchasing, Material Control and Accounts Payable. In addition there are vendors. To coordinate their actions they need to communicate their intentions to one another, as modeled in Fig. 6. But, because they cannot rely on the informal system to keep everyone informed of every step in the conversational cycles, they have to distribute various copies of messages. Accounts Payable

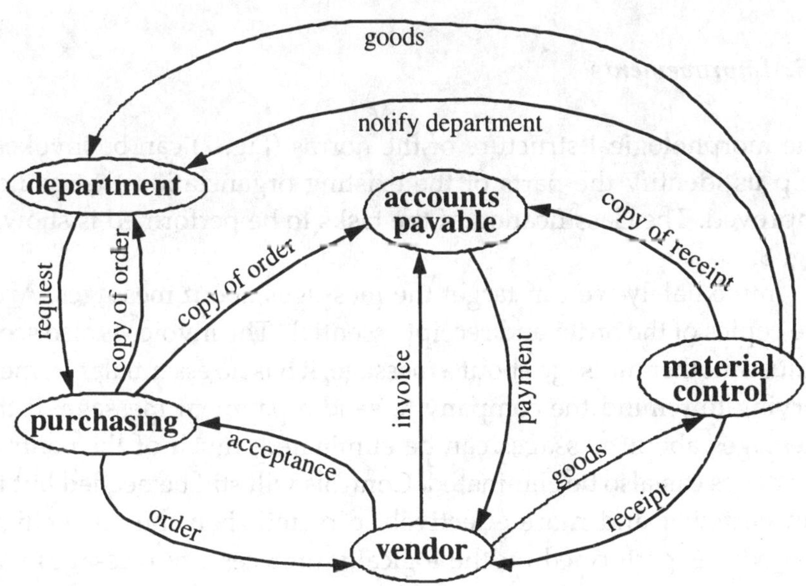

Figure 7 Ford's paper-chase process

are entirely dependent on these signals to make the logical deductions that the correct goods have actually been delivered according to contract before making the payment. Moreover, although they could also make the logical deduction that they then have a debt to pay, no payment is made until the vendor sends a reminder that effect, in the form of an invoice.

The classical 'dataflow diagram' used in systems analysis is like Fig. 7. It is sometimes described as representation of a part of the system's logic but it is nothing of the kind. It actually represents, in a rather abstract form, the physical level of analysis. The oval nodes in the graph show various locations and the arcs show physical routes labelled by the names of the documents that use them. Using this level of analysis, it is quite difficult to see what is fixed and what is variable in the situation that the organizational engineer must deal with. On the other hand, the Ontology Chart in Fig. 6 specifies only the organizational invariants.

5.5. Improvements

The morphological structure of the norms (Fig. 2) can be invoked to help us identify the parts of the existing organization that could be improved. The classification of the tasks to be performed is shown in Fig. 8.

Immediately we can target the messages about messages. Are all the copies of the order and receipt essential? The invoice is also seen to be just another message about a message, it has no essential role, merely serving to remind the company to send a payment message. If these messages about messages can be eliminated, much of the control of messages can also be eliminated. Controls will still be needed but they can be fewer and more effectively directed than the reconciliation procedures performed on the logically unnecessary messages which comprised most of the work in the accounts payable department at Ford. Although logically unnecessary, the reason for all these messages

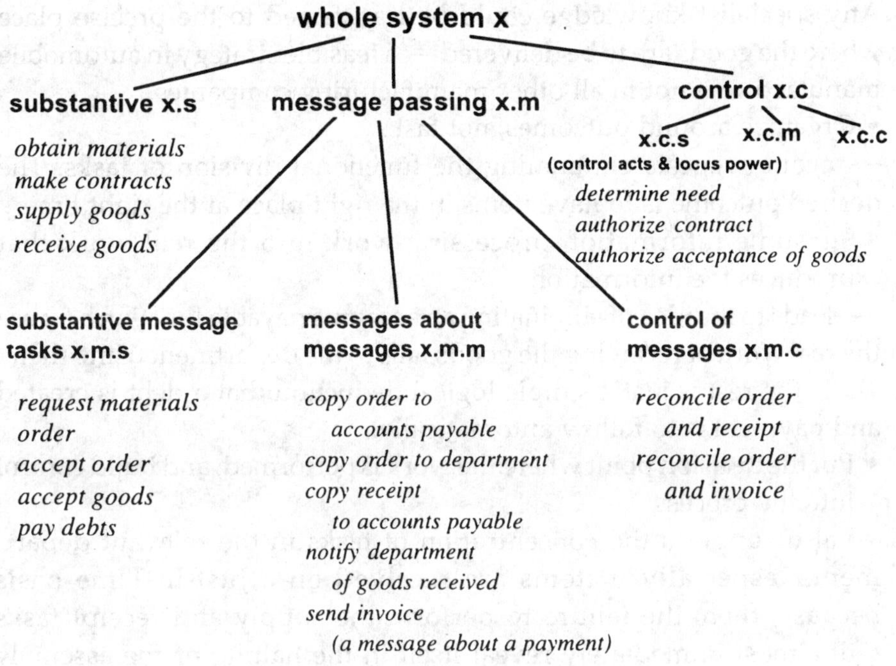

Figure 8 Organizational morphology for Ford's system

lies at the empirics level in the semiotic framework. Unreliable communications, the risk of fraudulent introduction of errors in the message stream and similar problems would have dominated the design of many original systems and procedures. The situation is radically changed now that we have telematic systems and shared databases. Too often, however, computer-based systems reproduce designs that paper-based technology would have justified. The above analysis gives us a basis for redesign at this empirics level.

Some of Hammer's six principles can be invoked.

- Have those who use the output of the process perform the process.

— suggests that the department using the goods received should perform that task instead of a separate materials control department.

Any specialist knowledge could be transferred to the precise place where the goods are to be delivered — a feasible strategy in automobile manufacture if not in all other manufacturing companies.

- Organize around outcomes, not tasks.

— again suggests eliminating the functional division of tasks. The desired outcome is to have items in the right place at the right time.

- Subsume information-processing work into the real work that produces the information.

— leads to the idea of eliminating an accounts payable function because the real work of receiving the goods falls to the department using them, while the rest is just a simple logical deduction that a debt is created and payment is to follow automatically.

- Put the decision point where the work is performed, and build control into the process.

— also supports the concentration of tasks in the relevant departments, especially if items are received on a Just-in-Time basis because, then, the failure to perform the supply and receipt tasks will almost immediately reveal itself in the halting of the assembly line.

The resulting, reengineered organization is shown in Fig. 9. This is essentially what Mazda was doing to such good effect. Note that the accounts payable function is now just an automatic process which a computer can perform. The next target of analysis would be the purchasing function. The negotiating of long-term contracts would still be a human activity but, within the contract, all the routine call-off orders could be handled by EDI, allowing us to put most of the purchasing function into a rectangular box to signify its being performed by computer.

5.6. *Syntactic aspects*

Continuing the decomposition of the problem within the semiotic framework, we turn briefly to the syntactic aspects. In classical methods

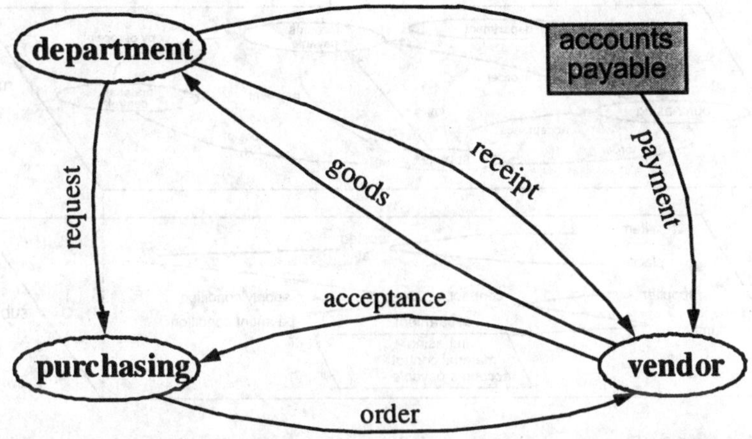

Figure 9 Mazda's invoice-less payment system

of requirements specification, a great deal of effort has to be devoted to syntactic details such as record and message structures, type of field, numbers of characters, algorithms for computer functions and definitions of clerical procedures. These issues are essential ones to consider but they are the most superficial from a *business* point-of-view.

The above analysis makes no assumptions at all about the ways in which the various messages and data structures or programs should be designed. The core of the analysis is the semantic schema in the form of the ontology chart in Figs. 5 and 6. It might be argued that the choice of terminology is an aspect of the syntactic design which comes close to specifying details of some of the fields, but in this case it is not so. The semantic schema is syntactically and linguistically neutral; the terminology can be switched quite easily into any other language or code, as explained below in Sec. 6. This is important when we have to consider how to reengineer systems that depend upon existing software that we do not yet want to change. And also when redesigning systems that cross organizational

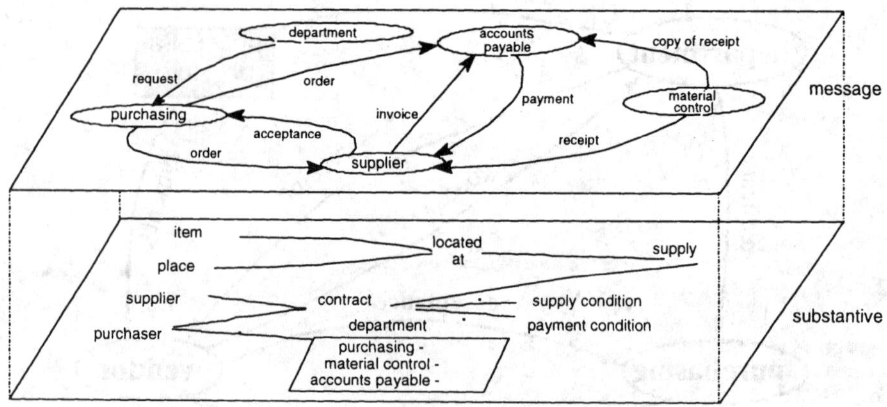

Figure 10 The procedural and the substantive levels of the system

boundaries. Inside the boundaries of a system or organization it is relatively easy to exercise total, arbitrary control of the syntax to be adopted. Hence the low priority given to syntactics in this kind of business-oriented analysis.

If we adopt a common standard based on the semantics and the pragmatics of the business activities under consideration, we can introduce any desired local solution for the syntactics. Figure 10 captures a fragment of the essential business structure without regard for syntactics. The lower layer shows the semantics for some of the relevant, substantive, physical and social features of the problem domain. The upper layer shows a number of agents and the messages they exchange. The meanings of these messages can be made explicit in a precise form by defining them in terms of the substantive layer. The language, the codes, the fields types, the record and message formats are relevant for the design of the technical system but irrelevant for the design of the business. This is also true in the EDI domain where the syntactic issues are the major concern of the standardization committees under the UN/EDIFACT Board. Our research begins to develop common, syntax-free standards for inter-organizational communications (see Ref. 28).

5.7. Allocation of norms

An important part of the systems architecture is the allocation of tasks (or norms, in the case of our method of analysis). Traditionally, this is regarded as the design decision for the allocation of functions between man and machine, or defining the human-computer interface (HCI). This is certainly important but it neglects another, possibly more important interface design issue: defining the balance between the informal and the formal components of the system. Both these interfaces are essential aspects of the morphology of an organization.

The analysis outlined above has said nothing about the execution of the norms, only classifying them, on the dimension of *reference*, as substantive norms, norms about passing messages or about exercising control. Orthogonal to the dimension of reference lies the dimension of *execution*. Broadly the alternatives are

- to have the norms become a part of the culture of the organization so that they will be applied informally;
- to express the norms in explicit formal, bureaucratic rules which will be applied by people mechanically but not necessarily with understanding;
- to incorporate the norms in computer programs which can execute them automatically.

This is shown in Fig. 11.

It will be seen that the modes of execution are nested, with the formal norms depending upon an encompassing informal, cultural system and the automated system depending upon a bureaucratic system. The HCI is the innermost boundary but we also see the neglected interface between formal system and the informal system or cultural infrastructure. The HCI receives, rightly enough, adequate attention from experts in ergonomics, for which there is a strong commercial motivation: a well-designed interface makes software more attractive to the market. By comparison, the informal-formal interface (IFI) still receives relatively little attention from the research community.

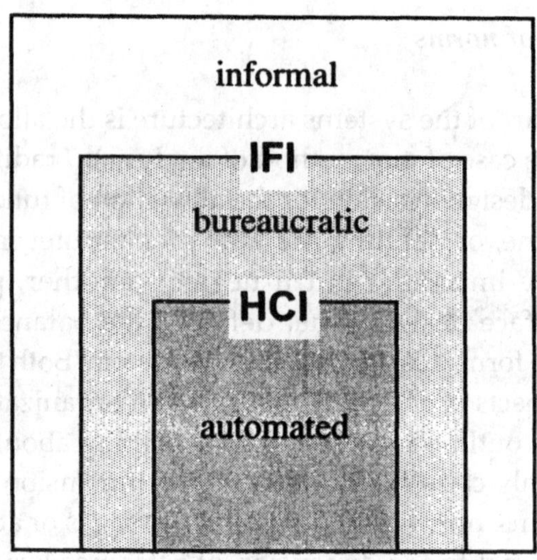

Figure 11 The IS architecture [21]

It does not even have a recognized place in the classical requirements engineering methods which all tend to encourage the formalization of tasks in order to automate them (however, see Jirotka *et al* [29]). The allocation of tasks between the informal and formal parts of the system should not act as a ratchet, continually increasing the size of the formal part. The designer should look for ways of implementing norms in the informal, cultural system, where it is appropriate to do so. Research on the IFI needs to be given much more attention.

The IFI is difficult to design unless the organization is prepared to alter its culture and the main structural determinants of its culture. Fortunately we have seen the growing use of small, semi-autonomous teams, responsible collectively for organizing and controlling areas of activity. This provides a social structure far more receptive to new, task-oriented norms than the hierarchical, machine bureaucracy which one tends to associate with centralized computer systems. A small team is better able to provide all its members with relevant, local information without bureaucratic means. A small team, where the members are jointly and severally responsible for the whole team's performance, will apply most of the necessary controls quite informally, without the need for an explicit system of rewards and sanctions. These developments, associated with the concept of organizational learning and 'lean' organizations, provide new opportunities during organizational reengineering to shift the implementation from the bureaucracy into the informal organization, often with at least as much benefit as might be obtained by the use of computers.

6. Implementation

The Semantic Temporal DataBase (STDB) and the Normbase are currently under development to provide tools for direct implementation of the information systems developed using MEASUR, the norm-oriented methodology.

The foundation of both these tools is a database management environment that accepts an ontology chart, as illustrated in Figs. 5 and 6, as a schema. The result is not a relational database but may be imagined as one in which every relation has the same structure, one for each element in the ontology chart. This common structure includes the one or two ontological antecedents, the start and finish times of every type and instance and their associated authorities (either an agent or a norm). These structures represent the behaviors of the people in the organization. And the authorities provide direct links to the right people. They can use a simple, common, default interface, which makes learning to use the system very easy.

The functionality of the system can be added to the STDB by linking a number of modules that are efficient enough to deliver software that will meet most ordinary, administrative data-processing needs. The syntactics and empirics are easily adapted because the internal structures have nothing to do with these aspects of the information system, being only concerned with the social behavior of people. The elements in the ontology chart represent semantic units which can be named in any language, making it easy to switch between them. The codes are handled in the same way. We can instantly switch, for example, between English, Dutch and Arabic. The syntax of the screens can be defined as a complex object, using the same analysis methods and the contents defined using the semantic schema. Exactly the same strategy could be used for communicating with other, preexisting systems. The use of MEASUR supported by the STDB has proved itself to be quite spectacularly more efficient for implementation, support and maintenance than classical methods (see Ref. 30).

The Normbase adds sophistication to the STDB by providing an interpreter for the language we have for manipulating the data in the STDB. Whereas Semantic Analysis and the ontological structures are based on Norma [31] the manipulation language is called Legol (a legally oriented language) which was developed for expressing and manipulating social norms, and was the predecessor for Norma. For more about the Normbase see Stamper [24]. It functions as a Fifth Generation Language. It allows queries to be expressed far more simply than is possible in 4GLs such as SQL: for example, the three elements in the Legol expression *item while requests*, require 99 operators and operands in SQL. The explanation for much of this efficiency is the ease with which time is handled by the STDB and Legol. Another user-friendly feature of the Normbase is its use of the Ontology Chart as an interface for designers and users. These structures are easy to build and browse using a mouse. For most users little other documentation is necessary for quite sophisticated levels of operation. The Normbase will be used as the workstation on a network served by any number of efficient STDBs.

7. Conclusions

The need for organizational reengineering results from ever-changing social, cultural and business environments. The world has become increasingly hostile to inflexible business organizations as political and economic crises occur more frequently, and as the marketplace becomes more competitive. The development of electronic commerce offers a promising way for improving the conduct of business by inducing and enabling organizations to redesign their business processes and organizational structures to meet the new business environment.

However, the lack of structural approaches in this process has caused many reengineering projects failed and prevented organizations from realizing those potential gains. To reengineer an organization systematically, the norm-oriented methodology MEASUR offers Organizational Morphology as a conceptual framework to identify organizational behavior with respect to substantive, communication and control purposes. In this framework, one can distinguish the relatively stable and unstable parts of the system. This improved understanding will help in solving business problems, regardless of any technical issues, and it will help in designing a flexible organizational infrastructure for continual organizational reengineering.

The effective management of information systems depends upon treating the organization as the information system to be designed. Organizational reengineering is then an integral part of work on information systems. Advanced IT can enhance performance and productivity of businesses. But the lack of flexibility and the difficulties of modifying large and complex computer-based information systems have limited the benefits from IT. Changing the functions of information systems in order to match changing business requirements is normally a costly exercise. The methods presented in this chapter increase the flexibility of the technical systems and facilitate reengineering. In this approach, the design of the technical system is a by-product of designing an organization, and reengineering an IT system is a by-product of business reengineering. Information systems become more comprehensible and manageable by non-technical people as organizational issues replace technical issues as the central concern. The computer-based system becomes comprehensible, not only for technologists, but also for business executives and managers so that quality assurance and control over technical systems can be exercised with great confidence.

We hope that the reader will also find, in the work as a whole, the general message that information systems *are* organizations. Therefore information systems do not necessarily incorporate computers. The classical methods of analysis for software development do not reveal the rich morphological structure of organizations which underlies the approach presented here.

References

1. P. S. Weltevreden, The development of EDI in the European scheme, Commission of the European Communities, Directorate General Telecommunications, Information Industries and Innovation, Rue de la Loi 200, B-1049 Brussels, Belgium (1991).
2. B. Hedberg, The role of information systems in imaginary organizations, in *Collaborative Work, Social Communications and Information Systems*, Stamper, Kerola, Lee and Lytinen (eds.) (IFIP, Amsterdam, 1991).
3. M. J. Earl, Approaches to strategic information systems planning in twenty-one UK companies, *Proceedings of the 11th ICIS, December 16–19*, Copenhagen, Denmark, 1990.
4. T. Reponen, Organizational information management strategies, *Information Systems Journal* **4** (1995) 27–44.
5. N. Venkatraman, IT-enabled business transformation: from automation to business scope redefinition, *Sloan Management Review* (Winter 1994) 73–87.
6. M. Hammer, Reengineering work: don't automate, obliterate, *Harvard Business Review*, July-August 1990, 104–112.
7. K.-Y. Huang, The impacts of electronic commerce, *Proceedings of the 1997 ACM SIGCPR Conference* (ACM Press, San Francisco, 1996).
8. K.-Y. Huang and Kaiyin, Towards an open EDI, working paper, Enschede, 1996.
9. V. Leyland, *Electronic Data Interchange, A management View* (Prentice-Hall, 1994).

10. R. K. Stamper, Information system modelling myopia, *Information System Concepts, Towards a Consolidation of Views Proceedings of the IFIP International Working Conference on Information System Concepts,* E. D. Falkenberg, W. Hesse and A. Olive (eds.), (1995) pp. 311–315.
11. J. L. G. Dietz, Automatiseringsgids 21 June, 1996.
12. R. K. Stamper, Signs, information, norms and systems, in B. Holrnqvist, P. B. Andersen, H. Klein and R. Posner (eds.), *Signs at Work* (De Gruyter, Berlin, 1996) pp. 349–397.
13. H. Mintzberg, *The Structuring of Organizations* (Prentice-Hall, Inc., Englewood Cliffs, N.J, 1979).
14. J. Woodward, *Industrial Organization: Theory and Practice* (Oxford University Press, 1965).
15. O. Williamson, *Markets and Hierarchies: Analysis and Antitrust Implications* (Free Press, New York, 1975).
16. O. Williamson, The economics of organizations: the transaction costs approach, *American Journal of Sociology* 87(3), (1981) 548–577.
17. M. Douglas, *How Institutions Think* (Syracuse Univ. Press, New York, 1986).
18. M. Douglas and W. Aaron, *Risk and Culture: An essay on the selection of technical and environmental dangers* (Univ. of California Press, Berkeley, 1982).
19. M. Boisot, *Information and Organizations: The Manager as Anthropologist* (Fontana, London, 1987).
20. R. Stamper, *Information in Business and Administrative Systems* (Batsford, London & Wiley, New York), 2nd edition forthcoming from Basil Blackwell, Oxford.
21. R. K. Stamper, K. Liu and K.-Y. Huang, Organizational Morphology in Reengineering, *Proceedings of Second European Conference of Information Systems* (Nijenrode University 1994) pp. 729–737.
22. K.-Y. Huang, *Organizational Aspects of EDI, A Norm-Oriented Approach,* thesis Enschede, The Netherlands, (1998) pp. 17, 170.
23. J. P. Womack, T. J. Daniel and R. Daniel, *The Machine that Changed the World — The Story of Lean Production* (Harper Perennial, New York, 1990).
24. R. K. Stamper, Social norms in requirements analysis — and outline of MEASUR, in Jirotka, *et al* (1994).

25. J. L. Austin, *How to Do Things with Words,* the William James Lectures delivered at Harvard University in 1955 (Oxford University Press, Oxford, 1980).
26. J. R. Searle, *Speech Acts — An Essay in the Philosophy of Language* (Cambridge University Press, Combridge, 1969).
27. J. R. Searle and V. Daniel, *Foundations of Illocutionary Logic* (Cambridge University Press, Combridge, 1985).
28. K.-Y. Huang, The study of semantic standard for EDI, *Academic Research on Electronic Commerce,* the 2nd EDISPUUT workshop, the Netherlands, 1995.
29. M. Jirotka, J. Goguen and M. Bickerton (eds.), *Requirements Engineering: Technical and Social Aspects* (Academic Press, 1994).
30. K.-C. Liu, A. Yasser and S. Ronald, Simplicity, uniformity and quality — the role of semantic analysis in systems development, *Software Quality Management Conference, SQM'94,* Edinburgh, UK, 1994.
31. R. K. Stamper, A logic of social norms for the semantics of business information, in Steel and Meersmann, *Knowledge and Data* (North Holland, 1985).
32. EDIFACT Board, *Introduction to UN/EDIFACT messages,* 7th revised issue, 1993.
33. P. G. W. Keen, *Shaping the Future — Business Design Through Information Technology* (Harvard Business School Press, 1991).
34. R.-M. Lee and R. W. H. Bons, Soft-coded trade procedures for open EDI, *Electronic Commerce for Trade Efficiency, Proceedings for 8th International Conference on EDI and Inter-Organizational Systems,* Bled, Slovenia, 1995.
35. A. Mitrakas, Ways to draft an interchange agreement (Erasmus University Rotterdam, 1995).
36. R. K. Stamper, K. Liu and K.-Y. Huang, EDI systems design from semiotic perspective, *Proceedings of the International Conference in Communication Technology, Communication: Highway of Economic Growth and Social Progress,* Shanghai (1994) pp. 933–942.
37. P. H. M. Vervest, Communication, not information — an *ad hoc* organization of the value chain, Inaugural speech, Erasmus University Rotterdam.

Chapter 11

Capitalizing on the Improvements in Software Development with Object-Oriented Models

LUIGI BENEDICENTI
DIST — Università di Genova,
Via Opera Pia 13, 16145 Genova, Italy
E-mail: Luigi.Benedicenti@dist.unige.it

GIANCARLO SUCCI
Department of Electrical & Computer Engineering, The University of Calgary,
2500 University Dr. N.W Calgary, AB — CANADA T2N 1N4
E-mail: Giancarlo.Succi@enel.ucalgary.ca

TULLIO VERNAZZA
DIST — Università di Genova,
Via Opera Pia 13, 16145 Genova, Italy
E-mail: Tullio.Vernazza@dist.unige.it

This chapter presents Gertrude, a methodology for business process modeling. Gertrude uses Object Orientation, and conjugates it with Activity Based Costing. The methodology is simple, easy to use and understand, and concise. It accounts for what-if analysis, and variation in the perception of the firm. It can serve as enabler for a BPR process, or monitor a continuous improvement in the production process. It is the basis for corporate experience capitalization.

1. Introduction

In this chapter we present Gertrude, a methodology for business process modeling. This methodology is based on both object orientation and activity based costing. We proceed as follows: first we outline the existing proposals for business modeling, then we outline our approach, and eventually we provide a sample application of Gertrude. Gertrude has been selected as the target methodology of the Esprit Project 23699 Deco: it will be validated inside a software firm. The chapter is organized as follows. Section 3 presents some background on the subject. Section 4 describes our methodology. Section 5 presents an example that employs our methodology.

2. Background

The software production process has been modeled in several different ways. The proposals range from very theoretical paradigms to very practical techniques.

The software engineering group at Politecnico di Milano has proposed SPADE, a formal approach based on extended Petri nets [1]. SPADE describes a process in terms of the actions performed and the deliverables produced. Since each token can be labeled by attributes, the deliverables can be adequately represented. The placement of each token is subject to guards. The guards can determine whether tokens can flow among places, thus enabling transitions. SPADE supports time semantics by means of special transitions called TO transitions. The TO (Time Out) transitions occur in case the required places are not occupied by tokens within a time interval.

SPADE can model a process in a very effective way. Moreover, it lets users specify the tool they use and it guides new users into the modeled software development process. However, SPADE is rigid, it is very difficult to make the model reflective, that is, able to modify its own structure to cope with process changes. Furthermore, human activities such as the creative phases are excluded; this means that the only way for humans to interact with the model is via predefined input points.

Ivar Jacobson has been working on a technique based on object orientation. The modeler collects typical scenarios in the organization to be modeled. The scenarios are structured in use cases, and these form the basis of the model. The use cases develop in activities, performed by actors. Activities do not relate to the 'vertical' hierarchical structure in the organization, stretching 'horizontally' in more than a single department. The Jacobson Model is much simpler than SPADE. It does not require a deep knowledge of theoretical abstractions. However, it does not concentrate on the modeling technique, but only on the reengineering of the firm. Moreover, there is no connection with Activity-Based Costing.

Several further proposals exist for business modeling, such as Adele, ISPW6, EPOS, etc., but they mostly share the features of the two presented above.

3. Our Work

We think that all the past work has been extremely significant in terms of capturing some relevant aspects of the business. However, they all fail to supply a comprehensive view of the firm.

As Kaplan and Norton say in Ref. 2, a financial perspective is not a plus. Operational improvements alone do not imply better businesses. Several examples exist, in which improved performances have not resulted in increased profits. Reference 2 provides the example of a NYSE electronics company that between 1987 and 1990 has significantly improved all its performance figures (defect rate, on time delivery, and so on) but failed to succeed, since it did not manage to capitalize on such improvement.

On the other hand, it is widely known that financial perspectives alone fail to provide a sound view of the business.

Our model integrates object orientation and activity-based costing in a very natural way. The business modeler starts with a description of the interactions among the components (people, their roles, the activities and the infrastructures). Variations of Jacobson use cases and scenarios are employed. Then people, roles, activities, and infrastructures are organized in hierarchies; we use an OMT-like notation. The joint usage of OMT and use cases does not create any confusion: use cases are powerful in identifying the components and their dynamics. OMT is best used to model the static nature of each one. Once each component is identified and modeled, we attach to it the information about its cost, if any. Thus, each person gets a salary and each infrastructure the fixed and the variable costs for its use.

The next step is to deduce the activity-based costing form. This can be easily performed in an automatic way from the object model. The ABC forms are distributed among the employees. They are requested to fill them day by day. It has been widely recognized that this constant bookeeping is a means to improve the performance *per se*, rather than being a waste of time. The collected data are used to perform a sequence of analysis.

The application of the Activity-Based Costing methodology requires an activity-oriented description of the firm's processes. The technique we have developed constructs an object-oriented graphical description of the processes in order to make the costs distribution visible and assessable. The object-oriented approach is particularly adequate for this kind of problem because the objects that are represented correspond to real objects in a firm.

4. A Sample Application

This section uses Gertrude to describe a restaurant. Consider the diagram in Fig. 1; it is a Processes-Actors-People (PAP) snapshot and represents a typical restaurant process for serving lunch or dinner. Some objects, like the activities in round cornered boxes, are not

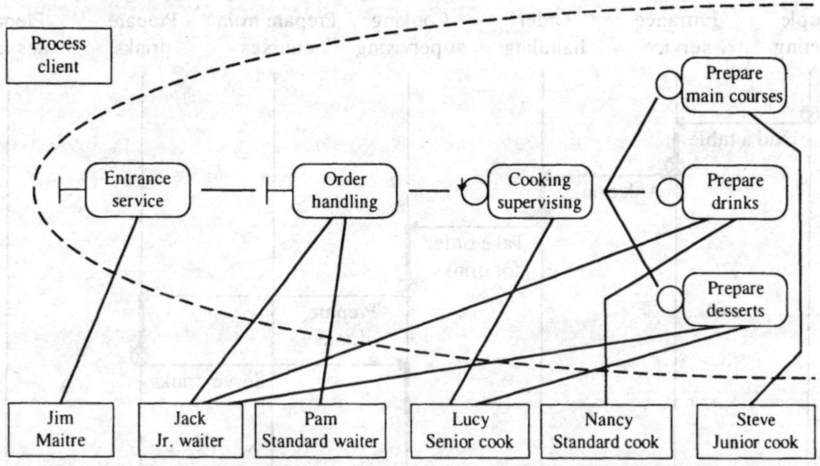

Figure 1 PAP snapshot of a restaurant process

physical, yet they are actual and important objects in the process. The links show interactions between objects. A link between a restaurant worker and an activity states that the worker performs the activity. A link between activities shows a message exchange (e.g. the 'cooking supervising,' which is a control process, interacts with the three rightmost activities it controls).

The PAP snapshot can be obtained by means of interviews of people in the firm. They are required to give a description of the processes in terms of use cases. A use case is a typical scenario of a process and involves the people and the activities that are needed to implement the process. The result of an interview is a textual description of a use case. Since people tend to present their descriptions from a personal point of view, the collected information should be verified in order to give a unique, consistent and unifying description. A Process Interaction Diagram (PID) is a more formal representation of the use cases. The example (Fig. 2) shows the flow of events and message exchange of the 'serving a drink' use case.

It is important to choose the right use cases. The PIDs should be used to represent typical use cases. Unusual situations, though partially

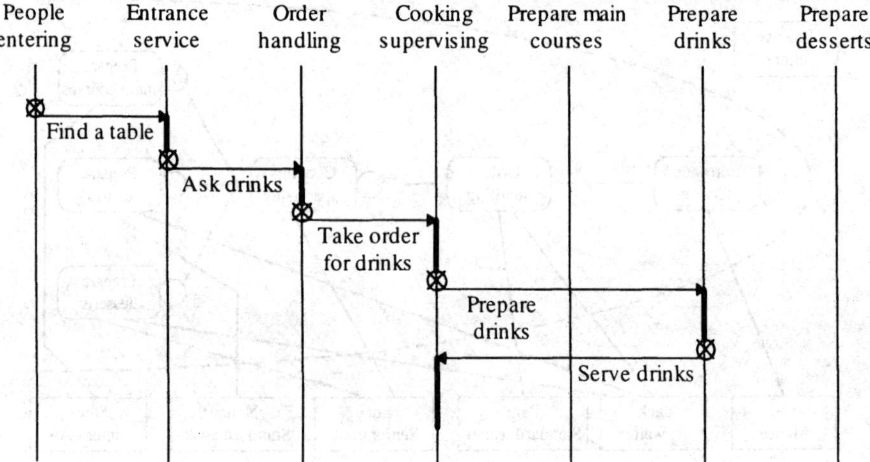

Figure 2 Process interaction diagram

predictable, are not considered in this modeling technique. What we want here is a good basis for the ABC analysis, not a thorough process specification. A simple yet significant description allows an automatic generation of the forms required to support the ABC activity.

One further step is to describe the processes and actors' hierarchies with an object-oriented technique.

It is necessary to make a distinction between classes and objects. The adopted process modeling technique represents objects as terminal nodes and classes as non-terminal nodes in the diagrams. Objects appear in the use case descriptions so they are concretely present in the described processes. Classes are not present in the use cases but they are needed to give a conceptual structure to a set of objects. This distinction is useful in the following diagrams.

Actor classes are actually used in the processes actors links diagram (Fig. 4). The solid lines represent an 'actual actor' relationship while the dashed lines represent a 'most generic actor' relationship. These relationships model actual and possible allocations of people to processes. The former involves only terminal nodes of the hierarchies; this limitation does not hold for the latter because it expresses potential

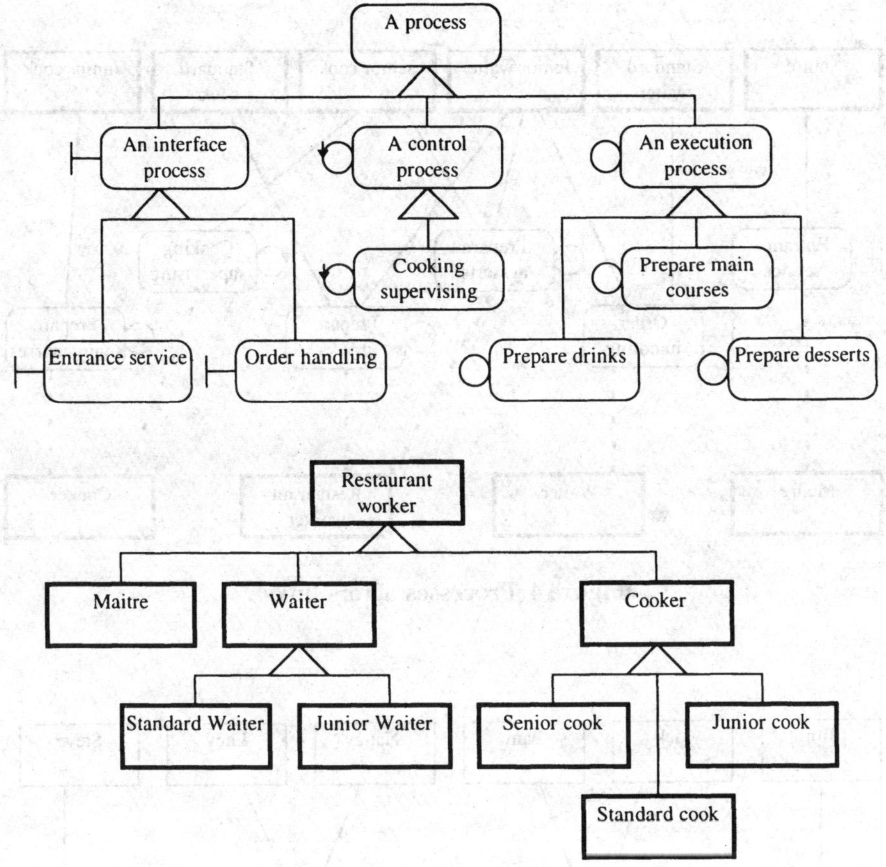

Figure 3 Processes and actors hierarchies

relationships between processes and actors, so it may involve classes at a higher level of abstraction.

In many cases a person can perform more tasks than he or she is actually assigned to. These unused capabilities are modeled in Fig. 5 with a dotted line.

The ABC technique requires a description of the infrastructures to properly manage their costs. Infrastructures are the physical facilities

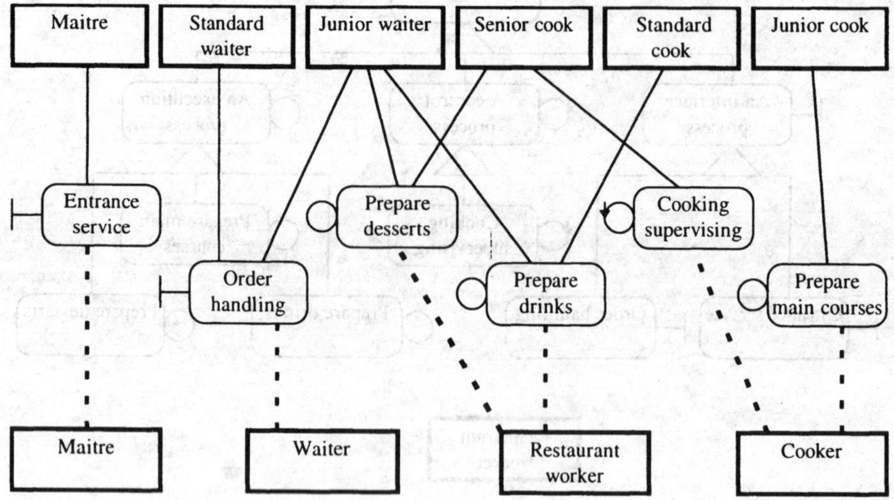

Figure 4 Processes actors links

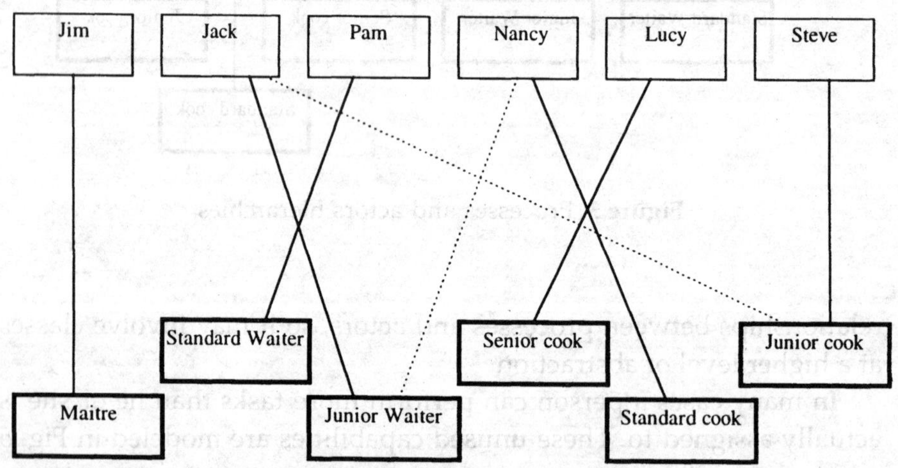

Figure 5 Actors people links

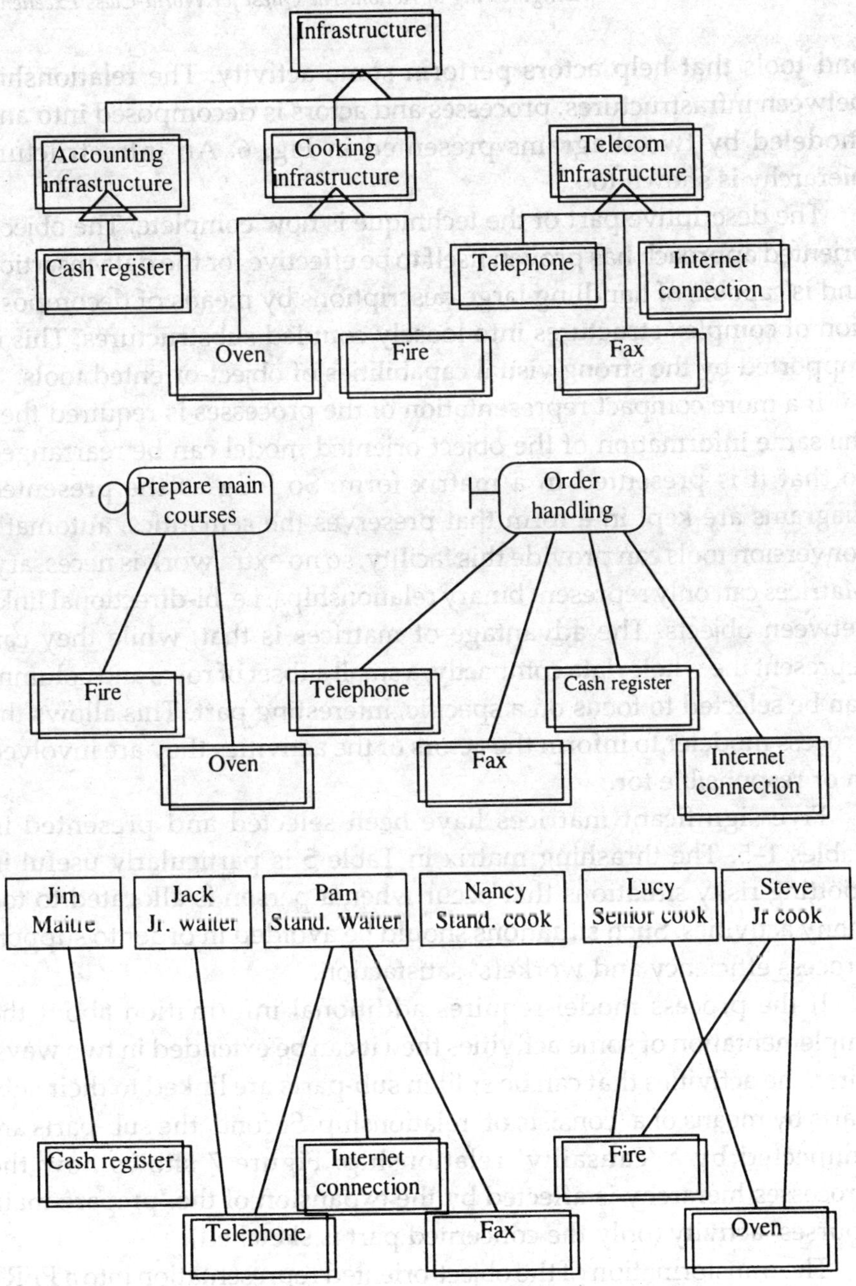

Figure 6 Infrastructures hierarchy and links

and tools that help actors perform some activity. The relationship between infrastructures, processes and actors is decomposed into and modeled by two diagrams presented in Fig. 6. An infrastructure hierarchy is shown too.

The descriptive part of the technique is now complete. The object-oriented approach has proven itself to be effective for the data insertion and is capable of handling large descriptions by means of decomposition of complex structures into loosely coupled substructures. This is supported by the strong visual capabilities of object-oriented tools.

If a more compact representation of the processes is required then the same information of the object-oriented model can be rearranged so that it is presented in a matrix form. So long as the presented diagrams are kept in a form that preserves the semantics, automatic conversion tools can provide this facility, so no extra work is necessary. Matrices can only represent binary relationships, i.e. bi-directional links between objects. The advantage of matrices is that, while they can represent the whole data compactly, a small subset of rows and columns can be selected to focus on a specific, interesting part. This allows the process modeler to inform the actors of the activities they are involved in or responsible for.

Five significant matrices have been selected and presented in Tables 1–5. The thrashing matrix in Table 5 is particularly useful in spotting risky situations that occur when a person is allocated to too many activities. Such situations should be avoided in order to support process efficiency and workers' satisfaction.

If the process model requires additional information about the implementation of some activities then it can be extended in two ways. First, the activities that can be split in sub-parts are linked to their sub-parts by means of a 'consists of' relationship. Second, the sub-parts are connected by a 'causality' relationship. Figure 7 shows how the processes hierarchy is affected by the expansion of the 'prepare main courses' activity (only the concerned part is sketched).

The transformation of the object-oriented representation into a PERT chart is straightforward. This is shown in Fig. 8.

Table 1 Potential skills matrix

	Maitre	Stand waiter	Junior waiter	Senior cook	Stand cook	Junior cook
Jim	√					
Jack			√			√
Pam		√				
Lucy				√		
Steve						√
Nancy			√		√	

Table 2 Actual skills matrix

	Maitre	Stand waiter	Junior waiter	Senior cook	Stand cook	Junior cook
Jim	√					
Jack			√			
Pam		√				
Lucy				√		
Steve						√
Nancy					√	

Table 3 Most general actor placement matrix

	Restaurant worker	Maitre	Waiter	Cook
Entrance service		1		
Order handling			2	
Cooking supervising				1
Prepare main courses				1
Prepare desserts	2			
Prepare drinks	2			

Table 4 Actual actor placement matrix

	Maitre	Stand worker	Junior cook	Senior cook	Stand cook	Junior cook
Entrance service	1					
Order handling		1	1			
Cooking supervising				1		
Prepare main courses						1
Prepare desserts			1	1		
Prepare drinks			1		1	

Table 5 Thrashing matrix

	Entrance service	**Order handling**	**Cooking supervising**	**Prepare main courses**	**Prepare desserts**	**Prepare drinks**
Jim	√					
Jack		√			√	√
Pam		√				
Lucy			√		√	
Steve				√		
Nancy						√

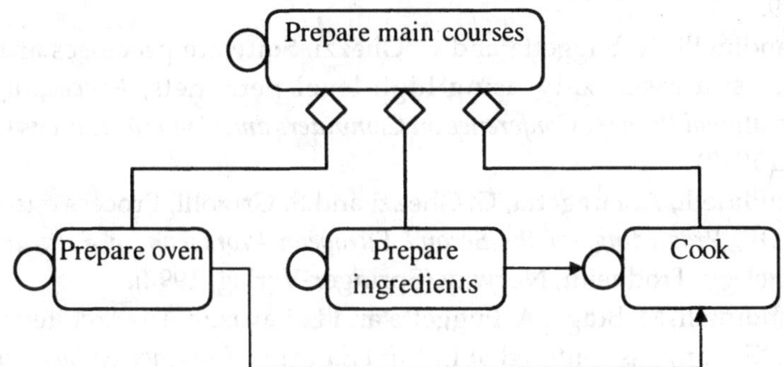

Figure 7 A process consisting of three activities

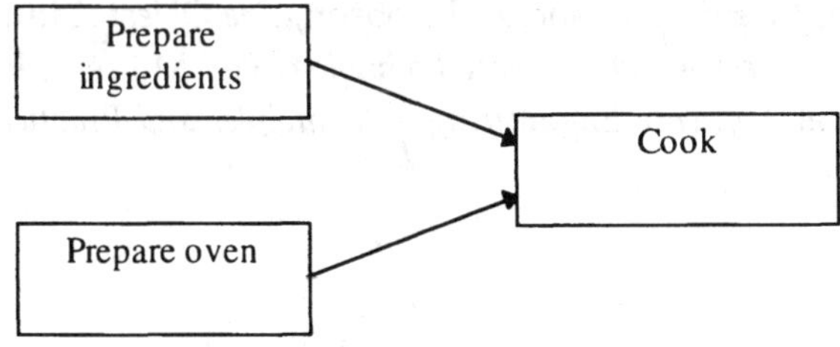

Figure 8 PERT chart

PERT charts play the same role as the matrices, since they summarize the information of the object-oriented diagrams. Moreover, PERT charts can be used to identify critical paths of activities. The cost of such paths can be assessed by means of the ABC methodology. Alternatives can be looked for and the advantages or disadvantages of a change can be evaluated.

References

1. S. Bandinelli and A. Fuggetta, Computational reflection in software process modeling: the SLANG approach, *Proceedings of the Fifteenth International Conference on Software Engineering* (Baltimore, USA, 1993).
2. R. S. Kaplan and D. P. Norton, The balanced scorecard — measures that drive performances, *Harvard Business Review*, January-February 1992, 71–79.
3. S. Bandinelli, A. Fuggetta and C. Ghezzi, Software processes as real time systems: a case study using high-level petri nets, *Proceedings of the International Phoenix Conference on Computers and Communications* (Arizona, April 1992).
4. S. Bandinelli, A. Fuggetta, C. Ghezzi and S. Grigolli, Process enactment in SPADE, *Proceedings of the Second European Workshop on Software Process Technology*, Trodheim, Norway (Springer-Verlag, 1992).
5. S. Bandinelli, M. Braga, A. Fuggetta and L. Lavazza, The architecture of the SPADE-1 process-centered SEE, *Third European Workshop on Software Process Technology* (Grenoble, France, 1994).
6. S. D. Conte, H. E. Dunsmore and V.-Y. Shen, Software engineering metrics and models (Benjamin/Cummings Publishing Company, 1988).
7. I. Jacobson, M. Ericsson and A. Jacobson, *The Object Advantage —Business Process Reengineering with Object Technology* (ACM Press, 1994).
8. H. Van Vliet, *Software Engineering — Principles and Practice* (John Wiley & sons, 1993).

PART III

PUBLIC SECTOR EXPERIENCE

Chapter 12

Reengineering Practice in Singapore's Public Sector

CHAN MENG KHOONG
Centre for Strategic Process Innovation, National Computer Board,
71 Science Park Drive, Singapore 118253, Republic of Singapore
E-mail: chanmeng@ncb.gov.sg

In recent years, there has been marked increase in business process reengineering practice in Singapore's public sector. The 'PS21 — Public Service for the 21st Century' *movement, championed at high levels of government, is a key factor behind this phenomenon. This paper examines the application of reengineering to the Singapore public sector context, and discusses some critical success factors. We also present a holistic enterprise model and a change implementation framework, which has been used successfully in assisting several public sector agencies in their reengineering efforts.*

1. Introduction

The public sector in Singapore has been recognized as a major competitive advantage for the country. The efficiency of the public sector is a key enabling factor in Singapore's economic growth, because all economic activity of a domestic or international nature will have government functions as part of the entire process.

In the 1980s, computerization was aggressively pursued throughout the sector with generous government financing, bringing about the first 'S' curve in performance enhancement. In the early 1990s, effects of a plateau in the 'S' curve were beginning to be felt. In a sense, the returns from early computerization were reaching the limits, and radical innovations were sought that would bring about a second 'S' curve. This search for excellence received a major boost in 1995 with the launch of the high-powered *'PS21 — Public Service for the 21st Century'* movement in Singapore [1]. PS21 committees, staffed by very senior civil servants, were formed to drive service improvement and process innovation initiatives across the public sector [2]. All public sector agencies were also tasked to set new service performance targets and to undertake their own internal PS21 initiatives (e.g., [3, 4]).

A cornerstone strategy in PS21 is the *autonomous agency* (AA) concept [5], which converts most public sector agencies into entities that are more like business corporations, with autonomy in operations, employment policies, and expenditure control, and with budgets based on results promised for public services to be delivered. When the AA concept is fully implemented by the end of 1997, the central government is implicitly downsized, and the offering of some public services will be open to competition as well.

Such developments in Singapore's public sector have led to greatly expanded interest in business process reengineering (BPR) in government. Pioneering success stories are found in the Inland Revenue Authority of Singapore [6], the Tan Tock Seng Hospital [7], the Work Permit Department [8], and the Immigration Department. Today the BPR approach to public sector innovation is being pursued at the agency level, cross-ministry level, as well as the national level, fueled in particular by rapid changes in information technology.

In response to the escalating demand for BPR assistance, the Centre for Strategic Process Innovation (CSPI) was established in 1995, operating as an intra-government resource for BPR consultancy, research, and knowledge repository. To date, CSPI has facilitated BPR initiatives in agencies of half a dozen ministries, and has also provided inputs into cross-ministry and national-level BPR. The discussion in the rest of this paper reflects CSPI's experience in reengineering the Singaporean public sector.

This paper is organized as follows. The relevance of BPR to the public sector is examined, with reference to some cases in the Singapore context. Critical success factors for public sector BPR are discussed, based on our experience with these cases. We propose a holistic enterprise model that forms the centerpiece of the change blueprint arising from BPR. A framework for change implementation is also discussed. We have applied the enterprise model and implementation framework successfully in public sector BPR projects. We conclude with some remarks on the scenarios for public sector process management.

2. Relevance of BPR to Public Sector Practices

Besides PS21 movement and the autonomous agency concept, there are various other factors that have motivated the application of BPR to the public sector in Singapore. These factors include:

- *Restructuring*. From time to time, roles and responsibilities among agencies are rationalized. Mergers and splits of agencies may take place, and BPR is used to see how the resultant new organizations may be operationalized.
- *IT and other infrastructural revamps*. Such revamps are often trigger points for BPR as they provide opportunities for a clean-slate approach in process and information management.
- *Relocation/renovation*. This is also a good trigger point for BPR, in particular for restructuring and for putting into place new resource management strategies.
- *Performance concerns*. These are natural reasons for undertaking BPR, especially when incremental improvement approaches have failed to create significant impact on process performance.

- *Quest for world-class excellence.* Champions for world-class excellence in service delivery embrace the BPR paradigm easily. While these champions are often the politicians and very senior civil servants, the younger middle managers in the public sector are also increasingly motivated.
- *National/government-wide IT initiatives.* The government in Singapore is building up a national information infrastructure riding on the internet backbone. This infrastructure enables new ways for the government to interact and transact with industry and the public. Within the public sector, opportunities to streamline communications and workflow are enabled through the government-wide Lotus Notes implementation.

As is the case for BPR projects in general, public sector practices will benefit from BPR if the following principles are subscribed to:

- *Taking a fundamental re-look at ways in which work is being done.* Re-examining the ways people execute physical and knowledge activities, handle information, interface with internal and external partners, and use equipment and tools in their work.
- *Harnessing radical ideas and 'out-of-the-box' thinking.* Harvesting the 'creative juice' of management and staff in envisioning and designing the ideal business processes.
- *Aiming for quantum-leap improvements in time, cost, quality, value measures.* Exploiting the concept of stretch targets to eradicate sacred cows from mindsets of management and staff.
- *Vision-directed change.* Linking the performance of business processes to corporate mission and vision, and developing new corporate-level strategies for organizational excellence.
- *Organizing around outcomes rather than tasks.* Breaking down functional silos and reconfiguring the deployment of human resources to serve the desired outcomes of business processes better.
- *Building process orientation and customer focus.* Inculcating process thinking, viewing each process from end to end as beginning and ending with an external customer, and focusing the desired

outcomes of processes around the needs of customers and stakeholders.

- *Adopting a holistic approach to implementing and managing change.* Inculcating systems thinking, developing deep understanding of the interconnected causes and effects of various elements of the corporate 'organism.'
- *Using technology to enable new processes and capabilities.* Exploiting the latest IT innovations to enable the transformation, rather than to automate old habits.

In a separate paper, we show that the many variations and combinations of reengineering strategies in the public sector can be normalized into a taxonomy of reference models [9]. Depending on the nature of application of the model and the impact derived, the models may be classified as operational, tactical, strategic, or catalytic. Operational models are applied to front-line operations of the organization, with direct and immediate but not necessarily high impact. Tactical models are applied to medium-term initiatives, with direct but delayed and moderate impact. Strategic models are applied to long-term strategies, with direct and high but much delayed impact. Catalytic models do not directly implement change, but create environments within which high-impact change can be facilitated over time. The appropriate combination of models needs to be applied synergistically, possibly at different stages of the reengineering exercise. Near-term impact models (operational, tactical) can also be positioned as supporting long-term impact models (strategic, catalytic) within a broader reengineering agenda at the national or international level.

3. Some Public Sector BPR Projects

We highlight here some major BPR initiatives undertaken by the public sector in Singapore. These BPR projects were all executed successfully at the corporate level, subscribed to the principles discussed in the previous section, and involved a holistic treatment of hard and soft organizational issues, above and beyond the streamlining of processes.

3.1. *An infrastructure regulation agency*

Physical infrastructure projects require approval of their plans from this agency. The old approval process used to take 3–6 months to turn around, and often resulted in many cycles of re-submissions and hand-offs within the agency to handle different parts of project plans. The new approval process is expected to reduce the turnaround time eventually to 1 day. The new process depends on a coordinated strategy that involves self-regulation, introduction of a new workflow system linked to the national information infrastructure, introduction of a formal consultancy service, and consolidation of public interfaces into a one-stop, common-counters area. At the moment the process turnaround time has already been reduced to 1–4 weeks, the one-stop service centre is operational, and the consultancy service has been put in place.

3.2. *An employment regulation agency*

The BPR project covered the complete cycle from application, collection, to cancellation and renewal. A new process that hinges on an internet-based submission system has been designed, that reduces the application turnaround time from more than 7 days to 1 day, the number of trips that employers need to make to the agency from 5 to 1, and waiting time for counter service from 2 hours to 30 minutes. The blueprint was rigorously validated through a second phase of modeling and simulation, and the process redesign refined as change implementation was in progress, including the optimal configuration for a one-stop service counter. Today, a one-day in-principle approval for applications is in place, and the customer service facilities have been overhauled.

3.3. *A retail clearance agency*

This project comprised a ministry-level envisioning exercise, followed by analysis and redesign of core business processes for the clearance of some classes of goods for retail purposes. The outcome of the project was a BPR blueprint providing a quantum leap redesign of the clearance processes, reducing turnaround times from 1 month to within 4 days. The blueprint also included introduction of new workflow and data capture capabilities in the systems, realignment of responsibilities among staff, cross training, increased self-regulation, organizational restructuring, relocation, and policy change. At the moment, a one-stop customer service point has been established, staff have been cross-trained, some policy changes have taken effect, and process performance has been improving.

3.4. *A public hospital*

Accidents & Emergency (A&E) services form a major component of this hospital's business. A BPR study of the A&E process was commissioned in light of the ongoing renovation of the hospital and implementation of new IT systems. The BPR approach took a holistic view of patient flows from entry into, till exit from, the hospital. The BPR blueprint showed that end-to-end A&E service turnaround time can be reduced by 60% and waiting time by 75%, while administrative time savings by nurses can be about 50%, volume of paper handled can be reduced by 80%, and efficiencies of various departments involved in the process expected can increase by between 25% and 60%. More than 20 immediate improvement actions, with impact on process performance, were implemented early in the BPR project. The hospital's renovation plans and IT system requirements were also modified to take into account the BPR recommendations.

3.5. *An information services agency*

Building upon a long-range national vision, the agency embarked on a BPR project to optimize its core business processes. The focus areas for BPR were in information source development, information circulation, service delivery, and the setup of service outlets. The BPR blueprint arising from the project offers new process designs with quantum leap innovations that range from 4.5× to 24× improvement in turnaround times. Direct cost savings for the agency arising from BPR is expected to exceed $20 million over 5 years, and indirect economic gains on the part of its customers is expected to be in the range of $90 million. The change implementation process includes restructuring, the development of strategic IT applications, business development models, and supply chain management alliances.

4. Critical Success Factors for Public Sector BPR

Based on our experiences in the Singapore public sector, we have identified the following critical success factors, which should be generally applicable to public sectors in most countries:

- *Top management sponsorship.* In the Singapore context, the resolve of the agency CEO or ministerial Permanent Secretary is often needed to get the project going. Top management sponsorship is the single most critical success factor.
- *Involvement of all levels of management.* In the public sector, senior managers are often rotated across appointments and across agencies. It is thus important to involve all levels of management to insure continuity of the project.

- *Adopting a top-bottom-middle-out approach.* It is not possible to reengineer an organization in a purely top-down manner. Specific processes need to be identified. However, it is often not practical to study all processes at once. Some processes need to be selected for the BPR pilot, based on an initial top-down analysis. After the pilot processes have been studied bottom-up, a consolidation and review (middle-out approach) can take place to extend the reach of BPR implementation to encompass other business areas.
- *Adequate preparation before BPR.* Preparation for BPR is often overlooked. From educational and promotional activities to psychological 'tuning,' the range of preparatory activities needed can take up as much time as the BPR study proper. The importance of this preparation is examined in detail in a separate paper [10].
- *Government investment in infrastructure.* Public sector agencies normally cannot implement radical change on their own, but require linkages with other agencies and with the industry and the public at large to be addressed as well. Thus government-wide or national infrastructures must be in place. Such infrastructures cannot always be justified on commercial terms in the near term, and thus require government investment.
- *Hands-on, high-involvement approach.* We believe that useful BPR results cannot be achieved without the project team being hands-on into the details of operational activities. Management must similarly be highly involved, in order for them to know enough to be able to add value and make decisions that lead to the change blueprint.
- *Use of rigorous methodologies and tools.* There is much complexity to be managed in the BPR exercise. For instance, fully developed process maps often require A0-size paper (16 sheets of A4 paper) to be plotted on. Without methodologies and tools, the BPR project may run into productivity problems.
- *Public sector contextual sensitivity.* Reengineering application in the public sector differs from the private sector in various ways. Also, the experience from public sector cases in a different culture may not be readily applicable as well.

- *Understanding the downside of not doing BPR*. Public sector employees that see the BPR project as a directive from management would naturally ask about the downside of doing BPR. Employees need first of all to be convinced that there is a downside for *not* doing BPR. Once convinced, the costs and benefits of BPR will be ascertained through the project.
- *Change management follow-through*. The point when the BPR project crosses over from planning to implementation is a very risky period. This is often the time when external consultants terminate their involvement with the organization, and the time when senior management entrust the details of implementation to junior employees.

In addition to these factors, we have also previously developed a taxonomy of pitfalls to avoid [11]. This taxonomy is based on our experience as well as findings from published literature.

Invariably, BPR projects also uncover and eradicate many 'little habits' that, collectively, can mean big trouble for a public sector organization in its quest for excellence. These little habits include:

- *Hand-offs that go on for miles and miles*. Functional decomposition results in work being handed off from person to person in the process, often slowing the process, introducing errors, and diffusing responsibility. Process redesign can often reduce the number of hand-offs to half or less.
- *Layers and layers of checks and controls*. Traditionally, checks and controls are placed to insure that policies and procedures are adhered to. Unfortunately, they often fail to add value toward process deliverables, and instead thicken the bureaucracy, multiply the overheads, and overwhelm the employees. Process redesign can often reduce the number of layers to half or less.
- *Working with too little, too much, or erroneous information*. Despite the pervasiveness of IT productivity tools, human habits 'die hard' as far as the handling of information is concerned.

- *Not doing the right thing right the first time.* Doing the right thing wrong causes rework and customer satisfaction problems. Doing the wrong thing right (e.g. due to misinterpretation of objectives) causes even deeper problems.
- *Not processing information or making decisions at places where it makes the most sense.* Very often, the reasons for placement of information processing and decision making points are historical rather than practical.
- *Not optimizing the process from end to end.* A process is a set of activities that, taken together, produce a deliverable of value to a customer. Very often, employees are too caught up with their tasks to appreciate the process from end to end, starting and ending with the external customer.

5. A Holistic Enterprise Model

Our methodology for public sector BPR emphasizes a holistic treatment of all organizational issues. The methodology views reengineering as applicable not only to operational processes in the physical organization, but also to the partnerships and strategies in the encapsulating virtual organization. The holistic enterprise model is reflected in Fig. 1. The starting point of the methodology is a decomposition of the holistic enterprise model, while the ending point of the methodology is the assembly of the future enterprise model. The enterprise model comprises:

- The organization's raison d'être, or equivalently, core purpose. The raison d'être defines the organization's reasons for its existence, as governed by its social responsibility, and accountability to stakeholders. The raison d'être should reflect the 'eternal soul' of the organization. Very often mission statements put forth by public sector organizations have some (but insufficient) elements of their raison d'être.

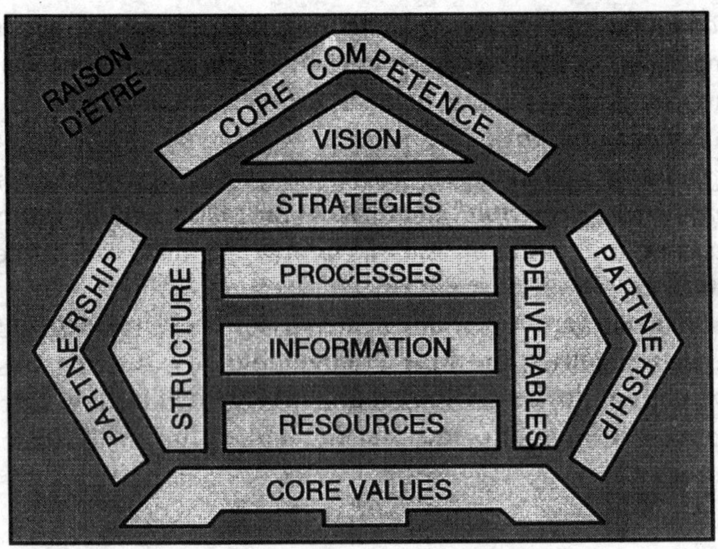

Figure 1 The holistic enterprise model

- The organization's core competence. The culture of public sector organizations has been such that the notion of core competence has rarely been addressed. However, in view of the inevitable need to right-size the government, core competence needs to be recognized as the basis on which to focus the limited resources of the organization.
- Vision, expressed in terms of the future level of excellence to be attained, and a time frame for the attainment. The corporate-level vision statement has to be translated into performance stretch targets for specific processes. The process of developing the vision statement and stretch targets may be called envisioning.
- Strategies, to move the organization from the current state toward the state expressed in the vision. The strategies must translate into operational processes, and must be dynamically adaptable to changes in the external environment in the future. We emphasize that these strategies are emergent from the entire reengineering project, rather than just a product of the envisioning exercise.

- The partnerships surrounding the organization, including customers (internal and external to the government), suppliers (internal and external to the government), and policy makers. The external customer is the most important category and should be segmented, and the various segments should be prioritized.
- The deliverables that the organization exchanges with its partners. These outputs need to be connected with outcomes that partners should derive from receiving them.
- The core business processes used in the organization to generate the said deliverables to the said customer segments. A process is a set of *activities* that, taken together, produce a *deliverable* of *value* to a *customer*.
- Information flows. Very often, information flows are a root problem and solution — be it lack of information, excess of information, information inaccuracies, or information flow bottlenecks.
- Resources (to be made) available in the organization. These include human resources, machines, material, and floor space. In the public sector, the lack of resources is often raised as a process problem, but the real issue may be capability.
- Structure, which includes the formal hierarchy as well as less formal setups such as committees, task forces, and discussion fora. In the public sector, informal setups are often used as channels to work around the red tape imposed on formal setups.
- Core values, often referred to as organizational culture, which are guiding principles for the way work should be carried out in the organization. Core values are intrinsic in nature and can be independent of external justifications. Core values provide an enduring form of spiritual bonding; they must be preached, and must be lived from day to day.

6. Change Implementation Framework

The change blueprint contains the future enterprise model and an implementation plan to realize the blueprint. The implementation plan should stipulate the transition strategy and implementation schedule and responsibilities for all aspects of the future enterprise model.

At the heart of change implementation is a conversion of the organization from a vertical, functional 'silo' into a horizontal, process-based setup. The conversion can be analyzed along two orthogonal axes, namely process integration and functional integration. To simplify the discussion of the framework, we consider the case of integrating two processes and two functions. A process may be duplicated or broken along two functions. We use the term 'function' generically, which may refer to sections, departments, divisions, or even agencies.

The change transition is illustrated in Fig. 2. In practice it is not possible to jump from the current state (A) into the future state of total integration (D). If the transition involves only functional integration (B), then the change may be cosmetic. If the transition involves only process integration (C), then the change is logical but may not be physical. The change implementation plan should be designed to move

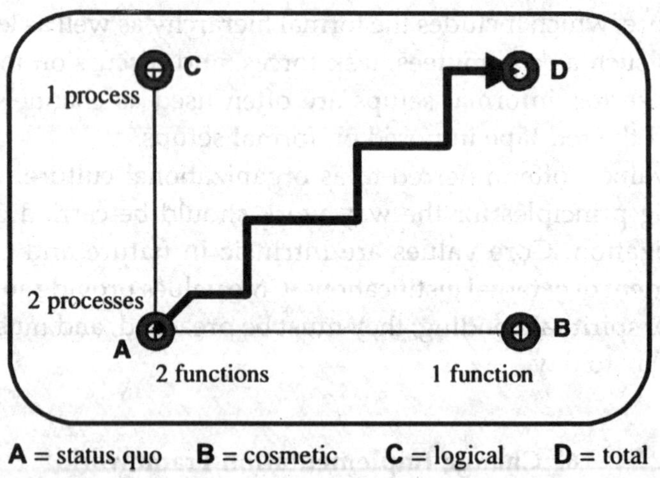

Figure 2 Evolution of BPR implementation. A, B, C, D are four possible final states of a merger between two entities

the organization efficiently toward total integration, while taking into consideration policy and operational constraints along the way. While policy issues normally take a while to be addressed, the organization must nevertheless bootstrap change implementation as soon as possible after the BPR planning phase.

Along the process integration axis, implications that need to be addressed in the implementation plan include:

- Location & layout
- Capabilities at counters & other public interfaces
- IT & other infrastructural capabilities
- Training road maps, including cross-training
- Alignment of standards
- Alignment of fee structures
- Amendments to laws and policies governing activities
- Internal cost management.

Along the functional integration axis, implications that need to be addressed in the implementation plan include:

- Organizational structure
- Job descriptions and career road maps
- Amendments to laws and policies governing roles and responsibilities
- Public relations initiatives — physical, print, electronic, etc.
- Public and political impacts
- External (customer) cost management.

The scope of integration may also need to be strategized. The processes that have been studied in the BPR project may have different end-points in the integration. It is also possible that integration takes effect at different times for different parts of the process. For instance, integration may first take place in the back-end administrative support functions, then at the front-end counter services and standards and guidelines used by the public, and finally along the actual processing activities behind the counters.

7. Future Vistas

The proliferation of BPR practice to the public sector in Singapore is still at the tip of the iceberg. By the end of 1997, 113 public sector agencies will operate autonomously. To date, at least a dozen or so among these have exploited the BPR paradigm to rethink their business processes. We expect a reasonable level of internalization in process thinking throughout the public sector before the turn of the century. Some convergence of public and private sector practices may also be expected.

As new processes take shape in individual agencies, inter-agency and sector-wide BPR initiatives will also begin to gain momentum. Although cross-agency initiatives should ideally be undertaken even before individual agencies re-look at their internal processes, practical considerations often make it difficult to do so. The effects of cross-agency initiatives will in turn feed back into intra-agency efforts. The cycle of change, once started, has become constant, if not accelerating.

While this paper has focused on the Singapore context, we believe that the framework discussed herein will be generally applicable to other public sector contexts as well.

References

1. Z. Ibrahim, Public service embarks on mission of excellence, *The Straits Times*, May 6, 1995.
2. Prime minister's office, public service for the 21st century (PS21), see http://www.gov.sg/ps21/.
3. National Registry Dept aims for better service, *The Straits Times*, April 18, 1996.
4. New police pledge to meet needs of better-educated Singaporeans, *The Straits Times*, January 26, 1997.
5. B. S. Koh, Whole civil service gets autonomy from this month, *The Straits Times*, April 9, 1997.
6. S. S. Emanuel, Reengineering for Mr Taxman, *Computerworld*, January 12–18, (1996) 20–21.

7. Reengineering a hospital, *The Straits Times,* November 6, 1996.
8. New $2.2m computer cuts work-permit processing time, *The Straits Times,* July 31, 1996.
9. C. M. Khoong, Models for public sector reengineering, *Proceedings of the International Conference Advances in Management,* Toronto, July 9–12, 1997.
10. C. M. Khoong, A framework for executing reengineering step zero, *International Journal of Business Performance Management,* Vol. 1, 1998, to appear.
11. C. M. Khoong, Culture-sensitive, strategy-level reengineering, *INFOR* **34,** (1996) 43–56.
12. J. Champy, *Reengineering Management: The Mandate for New Leadership* (Harper Collins, New York, 1995).
13. T. H. Davenport, *Process Innovation: Reengineering Work Through Information Technology* (Harvard Business School Press, Boston, MA, 1993).
14. M. Hammer and S. A. Stanton, *The Reengineering Revolution* (Harper Collins, New York, 1995).
15. D. Osborne and T. Gaebler, *Reinventing Government: How the Entrepreneurial Spirit is Transforming the Public Sector* (Addison-Wesley, Reading, MA, 1992).

Chapter 13

Reengineering Records and Information Management in the US Department of Defense: A Success Story

DARYLL R. PRESCOTT

Electronic Evidence Discovery, Inc. 6800 Versar Center,
Springfield VA 22151 USA
E-mail: corpsvcs@eedinc.com

The US Department of Defense, sponsored by the Assistant Secretary of Defense (Command, Control, Communications, and Intelligence) and funded through the Corporate Information Management program, has completed the reengineering process of its records management program. The program began in August 1993, published its last report in November 1996, and began test, evaluation and certification testing in 1997. Using IDEF0 and IDEF1X models, Functional Baseline Requirements for Records Management Application Software were established.

The requirements were enhanced to include additional functionality identified by experts at the University of British Columbia, Vancouver, Canada. During this same time, review of the program results by individuals from the National Archives and Records Administration and other Federal agencies suggested the results of the program could be a model for other agencies. Consequently, a testbed facility at the Center for Army Lessons

Learned, Fort Leavenworth, Kansas, coordinated by the National Media Laboratory, has been established.

Currently the Defense Information Systems Agency, Joint Interoperability Test Center, Fort Huachuca, Arizona is administering the first ever Records Management Application Certification Test and Evaluation program. It will test compliance with requirements established by the reengineering effort and specifically derived from the IDEF0 and IDEF1X models.

1. Established Objectives

The original project objectives [1] were to:

- Develop standard Department of Defense Retention Schedules.
- Reduce the number of retention periods used throughout the Department.
- Migrate to a single, standard coding scheme.
- Develop standard functional and automated system requirements.
- Incorporate records management requirements into all automated information systems development and redesign.
- Develop standard requirements for voice and e-mail records.

During the period of August 1993 through July 1996, additional objectives were added as a direct result of collaborative research with several academic institutions, government research laboratories, the National Archives and Records Administration, and other US Government Agencies. Additional objectives were identified as being necessary to implement a working program. They were:

- Create records management policy independent of technology.
- Develop procedures that are technology dependent.
- Develop training plans to insure an understanding of procedures.
- Generate audit mechanisms that document compliance.
- Establish an information architecture and migration plan.

- Establish a media migration plan that insures the economic maintenance and management of digitally stored information.
- Standardize policy for the backup of digital information.
- Establish standards for document conversion.
- Meet US Government Information Locator Service requirements.

2. The Department of Defense (DoD) Records Management Task Force

During 1993 and 1994, a DoD Records Management Business Process Reengineering (BPR) effort resulted in function and information models depicting streamlined activities that Department employees would perform by the year 2003. By the end of 1994, it became evident that additional models were necessary in order to fully realize the original intent of the reengineering effort: *Develop a single process for implementation across the entire Department.*

In January 1995, members of the Army, Navy, Air Force, National Security Agency, and the Defense Logistics Agency formed the core of the Task Force. Early into the year, Task Force members expanded their efforts and looked to academic professionals for help and answers. It was at this time that Dr. Kenneth Thibodeau, Director, Center for Electronic Records, National Archives and Records Administration (NARA), assumed the position of Director of the Task Force. Dr. Thibodeau's years of experience and leadership, along with newly formed academic relationships, would meet the goal of expanding the work to include Archival Science and Diplomatics.

3. University of British Columbia (UBC)

In 1995, the scope of work broadened to include consideration of research in Archival Science addressing requirements for electronic recordkeeping. These experts are working on a project addressing

"The Preservation of the Integrity of Electronic Records," funded by the Social Sciences and Humanities Research Council of Canada [2]. Their continuing research addresses the application of Archival Science and Diplomatics [3] to the derivation of functional and information requirements for electronic record-keeping to preserve the authenticity and reliability of electronic records [4].

4. Automated Records Management Systems

In December 1993, *The 47 Functional Requirements* were created from the first models developed by DoD participants [5]. This document evolved in 1995 into the first set of requirements for electronic records management software that were considered reasonable and testable. Task Force members determined that for this project *reasonable* meant that there was a high probability that over 50% of Commercial Off The Shelf (COTS) software could meet or exceed the initial set of requirements. The document established that any records management application sold to the Department:

- Meet a common set of functional requirements that insure the authenticity and reliability of digital records.
- Is certified that it supports the functional requirements for a given architecture, e.g. operating system, hardware, software.
- Has an estimated life-cycle cost.
- Can support the protocols and procedures established for interfacing with the Departments Defense Messaging System.

The report was the first of its kind within the US Federal Government and was reviewed immediately by many agencies for their use. In particular, the National Archives and Records Administration and the General Services Administration reviewed it as a basis for establishing government-wide standards for records management software.

5. Functional Requirements Derived from IDEF0 and IDEF1X Models

In 1995, Prescott, Kindl and Underwood would be the first to propose testable functional requirements and data elements to be used by the Department when purchasing automated Records Management Application (RMA) software [6]. The authors recognized early on that because of the broad-based nature of the requirements, it would be necessary for each organization to supplement the baseline set of requirements with mission specific requirements. The requirements allow maximum flexibility in software development while insuring that responses are testable. Activity and data models from the Department's reengineering effort were used as the genesis of the document. The document's intention was to constrain and to bind the requirement to insure standardization and although data elements are identified, it was not intended to specify the data type format.

There are two generic constraints on the RMA.

1. The RMA shall manage all organizational records regardless of storage media or other characteristics.
2. The RMA shall implement records management procedures to insure that authentic and reliable records are captured and preserved.

The first specifies the domain of the application. The second specifies the primary function of the application. The term *organizational record* is a departure from official record in that it connotes both the original and any migrated versions.

6. Implementation Derived from the Reengineering Effort

6.1. Real-world test and evaluation

Fort Leavenworth, Kansas will become the first test facility in the United States to incorporate and evaluate the best of class from industry and government for managing digital information. This evaluation will bring the right commercial technology to the government to get the right information to the right people at the right place at the right time.

Part of the initial focus will be on government-owned systems and software in support of Executive Order #12958. EO#12958 mandates the declassification of Federal records in excess of 25 years of age that will not jeopardize national security.

The testbed will incorporate the best components from the Central Intelligence Agency, Department of State, Department of Defense, Department of Energy and others. It will allow a single place to evaluate the value added and cost benefit to taxpayers of managing records under the concepts and standards of the DOD-STD-5015.2 Records Management Application Design Criteria Standard [7].

6.2. Test objectives

- Manage information as records.
    - Incorporate records management principles established in the Baseline Requirements for Records Management Application Software.
    - DoD Automated Document Conversion Master Plan.
    - Design Criteria Standard for Records Management Application Functional Baseline Requirements (DoD-STD-5015.2).
    - National Archives and Records Administration recommendation and guidelines [6].
- Incorporate automated tools for declassification of digitally stored records.
- Provide multi-level security access and distribution of digitally stored records.
- Develop and incorporate functional tools for:
    - Automated tool for record category and disposition.
    - User available classification guides.
    - Automated audit trails for document review and handling.

- Leverage existing digital library initiatives.
- Develop programs for multi-agency review and redaction of digitally stored records to insure *review once, use many times* concept can be realized.
- Share and transfer lessons learned to government agencies and industry.

6.3. *Worldwide mail messaging*

The Department is implementing a new worldwide architecture for its military mail messaging, the Defense Messaging System (DMS). The DMS Program Management Office recognized early in the design phase that records management considerations needed to be documented at the conception and development stages in order to implement them when the systems becomes operational.

The DMS protocols and procedures provide email systems:

- Are a transfer mechanism.
- Are for the point to point movement of digital information.
- Are neither designed for nor meant to be used as a records management system.
- Include the protocols for moving email out of the email system into a certified records management system.

There are only two types of mail messages:

- Organizational Mail Message (OMM)
  - Command and control.
  - Commits an organization.
  - Used as a release authority.
  - Used to determine mail message distribution.
  - All OMMs are identified and managed as organizational records.
- Individual Mail Message (IMM)
  - Sent between individuals.

- Does NOT commit or direct an organization.
- Used as a basic transport service.
- May be an organizational record.

The architecture and protocols are defined in the Allied Communications Plan (ACP) 123. The ACP 123 also specifies a content type (P772) adequate for military messaging. It has been adopted by the several NATO and other US allied nations. The US supplement to the ACP 123 specifies extensions that are necessary for DoD messaging and declare protocols and procedures for passing email that is a record to a certified RMA.

The US supplement to the ACP 123 proposes records management interoperability and protocol requirements for interface between an RMA and the DMS. DMS features the concept of a Records Management User Agent (RMUA) interfaced to an RMA that will receive and file records sent as messages and respond to requests for records by transmitting them via the DMS. Other features include the use of distribution code parameters in the header for recording classification code and message type. The US Supplement to ACP 123 also specifies the two aforementioned types of mail messages, Organizational Mail Message (OMM) and Individual Mail Message (IMM). The two mail message types are unique and designated to provide separate and distinct functions for the Department of Defense.

6.4. *DoD design criteria for testing software*

The Department has adopted and is utilizing the requirements established in the Functional Baseline Requirements and Data Elements for Records Management Application Software to develop the Department of Defense Design Criteria Standard for Records Management Application Functional Baseline Requirements DoD-STD-5015.2 [7].

The standard defines the minimum requirements for records management application software to satisfy operational requirements, the law, and federal regulations. The standard is not intended to be all inclusive. In fact, both documents state that additional operational requirements must be added to insure specific mission activities are supported.

DoD-STD-5015.2 defines the minimal functional requirements and data elements necessary to manage records throughout their life-cycle. A major challenge for the standard is to insure software purchased by the Department complies with legislation and policy directives, and supports records disposition schedules. The standard is implemented and applicable to all software that manages records regardless of the medium of storage.

The standard is meant to insure compliance with the NARA-issued regulations of August 1995 for managing email messages [6], 36 CFR, the Federal Records Act (44 USC.) and other applicable requirements.

The DoD-STD-5015.2 defines the basic requirements based on operation, legislation and legal needs that must be met by records management application (RMA) products that are acquired by the Department of Defense and its Components. The focus of the RMA is to enable the DoD to achieve its mission effectively and efficiently by providing access to information whenever and wherever needed.

The standard identifies features required for filing and retrieving records particularly in digital media. The standard covers three types of requirements:

Mandatory and implemented by the RMA.

- Mandatory, but may be implemented through another application.
- Not mandatory, but provided as information to assist in the acquisition of usable RMAs.

The standard test suite is maintained and managed by the Defense Information Systems Agency (DISA) Joint Interoperability Test Command (JITC).

7. The Beginning

The original director of the reengineering effort, Colonel Greg Florey, US Air Force, once wrote that the reengineering effort was just the warm up before the baseball game. It wasn't the start of the game yet. Since the reengineering efforts last publication in November 1996, there has been continued interest within the software development industry and from other governments and their agencies outside the United States.

The National Media Laboratory and the Test Facility at Fort Leavenworth, Kansas will test and insure that what is believed to be valid within the models and their subsequent functional requirements, can actually perform in a real-world environment.

The Defense Information System Agency, Joint Interoperability Test Center, Fort Huachuca, Arizona has begun evaluating software for procurement within the Department of Defense. Industry software developers and integrators are watching closely the performance and use of the certification process. The current certification will be enhanced when testing at Fort Leavenworth yields insight.

Between these two programs and the continued coordination with organizations such as the National Archives and Records Administration, the Department's Reengineering effort will undoubtedly be claimed as a success as it is evaluated by its future users.

References

1. US Department of Defense, Records management functional process improvement scoping session report (1993).
2. L. Duranti and H. MacNeil, The protection of electronic records: an overview of the UBC-MAS research project, *Archivaria* **43** (1996) 46–67 (see also www.slais.ubc.ca/users/duranti).
3. L. Duranti, Diplomatics: New uses for an old science, *Archivaria*, Part I, **28**, 7–27; Part II, **29**, 4–17; Part III, **30**, 4–20; Part IV, **31**, 10–25; Part V, **32**, 6–24; Part VI, **33**, 6–24 (1988–1992).

4. L. Duranti, Reliability and authenticity: the concepts and their implications, *Archivaria* **39** (1995).
5. US Department of Defense, DoD records management functional process improvement TO-BE report (1994).
6. D. Prescott, M. Kindl and W. Underwood, Functional baseline requirements and data elements for records management application software, Army Research Laboratory, Software Technology Branch, Atlanta, Georgia, (1995).
7. US Department of Defense, Design criteria standard for electronic records management software applications, DoD 5015.2-STD (1997) (*www.dtic.mil*).
8. National archives and records administration, electronic mail systems, *Federal Register* **60**(166), (1995) 44634–44642 (*www.nara.gov*).

Chapter 14

Extensions of IDEF Methodology Based on Reengineering Records Management

WILLIAM E. UNDERWOOD
Artificial Intelligence Atlanta, Inc. 119 E. Court Square, Decatur GA 30030 USA
E-mail: bunder4200@aol.com

L. DURANTI
School of Library, Archival and Information Studies, University of British Columbia, 831-1956 Main Mall, Vancouver BC Canada V6T 1Z1
E-mail: luciana@unixg.ubc.ca

DARYLL R. PRESCOTT
Electronic Evidence Discovery, Inc. 6800 Versar Center, Springfield VA 22151 USA
E-mail: corpsvcs@eedinc.com

M. KINDL
Army Research Laboratory, 115 O'Keefe, Georgia Institute of Technology, Atlanta GA 30332-0800 USA
E-mail: kindl@airmics.gatech.edu

This chapter identifies opportunities for improving Business Process Reengineering activities that are based on IDEF methodology. A method is sketched for developing a functional requirements specification from an IDEF0 activity model. Issues encountered in developing information and conceptual models for document structure, business activities and record categories are discussed. The concept of control completeness is introduced as a mechanism for developing and justifying an activity model. This concept is illustrated with experience in applying the principles of Archival Science and Diplomatics to the development of an activity model for records management.

1. Introduction

The US Department of Defense (DoD) has reengineered the process of managing its electronic records [1]. The IDEF0 modeling method was used to develop AS-IS and TO-BE business activity models for managing records. These models were developed by DoD experts in Records Management, Information Management, Computer Systems and Acquisition. IDEF1X was used to develop a model of information in the TO-BE activity model. Functional and information requirements for an electronic record-keeping system were derived from these models. The requirements were then formulated as a standard for testing and acquisition of software [2].

The DoD also collaborated with the School of Library, Archival and Information Studies at the University of British Columbia (UBC), Canada, in the development of IDEF activity and information models for *Manage Archival Fonds* [3, 4]. These models were developed by people conversant with the principles of Archival Science and Diplomatics.

The Army Research Laboratory has collaborated with the DoD and UBC in these efforts. It has also sought to reengineer the Army's records classification scheme and records schedule to support management of electronic records [5].

Figure 1 shows some of the IDEF methods used to support analysis and design during system development [6].

IDEF0	Function Modeling
IDEF1	Information Modeling
IDEF1X	Data Modeling
IDEF3	Process Design Capture
IDEF4	Object-Oriented Design
IDEF5	Ontology Description Capture

Figure 1 Suite of IDEF methods

This paper discusses issues encountered in deriving a functional requirement specification from an IDEF0 activity model. It also describes issues encountered in using IDEF1, IDEF1X and IDEF5 to develop information and conceptual models of document structure, business activities, and record categories. The concept of control completeness is introduced for the purpose of insuring completeness of activity and information models.

2. Activity Models and Functional Requirements

This section discusses the IDEF0 method, the need for a representation that describes the procedures controlling activities, the need for a standard representation of functional requirements, and a method for deriving functional requirements from an IDEF0 activity model.

2.1. *IDEF0*

IDEF0 is a method and graphical notation for modeling business activities [7]. One purpose of modeling business activities is to understand the structure of existing systems in order to identify through analysis opportunities for improving and automating some aspects of the activities.

The primary graphical device of IDEF0 is an ICOM, an acronym for Input-Control-Output-Mechanism (see Fig. 2). Arrows entering the left-side of an activity box are labeled with inputs to the activity. Arrows entering the top of an activity box are labeled with the controls of an activity. Arrows leaving an activity box on the right are labeled with the outputs. Arrows entering the activity box from the bottom are labeled with the mechanisms for performing the activity.

The method involves defining the ICOM of a primary activity and decomposing that activity into three to six sub-activities. The decomposition is continued until one reaches activities that can be defined by a procedure and need no further decomposition. A glossary is constructed that defines the inputs, controls, outputs, mechanisms and activities of the model.

An AS-IS activity model characterizes business activities as they are currently practiced. A TO-BE activity model is based on an analysis of the AS-IS model to identify opportunities for improvements in the

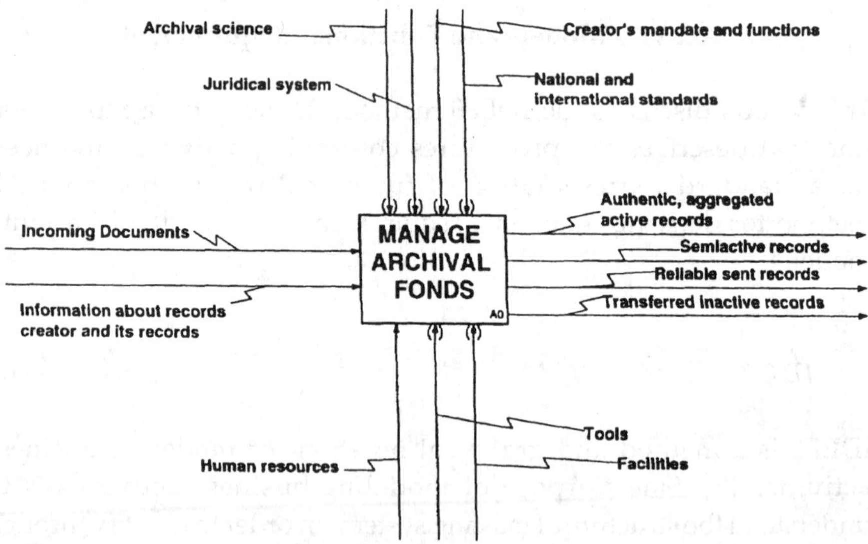

Figure 2 An ICOM for the primary activity Manage Archival Fonds

business activities through the redesign of activities or incorporation of new technologies.

2.2. *Definition of business activities*

IDEF0 prescribes that controls on the lowest-level activities be described as procedures, but does not prescribe a representation for these procedures. The DoD Records Management Task Force activity model for *Manage Records* described the lowest-level activities, but did not write procedures defining the function(s) performed at the lowest-level. If one of the purposes of the activity model is to specify functional requirements, procedures for the lowest-level activities must be defined so as to provide enough detail to generalize the required functions. Descriptions of activities are generally incomplete and often inconsistent. For the activity model to be useful, it must be complete and internally consistent.

Several representations have been proposed for specifying the procedures in activity models, for example, structured English, decision trees and tables, and finite state machines [8]. Structured English, also called pseudocode or program design language (PDL), is free-form English with reserved keywords with special meaning.

In the UBC/DoD activity model, procedures for controlling the lowest-level activities have been written in structured English. The procedures refer to the data elements that are parts of the inputs and outputs of the lowest-level activities.

2.3. *Functional requirements specified in natural language*

Figure 3 shows some functional requirements for Records Management Applications. The requirements are specified using natural language descriptions [2].

C2.2.2.1 RMAs shall provide users with the capability to select and assign a file code to a record.

C2.2.2.5 RMAs shall (for all records) capture or provide the user with the capability to assign, as appropriate, the following minimum profile data (metadata) when the record is filed:

Subject	Location of Record
Date Filed	Document Creation Date
Addressee(s)	Author or Originator
Media Type	Originating Organization
Format	Vital Records Indicator

C2.2.2.12 RMAs shall provide the capability to designate a record as a vital record.

C2.2.2.18 RMAs shall automatically date a document when it is saved as a record, and preserve the date of receipt on records received.

Figure 3 Example of functional requirements specified in natural language

It is best practice in the US Federal Government and the private sector to use natural language descriptions to specify functional requirements for systems. However, because they are descriptions, the functional requirements are often ambiguous, inconsistent, incomplete and redundant.

Requirement C2.2.2.1 prescribes the assignment of a file code to a record. Is file code a part of the profile data described in C2.2.2.5? In other words, requirement C2.2.2.5 may be incomplete.

Requirement C.2.2.2.5 describes attributes of the record profile that are output by the filing function. However, it does not specify the filing function. The requirement statement is ambiguous. There are many possible behaviors that could satisfy the statement, if it is a functional requirement. Possibly a better interpretation of the requirement is that it is an information requirement, that is, a statement of information that will be captured, maintained and retrieved by the system.

Requirement C2.2.2.12 states that the RMA should provide the capability to designate a record as a vital record — a record essential to the continued functioning of an organization during and after an emergency or to protecting the rights and interests of that organization and the individuals affected by its activities. Given requirement C.2.2.2.5, requirement C2.2.2.12 seems redundant.

Requirement C2.2.2.18 states that a RMA must date a document when it is saved as a record. Is this the same as *date filed* in requirement C2.2.2.5? Do these requirements inconsistently describe the same data element?

A better representation is needed for specifying functional requirements. Consider the functional requirement specified in Fig. 4.

This specification may or may not be what the writers of the specifications shown in Fig. 3 had in mind. However, the expression

```
MAIN FILING MENU
IF USER WANTS TO FILE A RECORD
THEN USER RECEIVES RECORD PROFILE DIALOG BOX
IF RECORD IS A PAPER DOCUMENT THEN
USER ENTERS FILE CODE
USER ENTERS SUBJECT
USER ENTERS ADDRESSEE(S)
USER ENTERS MEDIA TYPE
USER ENTERS FORMAT
USER ENTERS DOCUMENT CREATION DATE
USER ENTERS AUTHOR OR ORIGINATOR
USER ENTERS ORIGINATING ORGANIZATION
USER ENTERS VITAL RECORD INDICATOR
SYSTEM ASSIGNS & DISPLAYS UNIQUE RECORD IDENTIFIER
SYSTEM ASSIGNS & DISPLAYS CURRENT DATE AS DATE FILED
SYSTEM STORES RECORD PROFILE DATA
MAIN MENU
```

Figure 4 A functional requirement for filing specified as a stimulus-response sequence

in Fig. 4 is unambiguous and there are automated tools for determining whether such specifications are consistent, complete and non-redundant [8]. A similar specification can be written for filing e-mail messages and other document types.

2.4. *A method for functional requirements specification*

IDEF0 does not provide a method for specifying functional requirements. Nor is there any other IDEF method for specifying functional requirements. A method is sketched below for specifying functional requirements based on an IDEF0 TO-BE activity model.

1. The controls on the lowest-level activities of an IDEF0 model must be defined as procedures that reference the inputs and outputs of the activity. The procedures should distinguish operations performed by people from those performed by the system. The procedures can be described in Structured English (PDL), as decision trees and tables, or as finite state machines. Limiting description to one or more of these provides a standard format for procedural definition. There are software tools for checking conformance to the format and producing a data dictionary from the procedures.
2. The controls and mechanisms of the lowest-level activities should include the technologies envisioned to be applied in automating the activity.
3. The glossary of the IDEF0 activity model must include definitions of all inputs, outputs and data elements referenced in the procedure. This subset of the glossary is essentially a data dictionary.
4. Functional requirements are derived from the procedural specification of the lowest-level activities by translating the procedures into a representation determined by the following rules.

   a) If the system function involves user's dialog with the system and user-oriented external functions, then use a stimulus-response sequence to represent the functional requirement.

b) If the function is decision intensive or if outputs are a nontrivial combination of inputs, then use decision tables or PDL.
c) If the function requires synchronization, then use a Petri net.
d) If the system is an embedded system, then use the Process-oriented, Applicative, and Interpretable Specification Language (PAISLey).

The rules in step 4 are based on Davis's taxonomy of types of software applications and types of functional requirements representations appropriate to those types [8]. Also see Davis for a description of these representations.

The lowest-level activities in the UBC/DoD activity model that correspond to the electronic record-keeping system involve a dialog of the system with either an action officer or an office records manager. They are functions such as classify record, register record, consign record to central records system, retrieve record, copy record, and annotate record. Since these functions involve a dialog of the user with the system, stimulus-response sequences are the appropriate representation for specifying functional requirements. The functional requirements specification shown in Fig. 4 is an example of a stimulus-response sequence.

A standard functional requirements specification language is needed for describing functions of different complexity. The functional requirements specification method sketched above points the way to a generic functional requirements representation and method. Stimulus-response sequences, decision tables and PDL are no more difficult for users to understand than IDEF0 or IDEF1X models.

3. Information Models and Information Requirements

This section reviews the IDEF methods for information and conceptual modeling. Issues encountered in developing information models for document structure, business activities and record categories are also discussed.

3.1 *IDEF1, IDEF1X and IDEF5*

IDEF1 is a method and graphical notation for modeling, analysis and formulation of an organization's information requirements. The primary graphical notation is an *entity class* box naming a class of entities of the application domain and their common attribute classes. An *attribute class* is a set of attribute-value pairs formed by one attribute and the values of that attribute for entity class members (entities). An aggregation of one or more attribute classes, which allows one entity in an entity class to be distinguished from another, is called a *key class*. A key class appears at the top of an entity class box. A *relation class* is an association between two entity classes. Such associations are discovered by noting that an entity class includes a key class attribute of another entity class. Relation classes are represented by labeled links between entity classes in an IDEF1 diagram. Diamonds, circles and bullets at the ends of the links encode other information about the relation (e.g. cardinality and dependency).

IDEF1X is a method and graphical notation for designing relational databases [9]. IDEF1X is derived from the IDEF1 method. The DoD uses the IDEF1X method for the development of conceptual schema. A conceptual schema provides a single integrated definition of the data within an enterprise that is unbiased toward any single application and is independent of how the data is physically represented.

One of the rules of both the IDEF1 and IDEF1X methods is that information models apply only to information that will be managed by the system, that is, information that is stored, maintained and manipulated by the system. No other information will be available to the system.

IDEF5 is a modeling method and graphical notation that enables the representation of knowledge about the application domain that is not included in the information model. There are four types of diagrams used to represent concepts. Classification schematics show three types of classification relations: generalization/specialization, a kind of (AKO), and description subsumption. Relation schematics represent relations between classes. Composition schematics are a special type of relation schematic that represent part-whole relations. Finally, an r-square schematic shows the axiomatization of a relation in the model.

The IDEF5 method is being used to represent concepts such as agency, archival fonds, business activity and record category which are part of the theory of Archival Science. It also allows us to represent information that is in documents, but does not need to be represented explicitly in the information model unless it will be used by the system.

3.2. *Specifying document structure*

Documents that are input to the activity model for managing records have different structures. For instance, e-mail has fields for originator's address, addressee(s), subject, body and attachments. Memoranda, contracts, forms and other document types have different structures. If a system function is required to automatically capture attributes of a document (see requirement C2.2.2.5 in Fig. 3), the document structures must be specified.

If one models the document structure in IDEF1, the information in the documents themselves will be managed by the system. The information content of the document will be retrievable by the attributes characterizing the document's structure.

This concept is implemented in word-processing or publishing software as document styles or templates. Document specification languages such as SGML embed the description of the document structure in the document [10]. Document-based or object-oriented databases can index documents by the values in the text of the document. Such object-centered implementations eliminate the need for a redundant profile of the document and reduce inconsistencies that can arise with such redundant information.

This approach to representing document structure is being pursued by the Army Research Laboratory [5]. It requires modeling, specification and standardization of the types of electronic documents used in the US Army.

3.3. *The structure of business activities and record categories*

Record categories in agency file plans and record schedules are described by relating documents to the activities that receive, make or use the documents. These descriptions are often incomplete and inconsistent, due in part to the fact that they are descriptions rather than definitions [5].

Record category descriptions in the US Army's integrated record classification scheme and records schedule (MARKS) were analyzed. Syntactic and semantic models were specified for the structure of record category definitions and disposition instructions [5, 11]. Descriptions of record categories in MARKS were restructured according to these models. An automated capability to support categorization of documents and disposition of record categories according to the restructured descriptions was demonstrated [12].

IDEF1 and IDEF5 models have been developed that represent the structure of business activities, records, record categories and their relations [4, 13]. An implication of representing business activities in an IDEF1 information model is that the system can use the information about the activities to support the business activities themselves. If the information structure supports those business activities, the records management functions of associating a document with an activity, filing those documents, and retrieving them can be accomplished by the functions supporting the activities themselves. This implies a significant improvement in the records management activities — accomplishing records management activities as a by-product of supporting the primary business activities.

Among the difficulties encountered in modeling the information required is that IDEF1 and IDEF1X provide weak support of business rules — the rules relating entity classes such as activity, record and record category. The methods only provide for representing such rules as natural language descriptions in a glossary. Extensions to IDEF1 have been made to provide more explicit representations of business rules.

4. Justifying Activity and Information Models

In this section some concepts of Archival Science and Diplomatics are defined that are used to illustrate how activity and information models can be based on theories of the application domain and the other controls on the activities.

4.1. Archival science and diplomatics

Archival Science comprises the concepts, principles and methods governing the treatment of records. It includes the concepts, principles and methods developed by Diplomatics. *Diplomatics* is the study of the genesis, inner constitution and transmission of archival documents (records), and of their relationship with the facts represented in them and with their creator [14].

An *archival fonds* is the whole of the records created and preserved by an agency or by its legitimate successor. *Aggregated records* are records that accumulate in interrelated groups according to the way in which an agency carries out its activities.

A *juridical system* is a social group organized on the basis of a system of rules (statutes, regulations and mores). A *record* (*archival document*) is a document created by a person as means and by product of their practical activity.

The *reliability* of a record is determined by its degree of completeness, the degree of control on its creation procedure, and the author's reliability. Reliability refers to the trustworthiness of a record's content.

A *complete record* is a record that has all the elements of intellectual form required by the juridical system in which it is created. The *intellectual form* of a record is its internal composition, e.g. date, author, addressee, action. An *author's reliability* is the competence and authority of the author to issue a specific document and/or the degree to which an author can be trusted.

An *authentic record* is one that can be proved to be what it purports to be. Differently from reliability, authenticity does not relate to the content of the record but to the genuineness of the record as a whole. It can be insured by controls established on the record's mode, form and state of transmission, and on its manner of preservation and custody. A record may be more or less reliable, and is either authentic or inauthentic. Records should be created reliably and maintained authentic. The most reliable records are those that are complete, have the most control over their creation procedure, and have the most reliable authors. The least reliable records are those in which part of their intellectual form is missing (e.g. date or author), or the author had neither the capacity or authority to issue it.

4.2. An activity model as a model of a theory

Archival Science, as inclusive of Diplomatics, is among the controls on the primary business activity in the UBC/DoD activity model. The other controls are juridical system, creator's mandate and functions, and national and international standards. An attempt has been made to create procedures and data elements in the UBC/DoD activity and information models according to the concepts and rules of Archival Science, Diplomatics and the other controls.

In the activity model, reliability is conferred to records through inclusion of activities to insure that business procedures are integrated with documentary procedures, officers are trained in business and documentary procedures, competent persons are assigned to offices, and register entries are accumulated that can serve as surrogate records, even if the original record is interfered with or destroyed. In the activity model, authenticity is conferred to records by prohibiting modification of records once they have been classified and consigned to the central records system, and insuring that the intellectual form of a record is preserved when migrating to a different system, while modifications to the physical form of records are properly documented.

The intellectual form of a reliable record must include date, author, addressee and action. These attributes and others are necessary in the profile of the record, and also for insuring that records are retrievable.

The record creator's mandate and functions determine the contents of the record classification scheme. The laws and regulations of the juridical system influence the retention periods of record series in the integrated classification scheme and records schedule. National and International information processing standards constrain the activities and data structures [e.g. 10, 15].

Lehman has described a computer program as *a model of a model within a theory of a model of an abstraction of some portion of the world or of some universe of discourse* [16]. This means that a program is a model of a program design within a theory (functional requirements) of an activity model of an abstraction of some portion of the world or universe of discourse (Archival Science, Diplomatics and Records Management). The UBC/DoD IDEF0 activity model for *Manage Archival Fonds* is a model of the theories of Archival Science and Diplomatics, and the other controls on this activity.

Let us say that IDEF0 controls are *complete* for the purpose of developing activity and data models, if they can justify every procedure and every data element in the activity and data models. A few examples justifying procedures and data elements of the *Manage Archival Fonds* activity and information models have been given. Establishing completeness involves justifying each procedure and each data element in terms of the controls. A positive result establishes the controls as complete for explaining the activity model. A negative result probably identifies other areas in which additional controls are needed.

5. Summary

Functional requirements specification is a weak link in Business Process Reengineering. US and International organizations that are reengineering their business activities would all benefit from a standard methodology and representation for functional requirements specification. A representation is proposed for describing procedures controlling the lowest-level activities in an IDEF0 activity model. A method is sketched for specifying functional requirements from these procedures. The concept of *control completeness* is introduced as a mechanism for justifying the inclusion of activities and data elements in IDEF0 activity and IDEF1 information models.

Information models of document structure, business activities, and record categories are described. These models offer opportunities for improving business activities by reducing redundancy of representation and accomplishing required administrative (records management) functions as a by-product of accomplishing primary business functions.

6. Acknowledgments

The research of Capt Prescott, US Air Force, COL Kindl, US Army and Dr. Underwood was funded by the DoD Records Management Program Office. Prof. Duranti's research was funded by the Social Sciences and Humanities Research Council of Canada. The findings in this paper are not to be construed as an official Department of Defense position unless so designated by other authorized documents.

References

1. P. Prescott, Reengineering records and information management in the US department of defense: a success story, *Reengineering In Action: The Quest for World-Class Excellence* (Imperial College Press, London, 1998).

2. US Department of Defense, Design criteria standard for electronic records management software applications, DoD 5015.2–STD (1997) (*www.dtic.mil*).
3. L. Duranti and H. MacNeil, The protection of electronic records: an overview of the UBC-MAS research project, *Archivaria* **42** (Fall 1996) 46–67 (see also *www.slais.ubc.ca/users/duranti/*).
4. US Department of Defense and University of British Columbia, Applying IDEF methodology to describe archival science, Reports 2–5 (1995–1996) (*www.dtic.mil*).
5. W. Underwood, The language of records classification, AIAI TR 97–02, Army Research Laboratory, Atlanta GA (1997).
6. R. J. Mayer, M. K. Painter and P. S. deWitte, IDEF family of methods for concurrent engineering and business reengineering applications, technical report, knowledge based systems, Inc. College Station, Texas, 1993.
7. US Department of Commerce, FIPS Pub 183, *Integration Definition for Function Modeling (IDEF0)*, 1993.
8. A. Davis, *Software Requirements: Objects, Functions and States*, 2nd Edition (Prentice-Hall, 1993).
9. US Department of Commerce, FIPS Pub 184, *Integration Definition for Information Modeling (IDEF1X)*, 1993.
10. US Department of Commerce, FIPS Pub 152, *Standard Generalized Markup Language (SGML)*, 1993.
11. W. Underwood and S. Laib, The language of records disposition, AIAI TR 95–01, Army Research Laboratory (1997).
12. W. Underwood, S. Laib and J. Underwood, Managing electronic records in an army office: final report, AIAI TR 97–07, Army Research Laboratory, Atlanta GA (1997).
13. W. Underwood, Formal models of business activities and records classification, filing and retrieval, Annual Meeting of the Society of American Archivists, San Diego, August, 1996.
14. L. Duranti, Diplomatics: New uses for an old science, *Archivaria*, Part I, **28**, 7–27; Part II, **29**, 4–17; Part II, **30**, 4–20; Part IV, **31**, 10–25; Part V, **32**, 6–24; Part VI, **33**, 6–24 (1988–1992).
15. US Department of Commerce, FIPS Pub 127–2, *Database Language SQL*, 1993.
16. M. M. Lehman, Programs, life cycles, and laws of software evolution, *Proceedings of the IEEE* **68** (1980) 1060–1075.

Chapter 15

Resource-Use Efficiency in the Public Sector: A Study of Civil Services in Taiwan

PIN-YU CHU
Institute of Public Affairs Management,
National Sun Yat-sen University 70 Lai-Hwai Rd.,
Kaohsing, Taiwan, R.O.C.
E-mail: vchu@mail.nsysu.edu.tw

This paper discusses an empirical study that combines Data Envelopment Analysis (DEA) with regression modeling to evaluate operating efficiency of civil services, household registration offices (HRO), in both Taipei and Kaohsiung, Taiwan, R.O.C. Factors affecting performance include HRO inputs and other nondiscretionary socio-economic factors. The results of this study indicate that the DEA approach is not only a helpful alternative to the traditionally used Analytical Hierarchy Process (AHP) but also a practical decision tool in allocating resources among these offices in order to achieve higher service efficiency.

1. Introduction

Rosenbloom (1993), in *Harvard Business Review*, clearly mentioned that the real productivity crisis is in government [1]. This astonishing statement also reveals Taiwanese scholars' heartfelt view. According to the China Productivity Center, Taiwan, 60% of Taiwanese consider the public sector the least efficient sector. From time to time there have been desultory drives to improve efficiency in the Taiwanese public sector. However, a sense of urgency was finally introduced in 1993 by Lien Chan, vice-president of the R.O.C., who advocated the idea of reinventing the government and required the public sector to achieve higher levels of efficiency. The Administrative Reform Program has been implemented since then.

The overall goal of the program is to establish an honest and efficient government. Under the goal, three important items, 'integrity,' 'effectiveness,' and 'better service to people' are advocated. The main foci of the program include:

1. Elimination of corruption and malfeasance; promoting an ethical government;
2. Reorganizing government units and re-evaluating manpower allocation;
3. Putting government finances on a sound basis and reducing budget deficits;
4. Increasing administrative efficiency and enhancing public productivity;
5. The realization of systematic reform and enhancement of service.

Government Service Network (GSN), the division promoting integrated automation of public services and implementing inter-organization information networks, is newly developed. The tasks of GSN involve the utilization of various types of information apparatus for broadened services including government online, electronic purchasing, electronic benefit transfer, net-izen, digital publications, etc. Among them, a network service for the household registration office (HRO) has been completed first and provided to the public since 1997.

The operating performance of the public sector in Taiwan is usually measured using multi-attribute utility methods such as Analytical Hierarchy Process (AHP). These methods of course provide a great deal of information about a HRO's administrative performance when compared with prior periods and with other HROs. There are, however, shortcomings with these measures. One is that they fail to provide useful information for inefficient HROs to improve their performance. Another limitation is that there are no standard rules for deciding the weights of these models; therefore, these methods appear to be wholly subjective.

It is necessary for management to identify and develop a means of comparing and improving the performance of the local civil service in Taiwan (in particular, HRO in our case). Despite the facts that besides AHP there are many conventional approaches for evaluating productivity, e.g. ratio analysis and multiple regression techniques, there are shortcomings with employing these measures to evaluate HRO due to the nature of public sector service [2].

In this chapter, we describe our aims in managing these problems using Data Envelopment Analysis (DEA) since it is particularly appropriate for identifying the sources and amount of inefficiency as well as characterizing the nature of the production function for each HRO objectively. The remainder of this paper is organized as follows. In Sec. 2, we discuss a theoretical account of DEA and its application. Section 3 gives a background of the household registration sector in Taiwan. Section 4 describes a field study applying the DEA method in 25 HROs. The conclusions are summarized in Sec. 5.

2. Data Envelopment Analysis

2.1. *Fundamental DEA models*

DEA is a mathematical programming technique introduced by CCR [3, 4] to evaluate the relative efficiency of *not-for-profit* organizations where multiple outputs are produced with multiple inputs, and the production or standard input-output relationships are neither known nor easily identified. If civil service is viewed as an industry transforming inputs into outputs, each HRO (treated as a decision-making unit, DMU) can be viewed as a multi-product firm. As suggested by CCR [3], a scalar measure of the productive efficiency of DMU can be obtained as the optimal solution of the following model:

$$\text{Max } h_{jo} = \left\{ \sum_{r=1}^{s} u_r y_{rj0} \right\} \Big/ \sum_{i=1}^{m} v_i x_{ij0}$$

$$\text{Subject to} \left\{ \sum_{r=1}^{s} u_r y_{rj} \right\} \Big/ \left\{ \sum_{i=1}^{m} v_i x_{ij} \right\} \le 1$$

$$u_r,\ v_i \ge \varepsilon > 0,\ i = 1,\ldots,m,\ r = 1,\ldots,s,\ j = 1,\ldots,n$$

where x_{ij} = observed quantity of input i used by HRO j,
y_{rj} = observed quantity of output r used by HRO j,
u_r = the weight (to be determined) given to output of r,
v_r = the weight (to be determined) given to input of i,
h_{jo} = relative efficient value,
ε – non Archimedean quantity (a sufficiently small number).

The DEA model has the following interpretation within the context of our HRO case. There are n HROs, each of which produces different outputs using different inputs. We are interested in determining the relative efficiency h_{jo} of HRO_{jo} with respect to all other HROs. The relative efficiency is the ratio of weighted output of the HRO_{jo} to its weighted inputs. The measure of the efficiency is to transform the multidimensional inputs and outputs into a single scalar ratio of single virtual output to single virtual input. The objective is then to assign the highest possible value to h_{jo} by comparing the observed outputs and inputs of all HROs such that none of the HROs has an efficiency index greater than 1. The above fractional program is often transferred into an ordinary linear program for actual computation because it has intractable non-linear and non-convex properties. In line with all linear programs, it has two components — a primal and a dual:

A primal model

$$\text{Max } h_{jo} = \sum_{r=1}^{s} u_r y_{rj0} \,,$$

$$\text{Subject to } \sum_{j=1}^{n} v_i x_{ij0} = 1 \,,$$

$$\sum_{r=1}^{s} u_r y_{rj} - \sum_{i=1}^{m} v_i x_{ij} \leq 0$$

$$u_r,\ v_i \geq \varepsilon > 0,\ i = 1,\ldots,m,\ r = 1,\ldots,s,\ j = 1,\ldots,n$$

A dual model

$$\text{Min } h_{jo} = \vartheta - \varepsilon\left(\sum_{i=11}^{m} s^{-}ijo + \sum_{r=1}^{s} s^{+}rjo\right)$$

$$\text{subject to } \sum_{j=1}^{n} \lambda_j x_{ij} - \vartheta x_{ij0} + s^{-}ij0 = 0,\ i = 1,\ldots,m$$

$$\sum_{j=1}^{n} \lambda_j y_{rj} - s^{+}{}_{r0} = y_{r0}\,,\ r = 1,\ldots,s$$

$$\lambda_j, s^{-}{}_{ij0} \geq 0,\ j = 1,\ldots,n$$

where s^{-} *ij0*, s^{+} *rjo* are slack variables.

Besides the CCR model, various DEA models such as BCC [5], CCGS [6] etc. have been proposed for solving various problems.

2.2. *Non-discretionary inputs and efficiency*

Different variables, i.e. non-discretionary inputs, measuring the socio-economic characteristics of the communities served by an individual HRO are expected to affect its achievement and should be separated from the HRO inputs and excluded from our DEA models. Ray [7] discusses the linkage between the non-discretionary inputs in the production process and the measure of efficiency obtained by DEA. The concepts are as follows.

For DMU HRO_j, let x_j represent the controllable inputs, and w_j the non-discretionary inputs. Consider a multiplicate separable production function of HRO_j, $F(x_j, w_j) = g(x_j) \bullet h(w_j)$. If $h(w_j)$ lies between zero and 1 for all values w_j and the function $g(\bullet)$ is linear, Ray [7] shows that the DEA measure of efficiency h_j corresponds to the component $h(w_j)$. If there exists mismanagement a regression model, $h_j = h(w_j) + \varepsilon$, can be used to relate h_j to the non-discretionary inputs w_j. Here ε represents pure and avoidable inefficiency caused by poor management. If h_j equals $h(w_j)$ we should conclude that there is no managerial inefficiency and failure to reach 100% efficiency (if $h_j < 1$) is due to external factors beyond the control of the DMU [7].

2.3. *Applications of DEA*

DEA models were initially developed to assess the relative efficiency of *not-for-profit* organizations such as public projects and programs [4], hospitals [5, 8], schools [9, 10], the military [11], etc. However, the applications of the DEA models have been extended to profit oriented organizations [12, 13]. There exists a very large volume of literature on DEA, and readers are referred to the bibliography complied by Seiford [2].

3. HRO in Taiwan: A Background

In order to put later discussions in perspective, this section addresses a brief description of the household registration office in Taiwan for the purpose of providing a minimal background.

Population affairs administration in Taiwan, similar to other countries, supplies the necessary demographic information for all aspects of government administration. Although household registration affairs had been transferred to the jurisdiction of the police during the rebellion suppression period of 1969, this function currently belongs to the civil affairs system. According to the Household Registration Law, the agencies in charge of household administration are the Ministry of Interior (Department of Population Affairs) at the central level, the provincial government (Department of Civil Affairs) at the province level, and the county (city) government (Bureau of Civil Affairs) at the county level. Household registration is handled by the household affairs offices of the county government, with each office serving a town or township, e.g. 'Chiu' in Taipei and Kaohsiung and 'Shiang' in Taiwan. Figure 1 shows the system of household registration administration.

The purposes of household registration are to collect and supply population information and to identify a person's civil status. The four kinds of household registration are as follows [14]:

1. Personal identification registration takes charge of the registration of birth, death, declaration of death, legitimization of children, adoption, termination of adoption, marriage, divorce and custody;
2. Migration Registration handles the registrations for immigration, emigration, change of address, and transience;
3. Industrial and occupation registration;
4. Educational attainment registration.

In addition, the HRO conducts a census to collect relevant information on the quality and quantity of the national population

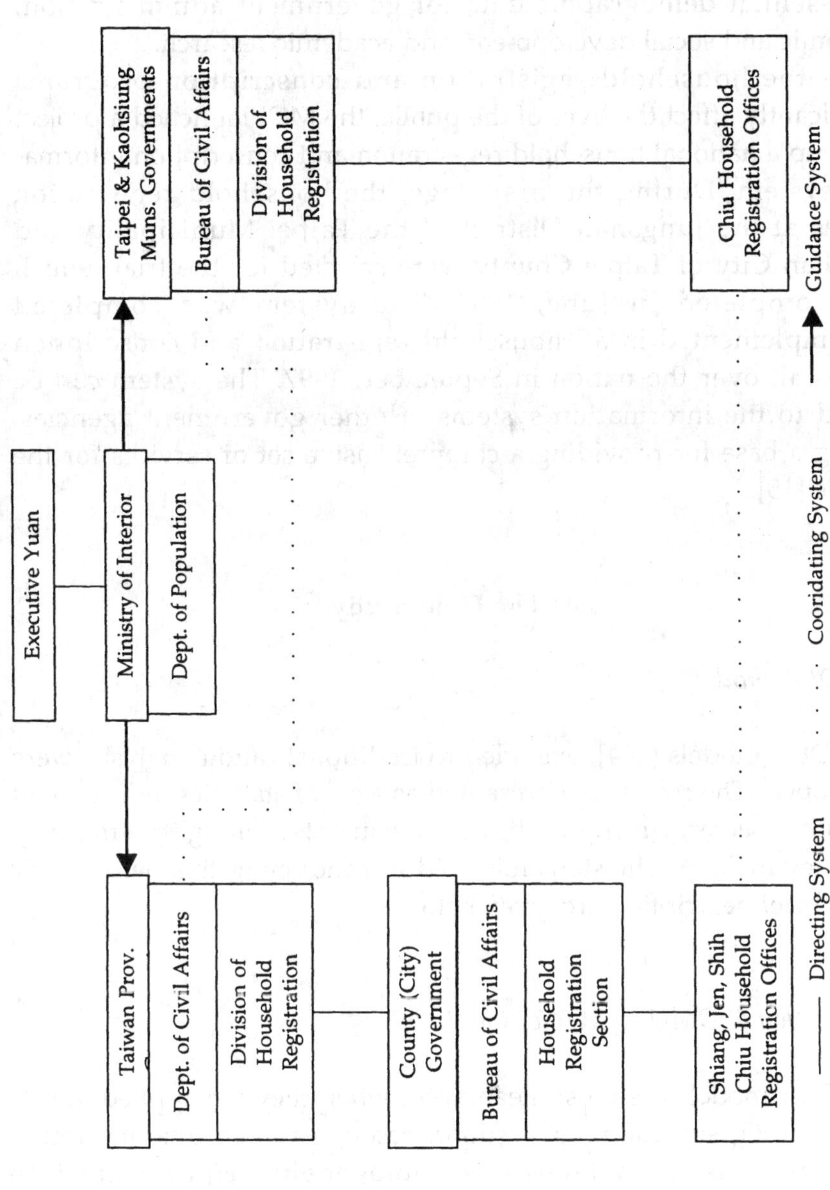

Figure 1 The system of household registration administration, Taiwan

and housing conditions at a specific time. This information serves as the essential demographic data for government administration, economic and social development, and academic research.

As the household registration and conscription programs significantly affect the lives of the public, the MOI launched a project to set up a national household registration and conscription information system. During the first stage, the household registration offices at the Jungshan District of the Taipei Municipality and Shindian City of Taipei County were selected for the trial, which was completed in June, 1993. The system was completed and implemented in all household registration and conscription offices all over the nation in September, 1997. The system can be linked to the information systems of other government agencies, setting a base for providing a comprehensive set of services for the people [15].

4. The Field Study

4.1. DEA model

Two DEA models [2–4], extended to traditional ration analysis, were developed. The results are presented as a set of statistics indicative of the public sector, which may be of value in determining the efficiency of policy making. The steps followed in conducting this fields study and a brief description are given below.

1. Selection of DMU (HRO) for the study

The DEA models are most meaningful when they are applied to sets of units or organizations using similar resources and providing similar services. This study takes this homogeneity requirement into consideration and chose 25 district household registration offices in two municipal cities, i.e. Taipei (14) and Kaohsiung (11), where HRO information systems were newly implemented in 1996. In addition, we examined a cross-section of data from 1995 and 1996 since we were particularly interested in comparing the efficiencies before and after the systems were implemented.

2. *Identification of input and output variables*

The empirical model of HRO performance developed in this study contains three input variables and three output variables. This study identifies these variables to reflect important characteristics in household registration service as indicated in the related literature and government policies and experts' opinions more generally.[1] The definitions of these variables are contained in Table 1.

Table 1 Operationalization of input-output variables

	Variable	Operationalization
Input	Personnel	The number of public staff in each HRO.
	Regular Expense	The expenditure of capital accounts (NT) in a given year.
	Computer Expense (for '96 analysis only)	The expenditure on information systems (NT) in 1996.
Output	Case of approval	The number of approval cases in a given year.
	Case of registration	The number of registration cases handled in a given year.
	Level of documentation completion	The percentage of completion of official documents in a given year.

[1]We consulted experts both at the MOI and Bureau of Civil Affairs in Kaohsiung to finalize the terms of input and output in the DEA model.

3. Calculation of efficiencies

Two series of calculations were made, one for overall efficiency analysis and one for technical efficiency analysis.[2]

4. Analysis of the sources of inefficiencies

Based on the efficiency calculations and efficiency reference sets, the weakness of the inefficient HROs were identified, albeit in general terms. This study also performed slack variable analysis and sensitivity analysis.

5. Formulation of suggestions

A set of suggestions for managerial decision making, thought to be most helpful in improving the performance of the inefficient HROs, are discussed.

4.2. *Empirical results*

This section includes a discussion and interpretation of the computational results. We will present the general observations and findings of our DEA model and then the managerial implications of the slack variable analysis and sensitivity analysis.

4.2.1. General observations and findings

In the comparison of 1996 data, the average performance of the

[2]Readers are referred to Banker *et al* [4] for the technical jargon used in this paper. Here the number for CCR stands for the overall efficiency, BCC for the technical efficiency, and SE for the scale efficiency. Also, overall efficiency = technical efficiency • scale efficiency.

HROs in Kaohsiung (including the overall, technical, and scale efficiencies) was better than that in Taipei. The results also suggest that overall there was a decreasing return to scale for all of the inefficient HROs in Taipei. A potential explanation is that since these HROs operated in highly mature communities, augmenting the controllable resources is likely to lead to a less than proportionate increase in the outcomes. In other words, deploying more personnel and increasing expenses does not enhance the service.

Table 2 shows the results of the DEA relative efficiency analysis in the context of cross-section data. These results were instrumental in reaching the following conclusions:

1. Although more than half of the HROs' (14) overall efficiencies increased after the information systems were implemented, the average overall efficiencies decreased from 0.865 to 0.875;
2. After the information systems were implemented, the average technical efficiency increased from 0.899 to 0.925;
3. After the information systems were implemented, the average technical efficiency decreased from 0.973 to 0.938.

From the above results, we may claim that inappropriate operating scale primarily caused the decrease in overall efficiency temporarily. On one hand, consider the set-up of the information systems and expansion of necessary infrastructure which would create a prompt increase in the operating scale. On the other hand, the cases served would not increase in such a short period.

4.2.2. Computational analysis

The slack analysis indicated the simultaneous changes required in inputs and outputs to make an inefficient HRO efficient. For example, for Kaohsiung to become relatively efficient, it should decrease 4.19

Table 2 The DEA efficiency results

DMU (Taipei)	CCR-'95 (BCC)	CCR-'96 (BCC)	SE'96 (SE'95)	DMU (Kao-hsiung)	CCR-'95 (BCC)	CCR-'96 (BCC)	SE'96 (SE'95)
Sung-shan	0.728 (0.732)	0.814 (0.869)	0.937 (0.994)	Yen-cheng	1.000 (1.000)	0.997 (1.000)	0.997 (1.000)
Hsin-yih	0.945 (1.000)	0.984 (1.000)	0.984 (0.984)	Ku-shan	0.915 (0.918)	0.921 (0.921)	0.999 (0.997)
Ta-an	0.712 (0.758)	0.815 (1.000)	0.815 (0.938)	Tso-ying	0.993 (0.996)	1.000 (1.000)	1.000 (1.000)
Chung-shan	1.000 (1.000)	0.932 (1.000)	0.932 (1.000)	Nan-tzu	0.985 (1.000)	1.000 (1.000)	1.000 (0.985)
Chung-cheng	0.724 (0.725)	0.819 (0.820)	0.999 (0.999)	San-min	0.957 (1.000)	0.945 (1.000)	0.9445 (0.957)
Ta-tung	0.731 (0.732)	0.733 (0.735)	0.997 (0.999)	Hsinhsin	1.000 (1.000)	0.793 (0.799)	0.993 (1.000)
Wan-i	0.792 (0.794)	0.800 (0.924)	0.865 (0.997)	Chien-chi	0.943 (0.981)	0.969 (0.972)	0.997 (0.961)
Wan-erh	0.741 (0.741)	0.702 (0.711)	0.987 (0.999)	Ling-ya	0.974 (1.000)	0.901 (0.974)	0.925 (0.974)
Wen-i	0.845 (0.846)	0.796 (0.855)	0.932 (0.999)	Chien-che	1.000 (1.000)	0.826 (0.840)	0.984 (1.000)
Wen-erh	0.761 (0.986)	0.767 (0.958)	0.801 (0.771)	Chi-chin	0.991 (1.000)	1.000 (1.000)	1.000 (0.991)
Nan-kang	0.715 (0.715)	0.735 (1.000)	0.735 (1.000)	Hsiao-kan	0.979 (0.980)	0.970 (0.973)	0.997 (0.999)
Nei-hu	0.826 (0.864)	0.896 (1.000)	0.896 (0.997)				
Shih-lin	0.715 (0.731)	0.758 (1.000)	0.758 (0.978)				
Pei-tou	0.866 (0.974)	0.765 0.775)	0.986 (0.889)	Total in average	0.875 (0.899)	0.865 (0.925)	0.938 (0.973)

personnel (from the current level of 60 to 55), $17,594 (NT) in regular expenses, and $253,998 (NT) in computer expenses. However, organizational downsizing or manpower simplification proves to be difficult and requires the amendment of the current Household Registration Law.[3]

A word of faith is emphasized. Based on the following facts, we may conclude that the decline of efficiency due to reasons like resistance to new technology may be temporary, and that the government network information system may still be helpful and necessary in the long run.

1. The average number of public staff decreased from 49 to 48, and on the contrary the average number of cases handled increased from 253,551 to 259,287 in 1996.
2. Our DEA model is most sensitive to one particular input — computer expense. The results of one-way sensitivity analysis indicate that without the input of new computer systems, input the average overall efficiency decreases from 0.956 to 0.896.

4.3. *Regression analysis*

Three variables measuring the socio-economic characteristics of the communities served by individual district (Chiu) HROs were identified as non-discretionary inputs to be used in our regression model with the DEA efficiency measure h_j as the dependent variable. They are: (1) the percentage of staff with four or more years of college education (*SCOLL*); (2) the average age of the staff (*AGE*); (3) the percentage of the citizens in the individual community served with four or more years of college education (*CCOLL*).

A linear regression model incorporating all of these three variables proved to be less satisfactory. Judging by the goodness of fit R^2 and the

[3]According to the law, at least one member of staff is required for serving every 3,500 citizens.

significance p values of individual coefficients, the most preferred model is ($R^2 = 0.638$):

$$\hat{h}_j = 1.9612 - 0.03253AGE_j + 1.4154CCOLL_j\,.$$
$$(p = 0.0028) \qquad (p = 0.0146)$$

The estimated regression model does provide some help in this respect. For example, the regression results indicated that the average age of the staff turns out to be a disadvantage factor to the overall efficiency. A potential explanation is that the elder people are less willing to learn and accept new information technology and therefore are less capable of providing efficient service. Also, the coefficient of the variable *AGE* indicates that if the average age of the staff is one year younger, the predicated efficiency of HROs would increase by 0.03253. Special plans directed toward hiring younger staff can be considered as a means of improving efficiency at HROs.

Greene (1980) has shown how to adjust the estimated value from the above regression by adding the largest positive residual [16]. The adjusted predicted value estimates the maximum efficiency in the use of HRO inputs attainable given a specific level of socio-economic characteristics. For the Chiu having the adjusted efficiency is replaced by 1 since it is 1.32335 ($\hat{h}_j = 0.7998$ and the largest residuals 0.5335), and the realized efficiency h_j is 0.6976. The overall inefficiency 0.3204 ($1 - h_j$) is primarily caused by the inefficient management of resources by the administration.

5. Conclusions

This chapter presented a data envelopment model for assessing the relative efficiency of the public sector in Taiwan before and after an information system was implemented. Although our study of the data from the household registration offices in Taipei and Kaohsiung shows that information technology has not yet improved performance given the relatively low levels of efficiency in cities in 1996, information technology proves to be a critical factor for improving the efficiency of HROs. In addition, our results show that efficiency in the utilization of HRO inputs varies with the socio-economic characteristics of communities.

Our comparison is based on input and output data since the information system was newly implemented. The results may have been influenced by random elements and measurement errors. Further research on cross-section data, e.g. panel study, is necessary.

References

1. D. H. Rosenbloom, Have an administrative Rx? Don't forget the politics! *Public Administration Review*, **53/6** (1993) 503–507.
2. L. M. Seiford, A bibliography of data envelopment analysis (1978–1990), Department of Industrial Engineering and Operations Research, The University of Massachusetts, Amherst, MA, USA (1990).
3. A. Charnes, W. W. Cooper and E. Rhodes, Measuring the efficiency of decision making units, *European Journal of Operational Research* **2/6** (1978) 429–444.
4. A. Charnes, W. W. Cooper and E. Rhodes, Evaluating program and managerial efficiency: an application of data envelopment analysis to program follow through, *Management Science* **27/6** (1981) 668–697.
5. R. D. Banker, A. Charnes and W. W. Cooper, Some models for estimating technical and scale inefficiencies in data envelopment analysis, *Management Science* **30/9** (1984) 1078–1092.
6. A. Charnes, W. W. Cooper, B. Golany and L. M. Seidord, Foundations of data envelopment analysis for Pareto-Koopmans efficient empirical production functions, *Journal of Econometrics* **30** (1985) 91–107.
7. S. C. Ray, Resource-use efficiency in public schools: a study of Connecticut data, *Management Science* **37/12** (1991) 1620–1628.
8. T. Y. Nunamaker, Measuring routine nursing service efficiency: a comparison of cost per patient day and data envelopment analysis model, *Health Service Research* **18/2** (1983) 183–205.

9. A. Bessent, W. Bessent, J. Kennington and B. Regain, An application of mathematical programming to assess productivity in the Houston independent school district, *Management Science* **28/12** (1982) 1355–1367.
10. A. Bessent, W. Bessent, A. Charnes and W. W. Cooper, Evaluation of education program proposals by means of data envelopment analysis, *Educational Administration Quarterly* **19/2** (1983) 82–107.
11. W. F. Bowlin, Evaluating the efficiency of U.S. Air Force real property maintenance activities, *Journal of Operational Research Society* **38/2** (1987) 127–135.
12. H. D. Sherman and F. Gold, Bank branch operating efficiency: evaluation with data envelopment analysis, *Journal of Banking and Finance* **9/2** (1985) 297–315.
13. C. Parkan, Measuring the efficiencies of service operations: an application to bank branches, *Engineering Costs and Production Economics* **12** (1987) 237–242.
14. Ministry of Interior, The introduction of MOI, 1993.
15. Ministry of Interior, Population Affairs Administration. http://www.moi.gov.tw/W3/xmoi1cc.htm/ (12 March 1998).
16. M. T. Greene, Long-term dependence and least squares regression in investment analysis, *Management Science* **26/10** (1980) 1031–1038.

Chapter 16

Customer Participation and Commitment in BPR

VERONIKA THURNER
Department of Computer Science,
Technical University of Munich
Arcisstr. 21, 80290 Munich, Germany
E-mail: thurner@informatik.tu-muenchen.de

Based on experience that was partly gathered in project cooperation with Siemens Nixdorf, we present a systematic approach to BPR, covering a methodology for information retrieval, process modeling and structuring, weakness analysis, and development and testing of concepts for improvements and change. Furthermore, we focus on our tactics for coping with psychological barriers of those employees of the client organization that are involved in and affected by a BPR project, and our way of motivating them to identify themselves with improvements and change.

1. Typical Goals and Starting Conditions for BPR

Of the many reasons for which BPR projects are set up, a frequently occuring one is the need to improve process efficiency and transparency. Quite often, this includes the introduction of information technology for the best possible support of the business processes [1], as well as a process oriented restructuring of the organization.

Usually, the process analyst or BPR consultant operates in an environment of project conditions that is determined by external restrictions such as legislation or regulations issued by the workers' council of the client organization on the one hand, and on the other hand by technical and social circumstances originating within the client organization itself. Basically, external restrictions are clearly defined, but out of reach of the BPR consultant's influence. In contrast to this, project relevant circumstances that are internal to the client organization and located in the social or political area will partly be implicit rather than established openly. These implicit internal circumstances are hard to get at sometimes, and endanger the project's success if not discovered and dealt with properly. However, once these hidden internal socio-political forces are detected, a skilled and sensitive analyst can influence them to a certain extent and turn them in a positive direction.

Vital for successfully introducing changes, no matter whether in the social or in the technical field, is the active participation and commitment of at least those of the client's employees that are affected by change measurements. To a considerable extent, failures of BPR projects that are executed by external consultants are due to the fact that the external consultants require the aid of the client's employees on the executive level for modeling AS-IS processes, but exclude them from the development of improvement concepts. As a consequence, they produce an improvement concept that is of high quality if measured with abstract theoretical principles, but does not take into consideration the specific situation within the organization and its business domain to an adequate extent, so that the application of the suggested improvements often is not feasible in the specific context. In addition, if they are not explicitly involved in the development of improvement concepts and changes, some of the client's employees tend to feel passed over in the improvement of their processes and will therefore block the new process concepts rather than being able to identify with them.

In order to motivate the client's employees on the executive level to actively participate in and commit to the improvement effort, it is essential to gain the employee's confidence at the beginning of the project that BPR will bring about changes for the better. Therefore, it is necessary to work with a BPR strategy that, on the one hand, lets the client's employees get involved in the development of improvement concepts to a fairly high extent, and, on the other hand, shows visible improvements at a very early stage and after rather little time spent on the project.

2. Embedding BPR in a Global Reengineering Process

In our approach, we embed BPR in a global reengineering methodology to insure an integrated realization of both quick, continuous improvements and more radical, complex changes in process and organization structure. Both are necessary: early improvement results keep employees motivated for the change effort, and radical changes enable innovation [1]. To achieve this, we structure our reengineering activities into four task domains (Fig. 1):

- immediate tactical change (ITC),
- extended tactical change (ETC),
- immediate strategic change (ISC), and
- extended strategic change (ESC).

Task domains are symbolized by rectangles with rounded corners in columns at the left of Fig. 1. Each task domain is realized by one or more processes, depicted by rectangles. Arrows visualize dependencies between processes [2].

Tactical improvements concentrate on detailed business activities and deal with local technological and operational changes, without impact on the business organization as a whole. By *immediate tactical changes,* we categorize small-scale improvements, tackling any problem where both its cause and a possible solution are somewhat obvious, and the solution is easy to implement. Usually, these are off the shelf solutions that can be realized within a short timeframe. In contrast to this, *extended*

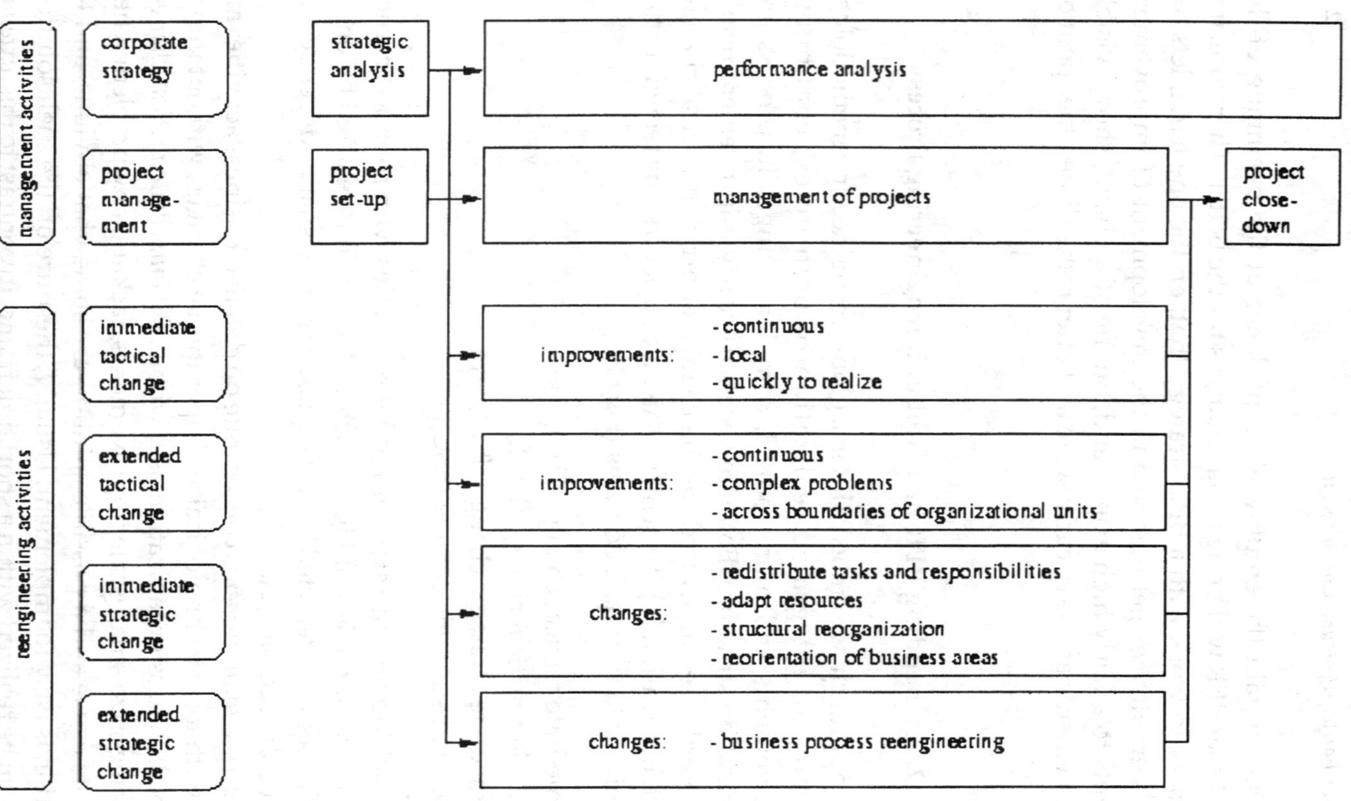

Figure 1 Embedding BPR in our methodology for business reengineering

tactical changes deal with problems that are mostly cross-functional, and therefore more complex, difficult to solve and whose possible solution takes some time and effort to be successfully implemented. They cover long-term improvements, which require a higher degree of error recovery and problem solving.

Strategic improvements are closely related to business objectives and a business's strategy of achieving them. Consequently, strategic improvements deal with global organizational and process problems. *Immediate strategic changes* tackle problems arising from flaws in the organization of an enterprise, e.g. due to the existing distribution of competence, responsibility and tasks. Finally, the task domain of *extended strategic changes*, focusing mainly on processes, is the most complex of the four; it incorporates and triggers all other reengineering tasks. All changes that extend over a rather long period of time and that globally affect the business organization, or the structure of its processes, or both, are dealt with here.

3. Business Process Reengineering

Figure 2 gives an overview of our methodology for business process reengineering, detailing the BPR process of Fig. 1. Phases structuring the process chain are depicted by rounded rectangles that are aligned horizontally in a row. In the following, we focus on process analysis, weakness analysis, design of improvements and test implementation, referring to the involvement of our clients' employees in each of these steps.

3.1. Process analysis

Identifying and selecting those business processes for modeling that are necessary and essential for achieving the BPR project goals is a crucial task of any BPR project. Preparatory to this decision and in

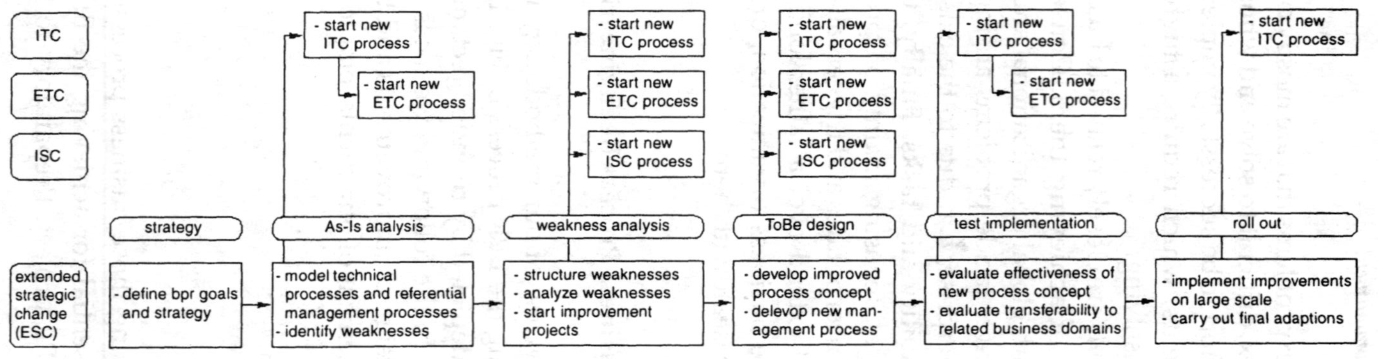

Figure 2 Overview of methodology for business process reengineering

order to embed the selected processes into the behavioral context of the overall system, we at first consider on a very coarse level of abstraction the key processes of the overall system in a cross-organizational way, starting from the major goals of the entire business system under consideration. We then specify which of these processes will be subject to detailed modeling, and correspondingly define the boundary of that part of the business system to be analyzed in more detail. Embedded into this system and process context, we model the relevant processes down to the required level of detail.

3.1.1. Modeling approach

As a basis for process improvement and redesign, we model typical system behavior that occurs frequently in similar ways. From our experience, process executives find it easier to narrate their process activities when following one specific instance of execution. Thus we collect sets of exemplaric process descriptions, which we generalize and integrate into a business process model.

Key questions in process modeling aim at identifying process triggers, process products and resources required for process execution. Furthermore, for each process, we determine its client and the client's requirements on the process and process products. This information helps focusing on those process parts that are relevant for achieving business goals, and give a first insight into improvements that help increase customer satisfaction.

Ideally, we would develop our process model hierarchically in a top-down fashion, starting from system and process boundary diagrams, adding level by level more detailed process information until the system behavior were well understood and documented in reasonable detail. However, in practice this procedure is usually inadequate for several reasons.

For one thing, information is often incomplete and usually comes across in an unstructured way. From our experience, most business organizations can fairly easily provide information on a coarse grain, strategic level, as well as on a rather detailed level close to the execution of everyday business. What is usually missing, however, is an intermediate layer connecting the abstract strategic and the much more specific execution level.

For another thing, information gathered from different sources may be inconsistent. In many business organizations, the awareness of the global context of a specific working position with respect to the business system decreases rapidly toward the lower levels of the organizational hierarchy. As a consequence, a single person's process knowledge on the execution level is usually limited to a very local working area. Connections to predecessor and successor activities in a process chain are only rarely understood. Thus on the execution level, process information comes in separate fragments, leaving at first numerous holes and inconsistencies.

Therefore, we employ a hybrid modeling approach, integrating both top-down and bottom-up steps to insure adequate granularity and consistency. The first version of some part of the process model will be subject to review and change in an iterative process, as gradually further information on the system's behavior is gained and the model becomes more stable and more and more complete. Whenever substantial additions to or changes of the process model are carried out, those levels of the model adjoining the changed or modified part are reconsidered. Thus changes that are local to some specific part of the model may propagate both top-down and bottom-up throughout the whole model hierarchy.

3.1.2. Documentation

To document a business process model, we use text as well as graphical notations derived from data flow diagrams [3] and the specification language GRAPES [4]. As tool support, we employ GRADE by Siemens Nixdorf [5].

In a process diagram, we visualize activities and their causal relationships, which manifest themselves in the exchange of material and/or information between activities, thus defining client-server relationships. Furthermore, in our process diagram we specify which business unit is responsible for a process's execution.

We structure our process diagrams by a two-dimensional grid, where time extends horizontally, partitioned into phases, and tasks are arranged vertically. Each task is carried out by one or more processes. Note that we separate value creating and supporting management activities related to a task, to visualize whether activities contribute directly to the value creation, or deal with organizational aspects that are not directly part of a process product. Within a single process, we visualize communication between different actors by aligning activities that are executed by different actors along differing imaginary horizontal lines. Furthermore, processes are structured hierarchically by refinement.

3.1.3. Customer participation and information retrieval

The most accurate and up-to-date knowledge of processes and execution practices usually lies with application experts from different levels of the organizational hierarchy of the business system, whereas existing written documentation of processes and organizational structures tends to be out of date and not applied by the people on the job. Consequently, the customer's employees are the most effective source of information on a business organization and its processes, and should be included in the modeling process in an adequate way.

From our experience, questionnaires produce rather low-quality, superficial information. Especially when touching on process weaknesses, many employees are not ready to document their criticism in writing. Therefore, we gather information by workshops and interviews, which encourage a greater openness.

We begin each project phase with a kick-off workshop which informs the employees on goals and methodology of the new phase and motivates them to cooperate. Subsequently, we carry out interviews, which allow us to deal with insecurities on the employees' side on a more private basis than a group workshop would permit. Although these interviews are very time-consuming, they usually prove to be worth the effort as they render information and results that are less dominated by peer pressure and 'political' aspects than most workshop results, but are rather closer to the personal opinion of the interviewee. The minimum results to be obtained from an interview are the identification of local activities, and their positioning in a global process context, in terms of predecessor and successor activities due to input/output relations. Furthermore, a local working area is structured according to tasks and phases.

Toward the end of each project phase, we switch to workshops again to present, compare and unify the different results and to achieve a consensus on process concepts and measurements to be taken. Thus we are able to achieve a commitment even of diverse groups of employees on change and improvement programs, which is a vital precondition for successfully putting them into practice.

Whenever possible, rather than merely using them as 'information sources,' we involve our client's employees in the modeling process by offering them a condensed introductory training on the modeling techniques used in our methodology. Subsequently, we guide them to model their own process sections, first on their own and later on in integration groups. Thus, as far as possible, employees themselves produce their own business process model, which somewhat naturally leads to a high degree of commitment.

3.2. *Weakness analysis*

During weakness analysis, we examine both general weaknesses, which are global to the system, and process specific weaknesses, connected to certain activities or process structures. This set of weaknesses is then structured, and chains from problem symptoms to problem causes are derived.

3.2.1. General weaknesses

All along with process modeling, any weaknesses in the existing system that are touched in interviews or discussions are collected and documented. To insure confidentiality, named problems are transformed into general weaknesses that are independant of specific persons.

Generally, the most pressing problems are named in the first few minutes after the subject of weaknesses is explicitly touched. The employees' priorization of process and general weaknesses in the system indicates where the design of improvement measures should be started. Quick treatment of those aspects that impede employees most in their everyday work document at an early stage that the reengineering team takes the employees' concerns seriously, and can bring about effective relief. Visible success at an early stage again motivates the customer's employees. As a side effect, an increase of efficiency due to first improvement measures helps over-worked employees to find the time for getting deeper involved in the reengineering project.

In a next step, the collection of individual weaknesses is analyzed and structured into weakness domains, grouping similar and related weaknesses. On the basis of this set of problem domains, and of the process model previously developed, the collection and analysis of weaknesses that are specific to processes is carried out.

3.2.2. Process specific weaknesses

Process specific weaknesses supplement the collection of general weaknesses. They are detected by structured process evaluation and evaluation workshops. Typically, process specific weaknesses are interface problems, as well as frequently occuring difficulties with the production of some specific intermediate result of a process.

In our process evaluation, we consider a diversity of criteria. Structural aspects focus weaknesses that can be detected from an analysis of the graphical process representation as a whole, without looking into details of single activities. For example, process complexity and the number of communications are considered here. Furthermore, results that are created in a process chain but not used any further indicate potential for optimization. Finally, the differentiation of technical and management processes in the process model helps to detect delays in the overall process performance that are due to organizational and management overheads, rather than technical complexity.

Other aspects are analyzed on a more detailed level, incorporating the internal realization of activities. Here, the adequate usage of information technology is a key aspect. In addition, we look for work that is performed more than once in the system. Also, we detect activities which do not contribute to value production, i.e. which do not transform a process result.

All these aspects point out improvement potential, both in single activities, and in the overall process and organization structure. For a quantitative process analysis, queueing theory is useful for analyzing processing times as well as the load on resources.

3.2.3. Reducing weaknesses to problem causes

In a next step, these weaknesses are structured into related groups. The structure of the set of weaknesses is project specific, as it reflects the existing situation within an organizational unit to a certain extent. In a BPR project that we carried out within a German agency, on the coarsest level our structure differentiated between structural aspects of the organization, internal communication, communication with external partners, technology and infrastructure, processes and process regulations, training and education, and different aspects of project management.

Complex weaknesses are then analyzed to separate mere symptoms from problem causes, using creative problem-solving techniques derived from Ref. 6, to render possible solutions that tackle problems at their roots, rather than treating mere symptoms. Setting up the link between symptoms and problem causes helps us focus on problem solving instead of symptom fixing. For example, in the BPR project mentioned above, we thus could boil down our original collection of about 360 weaknesses to approximately 15% thereof, which included the major problem causes.

3.3. *Developing and testing improvement measurements*

According to our methodology, design and testing of changes and improvements are integrated in an iterative process. Closely linking design and testing of improvement concepts allows even roughly sketched concepts to be evaluated to a certain extent, before they have to be worked out in detail. For all improvement suggestions, it is evaluated whether the expected chance of their success and estimated gain is worth the cost of the improvement project. Measuring the progress of improvement projects supports early discovery of problems in improvement concepts, and thus is the basis for decisions on the further realization of improvement projects. For the development of improvement measures and design of optimized processes, best practices and quasi-standardized processes are viewed as referential processes [7]. Furthermore, studying processes that work on similar tasks within the same organization can provide additional information to support the development of effective change measurements.

A vital precondition for improvements to be successful is the commitment of a large number of those employees who are directly engaged in or concerned by the change. Therefore, we involve the client's employees strongly in the improvement process by cooperatively setting up a number of improvement projects for developing and realizing a selected set of improvement concepts. Each project is realized by an improvement team, where the roles of team leader, patron and mediator are of high importance.

The *team leader* holds the main responsiblity for team building and for the results of an improvement project, and insures the necessary flow of information. Not regarding the 'usual' organizational structure, the team leader directly reports to the project patron on difficulties and results in the improvement project. Thus team leaders are endowed with both more responsibility and possibility to achieve changes than in everyday business, which usually motivates them to take their job on the improvement team very seriously although it often means extra work.

The *patron*, usually a higher official in the business organization, backs the team leader and helps the improvement team to overcome difficulties in carrying out their improvement tasks that are due to the existing hierarchical organization structure. To execute this kind of support, the patron must have both the ability and the authorization to take decisions on budget, resources, infrastructure and so on.

The *mediator*, the role taken by the external consultants, accompanies the improvement team throughout the whole project, providing experience and giving advice on aspects such as project planning and measuring of progress, as well as the execution of the different project tasks. In addition, the mediator supports communication between and interaction of team leader and patron.

4. Overcoming Psychological Barriers

According to our experience, the success of a business reengineering process largely depends on the engagement and commitment of those people who have to put reengineering and improvement measures into practice in their everyday working lives. Here, difficulties occur and have to be overcome, which have little to do with technical or economical aspects of reengineering. Rather, they come from the psychological domain and are often somewhat fuzzy or on a subconscious level. Thus, they are usually only poorly tangible and much harder to detect and to deal with than any of the 'technical' problems, needing a mixture of intuition, experience and strategy to cope with.

In the following, we describe some of the more frequent problems originating from the psychological level, and sketch some basic principles in approaching them.

4.1. *Initial conditions*

Quite often, a reengineering project that involves external consultants is initiated by the organization's top management, which consequently is highly interested in the success of a reengineering project. However, although the top management is competent on the global context, they generally have only a vague idea, or none at all, of the details of business processes and their execution.

Information on the more detailed process level is best obtained from expert users, and to a certain extent from middle management, which also has a fairly good understanding of the more global context of processes and activities. However, although these two groups are essential for successfully accomplishing a reengineering project, they often oppose more or less openly for a number of reasons.

First, interviews and workshops in the reengineering project are often seen as an extra strain in addition to the regular business. Second, if there is little or no belief in the success of the reengineering project, the willingness to cooperate or get involved decreases even more. More subtle problems arise from insecurities due to the fear of loss of face, or even one's job. Quite often, the reengineering project is not understood as a means of improving the quality of one's work and working surroundings. Rather, the fear dominates that the detection of improvement possibilities automatically insinuates that previously, one did not perform one's job as well as possible.

Consequently, the modeler often moves in opposing surroundings, pending between insecurity, hidden or open resistance, or simply indifference. To obtain the necessary information despite of this situation, the customer's employees have to be motivated for cooperation. Also, it is essential to establish confidentiality and trust between the customer's employees and the reengineering team to insure that critical information is not withheld on purpose due to insecurity.

4.2. *Motivation and commitment*

One major step toward motivating the customer's employees is to show them that they will benefit from the results of the reengineering project. Here, it is important to quickly establish positive examples. Even if they are only improvements on a rather small scale, they highly increase the credulity of the reengineering team among the employees. Furthermore, they increase the trust towards the reengineering team, as these positive examples document that the reengineering team does not work *against* the employees' interests, but rather endeavors to work *with* them and, as a catalyst, in favor of an improvement of the employees' everyday working surroundings. Thus, the employees are given the chance to achieve improvements they desire with the help of the reengineering team.

When the first insecurities are coped with, efforts are made to gain the customer's employees for cooperation. Here, we again emphasize that the information provided by the employees is decisive for the quality of the achieved results and improvements, and that the reengineering team sees itself in a supporting role. Thus, the responsibility for the quality and extent of improvement measures, as well as the merit of successful implementations, is partly transferred to the customer's employees.

In addition, we target at achieving benefits for those employees who spend time and energy on the reengineering project. For example, we train them in our methodology and the usage of the supporting modeling tool. When the global organization attempts to establish the practice of continuous improvements in their everyday working processes, employees with an introductory training and first experience on process modeling and reengineering have a favorable starting position for good performance. Also, employees who show a quick-sightedness in the detection of improvement possibilities, and a sensitiveness in the design and realization of improvement measures, establish for themselves a better positioning within their departments as well as chances for further career moves.

Furthermore, it is important to determine the internal leaders, and to win their involvement for the reengineering effort, as their attitude is likely to influence the position of their colleagues. When an internal leader is convinced of the advantages of supporting the reengineering project, he or she can propagate this as an insider of the organization, who can usually reach more people, and is more likely to be trusted, than a representative from an external company.

Also, both to increase the employees' trust in the reengineering team, and to enable employees to achieve part of the reengineering tasks by themselves, we openly explain our modeling and reengineering methodology. Thus we make sure that the expert users understand what is going on both in the modeling project and in the enterprise as a whole. In addition, we regularly present the project's results that were worked out by different groups of expert users in cooperation with and with support of the reengineering team.

The employees' commitment to improvement measures is vital to insure that they will be applied and put into practice rather than blocked and ignored. Commitment is closely related to the chance for identification, and thus may be achieved via cooperation and participation, by sharing the analysts' knowledge and offering an active role to the client's employees throughout the whole reengineering process. Finally, we prevent sneaking out of one's responsibility by requiring each expert user who participates in the modeling project to sign in commitment his or her processes and suggested improvement measures.

4.3. *Ensuring confidentiality*

Throughout the whole project, and especially during weakness analysis, it is important to maintain confidentiality when desired by the client's employees. Critical information will often be provided only when it is insured that its conveyance cannot be sanctioned negatively by colleagues or superiors.

Furthermore, the employees involved in the reengineering project are usually sensitive toward improvement suggestions and criticism connected with their work. It is important to keep and protect the personal integrity of all participants in the project over all levels of the organizational hierarchy. If this is kept in mind, criticism can be discussed openly without endangering the employees' identification with goals and results of the improvement project.

5. Conclusions

To be successful on the long run, business reengineering has to systematically integrate aspects such as visioning, continuous improvements, radical change or the introduction of new technology. Because the people who have to put reengineering suggestions into practice are the organization's employees, they should be involved in the entire reengineeing process not only as sources of information on existing practices, but also in the design of reengineering measures. In order to enable these employees to actively participate in the reengineering project, they are introduced to the reengineering methodology and share both part of the responsibility and the merit for its results with the professional reengineering team.

6. Acknowledgements

We thank Günther Klementz and his consulting group at Siemens Business Services for continuous support. Especially, we are highly indebted to Michael Adler and Andre De Leeuw for close cooperation and many fruitful discussions.

References

1. T. H. Davenport, *Process Innovation — Reengineering Work Through Information Technology* (Harvard Business School Press, Boston, Mass., 1993).
2. R. Barker and C. Longman, *Function and Process Modeling* (Addison-Wesley Publishing Company, New York, 1992).
3. T. DeMarco, *Structured Analysis and System Specification* (Prentice-Hall International, Inc., Englewood Cliffs, New Jersey, 1979).
4. Siemens Nixdorf Informationssysteme AG, *GRAPES V3 — Sprachbeschreibung* (in German) (Siemens Nixdorf, Munich, 1995).
5. Siemens Nixdorf Informationssysteme AG, *GRADE V2.0 — Benutzerhandbuch* (in German) (Siemens Nixdorf, Munich, 1995).
6. A. B. VanGundy, *Techniques of Structured Problem Solving*, 2nd edition (Van Nostrand Reinhold, New York, 1988).
7. C. E. Bogan and M. J. English, *Benchmarking for Best Practices, Winning Through Innovative Adaption* (McGraw-Hill, Inc., New York, 1994).

Chapter 17

Empirical Evidence for a Yin-Yang Balanced Approach to Organizational Change

TIEN HUA YIM-TEO
Curriculum Development Division,
Institute of Technical Education,
10 Dover Drive, Singapore 138683, Republic of Singapore
E-mail: yimth@ite.edu.sg

Reengineering has taken off in response to the rising demands of customers and changes in technology and expectations of employees. A model that gives a macro view of how reengineering can be made to work is especially important in view of the multitude of problems reported of reengineering endeavors. This chapter discusses the importance of having a shared vision and an environment that facilitates double-loop learning. The proposed Model uses the Chinese philosophical yin-yang balanced concept to illustrate the need to balance the application of technology with the human factor. Commonly cited success factors are classified as yin and yang factors. The Yin-Yang Balanced Model was empirically tested by the first ever Singapore Public Sector Survey on Success Factors for Change, conducted in the first quarter of 1997. Analyses on the findings confirmed that having a shared vision is paramount to reengineering success and an organizational ability to learn as a mediator of the yin-yang contributions toward building this shared vision for organizational change.

1. Introduction

The 1990s is heralded as a decade of radical change brought about by the advent of information technology (IT), with reengineering widely promoted as the necessary evil for organizations to be viable in the 90s and beyond. Reengineering has been identified as a key change initiative for achieving business improvement for organizations in the 90s. Reengineering involves starting with a clean slate in redesigning yesterday's organization using today's technology to meet tomorrow's demands.

However, reengineering is associated with a high percentage of reported failures [1–6]. Many report on the causes of both reengineering failures and successes [7–9]. The lack of attention paid to change management is often cited as being responsible for the reengineering failures. Could success lie in the need to balance these hard and soft aspects of reengineering? This is identified as the gap which this research has aimed to bridge.

This chapter applies the oriental yin-yang balanced concept in the development of the Yin-Yang Balanced (YYB) Model for successful reengineering. It discusses the factors that contribute to reengineering success and reports the findings of a recent survey conducted to test the YYB Model in the public sector.

2. Definition of Reengineering

Though the term reengineering is associated with various change initiatives, they generally mean the rapid and radical redesign of strategic, value-added core business processes to optimize workflow and productivity in an organization [7, 10]. Reengineering is defined here as the fundamental rethink of how an organization effectively fulfills its mission. It results in the identification of technical changes, essential to achieve the target gain, and a corresponding degree of socio-cultural changes and associated risk, which can be significantly reduced with the increase in the organizational capacity for double-loop learning. The scope of reengineering may range from process improvement to ongoing renewal, though the extremes are often seen as not 'true' reengineering, as defined in the spectrum of Fig. 1 [11].

The technical aspect of reengineering involves the appropriate approach, exploitation and application of technology and knowledge to deliver the reengineering goals. It may include changes in the reporting structure, relocation of facilities and resources, and acquisition of new skills. This scope of change comes with an associated risk. The socio-cultural aspect of reengineering refers to the impact on the employees as individuals and teams as the result of the reengineering initiative and how such impact is being managed. It may include a degree of cultural change, ranging from minimal change to paradigm shift, necessary to attain a corresponding degree of target gain. For organizations with older and more ingrained cultures, most change initiatives undertaken would sit in the lower end of the reengineering spectrum [11, 12].

A paradigm capable of expounding the profound relationships between the technical and socio-cultural aspects involved in

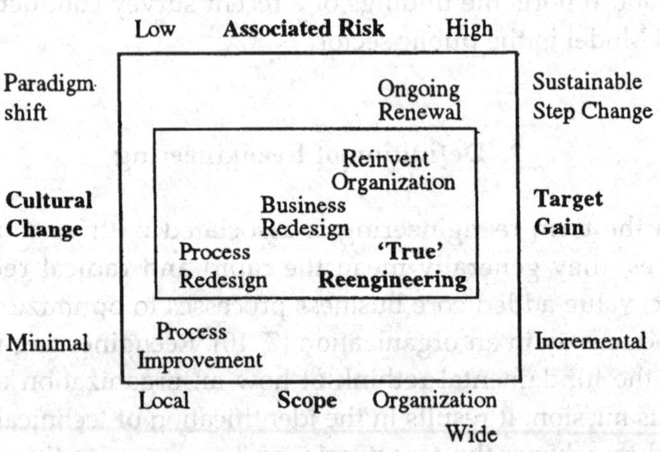

Figure 1 The adapted reengineering spectrum [11]

reengineering is necessary for the research on the effectiveness of organizational change. The oriental philosophical yin-yang balanced concept is identified as an appropriate paradigm to understand the complexity of organizational change and effectiveness in major change initiatives.

3. The 'Yin' and 'Yang' of Reengineering

Though there are reports of successes achieved by numerous organizations, the high failure rates experienced make the search for factors that make or break a reengineering project especially important. Reengineering has great potential for increasing productivity through improved service quality, greater customer satisfaction and reduced process time and cost. However, to attain these benefits, attention must be paid to achieving a balance between the application of technology and the human factor.

The literature review points to the need for a balance between the hard and soft success factors [7, 9, 13]. The yin-yang balanced principle can be used to illustrate the need for the balance [14–20]. 'Yin' and 'yang' are two principle forces of nature used to illustrate that while they are opposite elements, they are necessary for each other. The 'yin' is the feminine, passive and yielding, while the 'yang' is male, strong and firm [14]. *"The art of life is not seen as holding yang and banishing yin, but as keeping the two in balance, as there cannot be one without the other"* [15]. Any imbalance between these two forces will result in disorder [14–20]. The socio-cultural factors are classified collectively as the 'yin' while technical factors as the 'yang' of reengineering change.

The need to manage the 'yin' of reengineering is highlighted by several researchers [7, 9, 13]. Champy advocates that the limit of reengineering lies with the management which he identified as the main obstacle to reengineering [21]. Likewise Hammer and Shanton write to address the high reengineering failure which they claim, reflects a fundamental fact that reengineering is admittedly very difficult to do [22]. The Yin-Yang Balanced (YYB) Model (Fig. 2) advocates that a shared vision for change is paramount to reengineering success where balance between the yin and yang of reengineering is mediated in a conducive organizational environment where learning takes place.

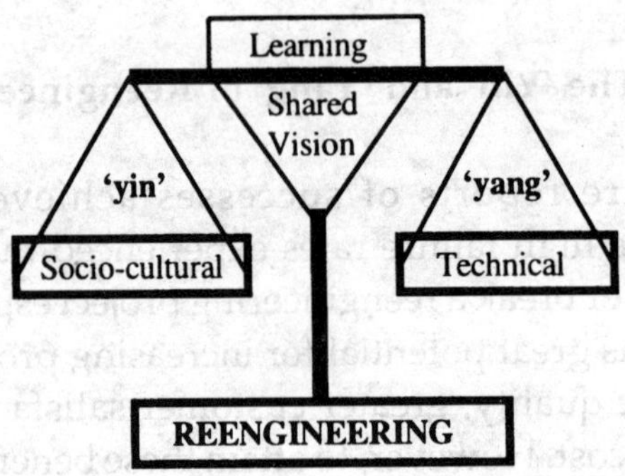

Figure 2 Yin-yang balanced model of reengineering

4. Key Factors Affecting Effectiveness in Organizational Change

Much research has been conducted on the various factors affecting organizational effectiveness in their change initiatives. This section reviews the commonly cited underlying issues beneath key factors under four main themes: shared vision, technical, socio-cultural and conducive environment [11, 12, 22–50].

4.1. Shared vision

Many researchers see having a vision as important to leadership, strategy implementation and change [27–31]. Some authors suggest vision as a form of leadership, where a visionary leader alters an organizational culture to bring members to understand, accept and carry forward his or her plans for the organization [29, 31]. Others view vision as one of the critical tasks top management performs [32, 33] and as a demonstration of leadership competencies [34]. Vision represents a pattern of organizational values that underlies a unique visionary pattern for an organization's future [35–40].

The importance of top management's commitment to change is in line with Sarason's Model of Strategic Transformation [51]. Sarason advocates that a shared vision of the organizational identity affects and is reinforced by policy and procedures which in turn influence the organizational structure. The notion of establishing a shared vision about the destiny of the organization undergoing change, from the standpoint of schematic approach to change, is a potent way of nurturing commitment of individuals to the organizational change [52]. Applying Giddens' structuration theory, top management's strategic role in setting the direction of change and their strong commitment to change will empower their 'agents' to successful effect organizational action and structure as the organization interacts with the changing environment [53–56].

One of the hallmarks of vision is the ability to share control and to create the feeling of self-control in subordinates [57, 58]. A visionary leader is seen as both empowering and empowered by the people [59]. Therefore, the more successful a chief executive is in including others to embrace his vision, that is to share his vision and move it rapidly forward, the greater is the tendency for his individual staff to want to re-assert and maintain control in the rapidly changing circumstances [40]. Building a shared vision is seen as an effective way of creating a common schema for all who are involved in the change, thus internalizing their locus of control and harnessing their organizational commitment to change [40].

Such major organizational change as reengineering takes time and resources, requiring clear top management commitment and determination to follow through the change [11, 22, 42–49]. In order for vision to be shared in the organization, clear and realistic reengineering vision and focus are determined as a result of the fundamental rethinking process of how the organization is to meet its mission in the context of its changing business environment [11, 22, 43, 44, 46–48]. Likewise, clear performance indicators are established and communicated to all staff affected by the change, so that success stories can be identified and shared to excite and sustain the momentum of change [11, 22, 44–46, 48]. The purpose of change and direction to which the organization is heading is constantly communicated within the organization [11, 22, 43, 44, 46–49]. In the case of the public sector, the critical role government plays in generating this vision for change can never be over-emphasized [5, 50].

> Hypothesis 1: Having a shared vision contributes significantly to the outcome of reengineering effort in meeting its expectation of improving the organizational performance and effectiveness.

4.2. *Technical factors (yang)*

Technical factors refer to the tangible or logical components that are cited as critical to improve organizational performances in areas such as process cycle time and cost of operation as outcomes of the change initiatives. The whole process of reengineering from the conception to implementation requires a number of technical success factors.

Reengineering needs to be pursued with clear vision and goals [4, 11, 22, 42]. Literature highlights the need for a holistic approach where organizations consider the whole and not just parts, as they think critically about the viability and relevance of their core processes in the context of the new business environment [11, 22, 45, 48]. A key differentiating feature of reengineering is the call for fundamental rethinking of the way organizations operate [4, 22]. In the process, organizations challenge existing and past held assumptions and adapt change strategies to meet the demands of their customers and compete in the changing business environment [11, 22, 43]. Reengineering is a serious undertaking that requires a systematic approach in the implementation of all related changes [22, 44–47]. Failure to adopt a systematic approach to change may result in organizations losing sight of their objectives, and is identified as a key cause of failures in reported reengineering efforts [5].

Likewise, reengineering initiative needs to be fully integrated with the corporate strategic context, with clear strategically integrated implementation plan [43–47]. Reengineering initiative undertaken is therefore an integral part of the organizational strategies to stay relevant and competitive in the changing business environment. The ability to exploit the power and effective use of information technology (IT) is essential in finding an optimum solution. The creative and innovative use of IT is advocated to be another critical area that contributes to success in reengineering [11, 43, 44, 46–48]. For maximum results, cross-functional reengineering project teams are preferred as they understand more fully the potentials for and implications of the change. To be effective, project teams need to be competent and knowledgeable in employing the appropriate methodology to effect the change [44–48].

Understanding both the internal and external processes that involve staff, customers and suppliers is an important prerequisite to reengineering success. This calls for an effective and logical decision making process with active staff participation and involvement at all levels who are affected by the change [11, 22, 42–49]. In order to deliver the requirements and expectations of customers, organizations must increase their customer orientation by involving customers in their reengineering efforts [22, 43–48].

> Hypothesis 2: The yang factors influence the outcome of the reengineering initiative in improving the organizational performance and effectiveness through their contribution to building a shared vision for the change.

4.3. Socio-cultural factors (yin)

Socio-cultural factors refer to the less tangible or the emotional components that are often neglected but are cited as critical to improve the organizational effectiveness in areas such as customer service and service quality as outcomes of the change initiatives. These are outcomes that are highly dependent on the quality of the human interface but will lack the necessary human touch if the organization neglects the socio-cultural aspect of reengineering change. Throughout the whole process of reengineering from conception to implementation, as the organization goes about implementing the technical changes, conscious attention needs to be paid concurrently to the socio-cultural success factors.

Change is often painful. Effective change management that gives assistance to staff affected to cope with the change is necessary for reengineering to succeed [11, 42–49]. To facilitate the transition to new processes, attention needs to be given to staff training. The organizational environment has to be consistent with the operational mode of the organization. A supportive organizational environment with appropriate reward system is often a potent way of reducing the pain that naturally comes with change [22, 43, 46, 49]. To be effective, management needs to be willing and able to empower the reengineering teams to recommend and make necessary and appropriate changes to organizational systems [22, 44, 45, 47–49]. Prior assessment of the organizational need for change is essential. As organizations are advised never to change for the sake of changing, members of the organization need to understand the rationale for the change [11, 22, 42–44, 47, 49].

If members of an organization not only feel the need for change, but also have a strong desire to succeed in the change, the organization is ready for the change and is well on its way to succeed in the reengineering effort [11, 22, 42–44, 47, 49]. Suspicious grows in the absence of trust. To garner the cooperation and support from staff in accepting the change, mutual trust between management and staff is critical to success [11, 22, 43, 46–48]. To gain the understanding and commitment of staff, the opinions and views of staff need to be actively sought during the reengineering process [11, 22, 42–44, 46, 48, 49]. An assessment of the organizational readiness is necessary before implementing a reengineering change. Organizations with collaborative culture are cited to be more conducive for reengineering to succeed [22, 42, 43, 45–49]. Programs to prepare the organization for the change are therefore necessary as part of the reengineering exercise.

Reengineering requires efforts to buy-in the commitment and understanding of staff affected by the change. Understanding the organizational culture, assessing its readiness and creating a trusting environment are integral parts of the change process, as these set the effective limit and extent to which reengineering is possible for the organization.

> Hypothesis 3: The yin factors influence the outcome of the reengineering initiative in improving the organizational performance and effectiveness through their contribution to building a shared vision for the change.

4.4. Conducive learning environment

Michael Hammer advocates that reengineering requires organization to redesign its processes from scratch. This calls for framebreaking, creativity and innovation, all of which imply the need for the organization to learn. Hammer's second principle is for the organization to embark on a program of continuous change. The latter principle requires the organization to be committed to learning [41].

Technical factors of reengineering need to be complemented by socio-cultural factors, so as to achieve the overall organizational performance and effectiveness in the reengineering effort. For the organization to reap the desired results of reengineering, competing demands of the yin and yang factors need to be balanced. To mediate the dilemma between these factors, literature advocates the need for a conducive environment that supports **organizational learning** [11, 42–46, 49]. At the heart of reengineering is the need to cultivate a conducive organizational environment where **double-loop learning** takes place.

In double-loop learning, organization challenges and redefines its purpose of existence, challenging past held and existing assumptions and modes of operation [60]. Such an environment is necessary to mediate the contributions of the technical and socio-cultural factors toward meeting the organizational expectations of the change. Organizational learning [61–69] is critical to produce the long-term desired results of major organizational change such as reengineering. Successful organizations pay attention to learning [60, 70].

The key factors affecting the effectiveness of organizational change, though discussed above under the four themes: shared vision, technical, socio-cultural and conducive environment, are in essence closely interrelated. In particular, the technical theme that refers to the rational and logical aspect of change can be seen as opposite and yet complementary to the socio-cultural that refers to the emotional and cultural aspect of change. Clearly a balance between the technical and socio-cultural aspects is necessary for either one to be effective. Developing a **conducive learning environment** is posited as critical to mediate for such balance.

> Hypothesis 4: The organizational conducive environment for learning mediates the contribution of the yin-yang factors to the organizational shared vision for the reengineering change.

5. Research Methodology and Results

The first ever Singapore Public Sector Survey on Success Factors for Change was conducted in the first quarter of 1997 [71–73]. The objective of the study was to empirically test the YYB Model as represented by the above four hypotheses.

5.1. Research methodology

The survey was piloted with 22 senior managers, from eight different public organizations, who were invited to complete the questionnaire based on the experience in their organizations. Personal interviews with ten reengineering practitioners were conducted to solicit detailed comments on the YYB Model and the questionnaire design.

The final questionnaire was mailed out to 500 senior public administrators of 235 government departments and statutory boards. 151 (30.2% response rate) from more than 80 different organizations responded. Respondents were asked to answer the questions based on one specific successful or failed project undertaken in their organization. They were asked to what extent they agreed with the items describing various variables on a Likert type scale ranging from 1 (Strongly Disagree) to 6 (Strongly Agree).

The items were constructed from the literature review and through focus group discussions, and validated in the pilot study. Appendix gives the multiple-item scale used. In addition, reliability tests were conducted on the actual survey data in parallel with factor analyses to confirm the scales used. Factor analyses using varimax rotation to extract the principal components of eigenvalue greater than one were conducted to verify the underlying latent factors represented by these items. These factors were subsequently used in regression analyses to test the four hypotheses.

5.2. Results of analyses

Factors examined before project: Twelve items were used to measure areas that were looked into before the organization embarked on the project. One item 'structure of the organization' had high factor loadings for both factors and was removed. Factor analysis on the eleven items gave two latent factors that clearly divide the socio-cultural items from the technical ones examined (Table 1). Reliability tests on the factors gave Cronbach alpha of .9186 and .8391 respectively, all showing high levels of reliability of the scales.

Table 1 Latent factors examined before project

Descriptions of items examined prior to project	Factor 1	Factor 2
SOCIO-CULTURAL (YIN) (α = .9186)		
Culture of the organization	.85651	.18353
Staff mindset	.84093	.27995
Mutual trust between management and staff	.80516	.23306
Management Mindset	.78961	.35923
Organizational readiness for change	.76870	.33489
Organizational need for change	.71165	.28457
Eigenvalue = 6.00816 Pct of Var = 54.6%		
TECHNICAL (YANG) (α = .8391)		
Workflow of the organization	.19313	.82556
Process management system	.24972	.81803
Information system of the organization	.24976	.76301
Service to customers	.24717	.63779
Customers' processes	.36661	.62613
Eigenvalue = 1.37955 Pct of Var = 12.5%		

Shared vision: Ten items were used to measure the extent to which vision for change was shared in the organization. Factor analysis confirmed these items as one latent factor of eigenvalue 6.47426, accounting for 64.7% of the variance. The scale had Cronbach alpha of .9383.

Organizational learning: Twelve items were used to measure the extent of learning that was taking place in the organization. Factor analysis confirmed the items as representing one latent factor of eigenvalue 6.60315, accounting for 55% of the variance. Reliability analysis of the scale gave an alpha of .9229.

Project met expectation: Respondents were asked to what extent they agreed, on the same 6 point Likert type scale, that the project had met the organizational expectation of improving the organizational performance and effectiveness.

Regression analyses were performed to measure the predictive power of each underlying success factor on the extent to which the organization met its expectation, testing the four hypotheses.

Shared vision: Simple regression analysis performed using the factor score for shared vision as the independent variable of the extent project had met expectation gave a beta value of .643 and a highly significant R^2 value of .413. Stepwise multiple regression analyses with the shared vision, included as one of the independent variables, consistently gave shared vision as the only variable in the regression equation. This result confirmed the paramount importance of having a shared vision in undertaking any reengineering initiative, hence supporting the Hypothesis 1, that having a shared vision contributes significantly to the outcome of the reengineering effort in meeting its expectation of improving the organizational performance and effectiveness.

Technical success factors: Simple regression analysis performed with the factor score of the 'yang' factors examined before the project as independent variables of the shared vision gave a multiple R^2 value of .197 and a value of F that was highly significant. The positive regression coefficient of 444 and significant R^2 value supported the Hypothesis 2, that technical success factors influence the outcome of the reengineering initiative in improving the organizational performance and effectiveness through their contribution to build a shared vision for the change.

Socio-cultural success factors: Likewise, simple regression analysis performed, using the factor score of the 'yin' factors examined before the project as independent variables, gave a multiple R^2 value of .213 and a value of F that was highly significant. The positive regression coefficient of .461 and significant R^2 value supported the Hypothesis 3, that socio-cultural factors influence the outcome of the reengineering initiative in improving the organizational performance and effectiveness through their contribution to build a shared vision for the change.

Organizational learning: Simple regression analysis, using factor score of organizational learning as independent variables of shared vision for change gave a highly significant multiple R^2 value of .282 with a regression coefficient of .531.

Stepwise multiple regression analyses confirmed the effect of organizational learning on the contributions made by the yin and yang factors. Table 2 summarizes the findings, showing a higher beta value for yin factor when learning was low, and lower beta value for yin factor when learning was high.

Table 2 Effect of organizational learning (1)

Variables	β values Learning < 0	Learning >= 0
yang factors examined	.343	.395
yin factors examined	.486	.186

The higher beta weight for yin factor when learning is low implies greater attention was needed to the socio-cultural aspect of project when the organizational environment is less conducive to learning. This mediating effect of organizational learning on the yin and yang factors supports Hypothesis 4, that the organizational conducive environment for learning mediates the contribution of the yin-yang factors to the organizational shared vision for the reengineering change.

6. Conclusions

The four hypotheses developed to test the proposed Yin-Yang Balanced (YYB) Model were empirically supported by the evidence collected in the Singapore Public Sector Survey.

Analyses confirmed that having a shared vision is paramount to reengineering success. Organizational learning has positive mediating effects on the yin and yang factors involved in undertaking the project. This mediating effect is also evident in the yin-yang contributions toward the building of a shared vision for change.

This chapter has provided some interesting insights into how reengineering is accomplished in the public sector of Singapore. An area for further research is to replicate the study in other countries and the private sector, so that the YYB Model can be refined and generalized for wider applications.

7. Acknowledgments

The Public Sector Survey on Success Factors for Change would not have been possible without the generous support and sponsorship of the Centre of Strategic Process Innovation of the National Computer Board, Singapore. A special vote of thanks is due to the staff of the Centre, in particular, Chan Meng Khoong for his support.

References

1. H. J. Harrington, *Business Process Improvement* (New York, McGraw-Hill, 1991).
2. D. K. Carr, K. S. Dougherry, H. J. Johansson, R. A. King and D. E. Moran, *Breakpoint: Business Process Redesign* (Coopers & Lybrand, Arlington, Va., 1992).
3. T. H. Davenport, *Process Innovation: Reengineering Work Through Information Technology* (Harvard Business School Press, Boston, Mass., 1993).
4. M. Hammer and J. Champy, *Reengineering the Corporation: A Manifesto for Business Revolution* (Nicholas Brealey, London, 1993).
5. S. L. Caudle, Reengineering strategies and issues, *Public Productivity & Management Review*, Winter 1994, **18**(2), (1994) 149–162.

6. A. Gore, *The Gore Report on Reinventing Government: Creating a Government that Works Better and Costs Less* (Times Books, New York, 1993).
7. A. Braganza and A. Myers, Issues and dilemmas facing organizations in the effective implementation of BPR, *Research Paper, Business Change & Reengineering* **3**(2), (1996) 38–51.
8. T. Bryant and D. Chan, BPR — to redesign or not to redesign?, *Research Paper, Business Change & Reengineering* **3**(2), (1996) 52–61.
9. R. Smeds, Successful transformation: strategic evolution management for competitive advantage, *Research Paper, Business Change & Reengineering* **3**(2), (1996) 62–72.
10. M. M. Klein, Reengineering methodologies and tools, *Information Systems Management* **11**(2), Spring (1994) 30–35.
11. R. Talwar, Reengineering — a wonder drug for the 90s? in C. Coulson-Thomas (ed.), *Business Process Reengineering: Myth and Reality* (Kogan Page, London, 1994) pp. 40–59.
12. B. G. Posner and L. R. Rothstein, Reinventing the business of government: an interview with change catalyst David Osborne, *Harvard Business Review*, May-June 1994, 133–140.
13. J. E. McKenzie, *Chaos, Paradox and Learning — Key Composites in the Revolutionary Change Process: Towards a More Holistic Strategic Paradigm for Transformation* Ph.D. thesis, Henley Management College, Brunel University, 1994.
14. H. Smith, *The Religion of Man (Perennial Library)* (Harper and Row, New York, 1965).
15. A. Watts, with the collaboration of Al Chung-Liang Huang, *Tao: The Watercourse Way* (Pantheon Books, New York, 1975).
16. E.-Q. Zhang (ed.), *Basic Theory of Traditional Chinese Medicine (I): A Practical English-Chinese Library of Traditional Chinese Medicine* (Publishing House of Shanghai College of Traditional Chinese Medicine, Shanghai, 1988).
17. S. Deng, Acupuncture treatment of syncope based on differentiation of signs and symptons, *Journal of Traditional Chinese Medicine* September, **10**(3), 182–188.
18. S. Tang and R. Craze, *Chinese Herbal Medicine: How to Use and Benefit from the Healing Power of Chinese Herbs* (Judy Piatkus, London, 1995).
19. X. Guang, *Chinese Herbal Medicine: A Practical Guide to the Healing Power of Herbs* (Vermilion, London, 196).

20. S. McNamara and X.-K. Song, *Traditional Chinese Medicine* (Hamish Hamilton, London, 1997).
21. J. Champy, *Reengineering Management: The Mandate for New Leadership* (Harper Business, New York, 1995).
22. M. Hammer and S. A. Stanton, *The Reengineering Revolution* (Harper-Collins, New York, 1994).
23. M. S. Scott-Morton (ed.), *The Corporation of the 1990s: Information Technology and Organizational Transformation* (Oxford University Press, New York, 1991).
24. C. A. Bartlett and S. Ghoshal, Changing the role of top management: beyond structure to processes, *Harvard Business Review*, January-February 1995, 87–96.
25. A. M. Khademian, Reinventing a government corporation: professional priorities and a clear bottom line, *Public Administration Review* **55**(1), (1995) 17–27.
26. Civil Service College, Ethos: harnessing change in the public service (Internal Publication, 1995).
27. Y. L. Doz and C. K. Prahalad, A process model of strategic redirection in large complex firms: the case of multinational corporations, in A. Pettigrew (ed.), *The Management of Strategic Change* (Basil Blackwell, Oxford, England, 1987) pp. 63–83.
28. S. R. Robbins and R. B. Duncan, The role of the CEO and top management in the creation and implementation of strategic vision, in D. C. Hambrick (ed.), *The Executive Effect: Concepts and Methods for Studying Top Managers* (JAI Press, Greenwich, CT, 1988) pp. 137–162.
29. M. Sashkin, The visionary leader, in J. A. Conger and R. N. Kanugo (eds.), *Charismatic Leadership* (Jossey-Bass, San Francisco, 1988) pp. 120–160.
30. J. P. Kotter, *A Force for Change: How Leadership Differs from Management* (Free Press, New York, 1990).
31. J. G. Hunt, *Leadership: A New Synthesis* (Sage, Newbury Park, CA, 1991).
32. A. E. Pearson, Six basics for general managers, *Harvard Business Review* **67**(4), (1989) 94–101A.
33. R. L. Phillips and J. G. Hunt, Strategic leadership: an introduction, in R. L. Phillips and J. G. Hunt (eds.), *Strategic Leadership: A Multi-organizational-Level Perspective* (Quorum, Westport, CT, 1992) pp. 3–14.

34. M. Sashkin, Strategic leadership competencies: an introduction, in R. L. Phillips and J. G. Hunt (eds.), *Strategic Leadership: A Multiorganizational-Level Perspective* (Quorum, Westport, CT, 1992) pp. 139–160.
35. R. Greenwood and C. R. Hinings, Organizational design types, tracks and the dynamics of strategic change, *Organization Studies* **9** (1988) 293–316.
36. R. Greenwood and C. R. Hinings, Understanding strategic change: the contribution of archetypes, *Academy of Management Journal* **36** (1993) 1052–1081.
37. C. R. Hinings and R. Greenwood, *The Dynamics of Strategic Change* (Basil Blackwell, New York, 1988).
38. J. M. Kouzes and B. Z. Posner, *The Leadership Challenge* (Jossey-Bass, San Francisco, 1987).
39. H. Aghassi, Organizational structures, people and technology, in C. Coulson-Thomas (ed.), *Business Process Reengineering: Myth and Reality* (Kogan Page, London, 1994) pp. 192–200.
40. L. Larwood, C. M. Falbe, M. P. Kriger and P. Miesing, Structure and meaning of organizational vision, *Academy of Management Journal* **38**(3), (June 1995) 740–769.
41. M. Hammer, Reengineering work: don't automate, obliterate, *Harvard Business Review*, July/August, **68**(4), (1990) 104–112.
42. P. Sadler, *Managing Change* (Kogan Page, London, 1995).
43. C. Coulson-Thomas, Implementing reengineering in C. Coulson-Thomas (ed.), *Business Process Reengineering: Myth and Reality* (Kogan Page, London, 1994) pp. 105–125.
44. W. G. Bennis and M. Mische, *The 21st Century Organization: Reinventing Through Reengineering* (Pfeiffer & Company, San Diego, CA, 1995).
45. D. C. Andrews and S. K. Stalick, *Business Reengineering: The Survival Guide* (Yourdon Press, Englewood Cliffs, NJ, 1994).
46. J. A. Edosomwan, *Organizational Transformation and Process Reengineering* (St. Lucie Press, Florida, 1996).
47. D. K. Carr and H. J. Johansson, *Best Practices in Reengineering: What Works and What Doesn't in the Reengineering Process* (McGraw-Hill, New York, 1995).
48. D. P. Petrozzo and J. C. Stepper, *Successful Reengineering* (Van Nostrand Reinhold, New York, 1994).

49. J. R. Caron, S. L. Jarvenpaa and D. B. Stoddard, Business reengineering at CIGNA corporation: experiences and lessons learned from the first five years, *Management Information Systems Quarterly*, September 1994 233–250.
50. D. Osborne and T. Gaebler, *Reinventing Government: How the Entrepreneurial Spirit is Transforming the Public Sector* (Addison-Wesley, Reading, Mass., 1992).
51. Y. Sarason, A model of organizational transformation: the incorporation of organizational identity into a structuration theory framework, *Academy of Management Journal* **38** (1995) 47–51.
52. C. Lau and R. W. Woodman, Understanding organizational change: a schematic perspective, *Academy of Management Journal* **38**(2), April 1995, 537–554.
53. A. Giddens, *New Rules of Sociological Method* (Hutchinson, London, 1976).
54. A. Giddens, *Central Problems in Social Theory: Action, Structure and Contradictions In social Analysis* (Macmillan, London, 1979).
55. A. Giddens, *The Constitution of Society: Outline of the Theory of Structuration* (University of California Press, Berkeley, 1984).
56. A. Giddens, *Modernity and Self-Identity* (Polity, Combridge, 1991).
57. J. M. Kouzes and B. Z. Posner, *The Leadership Challenge* (Jossey-Bass, San Francisco, 1987) p. 168.
58. H. P. Jr. Sims and P. Lorenzi, *The New Leadership Paradigm: Social Learning and Cognition in Organizations* (Sage, Newbury Park, CA, 1992) pp 296–297.
59. F. Westley and H. Mintzberg, Visionary leadership and strategic management, *Strategic Management Journal* **10** (1989) 17–32.
60. C. Argyris, Double loop learning in organizations, *Harvard Business Review* **55**(5), (September/October 1977) 115–125.
61. P. M. Senge, *The Fifth Discipline: The Art and Practise of the Learning Organization* (Century Business Books, London, 1990).
62. A. J. DiBella, Developing learning organizations: a matter of perspective, *Academy of Management Journal* **38** (1995) 287–290.
63. P. M. Senge, A. Kleiner, C. Roberts, R. B. Ross and B. J. Smith, *The Fifth Discipline Handbook: Strategies and Tools for Building a Learning Organization* (Doubleday, New York, 1994).
64. R. Fritz, *Corporate Tides: Redesigning the Organization* (Butterworth Heinemann, Oxford, 1994).

65. D. A. Garvin, Building a learning organization, *Harvard Business Review* **71**(4), (July/August 1993) 78–91.
66. B. Hedberg, How organizations learn and unlearn, in P. C. Nystrom and W. H. Starbuck (eds.), *Handbook of Organizational Design* **1** (Oxford University Press, London, 1981) pp. 8–27.
67. W. E. Schneider, *The Reengineering Alternative: A Plan for Making Your Current Culture Work* (Irwin Professional Pub., Burr Ridge, Ill., 1994).
68. E. Schein, *Organizational Culture and Leadership*, 2nd edition (Jossey-Bass, San Francisco, 1992).
69. C. Hampden-Turner, *Corporate Culture: From Vicious to Virtuous Circles* (Economist Books, London, 1990).
70. C. Argyris, *On Organizational Learning* (Blackwell Business, Cambridge Mass, 1993).
71. T. -H. Yim-Teo, Reengineering in the public sector (of Singapore): empirical evidence for a "yin" and "yang" balanced approach to organizational change, Conference Paper, in *Proceedings (Volume 2) of ISAS '97, World MultiConference on Systemics, Cybernetics and Informatics*, Caracas, Venezuela, 1997a.
72. T.-H. Yim-Teo, Singapore public sector survey on success factors for change, Survey Report, *Centre of Strategic Process Innovation*, Singapore, 1997b.
73. T.-H. Yim-Teo, *The Yin-Yang Balanced Concept of Organizational Changes Leading to a Double-Loop Learning Control (DLC) Model for Reengineering in the Public Sector Reengineering*, DBA thesis, Henley Management College, Brunel University, 1998.

Appendix

Relevant items used in the survey questionnaire:

Items for measuring socio-cultural (yin) and technical (yang) areas examined before the organization embarked on the project:

a. Service to customers
b. Customers' processes

c. Structure of the organization
d. Workflow of the organization
e. Information system of the organization
f. Process management system
g. Staff mindset
h. Management mindset
i. Mutual trust between management and staff
j. Organizational readiness for change
k. Organizational need for change
l. Culture of the organization

Items for measuring organizational learning (note item c is negatively coded):

a. Managers see staff development as their key responsibility.
b. Giving and receiving feedback is a normal practice.
c. People do not question proven ways of doing things.
d. Individuals are proactive in developing their own learning.
e. People are trained to give and receive feedback.
f. Individuals are supportive of their colleagues' learning.
g. People often try out new ways of doing things.
h. Rewards are established to reinforce the motivation to learn.
I. People always question past held assumptions and norms.
j. People focus on learning opportunities rather than the status of their job.
k. Individuals are empowered to apply their learning to the way they do their jobs.
l. The organization continually benchmarks itself against 'best practices.'

Items for measuring extent of vision for change is shared:

a. Goals and objectives of the project are clearly specified.
b. Goals are linked to the overall corporate vision and strategy.
c. Vision is tied to customer expectations and requirements.
d. Purpose and direction of change are clearly communicated.

e. Everyone affected understands the goals and shares the vision.
f. Clear performance indicators are set to measure the outcome.
g. Top/senior management is fully committed to the change.
h. Senior management played the active leadership role.
i. Progress and outcomes of the project are shared openly.
j. Staff are actively involved in making the project a success.

PART IV

PRIVATE SECTOR EXPERIENCE

Chapter 18

Information Technology Dimensions and Interdependencies in BPR Projects

ROGER SOR and DIETER FINK
School of Management Information Systems,
Edith Cowan University
Churchlands WA 6018, Australia
E-mail: r.sor@cowan.edu.au

Management increasingly are examining ways to redesign organizational practices to improve the quality of their products and services. This has led to the phenomenon of Business Process Reengineering (BPR). Business process reengineering purposefully discards existing tasks, processes and structures and replaces them with complete new ways of accomplishing work. The aim of BPR is to have innovative approaches to business operations rather than incremental improvements.

The study analyzed BPR projects conducted in four organizations. These organizations were a large construction company, a medium-sized manufacturer, a large multinational mining company and a large banking organization. First, BPR projects were examined along Information Technology (IT) dimensions determined by task variety and task knowledge. The findings indicated that technical-professional technologies, in the form of databases and transaction processing systems, were predominantly used to achieve organizational restructuring.

Second, BPR projects were examined in process interdependencies. The set of interdependencies between information processes themselves and with other processes is a major factor in creating organizational complexity because it is the factor that creates the need for coordination between tasks. The greater the interdependence, the more resources (rules, schedules, and line and staff officials) must be devoted to coordination mechanisms. The use of IT in BPR led to the absorption of sequential and reciprocal interdependencies thereby reducing the need for coordination and organizational resources.

1. Introduction

Management during the 1990s has been obsessed with improving the efficiency and effectiveness of its organizations. A common approach is to reduce costs, largely in respect to labor, whenever possible. However, as observed by Drucker [1], "Cutting staff to cut costs is putting the cart before the horse. The only way to bring costs down is to restructure work." Management has increasingly come to accept this proposition and is examining ways to redesigning organizational practices to improve the quality of its products and services. This has led to the phenomenon of business process reengineering (BPR).

Information Technology (IT) plays a key role in the restructuring of organizations. Scott [2] points out that the technology-structure relationship can be viewed from two points of view. One can look at the impact of technology on organizational structure and performance and one can look at how organizational structures vary in their capacities to appropriate or to generate new technologies. We examined the first relationship, and begin by discussing BPR and the opportunities offered by IT in reshaping the organization.

2. Business Process Reengineering

In one of management literature's 'classic' articles, Hammer [3] advocated that in the 1990s "We should 'reengineer' our businesses:

use the power of modern information technology to radically redesign our business processes in order to achieve dramatic improvements in their performance." He discussed seven principles of business process reengineering. Several of these can either be performed by IT or facilitated by it. The seven principles are:

Principle 1: Organize around outcomes, not tasks.
Principle 2: Have those who use the output of the process perform the process.
Principle 3: Subsume information-processing work into the real work that produces the information.
Principle 4: Treat geographically dispersed resources as though they were centralized.
Principle 5: Link parallel activities instead of integrating their results.
Principle 6: Put the decision point where the work is performed, and build control into the process.
Principle 7: Capture information once and at the source.

Business process reengineering purposefully discards existing tasks, processes and structures and replaces them with complete new ways of accomplishing work. The aim of BPR is to have innovative approaches to business operations rather than incremental improvements. Early experiences with BPR seem to indicate a range of outcomes; "The changes implemented by some organizations vary from simplifying to reinventing processes." [4]

The lessons to be learned by Australian firms, based on empirical research into BPR conducted by Broadbent and Butler [4], include the following:

1. The need for strong, visible executive management support.
2. The importance of constant communication of the motivation and progress of process changes.
3. The use of consultants and lateral thinking.
4. The need to manage consultants and insure skill transfer.

5. The importance of measurements for both current and redesigned processes.
6. The need for an external customer or supplier focus in the redesigned processes.
7. Education and support of all stakeholders in the process change.
8. Determining an appropriate role for technology.
9. Recognition of, and preparation for, the different phases of commitment to BPR which might be evident at different times.
10. The importance of focusing on the nature of work and the role of people, not the organization or its technology.

According to Broadbent and Butler [4] there are basically five motivations to seek out BPR. Two of the motivations are underpinned by IT. One is the utilization of the rapid advancements over the last decade of new technologies that are both flexible and affordable (e.g. imaging, EDI, mobile computing). The other is the renewal or migration of legacy systems and applications because older Information Systems (IS) no longer meet today's organizational requirements.

Interest in BPR has caused a number of themes to emerge in the BPR literature. Among them are the motivation for undertaking a BPR project, the communication process during a BPR intervention, and the outcomes of BPR projects [5]. Our study falls into the last mentioned domain. The study's objective was to observe the IT dimensions and interdependencies in BPR projects that had recently been completed.

3. Information Technology Dimensions

Perrow [6, 7] was among the first to identify the dimensions of technology as far as work is affected. According to Daft and MacIntosh [8] and Daft [5], Perrow identified two dimensions of activities that influence the type of technology employed. These are task variety and task analyzability. By treating these dimensions as coordinate axes, four quadrants were produced. Each quadrant represents a different type of technology. They are craft, routine, engineering and non-routine technologies. Daft and MacIntosh [8], by changing task analyzability to task knowledge, interpreted Perrow's quadrants in terms of information technology (see Fig. 1).

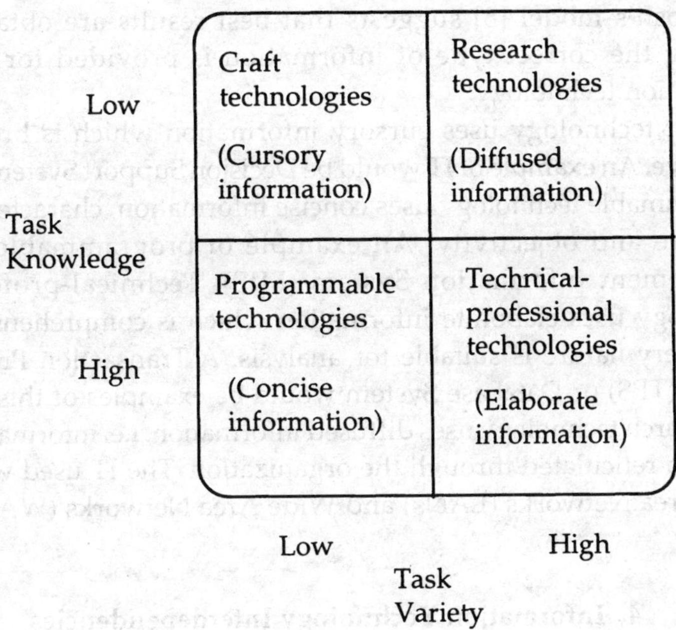

Figure 1 Information technology dimensions (Adapted from Daft and MacIntosh, p. 87 [7])

An IT task is perceived as a process in which input is converted into output. This process is determined by task variety and task knowledge. Task variety is the "frequency of unexpected and novel events that occur in the conversion process" [5]. High task knowledge implies that the conversion process is understood and known ways exist to respond to problems. However, for some problems the cause and effect relationships in the conversion process are not well understood and it is difficult to find a solution (low task knowledge).

The four quadrants were named craft, programmable (previously routine), technical-professional (previously engineering) and research (previously non-routine) technologies. Each type of IT is designed to cope with a qualitatively different class of information. Daft and MacIntosh's model [8] suggests that best results are obtained by insuring the correct type of information is provided for a given information technology.

Craft technology uses cursory information which is broad and subjective. An example of IT would be Decision Support Systems (DSS). Programmable technology uses concise information, characterized by structure and objectivity. An example of programmable IT is a Management Information System (MIS). Technical-professional technology uses elaborate information which is comprehensive and by its very nature is suitable for analysis. A Transaction Processing System (TPS) or Database System would be examples of this form of IT. Research technology uses diffused information, i.e. information that has been reticulated through the organization. The IT used would be Local Area Networks (LANs) and Wide Area Networks (WANs).

4. Information Technology Interdependencies

Scott [2] states that three dimensions of technology are most significant for predicting structural arrangements. These are complexity, uncertainty and interdependence. Our interest is in interdependence, which is the extent to which the items or elements involved in the work processes themselves are interrelated, so that changes in the state of one element affect the state of the others.

Thompson [9] described three types of technological interdependence; they were classified as pooled, sequential and reciprocal. In pooled interdependence work does not flow between units. Rather each unit or selected units contribute to a pool from which they and others take. According to Thompson [9] use is made of mediating technology. "A mediating technology provides products or services that mediate or link clients from the external environment, and in so doing allows each department to work independently. Banks, brokerage firms and real estate offices all mediate between buyers and sellers but the offices work independently within the organization."

Sequential interdependence could be called serial interdependence. The output from one unit is the input to the next. The second unit is dependent on the first performing to standard. Thompson [9] saw sequential interdependence occurring in long linked technologies. In these cases each stage of production is dependent on the previous for its input.

Reciprocal interdependence occurs when the output of unit A is the input to unit B and the output of unit B is then the input to unit A. Daft [5] gives an example of a hospital where a patient might move back and forth between X-ray, surgery and physiotherapy. Patient care requires several departments to be linked reciprocally. Thompson [9] sees reciprocal interdependence occurring in intensive industries.

The set of interdependencies between information processes themselves and with other processes is a major factor in creating organizational complexity because it is the factor that creates the need for coordination between tasks. The greater the interdependence, the more resources (rules, schedules, and line and staff officials) must be devoted to coordination mechanisms. Interdependencies should be reduced during BPR through the use of IT.

5. Coordination Tasks

March and Simon [10] presented three types of task coordination; standardization, the use of plans and schedules and by mutual adjustment. This is also the sequence of their use as a situation becomes more variable, less routine and less predictable. Thompson [11] concluded that the types of interdependence and the types of coordination parallel each other, so as the level of interdependence increases so does the type of coordination required, as shown in Table 1. Thompson also concluded that there are real costs associated with coordination, so reducing the level of interdependence also reduces the cost of coordination.

Table 1 IT characteristics of case studies

Case Study	IT Quadrants	IT Interdependencies	Coordination
CO	Craft Technical-professional	Pooled Sequential Reciprocal	standard planned/schedules mutual adjustment
MA	Technical-professional Programmable	Reciprocal	mutual adjustment
MM	Technical-professional Research	Sequential Reciprocal	planned/schedules
BA	Technical-professional Programmable	Pooled Sequential Reciprocal	standard planned/schedules mutual adjustment

6. Research Approach

The case studies discussed in this paper were obtained from a larger study to uncover what strategies organizations could use to implement downsizing. A series of semi-structured interviews was conducted with organizations in the Perth metropolitan area and its close environs. A number of case studies were completed.

A case study can be defined as "an empirical enquiry that investigates a contemporary phenomenon within its real-life context, especially when the boundaries between the phenomenon and context are not clearly evident." Yin [11], quoted in Trihajuwidjajani [12]. The case studies in our study capture the theoretical proposition of the research variables, namely IT dimensions and interdependencies. Relying on theoretical propositions helps to focus attention on certain data and to ignore other data [11].

7. Case Studies

In this section we outline the characteristics of organizational projects that we studied. A discussion of our findings is provided in the following section.

Large Construction Company (CO)

CO is a large to medium-sized engineering construction company. The major component of its work is fabricating buildings and parts of engineering plants. In addition, it seeks to perform maintenance work for the large manufacturers in their area and elsewhere. The majority of the skills it requires are available in the community of which they are a member.

Prior to implementing the new system, the company had to create a physical record for each employee, and potential employee (e.g. people who had worked for them previously on short contracts). Names had to be stored in an accessible form and needed to be regularly updated. It was necessary to keep multiple lists of people by skill and people by experience. Creating a list of potential employees for a contract or job was a major task, as was creating a mail and telephone list to check if they were available.

The computer system now creates and uses the information it needs. In the process of absorbing virtually all the tasks associated with the process it has also absorbed the interdependencies. A list of potential employees and a mailing/telephone list can be produced for many clients within the hour. They no longer need several typists, wages clerks and clerical assistants. The staff associated with the system consist of two receptionists/data input clerks and a systems manager. The head of the Human Resource Management (HRM) section was the main user at the time of the interview and was keenly associated with the system.

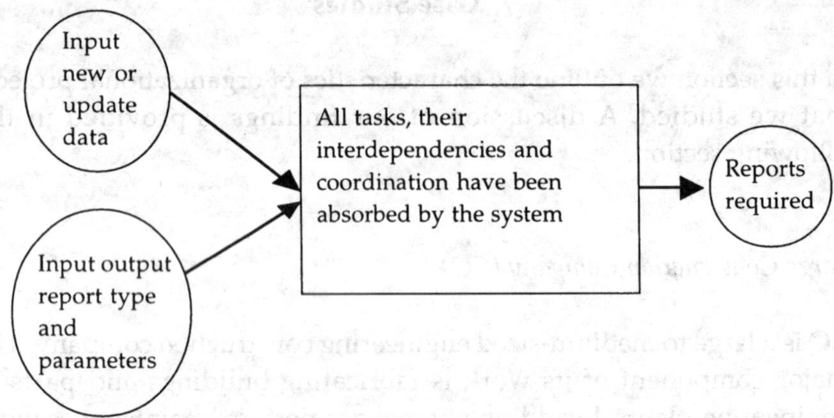

Figure 2 The reduced dependency relationships after the IT was implemented

Medium-Sized Manufacturer (MA)

This medium-sized organization manufactures an important basic chemical. Management had entered into a contract/alliance with a large equipment hire company to supply all of their non-plant and mobile equipment from small items up to items like fork-lift vehicles. In order to win the contract, the hire company had to develop a computer system that gave MA online access to their warehouse inventory system. This means that whenever MA needs an item they call it up on the hire company's system and place an order online. The item is delivered in the earliest possible timeframe.

The system also supplies MA with all the management information they need, like the total hours of usage for each class of item used, broken down by the site at which it was used, the time to get the items required and the breakdown rate for each piece of equipment. As a result of this facility MA do not have to purchase the equipment or hire the staff to maintain the equipment. In addition they do not need the clerical staff to collate the management information. The hire company benefits because not only do they have a satisfied and somewhat captive customer, but they also have a tool that gives them an edge when they tender to other large organizations. This was described as a win-win situation.

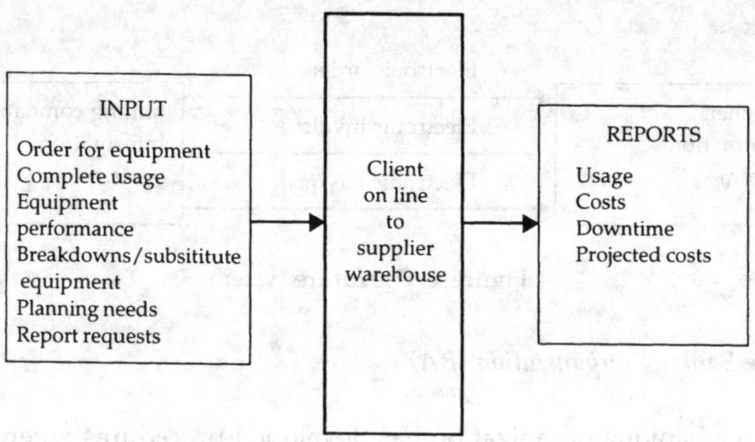

Figure 3 Reduced dependencies after implementing IT

Large Multinational Mining Company (MM)

MM is a large mining company. It assigned a manager with the specific task of reengineering his division to reduce the number of people and departments (there were eight) in the division. This meant that he had to find ways of simplifying and automating all accounting and clerical functions. To reduce functions, processes had to be reengineered so that people did not perform tasks just because they were performed previously. The division did not use more or new technology, they just used their current computer facilities more efficiently.

The interviewee reported that as a result of the reengineering project, 80% of tasks (steps in the process) performed in the Accounts Payable section were dropped. For example, only invoices above a certain level were physically checked. For others, comparisons were made by the computer against previous invoices and exceptions reported. The department head had entered into discussions with suppliers to arrange for electronic funds transfers (EFT). Eventually they hope to have no invoices, and no cheques.

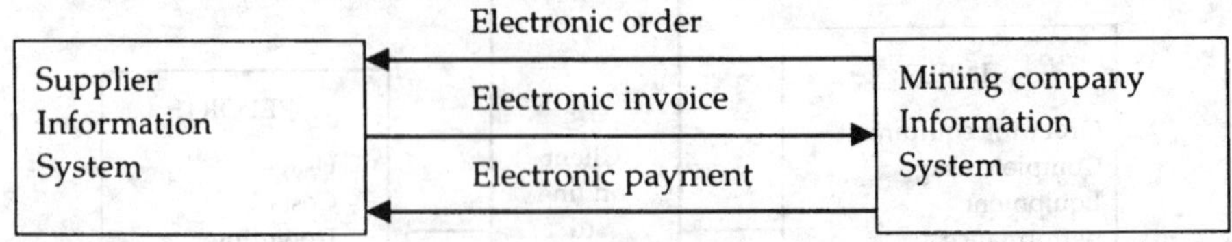

Figure 4 The future system

Large Banking Organization (BA)

A large banking organization has developed procedures whereby all queries come to the one central point and are then passed out to the appropriate people. This includes the administration of loans. Local branches accept details and pass them on by computer link to a nodal point which processes applications and makes decisions. Many of the decisions can be made by the computer. Another application uses widely distributed ATMs linked to a central accounting center for cash withdrawal.

Clients feel that they are receiving a better service, and the bank has reduced the number of highly paid and clerical staff in the branches. Less specialized skills and fewer supervisors are necessary; so less administrative layers are required. The difficulties previously experienced of having loan files at different places and different people qualified to assess loans at different levels has been largely removed. A multiskilled branch officer can process loan applications by either inputting the requisite information or passing the application request on to an officer at the central node.

8. Discussion

Within the Large Construction Company (CO) procedures are well-known but not simple. A database approach is used toward meeting the information needs of management. The IT process could therefore be classified as *technical-professional*. However, the reengineered system still has a component of the *craft* dimension in that staff often know employees and employers and use this knowledge to match people with jobs.

The IT in use at CO provides a database for the benefit of employees, potential employees and clients. IT mediates between the needs of external employees and clients and therefore supports *pooled* interdependence. The computer system now creates and uses the information needed by staff and management, thereby absorbing many of the *sequential* and *reciprocal* interdependencies connecting tasks. This has led to improved client service and fewer staff.

The Medium-Sized Manufacturer (MA), by entering into a strategic alliance relationship with a large equipment hire company, has access to IT resources to process its data and meet its information requirements. The order processing system is typical of a transaction processing system and hence reflects the *technical-professional* quadrant of IT. On the other hand, the production of management information by the system is a characteristic of MIS and is therefore an example of a *programmable* quadrant of IT.

MA exhibits a *reciprocal* IT interdependency with the hire company. The input of MA in the form of orders is reciprocated by the information that the hire company provides to MA in the form of equipment availability. Based on the information provided, MA is able to confirm or not confirm its order for equipment.

Within the Large Multinational Mining Company (MM) examples of two quadrants were observed. The automation of accounting and clerical functions (e.g. Accounts Payable) implies a *technical-professional* use of IT. However, evidence of the *research* quadrant exists in the form of the emerging electronic funds transfer system which eventually may lead to the introduction of Electronic Data Interchange (EDI). Through the use of networks, information is widely diffused, both within the organization and between associated organizations.

MM has reduced the number of tasks in its accounting processes, thereby reducing *sequential* and *reciprocal* interdependencies. The introduction of EFT and later EDI will play an important role in the future. These technologies are examples of so called 'long linked technologies' [11]. Organizations are becoming increasingly interdependent with themselves and with their customer through electronic links in the form of computer networks, particular the internet.

The Large Banking Organization (BA) uses IT in two ways. First, in a *technical-professional* way to process its banking transactions (e.g. ATMs) and second, in a *programmable* manner to produce management information (e.g. loan application processing). The computer system is used to make as many of the decisions as possible. If a greater human element had been present in the decision making, the IT quadrant applicable would have been more a craft rather than a programmable one.

By its business nature, BA demonstrates *pooled* interdependency. For example, the information is supplied by the customer and input to a database. The information is then available to all accredited bank officers as needed. IT absorbs *sequential* and *reciprocal* interdependencies in the way it performs tasks. For example, the task involved in allocating interest to customer accounts involves sequential interdependence; this is largely absorbed through the automation of interest calculation. Table 1 summarizes the findings of our study.

9. Conclusion

According to our findings, technical-professional technology was most commonly used to restructure the organizations included in our study. Through the introduction of a database approach and with the use of transaction processing systems, all four organizations were able to improve performance. Programmable technology was observed in two cases, indicating the importance of management information to organizations. The emergence of research technology within one firm points to a greater diffusion of information than before BPR was carried out. Craft technology has not completely disappeared, as indicated by one case study.

The real benefits of BPR are in the absorption of sequential and reciprocal task interdependencies. Evidence of this was found in all cases. Our study confirmed that IT enables tasks to take place and be coordinated with fewer resources than before BPR took place. The study provides evidence of a number of the BPR principles put forward by Hammer [3]. Tasks are increasingly organized around outcomes (e.g. case CO), information-processing work is subsumed into the work that produces the information (e.g. case MM), and geographical dispersed resources are treated as though they were centralized (e.g. case BA).

References

1. P. F. Drucker, Restructuring middle management, *Modern Office Technology* January 1993, 8–10
2. W. R. Scott, Technology and structure: an organizational-level perspective, in P. S. Goodman, L. S. Sproull and Associates, *Technology and Organizations* (Jossey-Bass Publishers, San Francisco, 1990).
3. M. Hammer, Reengineering work: don't automate, obliterate, *Harvard Business Review*, July-August 1990, 104–112.
4. M. Broadbent and C. Butler, Implementing business redesign: early lessons from the Australian experience, *Australian Journal of Information Systems* **2**(2), (1995) 63–76.

5. R. L. Daft, *Organization Theory & Design* (West Publishing Co., St Paul MN, 1995).
6. C. Perrow, *Organizational Analysis: A Sociological Approach* (Wadsworth, Belmont, California, 1970).
7. C. Perrow, A framework for the comparative analysis of organizations, *American Sociological Review* **32** (1967) 194–208.
8. R. L. Daft and N. B. MacIntosh, A new approach to design and use of management information, *California Management Review* **21** (1978) 82–92.
9. J. D. Thompson, *Organizations in Action* (McGraw Hill Book Company, St Louis, 1966).
10. J. M. March and H. S. Simon, *Organization* (Wiley, New York, 1958).
11. R. Yin, *Case Study Research Design and Methods* (Sage Publications, Inc., Beverly Hills, California, 1984).
12. W. R. Trihajuwidjajani, P. Marshall and J. McKay, Perceptions of success in a business process reengineering project, *EDPAC96 Conference* (1996) p. 481.

Chapter 19

Reengineering HR Development Systems to Support a New Computer Chip Factory: A Case Study

MATT BARNEY, ASHLEY PRINCE,
DARIN ARTMAN and SHARON O'TOOLE
Microelectronics International University,
Lucent Technologies, 9333 S. John Young Parkway,
Orlando, Florida 32819 USA
E-mail: mattbarney@lucent.com

Modern integrated circuit manufacturing requires employees with high levels and diverse types of knowledge, skills and abilities. This chapter describes an effort to support a new Lucent (formerly AT&T) chip factory with reengineered personnel selection, training, and performance appraisal systems. Each system described is fully integrated with each other, since all were based on the same rigorous job analysis. Results indicate positive benefits of the training and performance management systems, and one reengineering effort resulted in a 57% reduction in recruiting cycle time. The selection system validation effort was not supported, however, due to error-ridden criteria. The practical impediments to this major reengineering effort within a mature organization are also discussed.

1. Introduction

Semiconductor Manufacturing is a rapidly growing industry that requires highly skilled workers who can adapt to the frenetic pace of technological innovation [e.g. 1–4]. Chip factories employ thousands of technicians who operate machinery, perform preventative maintenance tasks, and solve problems in 'white rooms' that are thousands of times cleaner than hospital operating rooms [5, 6]. In order to perform effectively, technicians must have high skill levels in domains as diverse as robotics and interpersonal communication.

Bell Laboratories, the research and development section of AT&T (now Lucent Technologies), creates sophisticated semiconductor technology that has resulted in a strong surge in demand for AT&T's chips. Consequently, AT&T needed to build a new chip factory, and therefore needed to hire over 600 new employees. At the same time, there exists a serious shortage of skilled employees across the entire industry [7]. This skill deficit is an especially significant constraint for AT&T, because the new factory was built in Florida where only one other semiconductor manufacturer resides. Because AT&T's competitors build factories near each other (e.g. Austin Texas), they are able to recruit experienced employees from the community and inexperienced employees from specialized degree programs. In Florida, AT&T had neither resource from which to tap.

Additionally, AT&T's human resource processes were out of date. Originally designed when the existing factory was first opened in 1984, they could not accommodate a massive influx of new, inexperienced personnel. The entire recruiting process took over 3 months and could only select 20 employees at a time. The existing selection system contained a test used to measure electronics knowledge, and an assessment center. The assessment center was not based on a job-analysis, and contained elements that were not job-related. The activities in the assessment center were highly suspect in terms of the test's ability to predict effective performers, and participants questioned the assessment's validity. One activity involved affixing six small paper clips onto one large paper clip repeatedly. The other activity required applicants to gather in a group and construct a popsicle stick bridge. No empiricle studies had been conducted to establish either construct or criterion-related validity.

In order to support the aggressive performance goals of the factory, we needed higher quality, faster human resource processes. Our reengineering process focused initially on union-represented technical positions because technicians represent the largest number of new employees we needed to hire. Also, technicians typically only have an associate degree, whereas other employees already have significant training and education (i.e. engineers often have Ph.D.s).

2. Job Analysis

The first stage in the reengineering process involved gaining an understanding of the technician's (called Process Analysts) job requirements in order to maximize the success of the resulting HR systems. Rigorous job analyses were conducted using a modified version of the methodology recommended by Zedeck, Goldstein, Outtz, Cascio and Hogan [8]. First, we observed incumbents in the cleanroom. Next, we interviewed and surveyed other subject matter experts to determine the key tasks process analysts performed, and the knowledge, skills and abilities (KSAs) needed to perform those tasks. Next, we held critical incident meetings with supervisors and managers who provided examples of exceptionally good and poor work behavior. We inferred from these examples the attributes that differentiate average from exceptional performers, and included them in the KSA list.

Next, we compiled all of the information into a survey where we asked for ratings on task importance and frequency, and KSA criticality. We eliminated those tasks and KSAs that were unimportant and/or infrequent, and asked a different set of subject matter experts to rate which KSAs were needed to perform each task. These ratings created linkages between the attributes of the worker and the requirements of the job. Lastly, we asked a set of AT&T managers who are responsible for setting the future business strategy to review our results, and insure that this 'competency model' would serve the needs of the business for the next 5 years. We asked them to tell us how the occupational jobs/tasks would change in the future, and how those changes may impact new KSAs that will be required. This provided us with a model that showed which key KSAs are needed to perform important current and future job tasks. Figure 1 graphically depicts the entire job analysis process that was used.

The resulting competency model served as the foundation for our training curricula, personnel selection tests and interviews, and performance management systems. We created each resulting process in order of time priority. First, we engineered personnel selection processes designed to choose the most qualified applicants. Second, we created training curricula by considering the most effective and convenient methods and media. Third, we created job performance measures and performance management programs. The construction of each process is discussed in more detail below.

3. Personnel Selection System

The job analysis results clearly indicated that the existing selection process focused too narrowly. For example, in addition to the electronics knowledge it assessed, our technicians needed to have expertise in robotics, pneumatics, vacuum technology, electromechanical systems, silicon processing, statistical process control, interpersonal communications, writing, and teaching [5]. Additionally, technicians needed to effectively adapt to constant change, learn quickly, and perform their job tasks conscientiously. We constructed a matrix comparing the important job dimensions and the types of assessment available in cooperation with AT&T's corporate group responsible for company-wide selection. With an expert from the corporate group, we decided

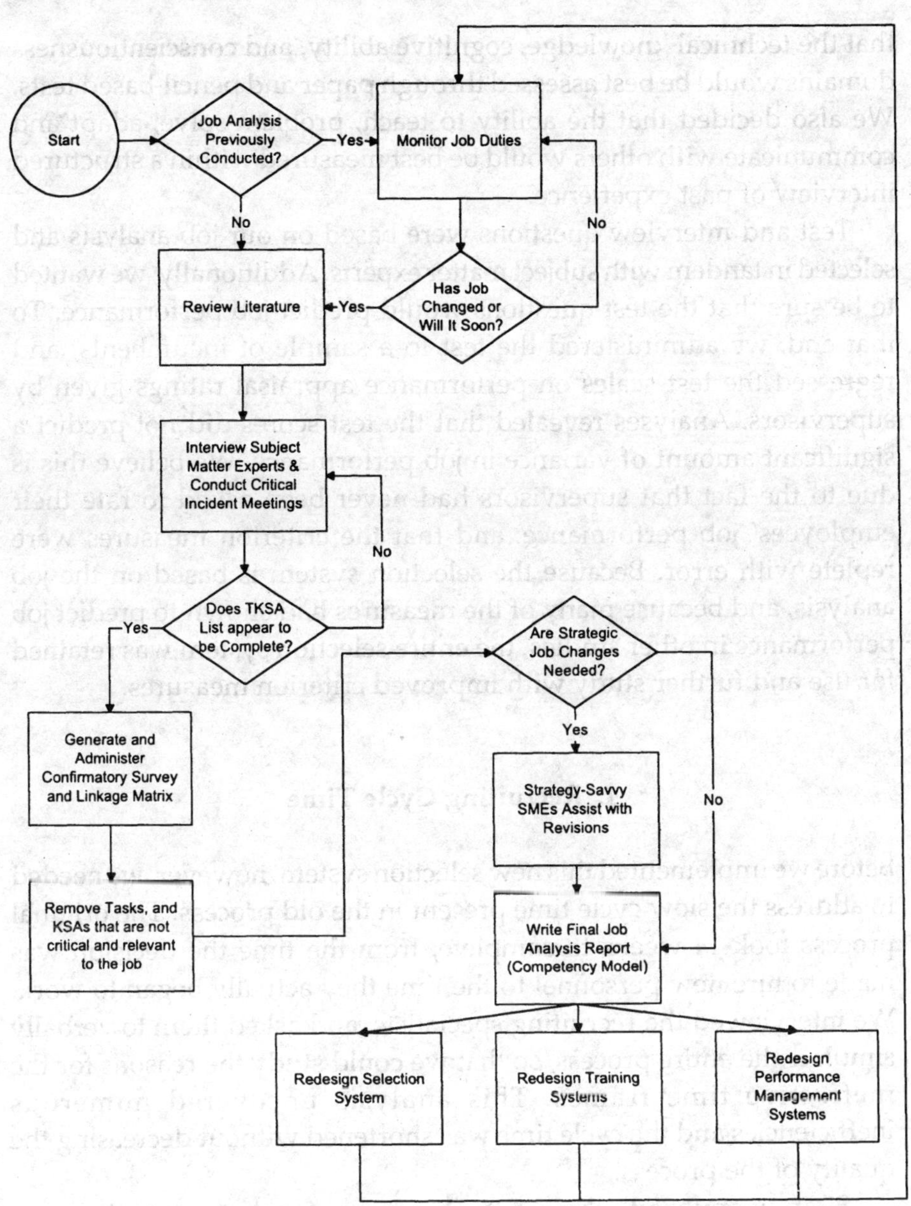

Figure 1 Job analysis process flow

that the technical knowledge, cognitive ability, and conscientiousness domains would be best assessed through paper and pencil-based tests. We also decided that the ability to teach, problem-solve, adapt and communicate with others would be best measured within a structured interview of past experience.

Test and interview questions were based on our job analysis and selected in tandem with subject matter experts. Additionally, we wanted to be sure that the test questions would predict job performance. To that end, we administered the test to a sample of incumbents, and regressed the test scales on performance appraisal ratings given by supervisors. Analyses revealed that the test scores did not predict a significant amount of variance in job performance. We believe this is due to the fact that supervisors had never been asked to rate their employees' job performance, and that the criterion measures were replete with error. Because the selection system is based on the job analysis, and because many of the measures had shown to predict job performance in other studies, the entire selection system was retained for use and further study with improved criterion measures.

4. Recruiting Cycle Time

Before we implemented this new selection system, however, we needed to address the slow cycle time present in the old process. The original process took 14 weeks to complete, from the time the decision was made to hire new personnel to the time they actually began to work. We interviewed the recruiting specialists, and asked them to verbally simulate the entire process, so that we could study the reasons for the ineffective time frames. This analysis uncovered numerous inefficiencies and the cycle time was shortened without decreasing the quality of the process.

First, we queued all job advertisements for the rest of the year. Historically, the recruiting specialist placed ads as needed in local papers. Florida newspapers required advance notice prior to placing advertisements. We were able to eliminate this time lag completely by giving the newspapers copies of the ads and a year-long schedule of dates on which we wanted to advertise.

Second, we automated the test scoring process. The old process involved three to five hours of labor to hand-score. Next, the prospective employees who passed the tests were called a few days later to schedule interview sessions. We determined that if we purchased an optical mark reader (i.e. Scantron machine) these two process steps could be combined. The mechanized system would allow the test administrator to score the tests as soon as the applicants were finished, and immediately schedule interviews for people who passed. The resulting process improvement at this stage was the elimination of two weeks of lag time and 4 to 20 hours of labor.

Third, we created multiple sources for the pre-employment physical/drug screen. Prior to the reengineering, the factory doctor was semi-retired, and worked three half-days per week. With his part-time schedule, the physician was able to perform about 10 combination physical/drug screens per week. We worked with the medical staff to identify alternative off-site physicians who would conduct the same procedures using AT&T standards. With this change, we were able to increase the volume of physicals/week to about 40, thereby shaving 2 to 3 weeks off of the overall cycle time.

Lastly, we restructured the orientation period for new employees. The pre-existing orientation process took about 5 weeks, including 3 weeks of classroom instruction, and 2 weeks of job shadowing. Using our new competency model, we determined the knowledge, skills, and abilities (KSAs) that new technicians needed before starting their jobs. This analysis indicated that a different set of courses for the first two weeks was needed, and that one week of the job shadowing could be incorporated into their initial entry onto the factory floor. For these reasons, we re-focused and shortened the orientation period from 5 to 3 weeks.

The combined effect of all the process improvements was an overall 57% cycle time improvement from 14 weeks to 8 weeks.

5. Training System

As the personnel selection process was maturing, we turned our attention toward the training curricula. Training curricula were also derived from the job analysis to insure job relevance. We grouped trainable KSAs into courses, and created behavioral objectives for each. Next, we searched for external vendors that sold courses in a variety of media (e.g. videotapes, computer-based training programs, or instructor-led courses). In order to maximize our chance of selecting the best possible set of courses for inclusion in our curriculum, we created a Multi-Attribute Utility Matrix [9] containing a weighted list of dimensions that were important to our organization (see Table 1). Our ideal courses would be: (1) flexible with respect to scheduling, (2) inexpensive, (3) shown to be effective in previous evaluations, (4) closely matched with the requirements of the job as defined by

Table 1 Multi-attribute utility matrix for training course selection

Rank-Ordered List	Rank-Ordered Sum	Mean	Weight
1. Scope of course	122	17.42	17
2. Flexibility	81	11.57	12
3. Teaching methods	80	11.43	11
4. Able to collect evaluation info	73	10.43	10
5. User friendliness	67	9.57	10
6. Evaluation info available	62	8.86	9
7. Duration (impact on production)	56	8.00	8
8. Cost	53	7.57	8
9. Upgradability	53	7.57	8
10. Strain on MEIU	29	4.14	4
11. Security	10	1.43	1
Total			98

(Note: means were truncated for simplicity and therefore do not sum to 100)

the job analysis, (5) brief, (6) sophisticated in using adult learning theory and/or instructional design principles, (7) customizable, (8) easy to collect AT&T-specific evaluation data, (9) highly readable, interesting and error free, (10) secure with respect test integrity, and (11) unburdensome to implement.

Table 2 Training decision matrix

Title of Program: ______
Provider: ______
Address: ______
Phone/Fax: ______
Cost: ______

Curriculum Area	Orientation ____	Basic ____
	Intermediate ____	Expert ____

Course Description:

Rank Ordered list of dimensions	Rating *x* Weight = Score
1. Scope of course	17
2. Flexibility	12
3. Teaching methods	11
6. Ability to evaluate course	10
5. User friendliness	10
4. Evaluation information is available	9
9. Duration (Impact on production)	8
7. Cost	8
8. Upgradability	8
10. Strain on MEIU	4
11. Security	1
Total Score	☐

Notes:

Once we agreed on the dimensions that were important to us, we asked 8 raters (including ourselves) within the department to allocate 100 points across all the dimensions, to indicate their relative importance. Table 1 depicts the result of this prioritization.

This weighting scheme was used to evaluate each course using an anchored rating scale (see Table 2). Courses receiving a zero rating on any dimension were eliminated from further consideration. After all courses were rated by at least two raters, we calculated the mean rating for each course. The course with the highest mean rating was selected for each set of behavioral objectives (course).

Next, pre- and post-tests were created for each course using the behavioral objectives, the instructional materials, and subject matter experts. These measures were used to demonstrate a change in students' knowledge, skills or abilities. After a sufficient number of students had progressed through the courses to create a sample size with enough power to detect moderate effects, we calculated standardized difference scores for each set of pre- and post-tests. Courses improved knowledge and skill by as little as a third of a standard deviation to as much as a half of a standard deviation for various courses.

6. Performance Management System

Finally, a performance management program was created, and included the development of a performance appraisal rating form. The tasks and dimensions derived from the job analysis were used to create the performance appraisal form. Dimensions include: task proficiency, job knowledge, oral/written communication, interacting with coworkers & others, instructing & teaching coworkers, decision making/problem solving, dependability, initiative, adaptability, professional conduct, planning/prioritizing, and general information processing. Supervisors rated each occupational employee's performance using a 5-point likert-type scale (i.e. 1 = very unsatisfactory; 5 = outstanding). The results from the performance appraisal had an impact on pay where low ratings resulted in no pay increase, and high ratings resulted in a pay progression.

Because supervisors had never rated their employee's performance and because performance appraisal ratings can be subjective, we developed a training course to insure reliable and valid ratings and responsible reporting of behavior. We hired a Ph.D.-level psychologist with extensive knowledge in performance measurement to lead the development of the course. The course included two sections: (1) frame-of-reference training; and (2) performance management training. For the frame-of-reference section, we developed videotaped examples of behaviors for each dimension at each level of performance (high, average, low). These simulations were used as an aid in calibrating participants' ratings. Supervisors were then taught performance management concepts and were trained in communicating job performance information effectively to their subordinates. The training was well received by supervisors in the factory.

7. Challenges and Obstacles

100-year old companies such as ours experience unique challenges to large-scale organizational changes. To omit a discussion of these issues would grossly oversimplify the complexity and difficulty of real-world interventions.

The most important political steps we took in the process of building the systems involved gaining and maintaining senior management support. We began the project during negotiations with our labor union. Once the new contract was complete, we noticed that it could serve as one justification for an integrated approach to HR systems. It required performance measurement systems and training curricula tied to pay. Since this agreement was negotiated by senior management, we showed how our approach would fulfill the requirements of the labor contract and support factory goals. Further, we pointed out legal and business shortcomings of the pre-existing selection system. While this approach was effective at gaining their initial support, we continued to keep them updated in order to continue that momentum.

Our local labor union was so supportive of a new selection system for our equipment technicians that the President helped us lobby the international union for additional support. Because the employment climate was different when we implemented the selection system for operators, however, we had staunch opposition from two international unions. Other locations were either being sold or dismantled, and the union wanted to secure employment for the displaced rank-and-file, regardless of their qualifications. The union held 'informational' pickets, and numerous meetings with managers at the executive levels. Because we had carefully documented each step taken to inform managers and union officials, we were able to get strong support from management to continue the selection program in spite of the resistance.

We also experienced challenges to our curriculum. Six months into the program, we discovered that some factory operations managers felt that employees were spending too much time off their jobs taking training courses. Also, because the initial course of the curriculum is at a basic, foundation-level, one manager was skeptical of its job-relatedness (e.g. "writing skills aren't getting wafers out the door". In response to these concerns, we re-reviewed the job analysis data showing the managers that the courses selected were related to performing critical job tasks effectively.

Secondly, our curriculum was constructed in expectation that jobs were being redesigned. Production process-focused technicians and equipment maintenance technicians traditionally shared few job tasks, but the redesign desired by management involved a merging of responsibilities. This combination has not yet occurred fully, so we have revised the curriculum accordingly.

8. Conclusion

AT&T succeeded at overhauling several business-critical human resource systems. Two key features of this Human Resource process reengineering effort are especially noteworthy. First, the job-relatedness and future focus of the processes help insure that the business will receive a return on investment. Second, all of the systems are completely integrated. If internal candidates seeking promotions fail a trainable portion of the selection system (e.g. interview), we give them feedback and direct them to an appropriate training system. At the same time, incumbents whose job performance is unsatisfactory are directed toward particular courses that address specific job-related deficiencies. The close integration between the processes gives the business a competitive advantage, because if error is present in one section of the system another serves as a backup.

References

1. V. M. Valvano, The evolution of skill demand and the nature of the employment relationship in a technology-intensive firm, in C. Brown (ed.), *The Competitive Semiconductor Manufacturing Human Resources Project: Second Interim Report, Report CSM-32,* University of California at Berkeley, Institute of Industrial Relations, 1996.
2. C. Brown, Human resource practices, in R. Leachman (ed.), *The Competitive Semiconductor Manufacturing Survey: Third Report on Results of the Main Phase, Report CSM-31,* University of California at Berkeley Engineering Systems Research Center (1996) pp. 208–218.
3. T. Willward, The $17 billion dollar search, *Corporate Location,* September/October 1995, 26–29.
4. S. Lear, J. Miller and P. Squires, A comparison of microelectronics manufacturers workforce with key competitors, AT&T Microelectronics International University, Technical Report, Berkeley Heights, NJ, 1995.
5. A. Prince, M. Barney and D. Artman, Job analysis report: process analysts,

AT&T Microelectronics, Microelectronics International University Technical Report, Orlando FL, 1995.

6. P. Chan, M. Barney and P. Roithmayr, Job analysis report on equipment-focused technicians, Technical Report, Intel Corporation, Albuquerque, NM, 1994.
7. C. Barton, Sematech workforce development report, Presentation to the Sematech Training Council Bi-Annual Meeting, Burlington, VT, October 3–4, 1996.
8. S. Zedeck, I. Goldstein, J. Outtz, W. Cascio and J. Hogan, *Job Analysis Manual*, Unpublished manuscript.
9. D. A. Artman, Doctoral Dissertation, University of South Florida, Tampa, FL, 1995.
10. M. F. Barney, Empirically demonstrating shared meta-mental models and their effects on team effectiveness, Doctoral Dissertation, University of Tulsa, Tulsa, OK, 1996a.

Chapter 20

Reengineering the End User Support

LAURI FORSMAN
Nokia Telecommunications Oy,
Upseerinkatu 3, FIN-02600,
Espoo, Finland
E-mail: lauri.forsman@ntc.nokia.com

This paper deals with reengineering End User Support in one of the Strategic Business Units of Nokia Telecommunications Oy. End users are software engineers using networked PCs as their main engineering platform. Operations take place in three geographical locations. In 1994, a period of rapid business growth began. Also, the IT environment changed radically, demanding new solutions for the distributed IS and particularly for supporting the users. A reengineering process was initiated in July 1994, resulting in fundamental changes to the support processes. The new solution was based on local Help Desks and service organization, replacing the previous unstructured support tradition in the beginning of 1996.

Changes improved the distributed IS services facilitating thus the planned business growth. Results indicate enhanced user satisfaction, higher motivation and improved productivity. Supporters adopted a more professional attitude and could manage their commitments more precisely. IS management became more proactive, confirmed by all key interest groups.

1. Introduction

A recent Help Desk research report claims the present customer support to be in crisis [1]. The main factors behind this are:

- Decentralization of the IS function.
- Moving away from mainframes toward client/server architecture.

We have faced similar challenges combined with exceptional business growth in our reengineering case. To answer them, we transformed the internal, technically-oriented PC support groups into a customer-oriented, structured service organization. The process started in July 1994 and in 18 months a new mode of operations was implemented. Since then, the effects of the transformation have been observed and tuned further. The writer works as the IS manager in the case organization.

Our target organization is one of the Strategic Business Units (Case-SBU = C-SBU) in Nokia Telecommunications Oy (NTC). This C-SBU presently employs 2000 knowledge workers on three geographical locations. End users are software engineers developing software for telecommunications products. Every user has a PC workstation with proper peripherals and software tools.

Business growth accelerated rapidly in 1994 due to market liberalization and global expansion of the demand. This created fast internal growth in the C-SBU that continued on an annual 50% level (all main indicators) for several years. New employees had to be equipped with IT tools and services, trained and made ready for the action. This happened while the IT management was under restructuring. Rapid technical transition took place toward client/server architecture. PC and LAN technologies were booming, causing the incoming components to become more heterogeneous. Technology set the rules for the game.

These factors had effects also on the business level. Poor quality IT services caused problems to the business and the users did not receive even the support they requested to overcome these problems. Business management saw these factors as severe IT-related risks for the anticipated business growth. A new approach was needed.

When a knowledge-work intensive organization grows at an exceptional speed and the computing landscape is experiencing a major evolution at the same time, some special measures are also required to align the computing services to meet these new contingency factors [2, 3]. The main cost item of PC ownership is the hidden costs caused by wasted EU time [4, 5].

Major challenges were to rethink the distributed IS structure, define its role as a service provider, and to balance these services with the requirements, key personnel groups and other IT players. Rethinking was the first step in the reengineering.

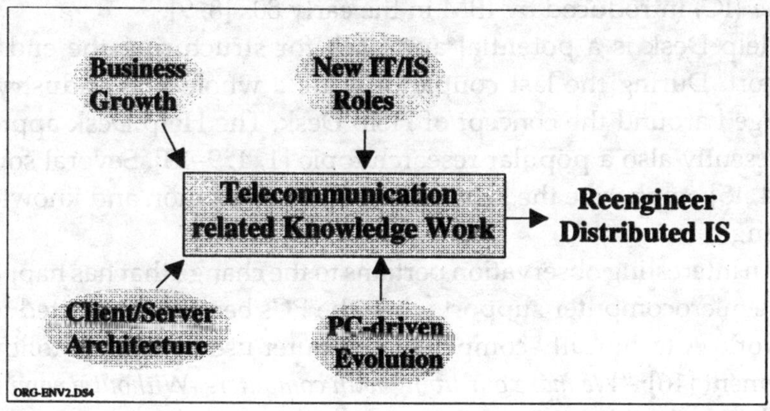

Figure 1 Original contingency factors

2. Earlier Research

During the past few years, Personal Computers and client/server computing have rapidly expanded their domain in the business environment. They challenge the conventional systems even in the mission critical application areas [6] and integrate the desk-top and organizational computing domains [7]. This development calls for enhanced support for all these distributed services, applications and systems.

End users spend too much time for unproductive purposes while learning the PC technology or being not able to complete their computing tasks. If support is asked from peers, further loss of time will occur [5]. Reynolds [6] remarks that *"the peers have been hired into the company to do something else other than support."*

The problem of supporting EUs has a short history. During the era of centralized batch processing, end users did not interact directly with the computers and there was no need for EUS. When the distribution eliminated the middleman between the user and the computer, support became an issue. The first solution for this need was the *Information Center* (IC) introduced by IBM in the early 80s [8, 9].

Help Desk is a potential approach for structuring the end user support. During the last couple of years a whole new industry has emerged around the concept of Help Desk. The Help Desk approach is presently also a popular research topic [1, 4, 9–13]. Several sources [6, 14, 15] emphasize the significance of specialization and knowledge sharing.

An interesting observation pertains to the change that has happened to the microcomputer support when the PCs became connected to the network. A technically competent computer user made the following statement [16]: *"We make our living with computers. Without a computer I couldn't do anything. I embraced computers long ago and until we got this network my view was, get me a computer and leave me alone. I knew how to maintain my own ...* ***When the network came in, all that changed*** *... It's very frustrating because if the computer's broken, I sit here because there's nothing I can do. I have no idea of what's going on. What I want out of support is simple: make my machine work and leave me alone."*

Definitions:

- End user: The ultimate consumer of a product, especially the one for whom the product has been designed [17].

- End User Support: EUS consists of all those services, reactive and proactive, needed to educate and assist the end users (EUs) to perform their computing duties [4].
- Help Desk: A source of technical support for hardware or software. Help desks are staffed by people that can either solve the problem directly or forward the problem to someone else. Help desk software provides the means to log in problems and track them until solved. It also provides the management with information regarding support activities [18].

3. The Case Environment

We shall describe next the characteristics of our business environment. We re-emphasize the four simultaneous changes which affected our reengineering. Combining the observations from the previous research with our reality we finally approach the alternative reengineering solutions.

Our research environment, NTC, is a highly dynamic, knowledge-work-intensive company. Most of the product development takes place in Finland and relies on complex, distributed computer systems. We have already explained the four exceptional contingency factors affecting both the business and IT in 1994. The anticipated business growth required radical rethinking of the IT services. Unstructured, technically-oriented support groups had to be transformed into a professional service organization. The main research question was: *How to align the distributed IS according to the business requirements?*

The computing landscape changed rapidly and became technically a networked client/server environment. To differentiate the managerial aspect from the technical one, we call this mode of computing ***Distributed-Organizational Computing*** (D-OC). We define it as follows: *D-OC is organization-wide, task-related computing, which is based on cooperatively managed, distributed services and resources.* Technically this transformation divided the IT infrastructure into the centrally managed and local domains. *End user computing* as a term, has got the emphasis of software development by the users [19, 20] and does not apply in our case.

We needed to have better control of the IT-related risks and to improve the support services for the end users. The other major element of the distributed IS-function besides EUS was identified to be the IS production. EUS should also prevent the problems in the first place. This gives us an initial view of the reactive and proactive components of EUS.

The definitions for the strategic alternatives are:

Reactive: "Act in response to some influence or stimulus" [21].
Proactive: "Acting in anticipation of future problems, needs, or changes" [22].
The reactive support is activated by a request, while the proactive EUS anticipates future problems and acts in advance [4, 9].

The alternative models for organizing EUS included the original unstructured model and several variations of creating a special focal point for managing the service requests. Analysis of the service requests proved that even a simple Help Desk could increase the service consistency, which was one of the fundamental expectations of users. They felt that supporters promised too much and did not meet their commitments. Some proposed in the first survey: *"You promise too much; please, promise less."* The problem was not just in the EUS performance but in the inconsistent communication.

Originally end users called any of the supporters at random. The alternative was a more structured model based on a common focal point. It would also provide managerial visibility at the service by reporting the service statistics.

3.1. Research method

Our approach is ***action research*** that contained intensive interaction with the environment to be studied.

Research questions are:

- How to align the distributed IS according to the business requirements?
- How to decrease the risks of the distributed IS?
- How to reengineer the EUS to increase the customer satisfaction?

The mission was divided into two major components: to reduce the risk of distributed computing and to improve the EU satisfaction. Higher satisfaction should have a positive impact also on EU motivation and productivity. The methods for data collection have been participating observation, end user and management surveys, document analysis and interviews.

4. Reengineering

We have given a description of our practical case environment and the previous research related to our challenges. We understand the need for reengineering the distributed IS. Now we show the method that we used in the reengineering and management of this process.

We base our reengineering approach on the ideas of Hammer and Champy [23, 24] and the interpretations of Boar [2]. The idea of reengineering is stated by Hammer [22]: *"It is time to stop paving the cowpaths. Instead of embedding outdated processes in silicon and software, we should obliterate them and start over. We should 'reengineer' our business: use the power of modern information technology to radically redesign our business processes in order to achieve dramatic improvements in their performance."* Reengineering is defined: "Business reengineering is the radical rethinking and redesign of business processes to achieve dramatic breakthroughs in speed, cost and service" [2].

Boar summarizes the principles of reengineering into five main guidelines [2]:

- start with a clean state — do not be encumbered by all the sludge that has accumulated over the years;
- rethink/redesign — do not tinker or modify; annihilate and build anew;
- aim for orders of magnitude of improvement — do not settle for double-digit percent increases;
- infuse the processes with the novel use of IT to automate and accrue the time, cost, or service advantages;
- drive reengineering by continual senior management involvement.

In our case reengineering included process redesign, job redesign, organizational restructuring, management oversight systems, cultural adjustment and adoption of a new IT system to enable the reengineering process. Strategic focus concentrated on enabling the service infrastructure to be aligned according to the business requirements and the internal market structure.

During the exploratory first year the contents of EUS were analyzed and some alternative solutions formulated. We studied the expectations of the key interest groups, which were the end users, management and IS-personnel. The first end user survey was implemented in May 1995 to understand their expectations for the IS services. Also a simple Help Desk was piloted during the spring of 1995.

A conceptual breakthrough in this development was the realization that there were two key entities in our market; the customer and the technology. In one of the early discussions, when we talked about PC support, a professional PC user made an enlightening statement: "*The PC does not need support, I do.*" This led to the dualistic architecture of the service organization. We label these two elements as End User Support (EUS) and the distributed production.

4.1. Actions

The main alternatives for the new EUS structure were:

1. continue the existing tradition and add manpower to the unstructured support teams = pave the cowpath;
2. divide the support responsibilities with the main players, which are the user departments, corporate IT and the local support teams = the rational solution;
3. allocate the main support responsibility for the local support teams by changing the basics = step to the unknown.

Each of the solutions had some strong arguments in favor and some doubts as well. We shall summarize these original views.

4.1.1. Pave the cowpath

The first alternative would be easy to implement just by adding manpower to the existing support teams. There was no risk getting it accepted. Both the users and the supporters had worked in this way for years. The concerns with this model pertained to its management. How could we plan, manage and develop a service without any visibility to its contents? So far the only feedback had come through business management, which relayed the departmental complaints to the IS organization. That was not an acceptable managerial approach.

4.1.2. The rational solution

The second alternative appeared a natural one for several reasons. The users were software engineers and eager to manage their own PCs. The user departments had also hired some supporters of their own, so why should we as the official IS organization get involved in those user-related support tasks? On the other hand, some of the support responsibilities clearly had corporate-wide demand. The primary candidate for organizing them would be the corporate IT. The local support teams would take care of the distributed servers, LANs and PC logistics.

This approach looked like the 'right' answer, but soon several pieces faded away from the structure. User departments and the business management refused to share the user capacity for the peer support. The corporate IT did not show any activity in building central support services.

4.1.3. Step to the unknown

The third alternative relied on the local support teams. These resources were at our disposal and thereby a solid ground. This would mean that each of our three locations would establish a local Help Desk to manage the user communication. The doubts related to the required expertise and level of ambition. Would it be realistic to establish local Help Desks with our existing support resources? We knew very little about the concept in general and there were just some demo systems available to test the Help Desk functionality. Would such approach be accepted by the users? Would it be accepted by the supporters? It seemed to have many open questions and a risky way. However, there was still one big benefit built in this alternative: it would create the desired visibility to the EUS reality and facilitate its management. That became one of the key reasons for pursuing this alternative forward.

4.2. *The new recipe*

Finally the third alternative, *step to the unknown*, was chosen. End users have a single point of contact to the support organization. Workflow is managed through a computerized system that reports the status also to the management. Distributed production is separated from the support services.

The main **reasons** for this choice were: it facilitated a professional service management, it excluded most of the peer support and could be implemented by ourselves. The risks pertained to the new communication model, but the piloting phase had succeeded without complications. In August 1995 several actions were launched to implement the targets. These included:

- Increased **number of IS staff;** the number of IS staff was increased from a 1.5% share of the total population to 3%.
- Introduction of the **Campus model;** after a preliminary support model was evaluated, the final Campus model was introduced. Management decided to eliminate the option of peer support. As the result the local IS organization has the primary responsibility for managing the local services and to support the end users. It has also development and administrative tasks within its domain.

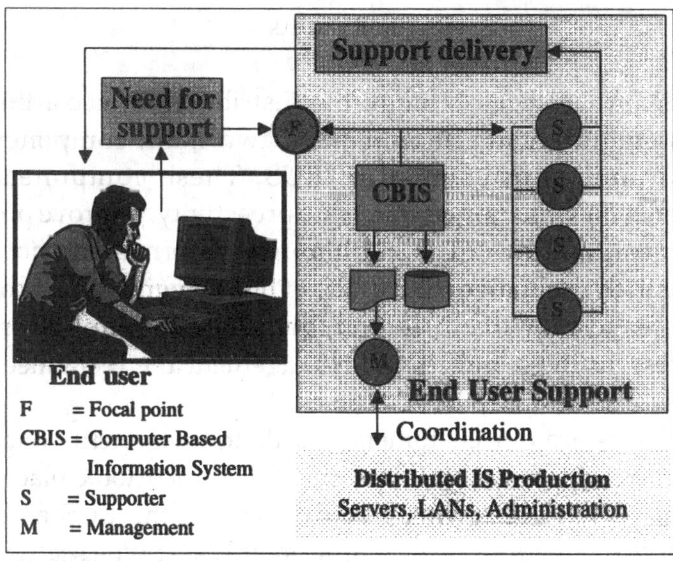

Figure 2 New process for end user support

- Implementing the **Help Desks;** pilot mode Help Desks were started on each of the campuses during fall 1995. Production mode was reached in January 1996. One of the Campuses allocated a professional supporter to run the Help Desk and two other campuses started with secretary-driven services.

The dualistic approach of ***support*** and ***production*** requires special qualifications from the respective personnel also. Supporters need a service orientation and production staff need expertise in their area of interest.

The main part of these actions was implemented during the second half of 1995. One year had been used to explore the problem and alternative solutions. During 1996 results have been observed. End users, supporters and management have evaluated the outcome of the reengineering. The final survey was implemented in January 1997 producing 1174 EUS answers (see Fig. 3).

5. Results

Our mission had been to align the distributed IS according to the business requirements. It contained two main components, risk aversion and improvement of EUS. These components were transformed into four targets: increase proactivity, improve production management, improve EUS and improve information and training. Here we shall summarize the results of this reengineering project. Our intention is to show that based on the feedback from the end users, supporters, business and the IS management the reengineering met its goals.

End users are our customers and their assessment weighs most. Feedback was gathered in three surveys, which took place in 1995, 1996 and 1997. Users were asked to assess the EUS among four other service categories using a four point Likert-type scale. Scale was 1 = good, 2 = fair, 3 = passable, 4 = poor.

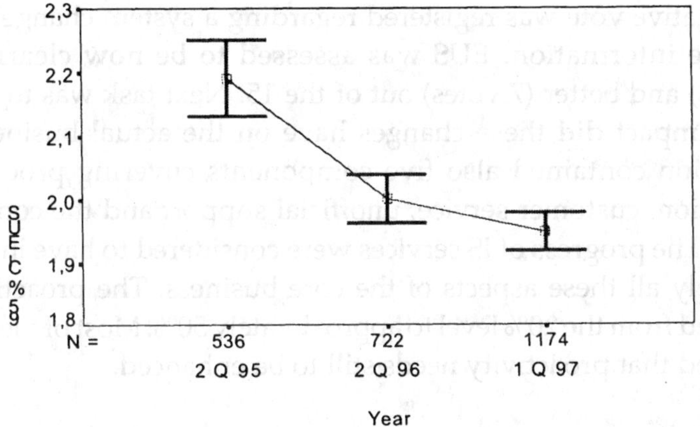

Figure 3 Error bar chart of the evolution of EUS. Lower ratings are better

The EUS assessment contained the following **components**: Service attitude, EUS availability, IS service point (open service center with standard workstations), Mode of operation (Help Desk), Material orders (e.g. new PCs), HD receipt and the EUS delivery (delivering the requested services).

As Fig. 3 indicates, the EUS services improved significantly between the three surveys. End users had accepted the new mode of operation. There had been the risk that users would continue to grab directly their old, familiar supporters in the neighborhood and avoid the extra trouble to communicate through the Help Desk. Most of the action took the new path. However, parallel procedures still exist to some extent.

The business management was interviewed in fall 1996. The interview was implemented as a structured discussion between the line manager and the IS manager applying a five point Likert scale for assessments. Each session took about one hour. The evaluation consisted of four major topics. Management was first asked to evaluate the changes in the IS services since June 1994. The average opinion was, that IS services have developed in the positive direction. Only one negative vote was registered regarding a system change without advance information. EUS was assessed to be now clearly better (8 votes) and better (7 votes) out of the 15. Next task was to estimate which impact did these changes have on the actual business. This evaluation contained also five components covering productivity, motivation, customer service, unofficial support and the competitive power. The progress of IS services were considered to have influenced positively all these aspects of the core business. The proactivity has increased from the 20% level to approximately 50%. Most of the answers indicated that proactivity needs still to be enhanced.

6. Summary

Here we shall summarize the results of our reengineering project. We review our mission, the exceptional contingency factors, what was expected from the process and what eventually came out.

The challenges for our organization were unique in July 1994. Business growth together with radical changes in the IT environment demanded a new approach for the distributed IS. Our 30-month long reengineering process changed the mode of EUS in a profound way. The changes affected both the end users and the IS staff.

Response confirms that end users, supporters, business and IS management consider the reengineering to have produced positive results. End users get better service, supporters are able to perform their commitments in a more professional way and the business management hears fewer complaints. Business management confirms also increased end user productivity and motivation. All key stake holders are satisfied with the outcome. The level of proactivity has increased.

Let us compare our accomplishments with the definition of reengineering: "*Business reengineering is the radical rethinking and redesign of business processes to achieve dramatic breakthroughs in speed, cost and service.*" The transformation in our case was not *paving the cowpath.* It was as radical as we could handle. So far our project fits into the definition. The results show clear progress in the EUS as well as the other vital service groups, which are not reported here. The radical elements are in the synchronization of the exceptional business context and the IS support services.

6.1. *Practical results*

In terms of practical results, the reengineering has reached the development targets and thereby fulfilled its mission. The business growth has been supported in these most dynamic circumstances. The IT-related risk level is brought under control. The data collection and piloting were vital processes for the success of the project. Proactive management was required to anticipate the problems and to shift the emphasis from fire-fighting to professionalism.

Our results confirm that the Help Desk concept works well even as a low profile implementation. The success factors are to be available, to manage the customer requests consistently and to have a positive service attitude. Our evidence supports the conclusion: proactive EUS has a positive impact on core business. The IS people have also a better managed work environment with less *ad hoc* interrupts.

In terms of management, our case is strongly built on the business interests for changing the distributed IS into a professional organization. The anticipated business growth was exceptional and there was a strong business demand to eliminate the potential risk for under-performing IT services. Our analysis has emphasized the practical steps we have taken to make these changes happen.

6.2. *Theoretical results*

Theoretically our research has identified some significant contingency factors in the support environment. These results indicate that the need for professional support increases when the IT services pose a risk for achieving the business goals. The more dependent the business is on IT tools and services, the more it needs to eliminate risks on those areas. The conclusion is still amplified in a situation where changes in the IT technology, architecture and responsibilities take place side by side. Such a combination may be planned and controlled to some extent, but the final insurance for sufficient IT performance is the professional support. Results show that the optimum level of proactivity in EUS management depends on several parameters. It is closely connected to other areas of IS/IT-management and to the main contingency factors.

6.3. Discussion

The concept 'D-OC' is presented as our contribution for focusing the attention more on the managerial, instead of technical issues of networked corporate computing. The Help Desk approach made the communication simple for the customers. The anticipated problems of specialization [25] did not emerge. Positive feedback from the business management was hardly free of bias. Management was interested to motivate the IS management to continue the active development and may exaggerate their comments. Therefore, the main evidence has been taken from the 'horse's mouth' i.e. from the end users.

The reengineering process created some additional benefits for the IS management. The new structured communication provided for the first time clear managerial visibility to this important service function. Help Desk as the focal point is important not only for the customers but also for collecting information about the service demand, its volumes, content and trends. This will facilitate rational service development on the long run and promote the proactive IS management.

Acknowledgement

The author would like to express his thanks to Professor Pertti Järvinen for his encouragement and constructive comments during the preparation of this paper and to Marjatta Forsman for her ongoing support and help.

References

1. R. Marcella and I. Middleton, *Key Factors in Help Desk Success: An Analysis of Areas Critical to Help Desk Development and Functionality*, British Library R&D Report 6247.
2. B. Boar, *Practical Steps for Aligning Information Technology with Business Strategies* (John Wiley & Sons, Inc., 1994).
3. G. Morgan, *Images of Organization* (Sage Publications, London, 1986).
4. L. Forsman, *Mikrotuen kehittäminen (Reengineering the PC support)* (Suomen Atk-kustannus Oy, Espoo, 1996).
5. J. Heikkilä, *The Diffusion of a Learning Intensive Technology into Organizations*, Doctoral dissertation, Helsinki School of Economics and Business Administration (A-104), 1995.
6. E. Reynolds, Client/server impact on enterprise support: an overview, presentation No 812 on *Support Services Conference East*, Help Desk Institute, March 9–12, 1997, Audio tape.
7. E. R. McLean, L. A. Kappelman and J. A. Thompson, Converging end user and corporate computing, *Communications of the ACM* **36**(12), December 1993, 79–92.
8. R. F. Bento, Life in the middle: an analysis of information centers from the perspective of their major stakeholders, *Information & Management* **30** (1996) 101–109.
9. N. Bruton, *Effective User Support, How to Manage the IT Help Desk* (McGraw-Hill, 1995).
10. C. Drew, *Tips on Evaluating & Reengineering The Help Desk* (Pine Hill Press, Inc., 1993).
11. R. Farrell and F. Tourniaire, *The Art of Software Support, Design & Operation of Support Centers and Help Desks* (Prentice-Hall Inc., 1997).

12. J. Keyes, The demise of the help desk, *Software Development*, February 1997, 29–31.
13. N. Khandpur and L. Laub, *Delivering World-Class Technical Support* (John Wiley & Sons, Inc., 1997).
14. R. Dugger, Supporting your support people, *Datamation*, March 1997.
15. J. McConnell, *Managing Client/Server Environments* (Prentice-Hall Inc., 1996).
16. R. Barley, Technicians in the workplace: ethnographic evidence for bringing work into organization studies, *Administrative Science Quarterly* **41** (1996) 404–441.
17. *The American Heritage Dictionary of the English Language, 3rd Edition*, (Houghton Mifflin Company, 1992).
18. Electronic Computer Glossary, Computer Select, 1997
19. J. C. Brancheau and C. V. Brown, The management of end user computing: status and directions, *ACM Computing Surveys* **25**(4), December 1993, 437–482.
20. J. Martin, *Application Development Without Programmers* (Prentice-Hall, Englewood Cliffs, N.J., USA, 1982).
21. Encarta dictionary, Microsoft, 1994.
22. Merriam-Webster's Collegiate Dictionary, Microsoft Bookshelf, 1995.
23. M. Hammer, Don't automate, obliterate *Harward Business Review*, July-August 1990, **68**, 104–113.
24. M. Hammer and J. Champy, *Reengineering the Corporation: A Manifesto for Business Revolution* (HarperCollins Publishers, New York, 1993).
25. W. Riley, Support generalization, *Datamation*, June 1, 1995.

Chapter 21

The Role of Information Technology, TQM and Business Vision in BPR – A Case Study of BPR in India

M. P. JAISWAL
Management Development Institute,
Post Box No. 60, Gurgaon — 122001, INDIA
E-mail: atul@iipm.delnet.ernet.in

This chapter analyzes the role of Information Technology (IT), Total Quality Management (TQM) and Business Vision in Business Process Reengineering (BPR). The study has been conducted in two large enterprises in India where BPR is being implemented. The study reveals that IT is the key enabler of BPR but is not sufficient in itself. Business Vision seems to be one of the critical preconditions and driving forces for BPR initiatives. TQM plays a complementary role in BPR.

1. Introduction

Business process reengineering (BPR), also termed as process innovation, is a fundamental rethinking intended to achieve dramatic improvement in the organizational performance by tackling cross-functional business processes, organization, human resources and information technology, all together [1]. BPR concurrently pursues breakthrough improvements in quality, speed, service and cost by leveraging the potential of information technology while addressing the issues of organizational strategies and vision for change. Breakthrough improvement means quantum gains of 5 to 10 times compared to incremental improvements of 20–30%. These improvements are generally characterized in terms of improvement of product and service quality at low cost and less time lag between product design to marketing. It is necessary to clarify that BPR and Total Quality Management (TQM) do share some common characteristics such as cross functional orientation and customer focus, but both are fundamentally different from each other. TQM tends to focus on continuous improvement and incremental change in the existing processes, while BPR seeks drastic improvement and radical redesign of the core business processes [2].

Business organizations in India are facing new challenges due to globalization and deregulation of the Indian economy. Global competitors are entering Indian markets, profit margins are shrinking, customers are becoming choosy and demanding, and products are experiencing shorter life cycles. The cooperative enterprises which play a very significant and critical role in the Indian economy, particularly in the fields of agriculture, food and rural banking will have to reconfigure themselves to be more effective, efficient and enterprising. The cooperative in these fields is perceived as the most suitable form of organization as it not only safeguards the interest of rural producers but also that of urban consumers. In the process it contributes in the growth of country's GDP. This has been witnessed particularly in the fields of milk, oilseeds, sugar, and chemical fertilisers. The liberalization of the Indian economy has brought a new challenge and a new market place for these cooperative enterprises, and it has become imperative for them to adopt the new management paradigm such as TQM and BPR. This paper attempts to analyze the linkages of BPR to TQM, Business Vision and IT by comparative study of two large agribusiness cooperative enterprises in India where BPR is being implemented.

2. Methodology

A study has been conducted in two large agribusiness enterprises to address the linkages of BPR to TQM, Business Vision and IT. One of these organizations is a leading chemical fertilizer production-cum-marketing firm in the country. The other one is a leading marketing cooperative enterprise for branded food products. Both these organizations are fairly large in terms of their business volume and manpower, and are the market leaders in their respective industries in the country.

An analytical framework is employed to analyze the linkages of BPR to TQM, IT and Business Vision of both the organizations. The framework's analysis is based on the quantitative and qualitative aspects of business data of the above organizations obtained through the discussions with chief/senior executives and through their business documents and reports. The aspect of business data are mainly in terms of their business volume, financial and material transactions, market share and growth. The qualitative aspect of business data are mainly in terms of management systems and organizational capacity for change such as professional leadership, cross-functional approach, flexible organization structure, business vision, customer-orientation, IT infrastructure and MIS culture, etc. Five core business processes of the organizations are considered for the analysis with the concept of reengineering principles suggested by Hammer and Champy.

3. About the Organizations Studied

This section describes the background of the organizations where the BPR study has been carried out.

Organization 1 is the largest fertilizer firm in the country with an annual turnover of about $400 million. At present it has five fertilizer plants and a nationwide market network. Fertilizers are marketed through about 33,000 cooperative societies and 168 farmers service centres throughout the country. The organization has a corporate office, 5 zonal offices, 21 state offices, 61 area offices, and 350 field offices in district levels to carry out the marketing operations. Since the organization has to market its products only through the cooperative institutions, it uses the services of state marketing federations, primary agricultural cooperative societies and cooperative banking systems to carry out its operations. The organization has drawn a long-term plan entitled 'Vision-2000' which aims to acquire, by the turn of century, the status of global fertilizer giant with an increased turnover of $1200 million by boosting production, sales, profit and productivity. This calls for a 100% sudden increase in the growth rate of the organization's turnover in a competitive and liberalized market. Thus the thrust is on making a radical improvement in the overall performance of the organization by employing the principles of the BPR paradigm using information technology as a strategic tool. The organization's Vision 2000 plan is putting pressure on its state and field offices to drastically increase the sales turnover by shifting from existing single to multiple marketing channels, and also by improving the efficiency and reliability in operational systems. The organization is in the process of implementing an enterprise-wide information technology infrastructure.

Organization 2 is the largest food-processing enterprise in the country with an annual turnover of $400 million. The organization markets the branded milk and edible oil products through its strong countrywide distribution network with 1,662 stockists and over 300,000 shopkeepers. It has 5 zonal and 35 depot offices to market the products of its member unions. The production as well as demand of the products have a seasonal variation. Since its inception, the organization's corporate plan has been growth-oriented, consistent with the national policy of self-sufficiency in milk and oilseeds production and improving the economy and social life of the farming community in general and strengthening the cooperative system in particular. The organization has a vision to become one of the largest food enterprises in the world. Realizing the threat from competition well in advance, its management has started taking steps. Total Quality Management is being implemented in the organization. The organization is in the process of implementing an enterprize-wide information technology infrastructure along with the reengineering initiative.

Organization 1 has adopted an IT strategy to implement BPR projects whereas Organization 2 has adopted IT, coupled with a TQM strategy to implement BPR.

4. Scope of BPR in Agribusiness Enterprises

The agribusiness cooperative enterprises have distinguished characteristics in terms of their operations. They deal with the commodities which have high fluctuations and uncertainty in terms of production and marketing. They have to operate and manage the procurement of commodities from a very large number of shareholders who are basically farmers. An analysis of transactions involving different core business processes in the above organizations reveals that more than 80% of the discrete flow of 'products' between functions was composed of information (e.g. forms, reports, charts, manuals, etc.), and less than 20% of product flow was that of goods. Therefore the crux of the problem is to redesign the information and workflow management systems associated with core processes. The analysis of the above cases reveals that most of the business processes, workflow systems, and control mechanisms of the management systems in the above organizations are outmoded and need to be redesigned or reengineered by leveraging the potential of modern IT. The business processes cut across the different departments, but due to demarcation of function of each departments its execution suffers adversely. There is a lack of coordination and integration among different departments/functions of the organizations to accomplish a process. The initial report on IT strategy prepared by the consultants for Organizations 1 and 2 highlights the redundancy and inconsistency of data and work at different levels of the organizations.

5. Critical BPR Issues

The above cases illustrate that BPR is about creating fundamental change within an organization and is context-specific. So, any such initiative would depend a lot upon the specific processes, people, and technologies of the organization. Therefore, there is no standard methodological approach for a reengineering initiative. However, an organization can initiate BPR in its core business processes on a pilot basis by forming multifunctional teams with information technology support. There are some critical issues such as organization structure, human resources management strategy, business vision, information technology strategy and infrastructure, etc. which needs special attention for BPR initiative in an enterprise.

5.1. Business vision and BPR

A business vision is a statement of the organization's values and beliefs, its overarching goals, and its overall business philosophy. Business vision not only provides a high-level sense of direction and statement of principle but it also provides a very essential input to the formulation of process visualization. Business vision seems to be one of the preconditions and driving forces for BPR initiative in the organization. Both the organizations where business vision plans have been drawn is putting pressure for a radical improvement in its operation's management. A correlation has been implicated between business vision and BPR in both the above cases. The business vision at Organization 2 is shared among its internal and external customers at all levels in the organization and therefore its impact is more visible and positive for BPR as compared to that at Organization 1 where it is confined to the top management.

5.2. *IT strategy in BPR*

Information Technology is found to be the key enabler of BPR in both the above cases. It has also been found that merely computerization or automation does not lead to BPR. IT and BPR have a recursive relationship which means IT capabilities should support business processes, and business processes should be in terms of capabilities IT can provide. IT needs to be used to innovate and not just automate the business processes [3]. Both the organizations have prepared IT strategy in alignment with their business. The focus of IT in Organization 1 is confined toward operational aspects of business whereas that of Organization 2 is spread from operational to strategic aspects. Organization 2 is employing Datawarehousing technology to identify and validate its external customers' current and anticipated needs, expectations and priorities for each major product and service of the organization. The study reveals that it is imperative to align IT vision and strategy along with the organizational business vision and strategy so as to get competitive advantage from IT. IT should be used to reengineer the strategic aspects of business too. This requires coordinated action in five areas such as process modeling, cross-functional integration (intra-organizational), setting up an inter-organizational systems, building an organizational memory, and initiating a change process in the organization with the extensive use of IT.

5.2.1. IT in process modeling

BPR is fundamentally about operational excellence and as such its focus is at the business process level of the organization. Organizational transformation occurs when the reengineered key business processes begin delivering superior performance results. Process visualization guides and inspires this superior performance. The key business process which needs to be reengineered can be depicted using some modeling tools [4]. In the present case five core business processes from both the organizations have been modeled using the Designer 2000 software engineering tool. The business processes were also modeled using the value chain framework of Michael Porter's [5] and processes were redesigned with optimized contemporary measures of performance.

5.2.2. IT in establishing intra-organizational business process

The reengineered organizations are envisioned to be networked across functions and designed around business processes rather than functional hierarchies. However, this requires redesign of organizational structure, workflow systems and management control systems with the full support and implementation of an enterprise-wide integrated information system. Organization 2 has been able to successfully initiate cross-functional integration in some of its core business processes, perhaps due to its organizational flexibility, versatile human resources and TQM implementation. This has yet not been possible in Organization 1.

5.2.3. IT in setting inter-organizational business process

The business processes not only cut across several functional units within the organization but in many cases also traverse several separate organizational units. Most of the core business processes of the above organizations traverse through 5 to 7 different organizational units of its suppliers, customers, transport's, warehouse's, etc. It is imperative to establish an integrated inter-organizational system (IOS) covering all the functions and units of the organization and its suppliers and customers with the use of the latest IT to derive the complete benefit of BPR. The IOS will bring a competitive advantage to the organization by significantly improving internal efficiency, customer services and bargaining power of the organization. The IOS are generally established by deploying electronic data interchange (EDI) technology along with the intra-organizational business process reengineering. The IOS is being established in Organization 2 initially with its suppliers and distributors.

5.2.4. IT in building organizational memory

Knowledge is the key asset in any organization. The computerized organizational memory extends and amplifies this asset by capturing, organizing, disseminating and reusing the knowledge created by its employees. The information is retained by an organization's individuals, culture, procedures, structure, and ecology. Individuals in particular are involved in the complete process of acquiring, retaining, and processing information and are considered the 'sensor' and 'cognitive' units of an organization. The information and the knowledge they acquire form a significant portion of an organizational memory. The advanced information technologies such as knowledge-based information retrieval systems, object-oriented database and machine-learning systems play a critical role in creating timely, comprehensive, and accurate organizational intelligence and in capturing organization-members' expertise. This is being initiated in Organization 2 but in a limited sense.

5.2.5. IT in change management and creating a learning organization

The innovation in business processes in the organization may be brought due to IT but it has to be ultimately implemented and managed by its human resources. The decision to reengineer the business processes is generally taken by the top management, but the lower-level management is made responsible for design and implementation. Therefore it becomes necessary for an organization to make aware to its line managers about the need for BPR. The process design job requires an innovative and creative skill apart from good understanding of the existing process as well as IT capability. To sustain enhanced business performance, organizations must ultimately create learning organizations that thrive on change, become more flexible, adaptable and responsive to a changing competitive landscape. In a learning organization, ideas and solutions come from everyone in the organization, no matter what their functions, job descriptions, or locations. The organization taps into the cumulative knowledge of its entire value chain, suppliers and customers, to create shared vision and value [6, 7]. The reengineered organization will take the shape of matrix structure in which the supervisory power and command of middle managers over their subordinates will be eliminated. Therefore middle managers may resist such drastic change. The operational managers and workers will have to be provided with a strong information support through enterprise-wide information technology infrastructure.

IT should be deployed to initiate and manage change processes in the organization. IT needs to be deployed not only to improve the internal and external operational efficiencies, but also to provide a strategic and competitive advantages. IT is considered to be an essential enabler of BPR — a major change process in the organization. To succeed, business and IT managers must view BPR and the deployment of IT as mutually supportive and synergistic.

5.3. *Role of TQM in BPR*

The reengineered organization (new organization) intends to be process-oriented, customer-focused and outcome-controlled, whereas the traditional hierarchical organization is functional-oriented, product-focused and procedure-controlled. In the new organization the customers are considered as its partners. The innovation in business processes in the organization may be brought due to IT but it has to be ultimately implemented and managed by its human resources. The decision to reengineer the business processes is generally taken by the top management, but the lower-level management is made responsible for its design and implementation. Therefore it become necessary for an organization to make aware to its line managers about the need for BPR. It has been found that due to TQM initiative in Organization 2, there is a shift from functional orientation to process orientation. The works are organized around processes which are managed by a competent team led by a process leader. The employees are grouped according to their area of competence and are managed by resource owners. TQM has instilled a mindset for change at all the levels of the organization, and has made BPR implementation conducive.

6. Conclusion

The agribusiness enterprises in India are facing new challenges and competition due to liberalization of the Indian economy. Some of these organizations are in the process of implementing TQM and BPR to achieve their business visions and compete globally. The study conducted in two such organizations reveals that although IT is the key enabler of BPR it is not sufficient in itself. Business Vision and TQM play a complementary role in BPR. Business Vision drawn by the top management of the organizations is found to put pressure for radical improvement on its operations. TQM is found to promulgate a mindset for change from bottom to top of the organization and helping in establishing cross-functional integration.

References

1. T. H. Davenport, *Process Innovation: Reengineering Work through Information Technology* (Harvard Business School Press, Boston, 1993).
2. M. Hammer and J. Champy, *Reengineering the Corporation* (Harper Collins, New York, 1993).
3. M. Hammer, Reengineering work: don't automate, obliterate, *Harvard Business Review*, July / August 1990, 104–12.
4. I. Jacobson, M. Ericsson and A. Jacobson, *The Object Advantage —Business Process Reengineering with Object Technology* (ACM Press, 1994).
5. M. E. Porter, *Competitive Strategy* (The Free Press, New York, 1980).
6. P. Senge, *The Fifth Discipline: The Art and Practice of the Learning Organization* (Doubleday, New York, 1990).
7. D. R. Tobin, *Re-educating the Corporation: Foundations for the Learning Organization* (Oliver Wight Publication, NC, 1993).
8. R. W. Belmonte and R. J. Murray, Getting ready for strategic change, surviving business process redesign, *Information Systems Management*, Summer 1993.
9. T. H. Davenport and J. Short, The new industrial engineering: information technology and business process redesign, *Sloan Management Review* **32** (1990) 11–27.

Chapter 22

Business Process Reengineering Using SAP R/3 in a Textile Manufacturing Environment

MONIKA B. CALITZ
University of Port Elizabeth,
Private Bag X1600, Port Elizabeth 6000, South Africa
E-mail: mbc@mweb.co.za

ANDRÉKWEN P. CALITZ
University of Port Elizabeth,
Private Bag X1600, Port Elizabeth 6000, South Africa
E-mail: csaapc@upe.ac.za

Business Process Reengineering (BPR) generally implies the redesigning of business processes and the way a business works, in order to achieve substantial improvements and financial benefits. With the introduction of modern integrated software packages, such as SAP R/3, best business practices are already incorporated into the package. BPR tools are provided both within SAP R/3 and other third party products, to assist companies in reengineering their business processes. In developing countries, reengineering business processes is generally perceived as a threat, the result being the elimination of unnecessary positions and the reduction in the staff complement. This paper describes a BPR project within a textile manufacturing company in a developing country; the use of BPR tools and an integrated software package; the experienced gained and the successful implementation of the project.

1. Introduction

Business Process Reengineering (BPR) generally implies going back to the drawing board and fundamentally redesigning the way work is performed within an organization [1]. This usually involves the introduction of information technology (IT) and bringing about organizational changes such as several jobs being combined into one, the empowerment of workers, multifunctional teams and other financial and operational benefits.

Inventing radically new ways of working is a non-trivial task. It requires critically evaluating current business processes and procedures and is usually accomplished employing consultants with extensive industry experience. However, many organizations have already successfully reengineered value-chain and mission-critical processes. This has resulted in industry-specific ways of performing certain tasks, which collectively have become known as best business practices.

Best business practices can be used as a basis to evaluate, compare and reengineer current business processes in an organization. The difference between reengineering to best business practices as opposed to clean slate reengineering is that there is a blueprint available, saving considerable effort, cost and time. This approach to BPR was applied in a medium-sized textile manufacturing company in South Africa to reengineer the materials management, purchasing and accounts payable processes.

Reengineering was achieved by studying BPR literature and implementing the SAP R/3 integrated software package, which incorporates best business practices. This chapter describes the BPR project, the experiences with reengineering according to best business practices, and the results achieved and experiences gained by implementing a BPR project in a developing country.

The following section gives an overview of the Textile Manufacturing Company (TMC), the business environment within South Africa and the specific problems with BPR in a developing country. In subsequent sections the BPR project is described, the experiences gained are discussed, and the results of the project are highlighted.

2. The Textile Manufacturing Environment in South Africa

Throughout the world today, companies are faced with the reality of competing in an increasingly global economy. This global marketplace is a place of rapid and relentless change. Product cycles are diminishing, customer service and quality are of utmost importance and constant innovation is necessary. Customers are more discerning, demanding excellence service and quality products [2]. Information about competitive products and services is more accessible to customers, for example through the internet, and price comparisons can easily be made. As one company innovates and expands the limits of possibility, it raises customer expectations for all companies in the market. Many companies in the world are responding to these changes, and some even initiating these changes, yet countries in developing countries are lagging behind.

Textile manufacturing, according to Byrne [3] continues to play an important part in the industrialization of developing countries. Among the older, established industries are the US, Japan and Europe. The technical textile industry is an industry with many variations in its resources, technologies and processing techniques and markets. During the past ten to fifteen years, the technical change and increased market growth has slowed down [4].

TMC is a medium-sized company located in a harbor city, Port Elizabeth, with two plants located in the region. TMC employs approximately 1800 people with an annual turnover of approximately R200 million. TMC is a manufacturer of household textiles (towels, face cloths, baby nappies) and industrial textiles, such as conveyer belting, geotextiles and tyrecord.

Many business processes at TMC were paper-based. Some isolated and non-integrated legacy systems are still operational on a mid-range computer. These legacy systems are to be phased out completely and replaced with SAP R/3 systems company-wide before the millennium change. The sales and distribution (SD) and financial systems (FI) have previously been implemented and are supported by the SAP R/3 software package. Some limited interfaces exist between the SAP R/3 and legacy midrange systems.

MacIntosh *et al* [5] state that mid-sized companies especially, are not radically different from larger enterprises in terms of their business processes. Medium-sized companies have complex business processes and high expectations with regard to information technology. Yet often, these companies do not have the budget to spend lavishly on consulting and high-cost business solutions, a statement that holds true for TMC.

The organizational structure of TMC can be described as complex. It operates as a group of five legal entities, each accounted for separately. Business areas within these legal entities include household textiles, technical textiles, tyrecord, geotextiles, coating, and a recently added retail division. Typical of a small to medium enterprise, TMC has a very small IT department, yet requires sophisticated IT solutions to support the complex business operations. The limited resources and packaged best business practices were the reason for choosing packaged software. According to Zencke [6], there has been a widespread acceptance of standard integrated software packages, such as SAP R/3.

TMC, being a company with limited resources as far as BPR is concerned, used current BPR literature, SAP R/3 and its best business practices as a blueprint for reengineering. The area chosen for reengineering was the materials management process from procurement through to accounts payable.

2.1. BPR in a developing country

The introduction of new information technology does not entirely guarantee a successful BPR project [2]. Organizational structures and the nature of the work itself may have to undergo radical change. In order to change a business process, all parties involved need to share a common goal. As many as 70% of BPR projects are reported to have failed, and a main reason listed for this is resistance to change from people within the organization [7].

The role of information technology in organizational transformation is very important [2]. However, business systems consist of complex interactions between employees, technology, market forces and relationships with external entities such as suppliers and customers. The majority of the workforce in developing countries, as in South Africa, lacks internationally accepted first world educational standards. Consequently, in South Africa, the largest part of the workforce has an education level of Std 2 (four years of schooling) or less. Culturally, many of these employees are not technology-oriented, and possibly see technology as a tool of the privileged management to manage and control all business processes. The introduction of information technology and modernization of manufacturing methods is a necessity for South African companies to remain competitive globally, yet this drive is viewed with suspicion and opposed strongly by certain employees in the workforce. The government is sympathetic to trade unions' demands due to high national unemployment figures, and attempts to create or maintain jobs for a large unskilled or semi-skilled population group.

In South Africa, a new political dispensation has opened its economy to a world from which it has been isolated due to political and trade sanctions, since 1994. In 1994, Apartheid was abolished and South Africa 're-entered' the global economy. The result is that a protected economy is suddenly faced with an inflow of foreign trade and global competition. South Africa, once listed among the top ten in terms of competitiveness, has now slipped into the bottom third of the list [8]. While the competition is aligning themselves for the information age, South Africa is faced with a situation where the majority of the workforce regards technology and more specifically information technology as a major threat. BPR projects in this climate are faced with an even greater resistance to change and a fear of job losses, than would be the case in a developed country. In a country where job creation is of utmost importance, BPR is seen as counter-productive to national labor goals.

3. SAP R/3 and Best Business Practices

The SAP R/3 software system is an integrated enterprise resource planning system. It comprises various modules which can be run standalone, or in conjunction with the other modules. SAP R/3 incorporates best business practices as a series of transactions. The best business practices are documented in the form of process chains. The notation used is event-driven process chains (EPC). Every process depicted on the process chain is represented as a transaction within SAP R/3. Process chains, data maps, functions, objects and configuration templates are collectively referred to as the R/3 reference model.

Reference models can dramatically improve the implementation of SAP R/3 within a company according to a white paper by SAP and Intellicorp [9]. It facilitates BPR by providing a basis, or blueprint against which current business processes can be evaluated.

While incorporating functions to cover all areas of business operations and functions, SAP R/3 also includes a business engineering workbench (BEW) to assist companies in their reengineering efforts. The project team need not invent radically new ways of working, the BEW provides a framework to choose from a variety of scenarios, the ones applicable. The BPR team is then guided through the implementation and customization of these scenarios.

4. The BPR Project

The SAP R/3 system had been partly introduced at TMC in a previous project. The systems implemented during this first phase were sales and distribution and financial systems. This project comprised the implementation of the materials management module, incorporating procurement and invoice verification. The materials management function was targeted for reengineering due to a lack of control caused by outdated business practices, many of them paper-based or only minimally supported by information technology.

The project focused on identifying the best business practices within SAP R/3 applicable to the company and to customize SAP in such a fashion that the business scenarios occurring at the company were adequately covered by the software package. The team members were selected from business people in the operation, IT department members and consultants.

Tools provided within the SAP R/3 software, such as the R/3 reference model were used. Supporting documentation consisted of spreadsheets, graphic diagrams and word processing documents.

The project had a restrictive budget but a relatively generous deadline, so it was decided that consultants would be used on a minimal basis, with an emphasis on knowledge transfer, and the project would be handled mainly in-house.

This section describes the composition of the team, the methodology followed, and implementation.

4.1. The team

The core BPR team requires various different skills and knowledge. A structure suggested by Andrews *et al* [10] comprises executive sponsors, project director, core project coordination and support group, business unit champions, advisory and subject-matter experts, implementation groups.

The team structure at TMC was smaller than suggested by Andrews *et al*, and the positions mentioned were represented as follows:

Role	Team member
Executive sponsor	CIO
Project director	Group Engineer Consultant
Business unit champions	Materials Handling Manager Manufacturing Services Manager Buyer Retail Coordinator Costing Accountant Group Financial Accountant
Advisory and subject matter experts	Consultant
Implementation group	System Analyst CIO

The project management functions were shared between a consulting project manager and the internal project manager, however, shortly after the start of the project, the group engineer was assigned to another project and the majority of the project management was performed by the consultant.

Due to the team being so small, some of the functions overlapped, the most notable being the CIO's involvement in the implementation issues. One of the business unit champions assigned to the project failed to participate.

The function of the business unit champions was to provide business scenarios, test and validate that they were adequately catered for, and eventually to train the other staff in their respective departments. They were referred to as super users.

The two members from the IT team were responsible for the configuration of the SAP R/3 software package to cater for the scenarios supplied by the super users, support of the super users, loading of the data and technical functions. The IT staff was assisted during certain phases by the external consultants.

4.2. *The methodology*

The methodology followed contributed greatly to the success of the project. The methodology was provided by the consultants. It can be divided into four major phases:

- Scoping and Planning;
- System Design;
- Configuration and Testing; and
- Production Preparation.

Each of the phases is described in more detail below.

4.2.1. Scoping and planning

During the scoping and planning phase, the SAP R/3 reference model was used extensively to gain an understanding of the functionality of the SAP. The R/3 reference model was loaded into Visio and served as a basis for selecting the processes applicable to TMC.

The models were adapted to reflect the materials management processes at the company. Four main variations were identified:

- Consignment stock handling
- Procurement of stocked items
- Procurement of non-stock items
- Procurement of subcontracting services

Certain functionality provided within SAP was excluded. The reference models were updated to reflect the processes specific to the company. These models served as a basis for configuring the software.

4.2.2. System design

The system design phase uses the models generated during the previous phase as a basis for creating a blueprint for TMC-specific business processes. Among the issues that were addressed and resolved here were:

- Identifying forms and report requirements
- Specifying the configuration requirements
- Identifying business scenarios
- Developing prototyping master data
- Identifying infrastructure requirements
- Assigning business processes to specific job functions

4.2.3. Configuration and testing

This phase comprises applying the system design in the form of configuration settings, and testing whether the configurations have the desired outcome for each business scenario.

The business scenarios identified and described by each team member served were mapped with the assistance of the reference model onto specific processes within SAP R/3.

The configurations specified in the system design were applied, the prototyping master data was created, and each scenario was played out in SAP R/3 as a set of transactions, validating that the configuration had the desired outcome.

The scenarios were expanded into a set of test strings, each identified with specific SAP transactions, applicable master data, and expected outcomes.

The team members prepared the master data for the data take-on, and generated the training material.

4.2.4. Production preparation

This final phase comprised training the users, loading the master data and taking on the stock balances.

5. Results of the BPR Project

The BPR project focused on the implementation of SAP R/3 to support best business practices. As far as the implementation of the software is concerned, the project could be termed a success. It was implemented one week before deadline date, and approximately 10% under-budget.

In terms of organizational change, the project had the effect of eliminating job functions, such as:

- Capturing of journal entries;
- Matching invoices to purchase orders, delivery notes, and internal documentation; and
- Monthly reconciling of consignment stock movements.

There are also examples of empowerment in certain job functions, such as:

- Responsibility of recording stock movements and their financial implications by store people;
- Purchasing process added to administrative assistants' job; and
- Releasing vendor invoices for payment by accounts payable clerk.

Job functions such as receiving are now empowered to accept or reject deliveries because the purchase orders are available on-line. The accounts payable clerk can release invoices for payment on a goods-receipt based invoice verification basis.

Various persons were computer-illiterate before the start of the project. The training empowered them to use a sophisticated integrated information system effectively. The empowerment is expected to proliferate as more PCs are being deployed throughout the company.

An interesting feature of the project was that the implementation of IT was the driving force, and the project was seen essentially as an IT project. This stands in contrast to literature which states that BPR efforts should be driven by executive management [10]. However the implementation of SAP R/3 is essentially not a focus on IT, but on business issues, because the IT infrastructure is already provided.

A possible effect of this approach is that the business changes were not as dramatic as is suggested by proponents of radical reengineering [1].

Another reason for changes in the business process being on the conservative, rather than on the radical side could possibly be attributed to resistance to change in certain business unit champions. Work-saving processes supported by SAP R/3, such as self-invoicing, were not implemented.

The non-involvement of the one business unit champion resulted in many errors being made and a huge support load by the IT members at the beginning of the project, and was noticeably the only problem area.

Some other minor errors made after implementation could be attributed to inadequate training. Scheer [11], states that users need to understand the business background in order to interpret information on screen effectively. The training for the end users focused on transactional training rather than business process training. The effect of this was that many end users could not effectively identify which process to follow for specific business cases.

Shabana [12] lists among the reasons for using consultants their experience, providing a fresh look, an objective vision, and effective facilitation of a BPR project. TMC used consultants, specializing in SAP R/3 implementations during the project but not on a full-time basis. Knowledge transfer took place effectively, which is reflected in the fact that during the last phase of the project the consultants were hardly present at all. The decrease of consulting time during the last stages of the project was largely responsible for the project going in under-budget.

6. Summary

In this article, a BPR project in a textile manufacturing environment was described and discussed. The project team reengineered according to best business practices, using successful case studies from literature and implemented SAP R/3. The implementation of the project and experiences gained were discussed and the results of the project highlighted.

South Africa is a developing country and job creation is a national priority. Business process reengineering in developing countries can be successful, however training, education and communication with workers is essential.

References

1. M. Hammer and J. Champy, *Reengineering the Corporation* (HarperCollins Publishers, New York, 1993).
2. D. Schnitt, Reengineering the organization using information technology, *Journal of Systems Management*, January 1993.
3. C. Byrne, The industrial and social impact of new technology in the clothing industry into the 2000s, paper presented for International Labor Office, http://www.dratex.co.uk/publications/clotech1.html, 7/10/96, 12:09:42.
4. D. Rigby, Strategic thinking in technical textile companies: how to adapt business strategy to changing technologies and markets, paper June 1995 Techtextil Symposium, Frankfurt, http://www.dratex.co.uk/publications/techtex95.html, 7/10/96, 12:09:42.
5. Dr. R. MacIntosh and Prof A. Francis, The market, technological and industry contexts of business process reengineering in UK businesses, 1996 http://bprc.warwick.ac.uk/glasgow1.html, 05/29/96.
6. Dr. P. Zencke, Standards for customised solutions, SAP info, Issue 46/47, September 1995, 14–15.
7. D. M. Pittle, Business process innovation, http://www.krnr.com/bpr.html, 08/15/1996.
8. F. Heydenrych, So much time, so much money, *Information Technology Review* 3(2), (1996) 26–34.
9. SAP/Intellicorp, Business process design with the SAP R/3 reference model and object-oriented information engineering, white paper, http://www.intellicorp.com/ooieonline/sapwhitepaper.html, 7/10/96.

10. D. C. Andrews and S. K. Stalick, *Business Reengineering, The Survival Guide* (Prentice Hall, New Jersey, 1994).
11. A.-W. Scheer, *Business Process Engineering* (Springer-Verlag, Berlin, 1994).
12. A. Shabana, The effect of outside consultants involvement over the success of bpr projects, http://hsb.baylor.edu/~ramsower/acis/papers/ashabana.html, 5/7/1995.

Chapter 23

A Scientific Approach to Business Process Reengineering

CHESTER C. WARZYNSKI
Director of Organizational Development,
Cornell University,
E-mail: ccw7@cornell.edu

Many BPR projects fail because they attempt to initiate organizational change using an ideological rather than a scientific approach. A scientific approach to business process reengineering would be based on clear definitions, variables, hypotheses, research design and verification strategy. This chapter attempts to develop a more scientific approach to BPR through the application of an axiomatic model that standardizes language, methodology, and measurement. It is argued that a more scientific approach to BBR will help build a valid and reliable body of knowledge for making predictions, validating outcomes, and guiding future decisions. Three case studies are presented to illustrate how BPR can be applied more scientifically to understand and improve organizational performance.

1. Introduction

F. R. C. Northrop defines an ideology as "the ideas held in common by (people) in ordering their social institutions. Ideology includes doctrines and ideals held by any group of people, which purport to furnish normative guidance to the group's practices" [1]. Edward Shils identifies several distinguishing criteria of ideologies, including the following: (1) explicitness of formulation; (2) deliberate systemic integration around core values and cognitive beliefs; (3) imperativeness of manifestation in conduct; (4) accompanying affect or emotion; (5) consensus demanded of those involved; (6) authoritativeness of promulgation; (7) association with a corporate body identified to realize the patterns of belief. He goes on to say that ideologies seek "a purer, fuller, or more ideal realization of particular cognitive and moral values ... (they) impel their proponents to insist on the realization of the ideal ... through total transformation" [2].

Anyone who has been around a business process reengineering project, even for a short time, will recognize the ideological nature of the BPR methodology [3]. In fact, the visioning phase, which is an integral part of many BPR methodologies, essentially involves the creation of a new corporate ideology. And the whole area of change management, or what is sometimes called 'cultural transformation,' is an explicit attempt to inculcate values and beliefs in a target audience [4].

The present need for greater use of the scientific method in business process reengineering is vital. The human and financial cost of reengineering failures is staggering. It has been estimated that failures in reengineering result in billions of dollars in unnecessary costs each year, not to mention human suffering stemming from dislocations in the workplace [4–7].

This chapter examines the confusion surrounding business process reengineering and attempts to ground it in science rather than ideology. An axiomatic model is used to show how BPR can be approached more scientifically. Finally, three case studies in higher education are presented to illustrate successful applications of BPR and to indicate directions for future research and practice.

2. Confusion Over Reengineering

Business process reengineering has many proponents today. However, there is very little agreement and much confusion over what it really means, how it is measured, what it involves, and how it works to improve organizational performance. This is the first problem that must be addressed if BPR is to be approached scientifically and if we are to reduce the failure rate of reengineering projects.

The concept of reengineering has a variety of different meanings and uses. When viewed from a corporate perspective, it usually refers to the massive restructurings that have occurred in the business world in recent years. When viewed from a media perspective, it usually relates to the wave of downsizings and layoffs associated with corporate restructuring. When viewed from an organizational perspective, it involves redesigning work processes and jobs and enabling them with new information technology. When managers speak of it, they are generally referring to major changes that are or will be occurring in the organization, and when employees speak of it, they are generally referring to the elimination of jobs.

If variations in usage and terminology are not confusing enough, nearly every consulting firm in the field promotes its own 'unique' methodologies and techniques to differentiate its approach to reengineering from that of its competitors. Thus, methods and measures differ from project to project and consultant to consultant. This lack of precision and standardization is one of the major difficulties in developing a valid and reliable body of knowledge on business process reengineering.

Another difficulty is due to the popularity of the concept of itself. According to James March [8], many managers make decisions using a "garbage can decision process." When faced with a need to improve organizational performance, the manager searches through his or her 'garbage can' of possible ideas or solutions, including the latest fads and cures and then, through a sorting process, identifies and selects the solution that most closely matches the organization's needs or the manager's mind set. This kind of decision making often results in capricious decisions based on inadequate or erroneous information.

Moreover, because this 'garbage can' process of decision making does not employ a scientific evaluation of alternatives, it fails to make use of or develop a systematic body of knowledge for testing or validating decisions. Consequently, managers fail to learn why some solutions work and others do not.

3. Business Process Reengineering as Science

The scientific method uses analysis, synthesis and evaluation in a controlled logic structure that promotes objectivity and understanding. It is based on principles and rules developed, tested, and refined through numerous experiments and empirical studies. It proceeds systematically by assessing the situation, formulating hypotheses, testing hypotheses, creating models or theories, evaluating applications, and finally deducing decisions and actions. Assessments and adjustments are made at each step of the process to gain further insight and foster continuous learning. The outcome of this approach is a body of knowledge that is constantly being improved and can be relied upon for guiding future decisions and actions.

For BPR to become more scientific in its approach, it would have to meet the following requirements:

1. Common definitions of terms
2. Explicit assumptions regarding context and scope of effort
3. Clear identification of independent and dependent variables
4. Comprehensive review of available research
5. Clear statement of hypotheses and propositions
6. Clear research and validation strategy
7. Deduced management decisions and plans

One way to meet these requirements is to formalize the approach to organizational improvement. This can be accomplished through developing an axiomatic model of organization that can serve as a frame of reference for planning and evaluating BPR efforts. A model is an explanation of some phenomenon by means of concepts, definitions and hypotheses that form a closed system. Each hypothesis in the model posits a relationship between at least two variables and has the capability of being empirically verified.

An axiomatic model can take a few variables and generate all possible implications or relationships. It can reduce confusion about BPR by explicitly answering questions of definition, measurement and theory. More specifically, an axiomatic model of organization can provide a framework within which concepts, assumptions, variables, and research findings about the organization and the impact of BPR may be systematically integrated, organized, interpreted, applied, measured, tested, and verified [9].

An axiomatic model functions to generate hypotheses. Only a few variables are needed to generate a relatively complex system of hypotheses or propositions. A fundamental principle of this model is that given (n – l) basic hypothesis where n equals the number of variables, and given that all variables appear in at least one of the (n – l) hypotheses, then all other hypotheses within the system may be generated. The total number of hypotheses in the model is therefore n(n – 1)/2.

The axiomatic model of organization in this chapter consists of the following sections:

1. Frame of Reference
   1.1. Assumptions
   1.2. Basic Concepts and Definitions
2. Substantive Domain (independent and dependent variables)
3. Basic Hypotheses
4. Generated Hypotheses

3.1. *Frame of reference*

The frame of reference is the foundation on which assertions about organizations are made. It consists of the major assumptions, concepts, and definitions. For purposes of illustration, a few of the more important assumptions and definitions are represented below.

3.1.1. Assumptions

- Business process reengineering is a systematic approach to improving organizational performance.
- BPR aims at optimizing the value system of an organization over a pre-determined time period.
- Long-term performance (over five years) is as important to managers as short-term performance (under five years).
- People are a critical asset of the organization, i.e. the organization cannot succeed for very long without the support and commitment of its employees.
- Organizational performance can best be increased through the alignment of strategies, resources, work processes, technology, structure, employee competence, and culture with customer needs.

3.1.2. Concepts and definitions

- BPR is defined as: "The fundamental rethinking and **radical** redesign of the entire business **system** to achieve **dramatic** improvements in critical measures of performance" [10, 11].
- BPR involves radical change to the entire organization — work processes, information technology organizational structure, employee competence, and culture for the purpose of achieving dramatic improvements (30% or greater) in customer satisfaction, efficiency (reduced costs or cycle time), effectiveness (revenue generated), and innovation (new knowledge, products or services).
- Work processes are interconnected sets of functions, activities, and procedures performed by people or machines over time that lead to specific results.

- Technology consists of organizational systems and know-how structured to achieve practical objectives in an efficient and effective manner.
- Structure is the configuration and relationship of functions, jobs, tasks, and authority.
- Employee competencies are the underlying characteristics of employees, e.g. knowledge, skills, attitudes, traits, etc. that are causally connected to performance through roles and responsibilities.
- Culture consists of the beliefs, values, guiding principles, norms, and rules that direct an organization's behavior and people.
- Resources are the assets and means through which an organization carries out its mission.
- Strategies are the decisions and actions that an organization takes to accomplish its mission, goals, and objectives.
- Customers are the people or entities that receive and use the organization's products and services. Customer satisfaction is a measure of the degree to which customers continue to purchase an organization's products and services.
- Scope and magnitude of reengineering change include the following five levels:

    - Level 1: Localized exploitation, e.g. financial system;
    - Level 2: Internal integration, e.g. multiple systems;
    - Level 3: Business process redesign, e.g. processes/structures;
    - Level 4: Business network redesign, e.g. across institutional boundaries;
    - Level 5: Business scope redesign, e.g. mission [12].

- Effectiveness is a set of desired results measured in terms of both quality and quantity of units produced and profit generated.
- Efficiency is the amount of resources consumed to achieve a desired level of effectiveness measured in terms of costs or cycle time.
- Innovativeness is the amount of new knowledge created, measured in terms of new technologies, products and services.

3.2. *Substantive domain*

The substantive domain consists of the class of independent, dependent and mediating variables in the model. The variables indicated in Table 1 are examples of key variables associated with BPR. (This model is not inclusive as many other variables could be included.)

Table 1 Key variables in organization

Independent variables	Mediating variables	Dependent variables
Work processes	Leadership	Customer satisfaction
Information technology	Project management	Efficiency (Costs/Cycle time)
Organization structure	Resources	Effectiveness (Revenues)
Employee competence	Culture	Innovation

3.3. *Basic hypotheses*

The basic hypotheses are those propositions or assertions of relationships between variables in the model that are based on empirical research or logical argument. Some examples of basic hypotheses are:

- The newer the technology, the higher the customer satisfaction.
- The greater the simplicity of work processes, the greater the efficiency (lower cost and cycle time).
- The greater the employee competence, the greater the effectiveness (revenues).
- The flatter the organization structure, the greater the innovativeness (new knowledge, products and services).

Taken together these hypotheses suggest a theory that organizational performance, as measured in terms of customer satisfaction, efficiency, effectiveness, and innovativeness, can be improved by simplifying work processes, installing new technology, developing employee competence, and flattening organizational structure. In other words, organizational performance can be improved through business process reengineering project designed to accomplish these aims.

3.4. Generated hypotheses

In the four propositions indicated above, there are four independent variables: technology, work processes, employee competence, and organizational structure; and four dependent variables: customer satisfaction, efficiency, effectiveness, and innovativeness, for a total of eight variables. Thus, according to the equation $n(n - 1)/2$ there will be a total of 28 interrelated propositions or hypotheses.

Generated hypotheses are those propositions emanating from the basic hypotheses. For example, propositions 1 and 2 may be used to generate a third proposition in the model that is related yet different from the four basic propositions: the newer the technology, the greater the simplicity of the work processes. In this manner all logical possibilities or relationships between the variables in the system may be generated to form a complete model of organization.

An axiomatic model of organization can provide the basis for constructing a neural network to predict or forecast the performance of different changes to the organization. A neural network consists of a system of 'neurons' (computational elements) in which several inputs are interconnected and weighted to produce one or more outputs. As a dynamic network of mathematical relationships between several input variables and output variables, the network, when trained with data, is capable of recognizing significant patterns and forecasting organizational performance. A neural network can learn and change as new information is added; it can generalize and make predictions; and it can abstract significant information relating to organizational performance. In other words, such a network could be used to estimate the impact of specific organizational changes, evaluate different decision options, and make accurate predictions for optimizing organizational performance.

The use of neural networks as a decision support tool to aid managers in BPR is still in an early stage of development. To date, they have been used successfully by managers to analyze the financial health of organizations; recognize financial distress patterns such as bankruptcy; predict the performance of stocks, bonds and commodities; simulate market behavior, and forecast corporate performance [13].

Figure 1 is an example of a neural network architecture based on the eight organizational variables impacted by BPR in the axiomatic model above.

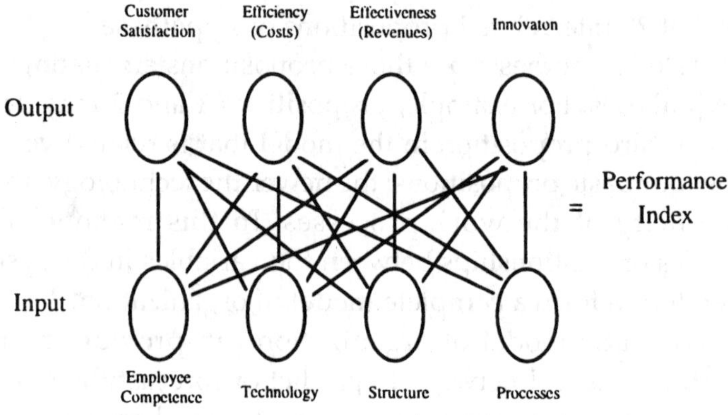

Figure 1 Neural network for predicting relationships between key variables

4. Empirical Research in Business Process Reengineering

The lack of a reliable body of knowledge, from which to evaluate the efficacy of various BPR methodologies and projects, has led to many ill conceived, unguided, and indiscriminate applications. The high failure rate of BPR projects may be attributed to the 'trial and error' approach adopted by many managers and practioners. With the exception of Booz, Allen and Hamilton's ten step methodology, which is grounded on the scientific method, most BPR methodologies fail to provide an adequate research design for determining why a particular approach worked in one organization and not in another. This undermines efforts to predict improvements in organizational performance and impedes the development of a reliable body of knowledge for making decisions and guiding BPR efforts.

Tables 2 and 3 below highlight some important empirical research findings related to the scope and methodology of BPR efforts. These findings clearly indicate that the scope of BPR effort needs to be cross-functional and include the full range of dependent and independent variables. The findings also illustrate the importance of the mediating variables of leadership, project management, resources, training, and employee involvement in the success of BPR efforts.

Table 2 How to make reengineering really work: a study of twenty organizations [14]

	Independent (Predictor) Variables	Dependent (Performance) Variables
Breadth		
	• Cross functional	• Change in earnings
Depth		
	• Roles and responsibilities	• Reduction in business costs
	• Measurements and incentives	
	• Organizational structure	
	• Information technology	
	• Shared values	
	• Skills	

Results: Breadth reduced overall business costs by as much as 17%
Depth reduced specific process costs by as much as 35%.

Table 3 Key factors for success in reengineering [15]

CSC (497 companies) ranked	Mercer (300 executives) %
1. Effective project management	1. Training — 31%
2. Executive commitment	2. Better communication — 25%
3. Adequate resources	3. Sr. mgmt. endorsement — 17%
4. Effective use of team	4. Staff aware of benefits — 17%
5. Team member commitment of time and resources	5. Reassurance & patience — 11%
6. Right focus (clear understanding of scope and goals)	6. Formation of teams — 11%
7. Strong communications program	7. Employee involvement — 10%
8. Realistic planning & schedules	
9. Effective education & training	

5. BPR Case Studies in Higher Education

James Porter [16] believes that BPR may not be possible in higher education. He states two reasons for this belief: (1) the mission of higher education is pretty much set and, in the opinion of most administrators and trustees, is not subject to dramatic change; and (2) initiating radical change in higher education is extremely difficult, if not impossible, because of the decentralized nature of educational institutions. He argues that "Administrative process redesign should not be attempted, since there is no demonstrated need, no documented benefit, and no organizational support for such an effort."

Others have said similar things about BPR in higher education. James Penrod [17] and Michael Dolence, quoting George Keller and Ann McCreery point out that

> "Universities have stressed the training of critical intellect; they have neglected the training of imaginative intellect. In addition, universities are ... 'loosely coupled' organizations. So the picture is one of confused, multiple-motivated people trying to advance

loosely coupled institutions with bounded rationality while hoping to find ways to express themselves without sustaining any losses."

Despite the warnings and difficulties of doing BPR in higher education suggested by these authors, many universities have embarked upon this perilous journey in an attempt — and sometimes desperate need — to improve organizational performance. The results of three recent case studies in higher education are summarized below.

5.1. *Reengineering the purchasing process at Carnegie Mellon University [18]*

Carnegie Mellon University recently reengineered its procurement-disbursement or purchasing process. This was a level 3 scope change in which a major cross-functional process was reengineered and the organization structure underlying that process redesigned. Prior to the reengineering effort, the acquisitions department was largely a transaction processing organization in which employees processed orders but had very little involvement in negotiating purchasing agreements or providing direct services to departments. According to one study conducted by a cross-functional team, the university was spending $48 to process each order with over 40,000 orders per year. The time involved in processing each order averaged 64 days from purchase decision to receipt of goods and services. 75% of staff time was spent in processing paper and record keeping, and 25% of the orders required re-work. The goals of the reengineering effort were to: (1) reduce the time and effort to process an order; (2) reduce total expenditures by leveraging the university's buying power; and (3) reduce costs of processing purchase orders. The independent variables impacted by the reengineering effort were process, structure, technology, and employee competence, and the dependent variables were cost, efficiency, and customer satisfaction. The basic hypothesis was that a more streamlined process, enabled by information technology, combined with a reduced number of highly trained and competent employees, could increase service to customers and reduce cost to the university.

The reengineering solution was to use a preferred list of vendors together with an electronic procurement card linked to responsibility centers. "To obtain a product or service, the cardholder looks through a paper or electronic catalogs and a list of preferred vendors. The order is placed by telephone, electronically, or in person; the procurement card number is provided; and the materials are received ... The bank forwards the details of the just-completed transaction to a data base and third-party provider of information technology services."

It was estimated that the reengineering effort resulted in approximately $8 million in savings to the university, including the net reduction of 19 positions from the accounts payable department and a drastic reduction in the role of receiving and central stores. In addition to streamlining the acquisition's process and organization structure, this effort also resulted in improved information for tracking purchases and for negotiating and leveraging buying decisions. Better service and quicker turn-around time for orders increased customer satisfaction.

5.2. *Reengineering administrative systems at UCLA [19]*

Like many other universities, the University of California at Los Angeles had developed a huge bureaucracy in which faculty, administrators, and staff spent a good deal of their time filling out, chasing down, and checking paper forms as part of their responsibilities. "It was not uncommon to see paper forms with 15 (or more) signatures, and business transactions took several weeks to complete." Faced with a fiscal crisis stemming from state budget cuts, UCLA launched a major reengineering effort aimed at reducing bureaucracy and costs. The goal of this level 3 change project was to streamline the administrative processes through restructuring and using information technology. The independent variables were administrative work processes, including organizational policies and procedures, and information technology. The dependent variables were costs and worker satisfaction. The basic hypothesis was that simplification and automation of administrative processes, in conjunction with a change in policies and procedures governing system access, transaction authority, and security, would result in increased efficiency and reduced costs.

The reengineering solution involved redesigning and automating administrative work processes and changing system access and transaction authorization. Redesigned processes were based on a post-audit function and distributed security system in which key business transactions could be initiated and finalized at the same time by the same person. The reengineering solution included the following elements:

- A post-audit mechanism to distribute completed transactions electronically to administrators for their reviews and approvals *after processing* rather than before processing.
- An audit file of all notifications forwarded to individuals for post-authorization reviews.
- A new policy outlining qualifications and responsibilities of individuals initiating transactions and those performing post-authorization reviews.
- A distributed access and control security system which would allow departments to determine and delegate security access and post-authorization to their staff.
- A front-edit to prevent errors based on institutional rules and funding restrictions.

The outcome of this reengineering effort was extremely successful. Based on some rough but conservative calculations, UCLA estimated annual savings at over one million dollars, including $600,000 in transaction time, $300,000 in data entry, and $100,000 in decentralized access controls. In addition to cost savings, processes that in the past took two to six weeks to complete are now being done in a matter of seconds; transactions that required numerous approvals are completed by one or two people in a post-audit mode; transaction errors have been reduced dramatically; and customer satisfaction has increased. These results were achieved with no loss of fiduciary responsibility or control. According to the university's external auditors, there were "no major control weaknesses which would significantly impact either the University's MIS general control or the ... control environment."

5.3. *Reengineering sponsored research at Cornell University [20]*

Another interesting case study in higher education is underway at Cornell University. The primary objective of this level 4 reengineering project (i.e. business network redesign across institutional boundaries) is to implement a comprehensive business solution to support sponsored research.

Cornell University is among the leading research institutions in the United States. It has approximately $325M of annual revenues related to research projects, which represents approximately 25% of Cornell's total budget. The university faces many of the same environmental challenges as its sister universities, including decreases in public funding, erosion of indirect cost recovery, increases in regulations from sponsors, and stiff competition from other universities for research dollars. Although Cornell has been very successful in sustaining its research growth and position as a leader in the industry, the current process and organizational infrastructure to support sponsored research programs is unable to meet the challenges of a changing research environment or the complex needs of the faculty.

In the current environment, there are no university-wide systems that support sponsored programs. Most activities conducted by units (departments, colleges and centers) are performed manually. Significant effort is expended in developing 'shadow' systems to supplement the information that is not readily available from central systems. Current systems are inadequate for tracking proposal and award information. Therefore much information is stored manually and re-entered during the proposal and award processing phases. The connection with sponsoring agencies is through inefficient manual paper systems in which everyone re-enters everyone else's data and administrative staff face great difficulty tracking, accessing, and using information to manage the system. Consequently, internal and external communications are often problematic, and relationships between primary investigators, sponsors, and administrative staff sometimes become strained.

The specific goals of this reengineering project are to: (1) improve stakeholder service and satisfaction; (2) reduce administrative effort required to manage sponsored programs; (3) maintain adequate communication and control to insure compliance with federal, state and sponsor regulations; (4) improve managerial and institutional reporting; (5) develop an infrastructure to establish and maintain best practices: and (6) provide a common tool set for proactively managing sponsored program activities in conjunction with sponsoring agencies.

The independent variables are work processes, information technology, and organizational structure (roles and responsibilities). The dependent variables are stakeholder satisfaction (primary investigators, sponsors, and administrative staff), and efficiency (cost and time savings). The hypothesis is that the redesign and automation of work processes across institutional boundaries together with a redesigned organization structure will improve stakeholder satisfaction and efficiency.

The following reengineering changes have been designed by the Sponsored Project Solutions (SPS) Team:

- On-line access to funding opportunities with capabilities for matching funding opportunities with professional information.

- On-line repository of standardized professional, sponsor, organization, subrecipient and unit information, and ability to interact electronically with other external systems.
- The ability to prepare proposals on-line and allow concurrent access during the review process with standard templates and guidelines to develop budgets and complete sponsor submission requirements.
- The ability to receive awards electronically, update the system with new information, and access on-line information.
- System edit checks for potentially unallowable costs; on-line award modification; tools to process standardized project management reports; and queries to obtain information critical to managing the projections and financial performance of the project.
- Automated processes for invoices, payments, tracking, and reporting. Reports are workflowed directly to certifying employees and changes are automatically processed through the human resources and financial system which are integrated with sponsored funds accounting and the office of sponsored research. Cost sharing information is captured in the system to insure compliance with federal regulations and there is electronic notification to all stakeholders responsible for final deliverables prior to the award expiration date.

In addition to new processes, policies, procedures, the reengineering solution will provide a new organizational model with clearly defined roles and responsibilities. This organization structure will be characterized by: (1) a strong customer service orientation; (2) clearly defined and delegated authority to carry out client-centered research administration activities; (3) comprehensive training in how to complete activities and provide service to stakeholders; (4) distributed signature authority to sign-off on proposals and expenditures; (5) an integrated team approach at the central and local levels; and (6) comprehensive research services to faculty.

The results of this reengineering effort portend significant improvements in the satisfaction of primary investigators in identifying funding opportunities, preparing and tracking proposals, processing awards, and getting accurate and timely information related to the financial status of awards. It is also hypothesized that the process and system changes will significantly reduced the non-value added administrative effort required to manage research across the system with sponsors. Key processes that should result in improved operational efficiencies for both sponsors and the university include establishing accounts, reviewing transactions, requesting payments, processing payments, monitoring accounts receivable, and preparing financial status reports. In addition, the redesign of cash management process should result in improved cash flow to the university.

Cornell's ability to link to new sponsor and agency systems will enable sponsors to review information in a more efficient manner. More timely submission of deliverables such as financial and non-financial reports will improve internal and external communications and relationships, increase sponsor satisfaction, and enhance the faculty's ability to acquire research funds.

Finally, in recent years, the federal government has significantly increased its scrutiny of higher education institution's ability to meet the regulatory requirements. The proposed process, policy, and structure improvements have addressed many specific compliance requirements that will help reduce Cornell's potential risk in the future by enhancing compliance with government and sponsor requirements.

6. Summary and Conclusion

This chapter has attempted to provide an overview of business process reengineering and to show how managers and practioners can adopt a more scientific approach to organizational improvement. It has been suggested that many BPR failures may be due to managers and consultants who use BPR as a strategy to promote culture change rather than as a scientific methodology to understand and optimize organizational behavior. A more scientific approach to BPR could be achieved through the use of an axiomatic model of organization and the use of a neural network as a verification strategy and decision support tool. This kind of formalization of BPR can help to standardize language, methodology, and measurement as well as build a reliable body of knowledge on which to base predictions and guide future decisions and change efforts.

The results set forth in this paper are tentative and require further research and refinement. The axiomatic model of organization presented included only a few variables. To expand the inclusiveness and scope of the model, it is essential that additional variables be added. Mediating variables relating to resources, leadership, and culture should be considered to make the model more comprehensive. The model then may be used to construct a neural network and trained with live data to assess relationships between variables. Once these relationships have been validated, the model could provide a dynamic tool for understanding and optimizing organizational performance [21].

References

1. F. R. C. Northrop, Ideological man in his relation to scientifically known natural man, in *Ideological Differences and World Order* (Yale University Press, New Haven, Chapter XIX) p. 3.
2. E. Shils, The concept and function of ideology, *Encyclopedia of the Social Sciences.*
3. S. Adams, *The Dilbert Principle* (HarperBusiness,1996). This book presents a satirical account of the ideological nature of reengineering.
4. F. Hilmer and L. Donaldson, *Management Redeemed: Debunking the Fads that Undermine Our Corporations* (The Free Press, New York,1996).
5. Bain & Company, Planning Forum, Management Tools & Techniques, Survey Reports Summary, London, 1995 pp. 3.
6. R. Johansen and R. Swigart, *Upsizing the Individual in the Downsized Organization* (Addison-Wesley Publishing Co., New York, 1996).
7. J. Micklethwait and A. Wooldridge, *The Witch Doctors* (Times Books, New York, 1996).

8. J. G. March, *A Primer on Decision Making: How Decisions Happen* (The Free Press, New York, 1994).
9. H. Zetterberg, *On Theory and Verification in Sociology* (Bedminster, New Jersey, 1963). Also see J. Hage, An axiomatic theory of organizations, *Administrative Science Quarterly*, **10** (1965) 289–320.
10. M. Hammer and J. Champy, *Reengineering the Corporation: A Manifesto for Business Revolution* (Harper Business, New York, 1993).
11. M. Hammer and S. Stanton, *The Reengineering Revolution* (HarperBusiness, New York, 1995) p. 33.
12. M. S. Morton, *The Corporation of the 1990s: Information Technology and Organizational Transformation* (Oxford University Press, New York, 1991), pp. 122–128 and quoted in James H. Porter, Business reengineering in higher education, *Cause/Effect* **16** (1993) 1–10.
13. R. R. Trippi and E. Turban, *Neural Networks in Finance and Investing* (Irwin Professional Publishing, Chicago, 1994).
14. G. Hall, J. Rosenthal and J. Wade, How to make reengineering really work, *Harvard Business Review,* November-December 1993, 119–131.
15. CSC Index, State of Reengineering Report — Executive Summary (CSC Management Consultants, Inc., Cambridge, MA, 1994), pp. 5–6; and Mercer Management Consulting, Business Improvement Initiatives — A Summary Report (Marsh & McLennan, Lexington, MA, November, 1994), p. 10.
16. J. H. Porter, Business reengineering in higher education, *Cause/Effect* **16** (1993) 1–10.
17. G. Keller and A. McCreery, Making difficult educational decisions: findings from research and experience, paper given at the Society for College and University Planning, Atlanta, Georgia, July 1990, pp. 14–15 and quoted in J. F. Penrod and M. G. Dolence, Concepts for reengineering higher education, *Cause/Effect* **14** (1991) 5.
18. P. Keating, *et al* Change as a constant: organizational restructuring at Carnegie Mellon University, *NACUBO Business Officer,* May 1996, 50–56.
19. E. Harel and G. Partipilo, Reengineering beyond the illusion of control, *Cause/Effect* **19** (1996) 38–44.
20. J. DeStefano, Project 2000 Master Plan Executive Summary, Sponsored Programs (Cornell University, Ithaca, New York, 1997) pp. 1–6. Also sec K. J. Hittelman and M. O'Connor, Research administration for the 21st century in *Managing the Academic Health Center Mission: The Search for*

Integration (Washington, D.C., 1997) for additional information on reengineering sponsored research.

21. V. Dhar and R. Stein, *Intelligent Decision Support Methods: The Science of Knowledge Work* (Prentice-Hall, New Jersey, 1997). Also see companion volume, *Seven Methods for Transforming Corporate Data into Business Intelligence* (1997).
22. L. M. Applegate, *Business Transformation Self-Assessment: Summary of Findings 1992–1993* (Harvard Business School, Boston, 1993).

PART V

FUTURE PROSPECTS

Chapter 24

Managing the Risks of Reengineering to Achieve Enterprise Excellence for the 21st Century

EDWARD G. LEWIS

Ted Lewis & Associates, 556 East Gill Way,
Superior, Colorado, USA
E-mail: elewis303@aol.com

By understanding why and how organizations have succeeded and appreciating the common pitfalls and misconceptions in implementing business process reengineering, executives, managers and employees will be better prepared to address critical organizational, management and technology issues in their organizations as we move into the 21st century.

Using data from many reengineering efforts in the private and public sectors, this paper will address the primary risks involved in reengineering and discuss five critical success factors for reengineering which every organization should consider: executives; environmental and cultural assessment; nine process change enablers; a structured methodology; and a change management program.

1. Background

As we move into the 21st century, the world is becoming even more complex and fluid. Frequent, and oftentimes drastic, changes in organization, management and technology have become the norm, if not *the* most important issue in both the private and public sectors. In many of today's organizations, there is tremendous pressure to reduce budgets, downsize/eliminate organizational structure, and use information technology more effectively. To address these rapidly changing critical issues, business process reengineering (BPR) has become the preeminent business performance technique used by today's visionary executives to achieve their strategic goals.

2. Reengineering Concepts

Through their extensive research, Michael Hammer and James Champy have done an excellent job in developing the basic tenets for business process reengineering, which emphasize fundamental rethinking, radical redesign, strategic and value-added business processes, dramatic improvements, and critical performance measurements [1]. Others, including Thomas Davenport [2] and Ray Manganelli [3], have also done extensive work in developing and refining the fundamental concepts of reengineering. Using these reengineering principles as a framework, organizations can strive for excellence in providing high-quality products and services at fair prices and reasonable cost in order to fully meet the needs and expectations of both their internal and external customers. They can, in fact, determine a better way to do work through their organizational structure, their work processes, their people, and information resources.

In implementing business process reengineering, organizations must realize that, on the one hand, tiptoeing through the reengineering maze one process at a time and in a 'vacuum' will be most difficult at best. On the other hand, casting reengineering within the organization as the way of life — a life-time journey to be traveled by all in the organization — will insure, although extremely difficult, that all changes as a result of the reengineering effort, all process redesigns, will fit together.

3. Reengineering Failures

Yet, evidence suggests that many reengineering efforts fail — why? To begin with, managers in general, in both the private and public sectors have only focused on:

- Reorganizing: Moving 'boxes' from one side to the other, up or down on the organizational chart,
- Downsizing: Major reductions in staff just to cut costs to meet quarterly profit/cost goals,
- Automating: 'Paving over the cowpaths,' doing the wrong things efficiently,
- Improving: Incrementally, one step at a time through quality circles.

But, is this reengineering — *absolutely not*! Then, perhaps, is breakthrough thinking, as embodied in business process reengineering, something so overwhelmingly and intoxicatingly new? *Not hardly*, these ideas have existed for centuries. But, business process reengineering is *not* a miracle cure. It offers no quick, simple or painless fix to organizational, managerial or technological challenges. It does entail difficult and strenuous work; and it still raises many questions, including the effective use of information resources.

But, in business process reengineering efforts that have not succeeded, the following categories do represent key reasons for reengineering failures:

- Undertaking a 'project' or change effort in the name of reengineering, but not following the concepts or principles of reengineering.

- Lack of understanding of reengineering concepts and principles by key executives — burying reengineering efforts in the middle of the 'corporate' agenda; unrealistic expectations and lack of adequate resources.
- Half-hearted reengineering attempt — lack of positive leadership and continuous support, commitment and involvement by executives.
- Reengineering effort seen as another cost-cutting, downsizing effort, emphasizing technology over people issues.
- Focusing on only a single reengineering effort as a short-term, narrowly-defined project; settling for minor results; neglecting people's values and beliefs.
- Not giving the organization or reengineering team a chance to succeed.
- Improper identification and use of process change enablers.
- Not using a structured, disciplined reengineering methodology.

By example, a large high tech company attempted to undertake a massive reengineering effort, focusing primarily on the consolidation of its many data processing centers. At the same time that they were implementing over 450 BPR projects, spending over $1 billion, they also undertook several new major business initiatives, as well as continued a major downsizing effort — separate and distinct from their BPR efforts. This company tried to do too much, too fast, committing many different and critical projects on their corporate agenda. Their senior executives failed to resolve this 'forest versus trees' syndrome, which severely hampered their reengineering efforts. They completely lost focus on their customer. During their reengineering effort, they also decapitated and reassigned many of their executives. As a result, their reengineering efforts have floundered, never achieving the necessary changes that were initially envisioned. Obviously, there are many lessons to be learned from this case in order to succeed at reengineering.

4. Critical Success Factors

In researching the reasons for failed reengineering efforts in many private and public sector organizations through interviews and analysis of documentation, five critical success factors have evolved on which organizations must focus in order to be more effective in their reengineering efforts. These factors include:

a) Educate all the organization's executives on reengineering.
b) Evaluate your organizational environment for reengineering.
c) Effectively identify and use key process change enablers.
d) Effectively use a structured, disciplined reengineering methodology.
e) Implement positive and dynamic change management process and procedures.

5. Executive Education

Management must not only do things right, but also do the right things if they are going to succeed in today's fast changing environment. Therefore, organizations must educate all of their executives at the very beginning of the reengineering effort on the concepts, principles and focus of reengineering and their reengineering efforts in order to evolve a consensus on what lies ahead for the organization and the commitment required of the executives. Not only must executives, managers and employees fully understand the anticipated dynamic changes, but they must also understand the methodology for reengineering and the critical role of key process change enablers, including information and information technology. To be prepared and more effective in managing innovative change, the executives must also appreciate the common pitfalls and misconceptions in applying reengineering concepts.

6. Organizational Environment

In order to give the organization and the reengineering team a better chance to succeed at their reengineering effort, the top executives must insure that the organizational environment, primarily internal, is first evaluated with respect to reengineering, *but* before the reengineering is undertaken. This evaluation should address many key issues as they would affect a reengineering effort. General categories for evaluation include the reengineering focus in the organization; the organizational culture and its acceptance of or resistance to reengineering; the support, commitment and involvement of top executives, managers and employees in their reengineering effort; the attitude, experience and knowledge of the reengineering leaders and team; and finally the time and support to be devoted to the reengineering effort.

The goal is to establish the best possible environment in which to undertake the reengineering effort. Through the evaluation, on the one hand, organizational strengths will be identified which then can be leveraged to support the reengineering effort. On the other hand, organizational weaknesses will be identified which could have an adverse impact on the reengineering effort. Once identified, courses of action should be developed and implemented to address these weaknesses before the reengineering effort starts in order to give the reengineering team and the organization a fighting chance to succeed at reengineering.

7. Process Change Enablers

Organizations can successfully enable this methodology in developing and implementing new business processes through the use of positive and powerful key process change enablers — factors that can shape and drive technological, behavioral and organizational change. These enablers will provide the means to successfully undertake the process of reengineering and contribute significantly to the successful implementation of the new, reengineered business processes.

Yet managers must also realize that each powerful process change enabler can both enhance and disable the organization's reengineering efforts. Therefore, managers must insure the judicious and careful use of process change enablers in exploiting new structural, cultural, management and technological capabilities. To succeed at reengineering, all process change enablers, including information and information technology, used in the reengineering effort must be aligned and in balance. They must work hand in glove with each other. To neglect a change enabler's importance or place more weight on the use of any given change enabler will prove detrimental, if not catastrophic, to the overall reengineering effort.

Process change enablers that should be considered within any business process reengineering effort include: people, education, communications and marketing, organizational structure and culture, funding, information, information technologies, and other technologies. The concept of information resources includes many of these process change enablers. Yet, other process change enablers may also be chosen depending upon the organization's mission, environment and situation. Each organization must determine for itself which process change enablers will successfully support their reengineering effort; but information resources will certainly play a key role in all reengineering efforts. Let us consider for a moment each of these process change enabler categories:

7.1. People

By far and away, the most important process change enabler. Reengineering efforts will succeed or fail based upon the people, both employees and managers — their skills, experiences, and attitudes. Attitude toward and motivation for reengineering will be crucial. Effective, dynamic and flexible teamwork will be essential in undertaking reengineering, as well as empowering all individuals involved in the reengineering efforts to 'think out of the box'; to break away from old traditions and paradigms; and to be imaginative, innovative, inductive and simply outrageous in their ideas for changing the way work is done through the creative use of key process change enablers. Proper education and training must be provided to insure that all employees and managers are properly prepared to participate in the process of reengineering and the future reengineered processes within their organization.

Positive, dynamic leadership is a must — all executives and managers throughout the government must be supportive, committed and involved if the reengineering efforts are to succeed. Management must insure a positive approach toward all human resource issues, including positive motivation, in order to use the full potential of all individuals in the organization.

7.2. *Education*

Everyone in a organization, including senior management, must be apprised of what reengineering is — the concepts, methodology, techniques and tools — and what reengineering actions will be taken. Everyone must be made aware of the importance and focus of the reengineering efforts. In order to make positive contributions to the reengineering effort, individuals must be kept informed. Education must begin during the initial phase and continue throughout the journey of reengineering within the organization.

7.3. *Communications and marketing*

Managers must insure that communication channels are kept open with everyone in the organization. Information on the reengineering efforts must be timely and accurate in order to create and maintain the necessary buy-in and commitment from the employees and managers. Management must gain their support, trust and confidence. Managers must also communicate openly with their organization's external stakeholders, including their suppliers and customers, in order to gain the necessary support and to insure consistency of purpose.

7.4. Organizational structure

The management infrastructure will either support or significantly hinder reengineering efforts. Within reengineering, focus will be placed on managing process boundaries; thus clarity in roles and authority must be clearly established. Emphasis will be on self-managed teams; thus the relationships, composition and location of the reengineering teams will be key.

7.5. Organizational culture

The historical culture within the organization must change if reengineering efforts are to succeed. The new culture must be fluid, flexible and adaptable, embracing change as the way of life, rather than maintaining the status quo and resisting any change. Management must emphasize individual initiative, imagination and innovation within the reengineering efforts. It also must empower more individuals in the reengineering decision-making process.

7.6. Funding

Reengineering cannot be done on the 'cheap.' Sufficient funding must be provided and maintained to see all reengineering efforts within individual organizations through to their completion. Continued funding must be provided if reengineering is to become the way of life within organizations.

7.7. *Information*

Are we in the Information Age or Knowledge Society, as some might suggest? I think not. When most people talk about the Information Revolution, they focus primarily on the information technologies that are exploding upon our society at breakneck speed. As this tremendous bow wave of information technologies continues to descend upon us, transforming our society, our businesses, and our governments, perhaps then we are only in the Information Technology Revolution. Since today, most organizations are inundated with data — a state of data overload. Yet many organizations continue to automate the current chaos and confusion that exists within our management and organizations without any focus on information.

In 1987, Peter Drucker wrote that information is data with purpose and relevance. At that time, he also declared that organizations were in a state of information blackout since individuals were not taking or accepting information responsibility [4]. Has anything really changed? In 1991, Shoshana Zuboff argued that organizations needed to informate, not automate, in order to understand, manage and create value from information [5]. Thomas Davenport suggested in 1993 that more than 85% of the information in organizations was not manipulated by any form of information technology; yet, he believed that information had considerable value as business process inputs and outputs [2]. At a 1994 CIO conference, Peter Drucker again exhorted the CIOs in attendance to focus, not on information technologies, but on information and its strategic role for today's organizations.

Today, many individuals in both the public and private sectors still do not understand or appreciate the significant role that information can play in their organizations. Most use the words *data* and *information* interchangeably; yet data is not information. In order to consider information as a key process change enabler for business process reengineering, let us consider an information paradigm and the characteristics of information-based organizations, as defined by Drucker [4] and Zuboff [5].

The information paradigm begins with raw, uncollected data that exists everywhere. Within organizations, individuals determine various parameters such that selected data can be collected and organized from the available raw data. Once data is collected (electronically in various types of databases or manually) or assimilated, individuals can now apply unique meaning and value to very specific data, defined as information, as they require its use within their work. Individuals will gain knowledge in the use of this information through positive or negative results. Through the accumulation of knowledge, individuals gain wisdom in the use of specific information.

In order for our society — individuals and organizations in both the private and public sectors — to effectively and fully evolve into the Information Age, we must understand and use information as data which has meaning and value to individuals, not organizations. Each individual will consider and view data differently, defining it as information only when they assign a unique meaning and value to the data as they need or use it. Specific roles for which individuals can use information include: measuring and monitoring process performance, coordinating process activities, customizing processes to meet customer needs, and decision making. It is in decision making that information will play its most important role. Individuals in the public and private sectors can use and leverage information, not just any data, to assist them in making positive decisions within their business processes. To do so will require timely, accurate and relevant information.

To be truly effective, all individuals must become fully aware of and assume responsibility for information — its identification, acquisition, storage, analysis, use, and distribution — a critical requirement for information-based organizations. These organizations can more effectively use information by opening up the information base of the organization to all people at all levels in the organization.

7.8. Information technologies

With the explosion of information technologies, the overall question must be asked: what direction is or should information technology be headed? Are we closing the gap between business requirements and information technology capabilities, or are we just "rearranging the deckchairs on the Titanic"? The past is replete with complex and undefined business processes with business functions supported through vertical systems development by using proprietary hardware and software — today's legacy systems in private businesses and in public organizations.

Rather than just automating old functions and processes with new information technologies, new capabilities must be determined in order to apply current and future information technologies more effectively in support of reengineering efforts. Information technologies must be placed in the proper perspective within reengineering — not as a sole 'driver,' but as a contributing enabler to allow us to do things in our business processes that we are not already doing. To more effectively use information technology as a positive process change enabler, Thomas Davenport suggests that organizations must first effectively define and use information. To do so will enable organizations to shift from predicting events to managing uncertainty, to shift from discrete to continuous processes, and to increase emphasis on the horizontal flow of information across the organization [2].

We must then search out and recognize the business possibilities latent within various information technologies by examining different functions, such as automational, informational, tracking, analytical and integrative, that they can support. Recent surveys by Deloitte & Touche and NAPA indicate that the types of information technologies used most often in business process reengineering projects include: shared databases, telecommunication networks, client/server architectures, e-mail systems, electronic data interchange, high performance computing, imaging systems, decision support systems, and multimedia.

To be most effective across an organization, information technologies used as process change enablers must be fully integrated into an enterprise-wide information resources architecture. The focus on and use of specific information technologies must be driven by the organization's data requirements which, in turn, should be driven by the accumulated information requirements of all individuals within the organization.

7.9. Technologies

Instead of just automating old functions and processes, such as manufacturing processes, with additional new technologies, new capabilities must be determined in order to apply current and future technologies more effectively in support of reengineering efforts. These technologies must be placed in the proper perspective within reengineering — not as a sole 'driver,' but as a contributing enabler to allow us to do things in our business processes that we are not already doing. Taco Bell in the early 1980s is a good example, using new technology to improve their ability to make better tacos, thus increasing customer satisfaction [6].

8. Reengineering Methodology

To address an enterprise-wide approach to business process reengineering, a simple and straightforward, yet structured and disciplined methodology must be used in order to give an organization and its people a better opportunity to succeed in their reengineering efforts. The following eight-phased methodology is an example of such an approach which may be used to implement reengineering.

1. *Planning*: Set foundation for future change activities; increase awareness, understanding and support for business process

reengineering; and establish mandate and provide direction for change.

2. *Organizing*: Mobilize, organize and train people to do business process reengineering; develop reengineering plans; initiate communication activities; and manage change.
3. *Evaluating*: Identify, measure and evaluate current business functions and processes; and ask the tough, yet fundamental questions of why and necessity.
4. *Identifying*: Identify and prioritize business process reengineering opportunities; complete process mapping analyses; and establish BPR project framework.
5. *Visioning*: Create vision of ideal business process; determine success criteria for new process; assess gaps between current and ideal processes: and gain approval.
6. *Designing*: Identify process change enablers; develop, test and evaluate process design alternatives; undertake detailed process design; and gain approval.
7. *Implementing*: Initiate pilot project; develop implementation plan; evaluate and train people; implement new business process; and measure and evaluate process performance.
8. *Managing*: Maintain BPR infrastructure; evaluate reengineering efforts; develop future reengineering objectives and priorities; and implement continuous quality improvement programs.

This methodology — planning, organizing, evaluating, identifying, visioning, designing, implementing, and managing — will allow an organization:

- To build the necessary 'bridge' from the on-going corporate strategic planning efforts to the process of reengineering — to tie its reengineering efforts to its strategic direction and control;
- To address its current business practices;
- To develop the vision and design for its future process-oriented infrastructure, emphasizing management, organizational, technical, and human resource issues;

- To coordinate all reengineering activities, providing flexibility and feedback throughout the process of reengineering;
- To build the 'bridge' from the implementation of the reengineered processes to the long-term management of these processes — to positively manage and continuously improve its new business processes;
- And to emphasize executive involvement and decision making throughout the reengineering effort.

9. Change Management

To effectively manage change through reengineering, executives and managers should understand why and how organizations, both public and private, have succeeded in implementing business process reengineering through the effective use of key process change enablers, including information resources, and a dynamic methodology. Key success factors include:

- Gain and maintain top management support, commitment and involvement; select the right people to undertake reengineering; have a BPR champion;
- Have the 'will' to undertake reengineering — absolutely critical; require extraordinary belief, dedication and effort — a huge, tough job;
- Recognize that change is a way of life, a value system, not just a process or project; recognize that BPR affects every person and every part of the organization;
- Focus on the customer at all times; focus on process before technology; focus on people before technology;
- Focus on strategic, value-added processes; use key process change enablers; focus on organizational core competencies;
- Provide a realistic BPR mission, clear direction and sufficient resources; organize properly; use disciplined BPR methodology; educate, train and communicate on continuous basis.

Reengineering can be done and done successfully. However, as a 'new' pioneering tool with many uncertainties, management must have the knowledge to understand, the courage to begin, and the will to succeed at business process reengineering if they are going to make a "positive and successful difference" in their organizations. To do so, managers must be able to move from having great thoughts about reengineering to making these ideas happen.

Successfully managing innovative change within the reengineering framework will require a heavy dose of the 4 Cs: commitment, coordination, communication, and cooperation. All levels of management must be fully committed to the reengineering efforts. Internally, they must work very closely together, engaging in active dialogue, insuring full and active participation, and actively and positively supporting the reengineering effort. Externally, managers must actively communicate with their organization's stakeholders to gain their support and cooperation.

Lastly, to be successful at business process reengineering through the use of a sound methodology and the effective employment of key dynamic process change enablers, including information resources, management at all levels must exercise positive and dynamic leadership. They must maintain a high degree of flexibility and bring a dose of common sense to the 'reengineering' table. And, above all, they must always focus on their people as the most important resource — the most important process change enabler — to address within their reengineering efforts.

References

1. M. Hammer and J. Champy, *Reengineering the Corporation: A Manifesto for Business Revolution* (HarperBusiness, New York, 1993) p. 171.
2. T. H. Davenport, *Process Innovation Reengineering Work through Information T echnology* (Harvard Business School Press, Boston, 1993).

3. R. L. Manganelli and M. M. Klein, *The Reengineering Handbook: A Step-By-Step Guide to Business Transformation* (American Management Association, New York, 1994).
4. P. F. Drucker, The coming of the new organization, *Harvard Business Review*, January/February 1988.
5. S. Zubroff, Informate the enterprise: an agenda for the twenty-first century, National Forum, Summer 1991.
6. M. Hammer and J. Champy, *Reengineering the Corporation: A Manifesto for Business Revolution* (HarperBusiness, New York, 1993) pp. 32–36.

Chapter 25

Into the 3rd Millennium

CHAN MENG KHOONG
Centre for Strategic Process Innovation, National Computer Board, 71 Science Park Drive, Singapore 118253, Republic of Singapore
E-mail: chanmeng@ncb.gov.sg

As we come to end of this book, it is fitting to discuss future prospects for reengineering practice, vis-à-vis visions of organizations in the 21st century and beyond. In this chapter, we shall paint scenarios of new age organizations, and discuss new challenges for reengineering practice in such organizations of the future.

1. Twenty-First Century Organizations

Many management gurus have formulated predictions on the look and feel of the 21st century organization. See, for example, the predictions in Refs. 1–6. Typical predictions envisage organizations that are flat, horizontal, small, nimble, knowledge-based, networked, virtual, global, and learning systems. Employees in these organizations are envisaged to be empowered, team-based, customer-focused, leadership-driven, and maximally value-added. The environments within which these organizations and people operate are envisaged to be chaotic and uncertain, with prosumers taking the place of producers and consumers.

It is hard to dispute any of these visions, until we have actually lived through the 21st century. What appears certain, though, is that the reengineering paradigm will remain relevant in the next century, albeit with some variations in scope and approach, as we will discuss in the rest of this chapter. Indeed, as the pace of change quickens around the world, reengineering projects may well be undertaken even more frequently in the 21st century organization, to support the dynamism that is needed to move the organization forward.

This is true even if all of the world's corporations have each been reengineered before. Apart from the constancy of change, there are many other good reasons why a reengineered organization may embark on repeated cycles of reengineering in the next century. For instance, the organization may be faced with horizon effects or unanticipated changes in raison d'être imposed by its stakeholders. Furthermore, postponement of organizational changes may be justifiable from an operational cost perspective. The bottom line remains to use reengineering as a tool for leading change.

2. Virtual Reengineering

In the next millennium, there are various ways in which the target scope of reengineering may be virtual. Firstly, organizations will be virtual in nature. Their business processes will be strung across time and space, and will also cut across logical organizational boundaries to include processes of partners. Secondly, the complex interdependencies of government, business, and society in the 21st century will naturally lead to unprecedented scope for inter-organizational, industry-wide, and even national-level reengineering.

An intriguing development lies in the virtualizing of resources that form organizations and communities. Increasingly, organizations and communities will be populated by non-human intelligent beings that co-exist with human beings. Organizations will become loosely interconnected networks of physical and virtual resources. If reengineering monolithic organizations are a challenge today, reengineering networks of communities to achieve a higher good will be even more challenging by orders of magnitude.

3. Psychological Reengineering

Gone are the days when the leadership of an organization is made up of wise old men. Today, Generation X professionals are beginning to make their presence felt in senior management positions. This is true even in government. In the next century, we can expect organizational leaders to be a full generation younger, yet operating with twice as much drive and ambition. In this sense, some of the problems associated with leadership in reengineering projects today may well become non-issues in the future.

The flip side, though, is that emotional issues may feature more strongly in 21st century reengineering. A younger leadership is likely to operate with a lower level of emotional maturity. The organization's 'emotional quotient' will be further held down by the fact that the young leaders will be dealing with employees who are twice their age. Thinking more radically: *what if everybody becomes a leader*? In that case, the preoccupation of reengineering may be in explosive psychological warfare.

Reengineering projects in the next millennium will have to address changing employee motivation factors. Employees today are motivated by the financial returns for performing their jobs well, and view employability as being defined in terms of skills acquired. Future employability will have to defined in terms of ability to learn and unlearn, and future employees should be motivated by learning opportunities more than anything else.

The concept of employment may also become obsolete in the virtual organization. In its place is the concept of membership. While organizational loyalty is a virtue today, it will be a non-issue in the next millennium. This has interesting implications for future reengineering initiatives. The challenge is to develop a new mindset for collaboration and trust among people who collectively may come together serve a common good but are otherwise not bound in any way to the demands of organizational change blueprints.

4. Public-Private Grand Unification

There are some fundamental differences between public sector and private sector practices today. For instance, public sector organizations are traditionally input-based in their performance measurement (e.g. demands on services and resources), while private sector organizations are traditionally output-based (e.g. revenue, products sold, market capture).

However, as governments take stock of their accountabilities and modernize their practices, they are quickly adapting private sector practices to seek quantum leap improvements in service quality and organizational efficiency. As a consequence, public sector organizations are increasingly shifting to outcome-based performance measures. Using reengineering as the tool for the transformation, public sector processes and systems are becoming more like private sector ones. Over in the private sector, organizations are also being nudged by government, public, and various competitive forces to build up some sense of public accountability. Thus private sector performance measures are also increasingly outcome-based.

The impending unification of public and private sector practices is eventful because it creates many unprecedented opportunities for public-private partnerships and radically new organization forms. The new complexities in stakeholder relationships and influences will generate fresh room for innovation in reengineering methodologies.

5. Rapid Re-Reengineering

Leading management gurus and futurists would like us to believe that the 21st century will be a period of uncertainty, disequilibrium, and chaos. In such a scenario, the performance of any organization will depend largely on how it 'seizes the moments' and make the most out of every opportunity. Time to market for products and services will approach zero, and processes for delivering these products and services will be compressed to the extent of being eliminated totally. As a natural consequence, reengineering scope will therefore extend increasingly beyond process change to strategy change, from operational transformation to total business repositioning.

In the 21st century, reengineering projects will have to be executed with much shorter turnaround times, if organizations are to maximize their returns from the paradigm in a period of intense dynamism. In a sense, the process of reengineering may itself be in need of reengineering! Any change-leading organization should see itself going through multiple cycles of reengineering in the next century. Thus the need to build up capability for rapid *re*-reengineering.

On the human side, rapid re-reengineering demands that learning skills, process management skills, creative thinking skills, and reengineering know-how be nurtured as the core competencies of people. Given the ever-increasing level of uncertainty surrounding organizations, the level of trust among people will have to increase in tandem, and checks and controls should be eradicated as much as possible, if organizations are to seek lasting order out of the chaos.

On the technical side, the organization's ability to have a handle on its own corporate memory is a critical success factor. One key impediment in reengineering today is the lack of corporate memory — information sources are scarce, filled with gaps, and unreliable. In the future, a different sort of challenge arises, in that corporate memories are expected to be huge in size and mature, but also distributed. Reengineering will have to be directed not so much at the central corporate intelligence, but rather at the sprawling networked intelligence within which the organization operates.

Another critical success factor is information technology. Many enterprise management systems are being implemented today to solve yesterday's problems. These include enterprise resource planning, workflow, document management, and knowledge-based systems. These systems can very effectively codify and entrench organizational practices, and thus enable radical change today. But the same systems will certainly become roadblocks in future reengineering initiatives unless they themselves are amenable to dynamic change. At it is now, the lifespans of IT applications are shrinking to as little as three years, to the extent that some expensive IT investments have to written off shortly after the IT projects complete the development life cycle. The IT enablers in 21st century reengineering will have to be extremely malleable.

6. The 22nd Century Organization

In the 22nd century, the number of organizations in existence may well exceed the number of intelligent living beings on the planet. Most of these organizations will be virtual, and constantly mutating in size and shape. Organizations will be created and destroyed all the time. Organizations will no longer be sources of employment but simply serve as platforms for activities to take place. Each intelligent living being may have membership in a vast number of organizations. And human beings may be a minority within the population of intelligent living beings operating in organizations.

A typical reengineering project takes several months to complete today. In the 21st century, we should expect each reengineering cycle to take just a few days. In the 22nd century, the cycle time should probably decrease to minutes. At the moment, it is quite unimaginable how an organization can be reengineered in minutes. But, then again, the reality in the 22nd century is equally unimaginable today.

7. Conclusion

Discounting name changes, fads, and marketing hype, I believe that reengineering is here to stay. However, we need to be cognizant of the new demands that will be placed on reengineering practice. As we step into the third millennium, we shall have to embrace discontinuous changes of an increasingly larger scale and with increasingly higher frequency. Therefore, to be successful, organizations should not treat each reengineering initiative as a safeguard against future needs to reengineer. Instead, organizations should use each reengineering experience to improve their preparedness and proficiency for the next wave of total transformation.

References

1. R. Gibson (ed.), *Rethinking the Future* (Nicholas Brealey Publishing, London, 1997).
2. F. Hesselbein, M. Goldsmith and R. Beckhard (eds.), *The Organization of the Future* (Jossey-Bass, San Francisco, 1997).
3. K. Kelly, New rules for the new economy, *The Sunday Times*, Singapore, September 14, 1997.
4. J. P. Kotter, *Leading Change* (Harvard Business School Press, Boston, 1996).
5. A. Penzias, 10 scenarios for the next millennium, *The Sunday Times*, Singapore, September 14, 1997.
6. D. Tapscott, *The Digital Economy: Promise and Peril in the Age of Networked Intelligence* (McGraw-Hill, New York, 1996).
7. J. Champy and N. Nohria (eds.), *Fast Forward: The Best Ideas in Managing Business Change* (Harvard Business School Press, Boston, 1996).
8. T. H. Davenport, Business process reengineering: where it's been, where it's going, in V. Grover and W. J. Kettinger (eds.), *Business Process Change: Concepts, Methods and Technologies* (Idea Group, Harrisburg, PA, 1995), pp. 1–13.
9. T. H. Davenport and L. Prusak, *Working Knowledge: How Organizations Manage What They Know* (Harvard Business School Press, Boston, 1998).

10. J. C. Glen and T. J. Gordon (eds.), *1997 State of the Future: Implications for Actions Today* (American Council for the United Nations University, Washington, D. C., 1997).
11. G. Hamel, Strategy as revolution, *Harvard Business Review*, July-August 1996, 69–82.
12. KPMG Peat Marwick LLP, Organizations serving the public: transformation to the 21st century, Study Report, January 1997. URL: http://www.us.kpmg.com/ps/march97/orgtrans.html.
13. H. Mintzberg, Musings on management, *Harvard Business Review*, July-August 1996, 61–67.
14. M. M. Waldrop, *Complexity: The Emerging Science at the Edge of Order and Chaos* (Simon & Schuster, New York, 1992).

List of Contributors

Darin Artman
Matt Barney
Luigi Benedicenti
Hélène Bestougeff
Freimut Bodendorf
Amel Bouaissi
Antony Bryant
Monika B. Calitz
Andrékwen P. Calitz
Pin-Yu Chu
Guido Dedene
Wolfgang Deiters
L. Duranti
José Luiz Fiadeiro
Dieter Fink
Lauri Forsman
Kaiyin Huang
M. P. Jaiswal
Leslie Johnson
Albert Jones
Chan Meng Khoong
M. Kindl
Kari Kuutti
Klaus Lang
Edward G. Lewis
Thorsten Löffeler
Sharon O'Toole
Daryll R. Prescott
Ashley Prince
Pedro Ramos
Roger Sor
Maria Stergiou
Rüdiger Striemer
Giancarlo Succi
Wolfgang Taumann
Veronika Thurner
Shigeki Umeda
William E. Underwood
Jurgen Vanhoenacker
Tullio Vernazza
Jaakko Virkkunen
Chester C. Warzynski
Tien Hua Yim-Teo

Index